HITLER'S
COMMANDER

HITLER'S
COMMANDER

Field Marshal Walther Model—
Hitler's Favorite General

S<small>TEVEN</small> H. N<small>EWTON</small>

DA CAPO PRESS
A Member of the Perseus Books Group

Designed by c. cairl design
Set in 11.25-point Sabon MT by the Perseus Books Group

Cataloging-in-Publication data for this book is available from the Library of Congress.

First Da Capo Press edition 2005

Library of Congress Cataloging-in-Publication Data

Newton, Steven H.
    Hitler's commander : Field Marshal Walther Model : Hitler's favorite
general / Steven H. Newton. — 1st Da Capo Press ed.
        p. cm.
    Includes bibliographical references and index.
    ISBN-13: 978-0-306-81399-3 (hardcover : alk. paper)
    ISBN-10: 0-306-81399-8 (hardcover : alk. paper)
        1. Model, Walter, 1891-1945. 2. Marshals—Germany—Biography.
3. Germany. Heer—Officers—Biography. 4. Germany. Heer. Armee, 9—Biography.
I. Title.
    DD247.M58N49 2005
    940.54'1343'092—dc22
    [B]
                                                                        2005022684

Published by Da Capo Press
A Member of the Perseus Books Group
http://www.dacapopress.com

Da Capo Press books are available at special discounts for bulk purchases in the U.S.
by corporations, institutions, and other organizations. For more information, please
contact the Special Markets Department at the Perseus Books Group, 11 Cambridge
Center, Cambridge, MA 02142, or call (800)255-1514 or (617) 252-5298, or email
special.markets@perseusbooks.com

1 2 3 4 5 6 7 8 9–09 08 07 06

For William H. Flayhart, PhD,
colleague, friend, and mentor

CONTENTS

ACKNOWLEDGMENTS

As always, no book (of mine at least) is produced in a vacuum. Without the support and expertise of Colonel Dave Wrenn, Keith Poulter, Ted Savas, and Yohuru Williams, this book would have been difficult, if not impossible, to write. Dozens of helpful staff members at the National Archives went out of their way over four and a half years to provide me with extra assistance; I just wish I could name them all. Akwasi Osei, my department head, made it possible for me to take release time to complete the manuscript. My long-suffering editor, Robert Pigeon, put up with repeated delays while demonstrating Job-like patience until he finally judged it to be time for me to put up or shut up.

In my house the computer often has to be shared with my wife Faith; my children Marie, Alexis, and Michael; my grandson Shane; and even the two cats (Momma and Donny), who allow us all to live in their house. Without their love and forbearance (especially for books and notes piled three feet high), this project would have remained a half-baked dream.

INTRODUCTION

Should history remember Walther Model as a tactical genius, a fanatic Nazi, both, or neither? That was the key question with which I began researching the German commander thrown by Adolph Hitler into so many of World War II's worst crises that his contemporaries nicknamed him the "Führer's fireman." The answer was surprisingly difficult to unearth.

Despite the fact that he is associated with the defense of Rzhev, Kursk, the destruction of Army Group Center, Arnhem, Hürtgen forest, the Battle of the Bulge, and the Ruhr pocket, Walther Model has remained a very shadowy figure in histories and memoirs dealing with the Third Reich. The three most famous works, penned by Heinz Guderian, Erich von Manstein, and F. W. von Mellenthin, barely mention Model at all, and when they do the references are not usually flattering. Most historians, introducing Model into the narrative of a given campaign or battle, make an obligatory reference to his driving energy, his foul mouth, his monocle, and his supposedly blind faith in Hitler, but provide few other details. Certain stories—most of them obviously apocryphal—are repeated ad infinitum to create a pasteboard character who succeeds either because of his bloodthirsty determination not to yield an inch of ground or because of his preferential treatment by the German dictator. Rarely if ever is there an inquiry into the concepts that underlay Model's methods, or an attempt to plot the ebb and flow of his relationship with Hitler.

As I began to examine Model's life more closely, I immediately discovered several reasons why his contemporaries chose to present him to history in such an unfavorable light. First and foremost, he was dead when they wrote, and dead generals (especially dead generals capable of being presented as pro-Hitler) make easy targets. The German generals who ended up in American or British captivity after the war found it necessary to whitewash their involvement in the less respectable aspects of their regime and to portray themselves as bridled geniuses who could have defeated (at least!) the Russians if Hitler had not kept interfering. Officers like Wilhelm Keitel, Alfred Jodl, and Walther Model made excellent scapegoats in this regard.

The second reason for emphasizing Model's supposed preferential treatment at Hitler's hands was to obscure a very unpalatable fact: Far from being elevated to Army and then Army Group Command because he spouted the approved National Socialist slogans, Model rose quickly because he was a highly trained General Staff officer. Having begun the Great War as a battalion adjutant, Model ended the conflict as a division chief supply officer (with a long stint attached to the supreme headquarters in between) and spent most of the interwar years in staff positions. Long before Hitler had even heard his name, Model had been selected as an army chief of staff if it proved necessary to attack Czechoslovakia. Nor did his promotions to chief of staff (Sixteenth Army), 3rd Panzer Division, XLI Panzer Corps, or even Ninth Army result from anything other than his performance in his current position and his General Staff education. To officers like Heinz Guderian, Franz Halder, and Hans Speidel, who were all attempting to paint the General Staff as an organization opposed to Hitler's most radical social agenda, Walther Model became difficult to explain. Better to spread half-truths (even outright lies) about him in order to obscure some uncomfortable truths about their own culpability for everything from the Commissar Order to Courts of Honor to slave labor and POW abuse.

Yet I have come to believe that at least one other aspect of Model's career drove the likes of Halder, Guderian, Manstein, and Mellenthin to discount his intellectual prowess and tactical acumen. The surviving German generals created a sort of "panzer orthodoxy" about the conduct of the war in Russia, especially during the defensive phase in the war's final years. Time and again they insisted that had Hitler given up his rigid insistence on holding territory and set them free to fight a purely mobile—*elastic*—defensive battle, they might have worn down the Soviet colossus before the Hammer and Sickle waved over Berlin. The fact that a number of quite successful senior German commanders (Model, Erhard Raus, Lothar Rendulic, and Hans von Kluge, to cite only the most prominent) had not subscribed to this philosophy became one of the best-kept secrets of the war.

Model and Raus in particular appear to have thought through carefully the tactical problems of defense along a broad front and to have developed a tactical approach that was the direct antithesis of that propounded by Guderian and Manstein. They concluded that going over to maneuver warfare on a large scale was—at least after 1942—a losing proposition for the German army, for its depleted infantry divisions lacked the mobility and firepower to survive in such fighting. Instead, they argued for the creation of thick defensive belts and "zone defense tactics" to prevent the Red Army from achieving an operational breakthrough in the first place. Their system, which has yet to be thoroughly explored by military historians still caught up in the worship of Panthers and Tigers, actually worked quite well at Rzhev, at Orel, along the middle Dnepr River crossings, in the Carpathians, in Estonia, and even in East Prussia.

Examining such questions about Walther Model and his campaigns has led me to write a biography whose structure needs to be explained at the outset. The first several chapters, which deal with his World War I experiences, his Reichswehr career, and his staff duties during the Polish and French campaigns, are relatively lengthy and detailed. This detail is necessary to make the case fully that Walther Model in fact followed the General Staff career template quite closely. Likewise, Model's command of the 3rd Panzer Division during the summer of 1941, followed by his appointment to lead XLI Panzer Corps outside Moscow, is carefully scrutinized to establish his leadership style and tactical preferences. Once Model assumes command of the Ninth Army, however, the focus necessarily shifts from the army's day-to-day operations to Model's larger defensive concepts. I still depict some battles (the first counteroffensive at Rzhev and Operation Citadel) in great detail, but use the rest as a backdrop to explain Model's evolving tactical doctrine.

Once Model is promoted to Army Group Command, the narrative slips even further away from a detailed tactical (or even operational) presentation to concentrate on the field marshal as commander in the military-political milieu of the disintegrating Third Reich. The proper focus in evaluating an army group commander is not tactical but strategic, political, and interpersonal. This especially becomes the case when considering Model's tenure of command in France and western Germany during 1944–1945 (the period in which he is most unfairly presented to history by former subordinates who neither respected nor understood him), when he inflicted at Arnhem and in the Hürtgen forest two of the most significant defeats that the Western Allies suffered throughout the entire campaign.

This shift of focus brings to light one completely neglected aspect of Model's career: his changing relationship with Adolph Hitler. Model's influence with the Führer undoubtedly reached its peak in August 1944, when the dictator credited him with singlehandedly putting a final stop to the Soviet summer offensive against Army Group Center. His success at Arnhem slightly enhanced this prestige, but that ephemeral gain was almost immediately overshadowed by Model's vocal reluctance to conduct the Ardennes offensive in a manner consistent with Hitler's wishes. By January 1945, Model's stock with the Führer had fallen badly; two months later the Reich propaganda apparatus would publicly label both the field marshal and his entire army group as traitors.

By the time Walther Model walks into the woods alone, loaded pistol in hand, it is my hope that the reader will have gained important insight into both the commander and the man. Viewed up close, Walther Model does not manage to come across as likable: He lacks the charisma of Rommel, the patrician air of Manstein, and the fast-driving flair of Guderian. On the other hand, Model emerges from the shadows as an intellectually capable soldier, a tough-minded pragmatist, and a man capable of being overwhelmed by depression and personal fear. He is an interesting and important figure in the history of World War II; to know him better enhances our understanding of that conflict.

PART ONE

The Rising Star

1

AN UNCOMFORTABLE SUBORDINATE

The Great War

THE GRINDING INEVITABILITY OF EUROPE'S MARCH TOWARD WAR during the summer of 1914 weighed heavily on the German people. A newspaper editor observed that Sunday, August 2, was a day of "brilliant sunshine," the kind of day in which "Berliners, parents and children, young men and maiden, would go out to the Grünwald, to the forests around Potsdam, along the Havel, out to Treptow, or on the Müggelsee." But on this particular Sunday, Kaiser Wilhelm having ordered a general mobilization twenty-four hours earlier, "nobody went into the country." Instead, the reservists stayed at home to pack their uniforms and personal equipment, or shopped frantically for those last pieces of equipment to complete their kit. Faces were drawn, voices subdued. Wives and sweethearts followed their men as they reported to barracks or railroad station. Editor Theodor Wolff noticed that when they walked out of their houses, many for the last time in their lives, "they all turned into 'field greys'—so they were now called. Suddenly in that grey uniform, which did not suit them, and under that strange steel helmet, they seemed changed, their individuality was lost, they were just a long grey procession." Gripped by fear and virulent xenophobia, the next night thousands of civilians mobbed the British embassy, nearly lynching the Spanish ambassador, who was mistaken for an English diplomat.[1]

The reservists and the regulars were rapidly moving into a grim new world, quite different from parades and maneuvers and barracks drill. The mobilization points, observed one young captain, "appeared to contain nothing but men—and horses." He witnessed the same transformation remarked upon by the newspaper editor, though he saw it from the other side, exulting in "endless streams of men in the streets, men from the factories, men from the towns and men from the country, workmen in their overalls, clerks in their black coats, foresters and peasants in their coarse cloth suits, all marching together, all singing together, all coming to the barracks, and the great iron gates opened and swallowed them up." "From east to west," the captain announced to his assembled company of reservists, "enemies are advancing on us to break up our beloved country. It is up to each one of us to fulfill the highest duty of German manhood, to defend his home, his wife, and his children."[2]

The military machine now sputtering to life was so immense that its size seemed to all observers to dwarf individual men into insignificance. Germany's fate had been wrenched out of the hands of politicians to be placed in the care of the Great General Staff and the 3,800,000 regulars and reservists cinching belts and donning helmets. Of these, 1,600,000 were headed for the borders of France and the Low Countries, preparing to execute the gigantic gamble envisioned by former Chief of the General Staff Alfred Graf von Schlieffen. Von Schlieffen had committed the Reich to a plan that would send the bulk of the German army careening through France in a desperate attempt to win the war in six weeks, before the Russians could mobilize and overrun the skeleton forces left in East Prussia. Although the operation had been diluted by von Schlieffen's successor, who reduced the strength of the right wing, which was supposed to sweep near the English Channel and envelop Paris, there were still five full field armies marching through Belgium in pursuit of victory.[3]

The army entrusted with the most critical objective—plunging across Belgium, brushing the Channel, and encircling Paris and the French army—was Colonel General Alexander von Kluck's *Armeeoberkommando 1*. Composed of four active and two reserve corps, the First Army was also the largest army deployed against the French, over 320,000 strong. Only Lieutenant General Georg von der Marwitz's Cavalry Corps, an independent force securing the army's far right flank, faced a longer and more arduous march, and the grand design expected of von Kluck's men a continuous pace that could jade horses and kill men. That the Schlieffen plan was deemed possible, even as an all-or-nothing gamble, was due to the meticulous planning done by the German army to push supplies by rail through Belgium in the wake of the attack. "Everything," admitted First Army Chief of Staff Hermann von Kuhl, "depended on the rapid reconstruction of the railways in enemy territory and on resuming railway operation as quickly as possible."[4]

One of the corps on the army's left flank was General of Infantry Ewald von Lochow's III (Brandenburg) Corps, celebrated since the Wars of Unification as "one of the elite units of the German Army" and "long . . . renowned for their dash and forcefulness on the attack." Von Lochow was considered an aggressive, capable commander, ably supported by his chief of staff, Colonel Hans von Seeckt, and his operations officer, Major Georg Wetzell, a competent if somewhat pedantic veteran staff officer. The corps mustered more than 40,000 men in the 5th and 6th Infantry Divisions plus attached artillery and cavalry—hard-marching regular units with proud histories, their ranks filled out with the best class of reservists. These were the troops upon whom the General Staff depended to destroy the Belgian army and defeat any divisions of the British Expeditionary Force that might contest their path. Spearheading the 5th Division (Lieutenant General Georg Wichura) was Major General Guido Sontag's 10th Infantry Brigade, which contained the Brandenburg 12th Grenadier and 52nd Infantry Regiments. The 52nd Regiment, commanded by Colonel Walther Fromm with a small regimental staff, had three battalions of four 250-man companies each. Critical to the proper functioning of the regiment, one of the tiny essential cogs in the great wheel, was the adjutant of the First Battalion: Lieutenant Walther Model.[5]

When first we glimpse him as a twenty-three-year-old junior officer, Model is an indistinct figure. His decision in 1945 to burn his personal papers successfully eradicated all but the bare facts of his early life. He was undeniably a Prussian, born in the village of Gentheim near Magdeburg on 24 January 1891 and christened Otto Moritz Walther Model by Lutheran parents. Prussian maybe, but hardly *Junker* nobility, the Model family had its roots in the emerging lesser bourgeoisie. His father taught at a girls' school and directed the choir, and as Carlo D'Este observed, "On his mother's side were peasants, horsetraders and innkeepers." Though the family moved around, we do have records of young Walther at the gymnasium in Erfurt; they indicate a somewhat sickly student with a facility for Greek and Latin and a growing interest in history. The day that changed Model's life seems to have come in 1906 when he witnessed drilling by a *jäger* battalion stationed in Naumberg and der Saale. For a family of such modest means, an officer's career might have been out of reach, but Walther's uncle, Martin Model, was a reserve officer in the 52nd Infantry. Two years later, in February 1908, the Models prevailed upon him to use his influence to gain his nephew admittance to the *Kriegsschule* in Neisse as an officer candidate in the 52nd (Brandenburg) Infantry Regiment.[6]

He had found his calling, but first he had to survive the initiation: two years of isolation and uncompromising discipline. The German military academy of the prewar years is described by Klaus Theweleit as "a place where the cadet lives behind iron bars. He has no right of exit from the prison; it is granted only in reward for strict adherence to its governing laws." Can we ever know the extent to which the *Kriegsschule* shaped the personality of Walther Model? We know that he nearly quit, and that he developed a life-long passion for riding, but neither tendency was unusual for Prussian boys in the Kaiser's Germany.[7] Other than that, there is only the reality of the academy itself from which to judge; again, Theweleit:

> All the cadets have a place within a direct order of rank. Each knows exactly which cadets are "above" him and which "below." Each has the power to command and punish those below and the duty to obey those above. The occupant of the lowest position in the hierarchy must find another whom even he can dominate or he is finished.
>
> If a cadet fails to exercise his rights over his inferiors, he is despised or demoted. Thus the situation never arises. Privilege is universally exercised. There are no gaps in the cadet's daily round of duties. . . .
>
> The cadet never receives instructions; he recognizes his mistakes only in the moment of transgression from the reactions of others who already know the score. With slight variations according to his cleverness, each newcomer thus necessarily repeats the mistakes of his predecessors, who in turn recognize and welcome the apparent opportunity to treat their successors as they themselves have previously been treated. Justice works on the principle of equal torment for all. The principle is strictly adhered to; there are no grounds on which a mistake might be considered excusable.[8]

Less analytically, another young man who passed through the academy recalled: "I was met at the gates of the barracks by one of the senior cadets, who roughly demanded my name. I introduced myself with as respectful a bow as I could accomplish, whereupon, without any display of feeling, but rather as one who does what he considers to be his duty, he struck me across the face with a dog-chain." Later this cadet evoked the memory of his room-corporal— "the most finished bully I have ever met"—who preferred punishing his charges by forcing them to stand on tiptoe with bent knees, holding three large books under each arm, until they toppled over from exhaustion; "when he fell he was kicked or thrashed with a foil." The cadet quickly learned the appropriate response: "On the first occasion when this happened to me I dropped the dictionaries, arose, and flew at the great man's throat. The subsequent penalties which I suffered were severe, but the tormentor treated me more leniently during the rest of my stay."[9]

"The system is not for ambitious people—only for average persons," another cadet—young Heinz Guderian—had complained in 1907. "It is tedious."[10] Fellow cadet Hans Hube later observed nothing about Model in his schooldays that predicted the sort of officer he would become, and one of his sergeants scolded him with the words: "You, Model, lack the severity which a soldier needs." Nonetheless, Model survived, and along with Hube he received his commission as a lieutenant in the Prussian army on 22 August 1910 and was assigned as a junior officer in No. 11 Company of the 52nd. (Hube went to the 26th Regiment.)[11]

Although the regiment that had accepted him was hardly one of the oldest or more prestigious in the army (it was no competitor, for instance, to the 3rd Regiment of Foot Grenadiers, into which young Erich von Manstein had been commissioned a few years earlier), the 52nd had a proud tradition nonetheless. It had distinguished itself sufficiently in the Franco-Prussian War—suffering 1,597 casualties in a single day—to be nicknamed "Regiment von Alvensleben," after General of Infantry Constantion von Alvensleben, one of the most capable corps commanders in Field Marshal Helmuth von Moltke's army. Such appellations were not taken lightly in the Prussian army, and Model's rank represented a "generally negotiable social currency," because his acceptance had to be unanimous among the officers already serving in the regiment. "Even the kaiser was reluctant to influence the process," notes Dennis Showalter, "and would rarely approve the commission of a man who did not have his future comrades' assent. Anyone without the right pieces of paper, the right connections, or the right recommendations, found himself on the outside looking in."[12]

He apparently had no problems getting inside and staying there. By August 1914 and the orders for general mobilization, Lieutenant Model had risen to become battalion adjutant. This was a critical post, for the adjutant was not just responsible for much of the unit's paperwork and forming the ranks at parade. On the march and in battle, the adjutant not only carried his commander's orders to the companies but also served as his eyes and ears. If events moved too rapidly for the colonel's messages to control them, the adjutant might actually have to make a split-second decision to modify the orders on his own initiative. Only junior officers already thought to possess the right personal qualities were selected for the job, which often served as part of the selection and training process for future General Staff officers.

Something of Model's aggressive, even abrasive personality begins to emerge during this period, glimpsed through the eyes of his comrades. His first close friendship in the regiment developed with another lieutenant who shared his passion for riding and the hunt, but with many other junior officers he was less than popular. Lieutenant Wilhelm Bohnstedt found Model overly ambitious, while Lieutenant Erwin Vierow recalled him as excessively critical of the smallest miscues in infantry training. Vierow noted that Model even had harsh words for more senior officers whom he felt had not made an effort to analyze the results of the Russian-Japanese War of 1904–1905, which also highlights the fact that his passion for studying military history began very early indeed.[13]

In August 1914, Model would have been caught up—like nearly every other officer in the Kaiser's army—in the excitement of the impending war. This was, after all, the great undertaking toward which all the years of training and war games had been directed, and despite the fact that the war had been sparked off in the Balkans, most German officers felt that the Reich's natural enemy was France. If there were concerns among the men of the III Corps for the safety of their Prussia homeland, left nearly unprotected in the face of huge Russian armies, these fears were submerged in the heady enthusiasm for the imminent march on Paris. Day and night the trains remorselessly rolled across the central German plain, and at each brief stop, while crowds cheered, bands played, and young women threw flowers, the soldiers scavenged energetically for newspapers. Any war news was consumed, disseminated, and endlessly debated, no matter how heavily censored or skewed by nationalistic propaganda it may have been. A captain in Model's brigade recalled the special burst of patriotic pride that arose when the soldiers "read of the fall of Liege: a giant gun of Krupp, with shells as big as a man, had blown the defences of the Belgian fortresses to matchwood."[14]

There was, however, a much darker side to this reading about the oncoming battle. One of the great gambles involved in the Schlieffen plan was its willingness to denude every secondary front to dangerously low levels of troops in order to mass the greatest possible weight on the left wing tramping through Belgium toward Paris. In the original draft plan for the operation, this entailed not only a ruthless reduction in the number of divisions deployed in East Prussia and along the Upper Rhine but also a drastic pruning of rear-area security troops behind the advancing armies. Given that the Germans were violating Belgium's neutrality, civilian as well as military hostility could be expected, and guarding over-stretched supply lines and maintaining control of the cities and towns in the rear represented a major problem. The General Staff determined to meet this challenge through a planned program of controlled terror and savage reprisals.

This decision responded not only to the existing situation but also to institutional memories of the *franc-tireurs* who had so effectively harassed the rear areas of the Prussian army in the 1870s. These irregulars had been organized at the behest of the French army and represented an integral component of French strategy. Stung by their attacks, the Germans denied belligerent rights to the guerrillas—performing summary executions when snipers and saboteurs were apprehended—and invoked the principle of collective responsibility. "Experience has established," Helmuth von Moltke wrote to one of his army commanders, "that the most effective way of dealing with this situation is to destroy the premises concerned—or, where participation has been more general, the entire village." To another general he observed: "The very severest treatment of the guilty as regards life and property can alone be recommended to your Excellency, whole parishes being held responsible for the deeds of their individual members when these cannot be discovered." The resulting German reprisals became so bloody—on both sides—that even Prussian officers blanched. "The war," said one, "is gradually acquiring a hideous character. Murder and burning is now the order of the day on both sides." "We are learning to hate them more every day," admitted another who had always prided himself on approaching war with detached professionalism.[15]

Thus predisposed to view any civilian or irregular armed resistance as being officially sanctioned and coordinated by the Belgian government, the Germans adopted a pacification and security program upon entering the country in 1914 that involved the immediate imposition of a draconian rule in occupied territories. Barbara Tuchman, in *The Guns of August*, observes that "as soon as the Germans entered a town its walls became whitened, as if by a biblical plague, with a rash of posters plastered on every house warning the population against acts of 'hostility.'" Almost any act that could be construed as hindering or sabotaging the German offensive merited the death penalty: sniping at German soldiers, approaching a balloon or aircraft post, or hiding rather than sur- rendering weapons. The principle of collective responsibility, specifically outlawed by the Hague Convention, was to be applied without exception to Belgian towns; when the specific guilty party could not be identified, all the civilians in the area were rounded up for mass executions. "The method was to assemble the inhab- itants in the main square, women usually on one side and men on the other," notes Tuchman, and "select every tenth man or every second man or all on one side, according to the whim of the indi- vidual officer, march them to a nearby field or empty lot behind the railroad station and shoot them." If an infraction took place between two villages, the inhabitants of both were to be placed in the pool of potential victims.[16]

The first executions took place within twenty-four hours of the violation of Belgium's borders and continued unabated through- out the summer and fall. On 5 August the chief of the Army Gen- eral Staff explained to his opposite number in Austria-Hungary that "our advance in Belgium is certainly brutal, but we are fight- ing for our lives and all who get in the way must take the conse- quences." One hundred and fifty civilians were shot in Aerschot on 19 August; a week later the entire city of Louvain was burned to the ground. "A dreadful thing has occurred at Louvain. Our Gen- eral there has been shot by the son of the Burgomaster. The popu- lation has fired on our troops," the city's commandant told a visiting delegation of Spanish diplomats, "and now of course we have to destroy the city." The Germans did: When Lance-Corporal Adolf Hitler of the 6th Bavarian Reserve Division marched through the city in November, he wrote, the town was "a heap of rubble." This was not an isolated example: Another rear-area commandant blandly announced in October 1914 that in reprisal for various "atrocities," "I ordered the town to be completely de- stroyed. Orchies, formerly a town of 5,000 inhabitants, exists no longer: Houses, town-hall, church have disappeared, there are no more inhabitants." The frontline troops often assisted in collecting the victims; when snipers fired at his regiment, a III Corps officer reported that the village was immediately set afire, "men were dragged out of the houses, and any found with a rifle were given short shrift. Others who were only suspected had their hands tied behind their backs with washing-cords, and were driven along with the column until later they could be tried by court-martial."[17]

The troops participated because they believed that their lives and those of their comrades were at grievous risk from Belgian civilians. The same newspapers that carried word of the great victory at Liege also informed Model and his fellows of "more and more stories of revolting cruelties on our troops by Belgian civilians." They read "of priests, armed, at the head of marauding Belgian civilians, committing every kind of atrocity, and putting the deeds of 1870 into the shade; of treacherous ambushes on patrols, and sentries found later with eyes pierced and tongues cut off, of poisoned wells and other horrors." An artillery lieutenant in the IX Reserve Corps, Fritz Nagel, confided to his diary: "There were stories of poisoned water, tortured prisoners, and other things which filled us with disgust." Lieutenant Hermann Balck of the 10th Jäger Battalion, which led the First Army into Belgium on 6 August, asserted in his memoirs that an officer in his battalion had been shot by civilians under flag of truce on the very first day of the war, and that rumors concerning the mutilation of wounded prisoners spread like wildfire throughout the ranks. In Aachen hospitals, by 11 August, there were widely believed to be thirty German officers whose eyes had been gouged out by the women and children of Belgium. The official reason for the destruction of Orchies was that "doctors, sanitary personnel and about twenty German soldiers have been attacked and murdered. The worst atrocities have been committed in an incredible manner (ears cut off, eyes torn out and similar bestialities)."[18]

The atrocity stories and the belief that the Belgian government had encouraged such action had little if any basis in reality; guerrilla activity was inconsequential on a strategic scale and not in fact officially sanctioned. But the rumors gained tremendous currency because senior officers either created or credited them, and thus they filtered down to the men in the ranks with the authority of official dispatches. General Erich Ludendorff, for example, defended the actions of the invaders by arguing that the Belgians had brought down this fate upon themselves by having the temerity to defend their country: "It was evident that Belgium had long been prepared for our advance. The roads had been systematically destroyed and barricaded, showing that a great deal of work had been done beforehand. No such obstacles could be found on the southwest frontier of Belgium. Why had Belgium not taken similar precautions against France?" The commander of the First Army wholeheartedly agreed, arguing in his memoirs that "from the moment the Belgian frontier was crossed the advance of the Army had suffered by treacherous acts on the part of the population, apparently instigated thereto by the local authorities." Von Kluck grew so angry at the thought of this irregular warfare that he ordered "severe and inexorable reprisals," including "the shooting of individuals and the burning of houses." Both men then took pains to portray their actions as a response to Belgian outrages, patently ignoring the fact that the German terror program had been designed before hostilities began. If the second part of the German program was not the intentional creation of a "Big Lie" concerning the behavior of the Belgians, it represented a shared, unconscious, reflexive rationalization by the German military mind, already predisposed to see war as a remorseless struggle for survival and to categorize whole populations in absolute terms.[19]

To Model and the other officers of the III Corps on the trains heading west, however, only the newspaper stories hinted at this aspect of the war before them, and disquieting or blood-curdling as the rumors may have been, they were for the time being subordinated to more pressing practical considerations. The big guns had opened on Liege on 10 August; the first elements of the III Corps arrived at the medieval German city Aix-la-Chapelle the following day. Cavalry and lightly armed jäger battalions had already preceded von Lochow's corps into Belgium, so military resistance was not the immediate problem—time was. Each succeeding hour brought more trains, disgorging more troops and equipment; if the Schlieffen plan was not to be stillborn in its first hours because of massive confusion at the railhead, each regiment would have to be started on the march as soon as it detrained. This was no small undertaking, since there were only three major roads leading through the town, which itself lay in a defile that at its narrowest point closed to less than 2,000 meters wide. Through this bottleneck the First Army had to move nearly 300,000 men with all their equipment and ordnance in less than forty-eight hours. "The complicated advance through Aix-la-Chapelle had to be begun before the ammunition and supply columns of the leading corps had finished detraining," von Kluck reported, "and before the fighting troops of the corps following in the second line had been assembled, so that the separate corps could not be given sufficient time to complete their concentration and close up." As each company arrived, its commander was given a strip map of his route, told what signs to follow, given a point at which he would reunite with his regiment on the other side of the border, and hustled on his way without regard to the remainder of his unit. Two of von Kluck's six corps shared each road, and each general officer who had been assigned to control one of the roads was fully empowered to make any decision necessary to keep the whole enterprise moving. The III Corps passed along the southernmost of the three routes, through Weiden, Aix-la-Chapelle, Eynatten, and Lontzerr, sharing the narrow road with the IX Corps.[20]

Once the regiments threaded the eye of the needle beneath the medieval church spires of Aix-la-Chapelle, they tramped into Belgium. Now the race was truly on, and the German soldiers would spend the next month matching flesh against the unforgiving timetables calculated by the General Staff. That is not to say that von Moltke and his subordinates had not done their best to equip the troops for the ordeal ahead. "Each soldier carried sixty-five pounds: rifle and ammunition, knapsack, canteen, extra boots, entrenching tools, knife and a multiplicity of implements and kits strapped to his coat," observes Tuchman. "In one bag was his 'iron ration' containing two cans of meat, two of vegetables, two packages of hardtack, one of ground coffee, and a flask of whisky which was only to be opened on permission of an officer and was inspected daily to determine if its owner had cheated. Another bag held thread, needles, bandages and adhesive tape; another held matches, chocolate, and tobacco." They had been trained to make sustained marches, to collapse at night on the side of the road instead of fanning out into the countryside, to forage for themselves and their horses from the fields rather than wait for tardy field kitchens or supply wagons, and to stagger on singing despite the fatigue that inexorably gripped them tighter and tighter.[21]

But the pace that von Schlieffen's grand conception demanded was something far beyond the imagining of the hardiest. Von Kluck's First Army had to average—without respite—thirty to forty kilometers per day, just to stay on schedule. The first day's march for Model's brigade exceeded the required distance—they covered nearly forty-five kilometers before sunset—and Captain Bloem reported that "not one of my lads fell out, not a single one. The thought of falling into the hands of the Walloons was worse than sore feet." That initial tally was the result of other things besides fear, including youthful enthusiasm and the pent-up energy now released after a week of train rides in confined railroad cars. Sustaining the pace was another matter. Hermann Balck's memoirs detail what was to become the typical day for more than 200,000 infantrymen. Roused by their officers at 5:00 A.M., the regiments of the First Army would march for three hours before breakfast, covering as much as twelve kilometers. The rest halt for the meal lasted less than an hour, and another twelve kilometers would be expected by noon. Here there was usually the opportunity for two hours of rest, but only if the men had so far attained their quota. The minutes spent sprawled along the roadway ended all too quickly, for at least another twelve to eighteen kilometers would be required before night.[22]

Sweating in the mid-August sun, neither the soldiers nor the officers of the 52nd Infantry knew that the great plan had already begun to misfire. First, the bulk of the Belgian army had been able to escape von Kluck's clutches and retire into the fortifications around Antwerp, forcing the First Army to detach the III and IV Reserve Corps to guard against a possible sortie against the German line of communications. Then, as the armies further to the left began to make contact with the French in the Ardennes, von Moltke decided that he could not coordinate single-handedly the operations of seven advancing armies and subordinated the First Army to the commander of the Second, Colonel General Karl von Bülow. Von Bülow's innate caution made him precisely the wrong man in the wrong place in an operation that depended on audacity, ferocity, and speed; his orders reined in von Kluck's hard-marching infantry by ordering them south to help his own army outflank the French Fifth Army rather than allowing them to continue striking southwest for the Channel. Worse still, he removed von der Marwitz's cavalry from von Kluck's control, leaving the First Army commander plummeting blindly in the wrong direction.[23]

The culminating misfortune in this series of miscues was the complete failure of the Germans—from the intelligence service of the high command down to the cavalry pickets in the field—to realize the speed with which General Sir John French's British Expeditionary Force (BEF) was marching up from the coast. The confusion at von Moltke's headquarters, the *Oberste Heeres Leitung* (OHL), is difficult to credit, even decades later. On the same day that the commanders of the three armies of the right wing were informed by the intelligence section that the British were landing at Ostend, other officers in that office telegraphed the commanders of the armies on the far left that the British had not crossed the Channel and might not enter France at all. As Barbara Tuchman muses, "Perhaps the staff officers at OHL who dealt with the left wing were a different group from those who dealt with the right wing, and failed to consult each other." Even von Kluck, who knew the BEF was somewhere on the continent, harbored the illusion that they had not yet entered Belgium in force. His order of the day for 22 August noted almost in passing that "a squadron of British cavalry was encountered to-day at Casteau, north-east of Mons, and a British aeroplane coming from Mauberge was shot down near Enghien," and von Kluck ordered a continued march in which the III Corps was to "reach St. Ghislain and Jemappes by Lens and Jurbise," which would place it in the rear of the French Fifth Army on the Sambre. Unfortunately for the Germans, four divisions of British regulars stood between them and their day's objective, defending along the sixty-foot-wide Mons canal.[24]

The area surrounding Mons was industrial rather than agricultural, and it was not lovely country. Novelist C. S. Forester describes the dreary landscape from the viewpoint of a British cavalryman: "There were slag heaps and enclosures. There was barbed wire in the hedges, and there were deep, muddy ditches—there could be no hell-for-leather charging, ten squadrons together, on this terrain." "The canal, bordered by railroad sidings and industrial back yards," says one historian, "was black with slime and reeked of chemical refuse from furnaces and factories. In among small vegetable plots, pastures, and orchards the gray pointed slag heaps like witches hats stuck up everywhere, giving the landscape a bizarre, abnormal look." But what it lacked in attractiveness the countryside compensated on 23 August by providing excellent defensive cover for British soldiers outnumbered more than two to one.[25]

When eight German divisions careened into the BEF, the day-long engagement resulted in a British tactical victory that bought several hours for the French on the Sambre and set the First Army a day behind schedule. To von Kluck the battle represented merely the first brush with the enemy in what he knew would be a bloody campaign. In his memoirs, he devotes only a single page to "the obstinate fighting for the crossings of the Mons-Condé Canal on the 23rd August, in which both sides suffered heavy losses." Almost grudgingly he admits that "the British Expeditionary Force fought excellently," though he cannot resist adding that "British prisoners extolled the Germans as attacking devils." Historian Correlli Barnett agrees that Mons was "militarily without great significance in the campaign of 1914," but notes that "it was the first battle fought in northern Europe by the British since Waterloo; it expressed in blood Britain's inevitable yet so long evaded commitment to the continent."[26] As such, it has entered the historic mythology of British arms along with such other dubious "victories" as Dunkirk, Crete, and Arnhem. For the soldiers on both sides it was a sharp if small-scale introduction to the carnage that would consume an entire generation over the next four years. The Tommies of the BEF experienced for the first time the ability of airplanes to direct the plunging fire of heavy field guns. Meanwhile, the Germans discovered the extent to which machine-gun and even well-aimed rifle fire could dominate a battlefield: "Well entrenched and completely hidden, the enemy opened a murderous fire . . . the casualties increased . . . the rushes became shorter, and finally the whole advance stopped . . . with bloody losses."[27]

Model's entire regiment bloodied itself at Mons. Shortly after noon, the III Battalion, 52nd Infantry, "contrived, with great skill, to pass men by driblets over the road into the reedy marshes alongside the canal, and even to send one or two machine guns with them." These companies were pinned down and suffered heavy casualties without achieving anything of significance. Two hours later the remaining battalions of the 52nd launched a futile attack with closed ranks of singing, cheering soldiers. John Terraine observes that "the fate of these two battalions was the same as that of every German massed attack; they were shot to pieces, and decisively repulsed, with small casualties to the East Surreys." Neither of these actions got the III Corps in strength any closer than two hundred yards of the canal.[28]

At the individual level, "shot to pieces" and "decisively repulsed" translated into smoke, screams, and blood. Throughout the war soldiers of both armies felt compelled to record the horror of that first shattering moment. "I should like to give you a complete picture of the whole battle," wrote a twenty-three-year-old German private of his initial battle,

> but only little isolated incidents thrust themselves into the foreground. It was ghastly! Not the actual shedding of blood, nor that it was shed in vain, nor the fact that in the darkness our own comrades were firing at us—no, but the whole way in which a battle is fought is so revolting. To want to fight and not even be able to defend oneself! The attack, which I thought was going to be so magnificent, meant nothing but being forced to get forward from one bit of cover to another in the face of a hail of bullets, and not to see the enemy who was firing them.[29]

Even when Adolph Hitler attempted for political purposes to portray his own first battle as some sort of *volkisch* catharsis, the undercurrent of sheer terror was still evident in his narrative when he spoke of "the iron greeting [that] came whizzing over our heads, and with a sharp report sent the little pellets flying between our ranks, ripping up the wet ground."[30] We do not know with any certainty how Walther Model met his baptism of fire, although his later well-documented reputation for coolness under fire suggests that any horror, moral paralysis, or trepidation he may have felt was swiftly mastered. Nor would the battalion adjutant have had the same amount of time for reaction or reflection as a soldier in the ranks; the discharge of those responsibilities required constant action. Lieutenant Model would have been busy carrying his commander's orders to the companies and overseeing the alignment of one of the battalion flanks. If he reflected at all on his first day of combat, it is likely that Model would have shared the sentiments of Captain Bloem of the 12th Grenadiers: "The only impressions that remained in our dizzy brains were of streams of blood, of pale-faced corpses, of confused chaos, of aimless firing, of houses in smoke and flame, or ruins, of sopping clothes, of feverish thirst, and of limbs exhausted, heavy as lead."[31]

But events continued at a breathless pace without consideration for the sensibilities of the soldiers on either side. Flanked by superior forces at Mons, with the French front on the Sambre River collapsing to the east, General Sir John French withdrew south of the canal that evening. Von Kluck expected him to make a stand the next day in the vicinity of St. Ghislain, and Model's battalion spearheaded the advance of the III Corps through the village. "At a street corner, in front of a grocer's shop, the door of which had been smashed open with an axe, stood General Sontag, our brigade commander," recalled one officer. "Busy hands kept passing out to him from inside masses of packets of chocolates, biscuits, and cakes, which he distributed to the troops as they passed. A hundred greedy hands stretched out to him, and greedy eyes from a hundred hungry faces tried to catch his." There was an expectation of battle in the air.[32]

But there was no full-scale engagement in the offing. Von Bülow refused to release von der Marwitz's Cavalry Corps to von Kluck, and thus the First Army lacked any force that could overtake the BEF's grudging retreat to pin French's divisions long enough for a stand-up fight. Instead, as Captain Heinrich Hübner observed, "in front of us there still swarmed a number of scattered English troops, who were easily able to hide in the large woods of the district, and again and again forced us to waste time in deployments, as we could not tell what their strength might be." Except for a brief stand at Le Cateau on 27 August, the Tommies remained tantalizingly just out of von Kluck's reach. Losing precious hours was

more critical to the Germans just then than losing soldiers in battle, and von Kluck knew it; he threw his divisions forward as recklessly as possible, in an increasingly futile attempt to catch the
British and stay on schedule. After the war he wrote: "The requirements of the strategic situation made it impossible to give any rest
days in the true sense of the word. Marches and fights, battles and
marches, followed one another without interval."[33]

The march requirement increased to as much as forty kilometers
per day, with von Kluck paying personal calls on each of his divisions to keep them up to the pace. But the unending demands of
von Schlieffen's strategic conception began to unravel the army's
supply organization at the same time that the First Army's soldiers
began to test seriously the limits of endurance. "As German lines
of communication stretched out and troops advanced farther from
the railheads," Barbara Tuchman notes, "food supplies often
failed. Horses ate grain directly from unharvested fields and men
marched a whole day on nothing but raw carrots and cabbages."
"We were all tired to death, and the column just railed along any-
how. I sat on my war-horse like a bundle of wet washing; no clear
thought penetrated my addled brain," wrote one company commander. When General von Lochow attempted to bolster his division's morale with a series of surprise appearances to make
speeches about the soldiers' contributions to the upcoming victory,
that same company commander remembered that, "as the much-
respected general waved his hand to us and drove away, we all
looked at each other slightly disconcerted"; they were unable to re-
late his airy comments to the grinding reality of their daily existence. By early September, when the men of the First Army had
been on the march for nearly four full weeks, another officer confided to his diary that

> Our men are all done up. . . . They stagger forward, their faces
> coated with dust, their uniforms in rags. They look like living scare-
> crows. . . . They march with eyes closed, singing in chorus so as not

to fall asleep. . . . Only the certainty of early victory and a triumphal entry into Paris keeps them going. . . . Without this they would fall exhausted and go to sleep where they fall. . . . They drink to excess but this drunkenness keeps them going. Today after inspection the General was furious. He wanted to stop this general drunkenness but we managed to dissuade him from giving severe orders. If we use too much severity the Army would not march. Abnormal stimulants are necessary to combat abnormal fatigue. . . . We will put all that right in Paris.[34]

Neither Lieutenant Model nor his comrades, however, were privy to the internal arguments between senior German officers and the desperate strategic redeployment by the French, which would ultimately prevent a triumphant march through Paris. Alternating between the conviction that the war had already been won and the paranoid belief that tens of thousands more British—and even Russians!—were debarking at Ostend to threaten the German right flank, Chief of Staff von Moltke and his inner circle of advisers committed a series of strategic blunders in late August and early September so egregious that they provoked army commanders to near-mutiny and drove the war minister to assert that "our general staff has completely lost its head." Von Moltke transferred critical reinforcements for the right wing to West Prussia, reducing the strength available to the First and Second Armies so much that von Kluck could no longer consider enveloping Paris and had to wheel his several corps east of the city. Von Kluck and von Bülow, for their parts, began to ignore the directions of the OHL (while not communicating with each other either), and their armies headed for the Marne River at divergent angles.[35]

Meanwhile, the French general-in-chief, Field Marshal Joseph Joffre, had decided to risk everything on a flank attack to turn the tables on the Germans at the Marne. General Maunoury's Sixth Army was hastily organized on the French far left, while General Gallieni was assigned to convert Paris into an armed camp and

General French was induced to halt the retreat of the BEF for a concerted attack on the German First and Second Armies. Assembling these forces was a masterpiece of strategic improvisation, perhaps best characterized by the wild ride to battle of an Algerian division that traversed Paris in taxis and buses; committing them to the decisive battle in the hopes that their lack of organization would be offset by German exhaustion was either a stroke of genius or desperation—or both.[36]

Von Kluck had masked Paris with only the IV Reserve Corps, and he was reluctant to believe that the attacks reported by its commander on 5 September represented a major French counteroffensive. He was forced almost immediately, however, to begin pulling troops away from the Marne front to reinforce the hard-pressed reservists; with his main line of battle in turn left weakened as the attack spread, the BEF hit his left flank in the gap between the First and Second Armies. Even so, if a staff officer representing von Moltke—Lieutenant Colonel Richard Hentsch—had not been present at von Kluck's headquarters during the most difficult moments of the battle and assumed on vague authority the right to order a retreat, there is substantial evidence that the First Army might have weathered the storm and remained in its position threatening Paris. Walther Görlitz concludes that von Kluck "retreated at the very moment when the French generals were themselves considering when their own retreat would become imperative, and nobody was more astounded at the German withdrawal than Joffre, Gallieni and Manoury."[37]

For the men of the 5th Division the five-day battle of the Marne became a feverish blur. They were countermarched from the Marne back to support the IV Reserve Corps, and then on 9 September ordered back toward the left flank of the army to resist the British. Hundreds and then thousands of exhausted soldiers fell in battle; so many officers became casualties that companies and battalions underwent drastic field consolidations. Morale, sustained to this point almost entirely by the vision of Paris and victory, plummeted. When the order for withdrawal finally arrived, late on the ninth, no one believed the rationalization of the staff officer, who insisted that "during the march we shall return through places already passed through, and the men are therefore to be told that the future movements of the corps are in no way to be regarded as a retreat. Having thrown back the enemy that was opposing it to the south, the First Army is now to advance against the east front of Paris to guard against hostile operations from that place."[38]

The retreat itself was a nightmare that not only ended any chance of a decisive German victory in 1914 but came close to unraveling the last threads that bound together the army. Lieutenant Balck left us one of the most evocative portraits of the near-disintegration in the rear areas of the First Army, which Walther Model must also have witnessed. "All the roads were clogged with baggage trains and ammunition columns, all moving without orders," Balck writes. "Nothing was able to pass through. Nobody seemed to know what was what. Nothing stood fast as the First Army retreated." Staff organization had disappeared, and the meticulous controls that had passed several hundred thousand men through Aix-la-Chapelle without a hitch were nowhere in evidence. Unit commanders, Balck notes, were on their own: "Toward 8:30 A.M., we slowly maneuvered through the baggage columns which were jammed together. By fits and starts we managed to get the whole mass moving forward. At least once every half hour there was a longer or shorter halt. Meanwhile there was a growing anxiety of uncertainty." There was no reconnaissance, and reports of the BEF on parallel roads were constant; soldiers could not avoid hearing the thunder of what were assumed to be English guns in the background. "Among the 'baggage knights' a wild panic broke out," as individual soldiers in their hysteria suddenly became willing to do anything to secure a horse. Balck recalls that "one brought an ambulance carrying a severely wounded sergeant from the Life Grenadiers to a halt at the point of a pistol."[39]

Fortunately for von Kluck and his First Army, this near-rout slowly resolved itself into a more orderly withdrawal. The French and British had been hurt badly enough at the Marne to preclude their pressing the rear of his disorganized columns; those phantom enemies on the German flanks were—as Balck found out later— simply other Germans heading in the same direction. Von Kluck's regiments, brigades, and divisions sorted themselves out when they arrived at hastily prepared positions on the north bank of the Aisne River, and from that point they held their ground. In operational if not strategic terms, defeat avoided becoming disaster.

There was only one last frenetic act to play out before the armies settled down to trench warfare in what Paul Fussell has so aptly characterized as "the Troglodyte world." During October the Germans and the Allies conducted the indecisive "Race to the Sea," in which each side attempted with a notable lack of success to slide around the other's flank in northwestern France. By the end of November this last phase of maneuver ended because there was simply no place left to go, and the parallel fronts congealed in an irregular line from Switzerland to the English Channel. A soldier in the 6th Bavarian Reserve Division described "the trenches of our infantry" as "a maze of dug-out, trenches with loopholes, entrenchments, barbed-wire entanglements, pitfalls, [and] landmines." "If one could have gotten high enough to look down at the whole line at once, one would have seen a series of multiple parallel excavations running for 400 miles down through Belgium and France," writes Fussell. There were "over 12,000 miles of trenches on the Allied side alone. When we add the trenches of the Central Powers, we arrive at a figure of about 25,000 miles, equal to a trench sufficient to circle the earth."[40]

After the Aisne/Marne campaign, the 5th Division, of which Model's regiment was a part, came to rest in a static position in the Vailly/Soissons region before participating in the Battle of Soissons in mid-January 1915. While stationed there, Walther Model was promoted to *Oberleutnant* on 25 February, despite the fact that the records indicate he did not get along particularly well with his battalion commander. The division, along with the rest of the III Corps, was next removed from the First Army and transferred to the Arras sector, where it took heavy casualties that summer, as well as in the German attacks in Champagne beginning in September. Model was severely wounded at Arras—a bullet hit his shoulder bone and deflected through his neck—but recovered in time to win the Iron Cross, First Class, at Champagne in October. Just before Christmas the corps was again pulled out of the line—the 6th Division for a brief sojourn in the Balkans, and the 5th Division dispatched to a quieter section of the line in Belgium.[41]

This rest, however, was all too brief, for the III Corps had been selected by the new chief of the General Staff, Erich von Falkenhayn, for participation in the ill-fated battle of attrition at Verdun. Von Lochow's III Corps (the 6th Division having returned from Serbia) now became a part of Crown Prince Wilhelm's Fifth Army and was assigned a spearheading role in the assault on Verdun. The corps was considerably smaller in early February 1916 than it had been when it began its march into Belgium eighteen months earlier. Part of the reason was of course the steady grinding attrition of the trenches—mounting losses that could never quite be filled no matter what expedients were attempted—but there had been a structural change as well. The old "square" infantry division of two brigades each containing two regiments had proven unwieldy in both maneuver and combat. The General Staff therefore had begun removing one brigade headquarters and one regiment from each division, leaving a "triangular" organization with three regiments under a staff now more often known as that of the *Infanterieführer*. The headquarters and regiments thus removed became the cadres for new divisions; the 5th Division had lost the 9th Infantry Brigade headquarters and the 48th Infantry Regiment.[42]

The 52nd Infantry Regiment was held in reserve during the first attacks at Herbebois on 23 February and Fort Douaumont on 26

February, after which the 5th Division was pulled into reserve for about ten days before being committed again from the eighth to the fifteenth of March, when the 52nd figured more prominently in the offensive. This alternation of hellish battle and brief rest continued until 22 April, when the division was thrown into the fight for six uninterrupted weeks, emerging as only a skeleton of its former self. Nonetheless, the shattered regiments enjoyed only about a month's rest before they were forced back into combat at the Somme.[43]

Walther Model, however, only participated in the opening rounds of the Battle of Verdun and did not see any action at the Somme. In April, despite the fact that his battalion commander did not like him and the division's *Infanterieführer*, Prince Oskar of Prussia, characterized him as "an uncomfortable subordinate," Model was recommended for and accepted into General Staff training. The casualties of two years of active campaigning as well as the expansion of the army required hundreds of new General Staff officers. Although it was completely out of the question to send these junior officers to the three-year course at the War Academy in Berlin in the middle of the war, an intensive eight-month training regimen was developed to introduce them to the fundamentals of staff work. Although some of the subjects that contributed to the wider education of an officer were necessarily omitted (civil government, political economy, public and international law, chemistry, physics, and foreign languages), the remaining core of "statistics, war history, tactics, fortification, siege operations, sketching, surveying and drawing, general staff service, and training in travel [and] means of communication" certainly acted as a sufficiently rigorous introduction to the Great General Staff. Graduating from the course, Model returned to his old division at the front as brigade adjutant of the 10th Infantry Brigade, followed by postings as a company commander in both the 52nd Infantry and the 8th Life Grenadiers, as well as a brief stint as an acting battalion commander. This was in keeping with the tradition of alternating the assignments of young officers between staff and line in order to give them the widest possible range of experience.[44]

What happened next, however, was the first of many fortuitous occurrences that would mark the career of Walther Model, eventually propelling him to the highest ranks of the German army. In August 1916, the Kaiser had relieved Falkenhayn and replaced him with Paul von Hindenburg as chief of the General Staff and Erich Ludendorff as first quartermaster general. The "Duo," as historian Robert B. Asprey refers to the collaboration between the victors of Tannenberg, slowly erected a de facto military dictatorship intended to bring the war to a victorious conclusion. Around them gathered an exclusive clique of senior staff officers who would carry out their plans, including Lieutenant Colonel Georg Wetzel in the Operations Department and Colonel Hans von Seeckt, who was routinely assigned as chief of staff to whichever army faced the greatest challenge. Wetzel had been the operations officer and Seeckt the chief of staff to the III Corps at the outbreak of the war, and it is evident that whenever possible they favored officers from their old command with choice assignments. One of the beneficiaries of their largess was Walther Model, who suddenly found himself lifted out of the trenches and seconded to OHL in early 1917 as an ordnance officer.[45]

Assignment to the *Oberste Heeres Leitung* represented not only a tremendous opportunity for the young Model but also a heady approach to the very center of power. He was present when "Operation *Alberich*," the withdrawal to the Hindenburg Line, was planned and executed. To forestall an Allied attack and buy time to organize greater reserves, Ludendorff ordered Crown Prince Rupprecht to pull back his army group from fifteen to twenty-five miles on a seventy-mile-wide front, occupying prepared positions and creating a zone of devastation to impede any quick advance by the enemy. Rupprecht argued strongly against the wholesale destruction of property and forced displacement of 100,000 civilians, but Ludendorff was unrepentant, insisting that "the destruction of all highroads, villages, towns, and wells, so as to prevent the enemy establishing himself in force in the near future in front of our new position," was a military necessity and

> the fact that so much property belonging to the inhabitants was destroyed was to be deplored, but it could not be helped. The bulk of the population was driven eastward, only a small proportion being collected in certain places, such as Noyon, Ham, and Nesle, and provided with rations for several days and left behind. On the one hand it was desireable not to make a present to the enemy of too much fresh strength in the form of recruits and laborers, and on the other we wanted to foist upon him as many mouths to feed as possible.[46]

Although the withdrawal has since been described as "cunning and cruel," "inhuman," and bordering on illegal under international law, it was a technical and tactical masterpiece that added thirteen divisions to OHL's reserves.[47] The operation must have been especially impressive for Model—heretofore a purely frontline officer—to observe from the vantage point of headquarters. He could not of course have guessed that nearly two and a half decades later he would execute a comparable maneuver as an army commander.

Among Ludendorff's other grand programs that Model probably witnessed, at least in the planning stage, was his drive for an armywide political education and propaganda program. As conditions inside Germany worsened, desertion rates increased, and the officers at OHL began to worry that their divisions were melting away. Thus, in July 1917, Ludendorff proposed a comprehensive "scheme of patriotic education for the troops," which envisioned the training and appointment of permanent propaganda officers and noncommissioned officers (NCOs) down to the company level. "Propaganda work should not try to drive natural currents of opinion underground, where they would only work mischief in secret," Ludendorff argued, "but should counter and silence the voice of scepticism."[48] Ultimately the plan fizzled, but it is again interesting to note that it would have distinct echoes in Model's later career, when he would be one of the most agreeable of Adolph Hitler's commanders to programs of direct National Socialist indoctrination for his own troops.

Lieutenant Colonel Wetzel performed quite effectively in the role of patron to Walther Model, thrusting him into several choice assignments. During late 1917, Model and several other relatively junior officers (including Erich Köstring, the future German army attaché in Moscow in 1941) found themselves assigned to an exclusive working staff under von Seeckt that was dispatched to Turkey. Von Seeckt's mission was to assess the steadfastness of the Constantinople government in the prosecution of the war, as well as to lay the foundations for a hypothetical German advance in the Middle East. The results of this sojourn were disappointing to von Seeckt but afforded Model a precious opportunity to make a personal impression on the man who would later have a virtual veto power in deciding which four thousand officers would be retained in the postwar army.[49]

Likewise, Wetzel ensured that when Model left the OHL he received a particularly good posting. On 10 March 1918, just eleven days before Ludendorff's "Operation Michael" offensive would tear open the front of the British army, newly promoted Captain Model was transferred to Major General Maximilian von Poseck's Guard Ersatz Division as the division supply officer (IIb). The Guard Ersatz Division had been created at the outbreak of the war from the replacement and training battalions of the elite Guard Corps, and along with the Guard Cavalry and Guard Jäger Divisions it was to be held under Ludendorff's direct control as a reserve unit to be thrown into battle at the decisive moment. The division was a solid unit—categorized as an "attack" rather than a "trench" division—but despite its name it was never considered an elite formation.[50]

Model joined the division at Arlons, where it was undergoing its final preparations for the offensive. His responsibilities included anything to do with supplying his division, especially with food, fodder, horses, and ammunition. With only a small section of officers and NCOs under him, Model now had to supervise the division's rail movement through Charleroi to Mons just four days after his arrival. Did he have time to think about this unlikely return to the scene of his first battle? Probably not, for as soon as each battalion detrained it began a series of might marches to Mauberge, in the rear of Army Group German Crown Prince Rupprecht; now he was the man responsible for ensuring that those unruly trains of supply wagons that had so impeded the retreat in 1914 did not hopelessly entangle its advance. The Guard Ersatz Division was assigned upon arrival to the third line of the XIV Corps of Colonel General Georg von der Marwitz's Second Army, which bore responsibility for the main attack toward Peronne.[51]

The Michael offensive was the beginning of Ludendorff's great gamble to employ the temporary numerical superiority vouchsafed to Germany on the Western Front by the collapse of Russia the previous year. The attack was made in pursuit of a victory in France before the weight of the rapidly arriving U.S. army could be brought to bear. The conception for the attack centered on the "infiltration" tactics developed in Russia and perfected in Italy to break the stalemate of the trenches. "Infantry will be instructed," Ludendorff insisted, "upon the following new lines: Fewer lines of skirmishers and masked attacks; more attacks by scattered machine gun groups supported by the fire of rifles, light and heavy machine-guns, rifle grenades, trench mortars, and accompanying artillery."[52] Combined arms assaults would breach the weakest parts of the enemy lines. Success would be reinforced, and flanks disregarded. The immediate objectives were to destroy the nerve system of the Allied armies—their artillery emplacements, headquarters, and communications—leaving their inert mass to be carved up at will.

The Guard Ersatz Division did not participate in the initial assault, which was phenomenally successful in the sector of the Eighteenth Army to the south, reasonably so in front of the Seventeenth Army to the north, and frustratingly indecisive during the first hours along the line of the Second Army. Although the British Fifth Army lost 293 pieces of field artillery and 89 heavy guns in the first twenty-four hours, the two outnumbered divisions of the XIX Corps bent but refused to break in their defense of Peronne. Unfortunately for the British, however, the line south of the XIX Corps dissolved into a gaping hole in the face of the German onslaught on 22 March, causing the loss of Peronne in heavy fighting the next day. On 25 March, the Guard Ersatz Division moved into the battle line near Proyant, by which time the Second Army's new objective had been set as Amiens.[53]

Walther Model would have had no way of knowing it, but even though the British would be pushed back several more miles in the ensuing days, the offensive had already failed in its strategic objectives by the time his division was committed to the fight. Ludendorff had made the costly error of reinforcing the early failures of the Second and Seventeenth Armies rather than the success of the Eighteenth, and his disagreements with Crown Prince Rupprecht resulted in each of the three armies attacking in a different direction. This gave the offensive, one historian has observed, "a skyrocket effect" from which great tactical gains might still be achieved but which eliminated any chance of a decisive strategic result.[54]

A more fundamental problem for the Germans was their inability to exploit breakthroughs with enough speed to convert an advantage into a victory. This shortcoming Model and other officers on the ground understood all too well. As the Guard Ersatz Division and other reserve units plodded forward to get into the battle, they had to traverse terrain that had been not only churned up by the recent fighting but also devastated during the previous year's withdrawal. Again, while we do not possess a record of Walther

Model's observations during this period, we are fortunate to have the diary left by another officer, Rudolf Binding, who held a similar staff position in the 199th Infantry Division in the XXIII Corps, which was advancing just to the north of the XIV Corps. Binding recorded the difficulties of marching "over the territory which we laid waste, and where there are neither roads, trees, nor villages," where "all the wells and streams have been wrecked, and the water for the attacking troops has to be brought up in water-carts. That applies to the men. The horses have got to wait until we cross the canal at Mois-lains-Nurlu; we are supposed to reach it to-day."[55]

"We are going like hell, on and on, day and night," Binding wrote. "The sun and moon help. One or two hours' halt, then on again. Our baggage is somewhere in the rear, and nobody expects to see it again." The soldiers passed days at a time wherein the only water available had to be scooped out of shell-holes. Dead and dying horses littered the battlefield. Finally, in early April, the attack petered out: "One cannot go on victoriously for ever without ammunition or any sort of reinforcements. Behind us lies the wilderness. It is true that the railway is running again as far as Peronne, but it has too many demands to meet." Equally important, the ever-slowing pace of the battle allowed the British to redeploy more and more troops into the battle zone, reducing and then eliminating the German numerical advantage. Although the Kaiser awarded Hindenburg the Blücher Cross in recognition of the army's achievements, Ludendorff called off the offensive on 5 April, turning his attentions to other likely segments of the line.[56]

Six times between late March and mid-July the German army struck Allied lines, following the same tactical recipe. Each time the results were similar: a quick breakthrough stymied by the inability of the Germans to exploit their successes before the Allies brought up reinforcements to blunt their offensive. Each time miles of progress were bought at the price of irreplaceable casualties and equipment, while General John J. Pershing's troops continued to disembark by the thousands. For a brief moment in June the ultimate success seemed to beckon: Ludendorff had divisions over the Marne and within thirty-nine miles of Paris. But the timely arrival of two oversized American divisions at Chateau-Thierry provided the weight that the French XXI Corps needed to throw them back on their heels.[57]

Model did not participate in these attacks because the Guard Ersatz Division was being refitted for "Operation Gneisenau," a desperate last-ditch effort to envelop Rheims, shore up the awkward salient around Chateau-Thierry, and possibly inflict enough French casualties to topple Georges Clemenceau's shaky government. General von Poseck's division had been transferred to the First Army in mid-June and assigned a leading assault role east of Rheims in Corps "Langer" (XXIV Reserve Corps). "Our period of rest is nearly over," complained Rudolf Binding, whose 199th Infantry Division was in the corps' second line. Sourly, he observed that "the preparations are not so elaborate and energetic as they were before the spring offensive of this year."[58]

The chief problems faced by officers like Walther Model were an inadequate supply of horses and fodder, insufficient numbers of trained, healthy replacements, and a general decline in morale, which had finally reached even frontline troops. Despite a thorough comb-out of the rear echelons, the Guard Ersatz Division was still short several hundred horses when the day of the attack arrived. Nor were the animals they did have available in the best condition. One supply officer wrote: "To keep up the fiction of a hard ration they are now offered two pounds of dried chopped turnips. All other nourishment they are supposed to get from grazing, and that is to go on until the day of the offensive. As if one could suddenly stoke up a horse's body like a boiler." The consequence for the assault divisions was that even though they had been assigned extra artillery for their initial breakthrough attack, they would not be able to bring more than a portion of their field batteries with them as they moved forward.[59]

This potential shortage of artillery support after the first hours was concealed from the troops, primarily because the German army was experiencing ever more severe manpower and morale problems. Not only were the replacements being sent forward to fill the ranks far less well trained than their predecessors, but they were also less healthy. The food shortages experienced by the home front during the "turnip winter" had begun to make inroads into the army as well, and increasingly malnourished soldiers demonstrated a significantly decreased resistance to typhus, influenza, and other diseases. Just a week prior to the opening of the Rheims offensive, the First Army reported that some of its first-line divisions had as many as 1,600 men on the sick lists—the equivalent of two infantry battalions![60]

Worse still, however, was the creeping loss of confidence infiltrating the German ranks. "It is impossible to feel as much confidence as at the beginning of the year," opined Lieutenant Binding. Captain Herbert Sulzbach of the 63rd Field Artillery Regiment (9th Infantry Division) was even less inclined to mince words in his journal: "We haven't the same morale that we had on 21 March or on 27 May." Kurt Hesse, a company commander in the 5th Grenadier Regiment (36th Infantry Division), found himself confronted the night before the battle by a private soldier who "asked if it were true that Americans were stationed over there and that our attack was betrayed." Hesse reassured his grenadier, but was discomfited enough to spend the remainder of the evening inquiring "carefully here and there what the general opinions on the attack might be. There was thorough confidence in the leaders; but there was an indefinite feeling that the affair would not succeed."[61]

Nevertheless, thanks to the herculean efforts of staff officers like Walther Model, the divisions of the First, Third, and Seventh Armies were in place on the morning of 15 July and gamely ready for the rolling barrage to begin. General von Poseck had every reason to be satisfied with his supply officer, who had coordinated much of the buildup. The Guard Ersatz Division entered the battle rated by the First Army as one of the strongest in the line: "effective infantry strength 839 men [per battalion]; 94% of horses fit for service; fully fit; 4 weeks rest." In addition, the division had been strengthened by the attachment of "one army light artillery regiment, a second light howitzer battalion, one mortar battery and one heavy gun battery." The last operational report prior to the attack listed the Guard Ersatz Division as "fit for all missions"—the highest rating in the German army.[62]

The predawn darkness was so complete that "in the woods one could not see one's own hand in front of one's eyes, and ran against trees." "The barrage makes an incredible din, you can hear nothing, and can't see anything either because of the smoke," wrote artilleryman Sulzbach. "Once again, the enemy do comparatively little firing, and don't bother us very much." Unfortunately, fumes from the Germans' own poison gas shells blew back across some sectors of the First Army line. Captain Hesse's grenadiers were caught in this opening misfire, and he evokes the chaotic feeling that prevailed:

> Put on the gas masks! One could not see anything before—now still less! Many are seized with a dull despair. They feel helpless: if it would only be day! The wounded scream. At last a hoarsely gasped command from the leader of the company, even now seriously conscious of his duty: "Begin! Has every man a gun?" Now forward on the narrow paths which are struck so fiercely, which, nevertheless, are the only ways that lead down to the river.[63]

The French, moreover, had finally digested the tactical lessons from the last four months and for the first time met infiltration tactics with an elastic defense. The war diary of Army Group German Crown Prince Rupprecht analyzed the situation with technical precision, observing that "the conduct of the enemy was an excellent example of the 'giving way' tactics that we had been more or less directed to pursue since the battle of the Somme; the result of this first day of battle had again shown that decisive, apt leadership can readily evade any superior hostile attack by a 'mobile' defense." In a less detached but equally accurate view, Rudolf Binding wrote that

> They put up no resistance in front; they had neither infantry nor artillery in this forward battle-zone, the full use and value of which they had learned from Ludendorff. Our guns bombarded empty trenches; our gas-shells gassed empty artillery positions; only in little hidden folds of the ground, sparsely distributed, lay machine-gun posts, like lice in the seams and folds of a garment, to give the attacking force a warm reception. The barrage, which was to have preceded and protected it, went right on somewhere over the enemy's rear positions, while in front the first real line of resistance was not yet carried.

Both, however, reached the same conclusion: "The attack came to a standstill along the entire front during the late forenoon hours."[64]

The Guard Ersatz Division stalled in front of the French main line of resistance on the Roman road east of Rheims, suffering particularly heavy casualties because General von Poseck's headquarters was poorly located in an easily visible position on the white chalk flats that covered the area. By noon, enemy artillery fire began hitting it, killing several officers, including the division adjutant, and severing all telephonic links to the regiments at the front. According to the liaison officer from the adjoining division, von Poseck "himself must needs be seized with a fit of impatiences [sic] and false courage and go off on foot," accompanied by the division operations officer, and "they ran about like that for hours, unattainable by anybody. No orders could be carried out, and none was given." Captain Model may well have been the senior officer left at the abandoned headquarters, and if so he certainly learned a valuable lesson about chain of command. As communications were restored, the flow of information, reports, and requests for orders from the front line resumed, but in the absence of the general and his senior staff, "all inquiries and all reports had to be sent on elsewhere at hazard. One could feel the panic of troops deserted by their Commanders gradually growing." Several hours later von Poseck and his operations officer found their way back, but "they were so tired out that they were of no use for the rest of the day. They never realized what they had done and what risks they had run."[65]

West of Rheims the attack made some early progress, but in the First Army sector General of Infantry Bruno von Mudra's divisions were ordered to "discontinue the attack and assume great depth for defense" in the evening of 16 July. Von Poseck's division was required to thin out its sector in order to release adjoining divisions from the line so that they would be available as reserves in case of a counterattack. For the next two days, however, the Guard Ersatz Division held its ground despite French gas barrages and probing infantry attacks. The army group's 18 July evening situation report rather laconically mentioned the fact that "the center of the Guard Ersatz Division defeated a hostile attack." When it was withdrawn from the front on 20 July, the First Army carried it as one of the five strongest divisions available: "Fit for all tasks: after receiving recruits and rest, officers especially needed: after 1 week."[66]

There was no rest in the schedule, however, for while the First Army had held its ground, the Seventh Army tottered on the brink of disaster. The assault divisions' momentum had dissipated in only three days, and this time the Allies counterattacked in force. Hidden in the woods near Villers-Cotterets, the French had assembled several hundred tanks to support their infantry. While the Germans paused to regroup, the tanks lumbered toward them. According to the war diary of Army Group German Crown Prince Rupprecht, it must have been the first combined arms attack in history to include so large a contingent of tanks: "The enemy attacked with very strong forces, supported by numerous low flying planes and tanks," preceded by a rolling "drumfire" artillery barrage. A wave of three hundred tanks rolled over the forward German positions, routing the jaded infantry. Quickly surmounting the torn-up terrain, the tanks trundled toward the German rear areas. Unlike Cambrai, a year earlier, assault groups of French and American infantry followed immediately in the wake of each tank, simultaneously safeguarding it and guaranteeing the captured ground would be held. Only the divisional and corps artillery of the Seventh Army, barrels depressed parallel to the ground and firing over open sights, staved off complete disaster. "July 18, 1918, marks a turning point in the history of the World War," predicted the army commander, General of Infantry Max von Boehn, as he prepared to withdraw his troops all along the line.[67]

Crown Prince Wilhelm managed to stabilize the Seventh Army's front only through a frantically improvised redeployment of relatively fresher troops from the First and Third Armies—among which were included the men of the Guard Ersatz Division—to create a blocking line behind von Boehn's retreating divisions. Calculating that it would take far too long to move the reinforcements as intact divisions, the prince and his chief of staff, Major General Hermann von Kuhl, decided on the expedient of seizing every available truck in the army group's rear area in order to transport just the infantry across the battlefield. As these regiments arrived, they were assigned to makeshift staffs and paired with artillery battalions out of army and army group reserves. "Bits and pieces of other people's units" were thus thrown together in what Captain Sulzbach characterized as "a hopeless jumble." And yet that jumble succeeded in halting the Allied attack: Gunners "pulled out into the open in that hellish fire and knocked out several tanks, firing over open sights," while exhausted infantrymen dug in and held their ground.[68] While Walther Model very probably missed the final confrontation, as division supply officer he was certainly involved in coordinating the transportation for his division's part in the maneuver.

The Rheims offensive of July 1918 was the German army's final strategic offensive, and the course of that battle had a significant if heretofore unnoticed influence on an unusually high number of officers who would become commanding generals and chiefs of staff in the next war. Aside from Model himself, more than a dozen other key figures of World War II participated at various levels. Future Chief of the Army General Staff Ludwig Beck served on the staff of Army Group German Crown Prince Rupprecht and helped direct the emergency redeployment, as did Hitler's first war minister, Werner von Blomberg, in 1918 a staff officer at Seventh Army headquarters. Karl Gerd von Rundstedt took over as chief of staff of the XV Corps during the battle, and Kurt von Hammerstein-Equord held a similar position in the LXV Corps. Friedrich Dollmann, Gotthard Heinrici, Ewald von Kleist, Erich von Manstein, Hasso von Manteuffel, Walther von Seydlitz-Kurzbach, and Erwin von Witzleben all held positions on division staffs, ranging from operations to intelligence. In the line were Hans-Jürgen von Arnim, Fedor von Bock, Hans Speidel, and certainly many others. Even in the larger March and May offensives there had not been such a gathering of future command talent.[69]

As the German army went over to the defensive, capable officers and men who had previously been concentrated in a few "attack" divisions had to be reassigned to lesser-quality "trench" or "position" to solidify them in the face of growing Allied pressure. Walther Model was thus transferred to the 36th Reserve Division on 30 August, again acting as the supply officer. This division, now resting in the quiet Meuse-Antwerp sector, was never rated higher by Allied intelligence summaries than "third-rate." It had spent the first three years of the war on the Eastern Front, transferring to France in May 1917, but did not participate in any of Ludendorff's offensives, except perhaps through levies of younger officers and NCOs.[70]

Despite its reputation, the 36th Reserve Division would give a good account of itself in the heavy but unheralded defensive fighting during the fall of 1918. On 15 October the division relieved the 16th Bavarian Reserve Division southwest of Roulers and fought a sharp action at Thief two days later, another at Deynze on 26 October, and yet another in the vicinity of Ecke on 2 November. Under the competent leadership of Major General Franz von Rantau, the 36th managed to hold its ground long enough to withdraw intact across the Brugge, Thielt, and Lys Rivers and be pulled into army reserve just a week before the Armistice. During this retreat Captain Model would once again have been one of the busiest officers in the division. As an officer in the 9th Infantry Division described the process, "There is an endless amount for me to do and very many orders to give, since it is the most difficult thing alive to prepare a withdrawal and detach one's forces from the enemy, if possible without being observed and without suffering any casualties. Everything has to go back. The first units to be cleared, behind us, are the field hospitals, field dressing stations, ration dumps, ammunition dumps and artillery workshops." Model would still have been enmeshed in a thousand pressing details when the guns fell silent at 11:00 P.M. on 11 November.[71]

2

SUITED FOR

HIGHER COMMAND

Between the World Wars

EVEN BEFORE THE ARMISTICE WENT INTO EFFECT, THE SHAKY edifice of the *Kaiserreich* began to crumble, beginning with the rebellion of the workers' and soldiers' councils at Kiel on 3 November, followed in quick succession by Kurt Eisner's *putsch* in Bavaria on 8 November and Wilhelm's abdication the following day. Reluctantly, Friedrich Ebert, "the Socialist who looked like a prosperous bourgeois businessman," declared Germany a republic rather than commit his nation to a bloody revolution of the Leninist variety. But the very next day the workers' and soldiers' councils in Berlin announced that, Ebert notwithstanding, the Council of People's Commissars now constituted the government of Germany. "Disorder, insecurity, plundering, wild commandeering and house-prowling have become the order of the day," observed the adjutant to the commander of the military garrison in Berlin.[1]

Even the presence of Field Marshal Paul von Hindenburg and General Erich Ludendorff could not intimidate Lieutenant Model (far left) who edged down onto the same step as Germany's commanding general in this group photograph taken at Bad Kreuznach in 1918.

The officers and men of the German army could not comprehend the rapidity with which the world they knew came crashing down in the last two months of 1918. In the summer they had been only a few dozen miles from Paris, and in their minds already dictating peace terms; in November German divisions still held their ground on foreign soil—albeit precariously—on every front. Nonetheless, following the failure of the Rheims offensive, a pervasive rot set in even among frontline troops, a decline in morale that was almost universally attributed to events at home rather than the disastrous leadership of von Hindenburg and Ludendorff. "Though the battlefield was the same, the men had changed," recalled Corporal Hitler. "For now 'political discussions' went on even among the troops. As everywhere, the poison of the hinterland began, here too, to be effective. And the younger recruit fell down completely—for he came from home." Although Hitler in *Mein Kampf* is hardly an impartial source, he nevertheless captured a prevalent feeling among the men who had lived in the trenches for years, a feeling that was echoed time and again by contemporary letters. "Our beautiful German Empire is no more. Bismarck's work lies in ruins," wrote Captain Heinz Guderian, three days after the Armistice. "Villains have torn everything down to the ground." "The people in the rear, most of whom never heard a shot," had betrayed the army, asserted Major Ludwig Beck a few days later. Initial vague suspicions of betrayal would soon crystallize into the "stab-in-the-back" theory of an undefeated army surrendered by cowards, traitors, and Communists at home. Unwittingly, Ebert himself contributed significantly to the development of this dysfunctional mythology with his well-intended but hopelessly maladroit address to the soldiers parading through Berlin: "As you return unconquered from the field of battle, I salute you."[2]

For Walther Model there was, however, little time to contemplate these developments, except as they affected the execution of his duties, for he now had to coordinate the withdrawal of the 36th Reserve Division from Belgium to its demobilization station in Danzig, West Prussia. The Allies had given the Germans a timetable of only thirty days to remove their army from French and Belgian soil, and on 20 November, when the division crossed the border at Aachen, both Model and his commander, Major General Franz von Rantau, realized that this would not be a simple undertaking. Four and a half years earlier the trains had all run west in precise alignment with General Staff schedules that had been calculated years in advance and revised on an annual basis. Now, however, a relative handful of officers had to scramble for space on haphazardly run trains that crept across a country in a state of near-anarchy. Where food, flowers, and the kisses of young women had greeted the soldiers at every stop in 1914, they found themselves passing through cities over which plumes of smoke now rose, and the civilians in the stations more often than not encouraged the troops to desert and take their rifles with them. Von Rantau would later credit the fact that the 36th Reserve Division reached Danzig mostly intact to the tenacity and improvisational skill of his supply officer.[3]

What the Prussian soldiers returning from the West found in their home provinces shocked them even more than the general condition of Germany. The army in the East had been gutted of its best soldiers for Ludendorff's offensives, and when the end of the war came it simply disintegrated. "The consequence was complete chaos and ignominious rout, although no united and determined foe faced the army," observes historian Harold Gordon. "The troops fled westward in hopeless disorder, the victims of any robber band which cared to harry them." A few cavalry units made their way home intact, "but the bulk of the troops were a panic-stricken mob. Many thousands of soldiers died needlessly, the victims of their own fear and indiscipline. Millions of marks' worth of war materiel and other supplies were abandoned." As the German army exited the Baltic, the Russians flowed in behind it, the soon-to-be-autonomous Poles attempted to grab as much territory as possible, and the homegrown revolutionaries tried to extend their struggle into the heart of Prussia. The weary troops detraining from France were met with "constant raids by bands of armed Poles, uprisings of pro-Polish groups, Communist-Independent Socialist riots, sabotage, and murder."[4]

Despite their mutual distrust, the moderate Socialists upon whom had been dropped the reins of government and the senior generals of the OHL found themselves with no choice but to cooperate, as they saw it, to return internal order to Germany and maintain her eastern borders. Calming Field Marshal Hindenburg, who was struck periodically with a last-minute determination to fight either the Allies or his own government "to the last ditch," Lieutenant General Wilhelm Gröner—Ludendorff's successor as first quartermaster general—negotiated an agreement with Ebert on the very first day of the new republic. Their telephonic conversation, as recounted by Groener in 1925, has become a famous interchange:

EBERT: What do you expect from us?

GROENER: The Field Marshal expects that the government will support the Officers' Corps, maintain discipline, and preserve the punishment regulations of the Army. He expects that satisfactory provisions will be made for the complete maintenance of the Army.

EBERT: What else?

GROENER: The Officers' Corps expects that the government will fight against Bolshevism, and places itself at the disposal of the government for such a purpose.

EBERT: (after a slight pause) Convey the thanks of the government to the Field Marshal.[5]

Despite the immediate impression of the army dictating terms to a weak civilian government that this transcript leaves, the army needed the support of the republic just as badly—at least the General Staff did. As pointed out by John Wheeler-Bennett, Groener "was aware that the great majority of the troops who had returned to Germany wanted to be in their homes for Christmas and that, if this were not arranged officially, they would simply go home anyway. . . . Once the troops were in Germany they would inevitably disperse." Those who remained were succumbing to the revolutionary urges of the soldiers' councils, demanding an end to the army's disciplinary system, the elimination of badges of rank, and other radical changes, while the officer corps itself had been struck to the core by the Kaiser's abdication, which rendered meaningless at the stroke of a pen the oath to which they had bound their lives.[6] The agreement with Ebert gave the General Staff a fighting chance—and only that—to maintain control of whatever the Imperial Army finally evolved into.

As Groener feared, the army unraveled with chilling speed. At Christmas the once-feared Division of Horse Guards attempted to evict the People's Naval Division (described by one of its own commanders as "an organized band of robbers") from the Imperial Palace. After an initial tactical success, the Guards found themselves faced by not only defiant left-wing sailors but a hostile civilian crowd; the division "threw down its rifles, took to its collective heels, and ran away." Faced with the specter of complete disintegration, Groener and Ebert mutually agreed to the appointment of Gustav Noske, a pro-military Socialist, as defense minister, giving him plenipotentiary powers to take whatever steps necessary to put down the Sparticist uprisings and secure Germany's borders. Noske quickly seized upon the rapidly organizing *Freikorps* (Free Corps) as the only effective military force immediately available for this purpose.[7]

The *Freikorps* coalesced out of former soldiers (as well as some students who had been too young for the war) who refused for a variety of reasons to accept the Armistice as a reason to lay down their arms and return placidly home in defeat. Many of them had been *Stosstruppen*, the elite stormtroopers who had spearheaded Ludendorff's 1918 offensives, for whom the bonds of loyalty to each other and their company officers were far stronger than to Kaiser or country. They were brutally effective soldiers in combat, but they also represented a weapon as likely to explode in the hands of the government as to destroy its enemies. Between 1919 and 1923, they fought Communists, Poles, and each other, supported the Kapp *putsch*, and instigated a series of political assassinations. Their leaders briefly acquired enough power to challenge for control of both the government and the army; many of the freebooters passed directly into the ranks of the newly organized Reichswehr.[8]

Throughout this period there was an ongoing struggle for control of the new army between the frontline radicals of the *Freikorps* and the well-trained professionals of the General Staff.

Groener's participation in forcing Wilhelm's abdication and his association with Germany's defeat led to his departure as first quartermaster general soon after Noske's appointment. His effective successor (bearing the new title *Chef des Truppenamt* [chief of the Troop Office] to disguise the position of chief of the Army General Staff) was Lieutenant General Hans von Seeckt, the officer who had begun the war as chief of staff to the III Corps. Von Seeckt, who never seemed to part from his monocle, had risen to prominence as chief of staff to Field Marshal Eberhard von Mackensen's Ninth Army in the East, achieving such a reputation for planning and conducting successful operations that the saying "Where Mackensen is, Seeckt is; where Seeckt is, victory is" gained common currency among junior officers. At the end of the war he had been dispatched as the military adviser to the German delegation at Versailles, where he was among the first to learn that the treaty would reduce his beloved army to a force of only 100,000 men (and just 4,000 officers) and would allow no trained reserves, general staff, heavy artillery, airplanes, poison gas, or tanks.[9]

Von Seeckt returned to Germany determined to build within these limitations (or at least within these limitations as far as Allied inspectors would be able to discern) a professional army that would become the prototype of a thoroughly modern, mobile fighting force, capable of slashing to ribbons a more ponderous adversary. To accomplish this task "the Sphinx"—as friend and foe alike knew him—had first to assert his domination over the army. This process consumed several years of dangerous infighting with senior *Freikorps* commanders whose actual military might often outweighed what was available to von Seeckt. But von Seeckt ultimately prevailed by reestablishing the General Staff (driven underground but hardly disbanded) as the brains and nervous system of any permanent army that Germany, regardless of her form of government, might possess. As his accomplices in this endeavor, von Seeckt enlisted a small clique of young staff officers whose names would become inseparably linked with the German army for the

next twenty years, including Ludwig Beck, Fedor von Bock, Werner
Freiherr von Fritsch, Kurt Freiherr von Hammerstein-Equord, Kurt
von Schleicher, and the brothers Joachim and Otto von Stülpnagel.
They helped von Seeckt consolidate his personal supremacy in the
army, bring the fractious *Freikorps* to heel, and select the exclusive
club of four thousand officers for retention in the shriveled ranks
of the Reichswehr.[10]

Model had already come to von Seeckt's attention in Turkey
during the war, and his immediate postwar assignments increased
his profile with at least one of the officers whose opinions
counted. After demobilizing the 36th Reserve Division, Model became the corps adjutant to the XVII Corps headquarters in
Danzig from January to June 1919; the operations officer was
Otto von Stülpnagel. When the Provisional Reichswehr was organized that summer—a temporary 400,000-man force that
formed the bridge between the Imperial Army and the handful of
divisions allowed by the Versailles Treaty—Model became the
General Staff officer for the 7th Brigade in Westphalia. This was
not at all an easy assignment, for the brigade was an uneasy con-
glomeration of local *Freikorps* companies and remnants from the
ill-fated "Iron Division," which had just returned from their Baltic
misadventure, "unruly and rebellious, to a Germany they detested
for having failed to support their claims in the manner they felt
they deserved."[11]

At the end of the year von Seeckt and his associates had to make
the final selections for retention in the permanent army. This was
no small matter, collapsing corps into divisions, brigades into regiments. Including regulars, reservists, those who received temporary commissions, and NCOs granted the dubious honor of
becoming "deputy officers," more than 270,000 men had served as
officers during World War I. Despite horrendous casualties in the
trenches, there were still nearly 11,000 regulars alone left to contend for only 4,000 positions. Von Seeckt managed to keep the selection of everything below general officer's rank out of the

government's hands, but that hardly finished the infighting. Given complete control, von Seeckt would have leaned toward creating an officer corps composed almost exclusively of General Staff officers, convinced as he was that the freebooters and their officers were far too explosive to be trusted in the new apolitical army he intended to build. But the Sphinx did not enjoy such unlimited prerogatives. He had to contend with the leaders of some of the larger *Freikorps*, who intended to take their outfits into the Reichswehr intact.[12]

One of the great strengths of the later Wehrmacht would be the dynamic mixture of officers produced by this haggling. From the General Staff side of the house came officers such as Heinz Guderian, the architect of the panzer divisions; Franz Halder, the chief of the Army General Staff who planned the early victorious campaigns of 1939 to 1941; and Albert Kesselring, who played an integral role in organizing the Luftwaffe. On the other hand, Hermann Balck of the Iron Division, Hasso von Manteuffel of *Freikorps* von Oven, and Ferdinand Schörner of *Freikorps* Epp emerged as some of the most skilled operational commanders in the German army during the last two years of World War II. That neither of these results is particularly astounding to military historians often renders them oblivious to some of the more ironic outcomes of this mix; Walther Wenck, for example, first enlisted as a private under both Reinhard and von Oven, but earned his greatest reputation as a staff officer.[13]

Walther Model's eventual rise to prominence as *primus inter pares* among the likes of Balck, von Manteuffel, and Schörner has obscured the fact that he was originally selected for the Reichswehr because he represented the epitome of the young staff officer. Aside from his connections with von Seeckt and von Stülpnagel, Model had the advantage of a sterling recommendation from General von Rantau, who characterized him in January 1920 as being by "disposition and performance" eminently "suitable for higher command."[14] In addition, how many other twenty-nine-year-old captains could claim to have won the Iron Cross, First Class, as a troop commander and also to have served at the OHL?

The Army Personnel Office notified Walther Model in early 1920 that he had been appointed a company commander in the II Battalion of the 14th Infantry Regiment—the consolidation of the 7th Provisional Brigade. The 14th Infantry Regiment had been formed from cadres of *Freikorps* Gabcke and Hacketau, and it is easy to suspect that the only kind of staff officer acceptable to these men would, like Model, also have been a decorated troop leader with experience in the trenches. Along with his former *Freikorps* soldiers, Model participated in April, as part of the *Münster* Division, in the bloody suppression of the Red Army uprising in the Ruhr. These actions were among the fiercest in the postwar period; for the first time the pro-Communist forces managed to organize and arm themselves on a scale comparable to their right-wing opponents. "If I were to tell you everything, you would say I was lying," one young volunteer wrote to his family. "No pardon was given. We shoot even the wounded. . . . Anyone who falls into our hands first gets the rifle butt and then is finished off with a bullet. We even shot ten Red Cross nurses on sight because they were carrying pistols."[15]

Model, for whom politics had no particular attraction, went into this battle motivated by a rather vague sense that no matter what government was in power the armed forces had the obligation to maintain order and crush communism. If he felt qualms about the blood of civilians and prisoners being shed, he did not express them, no more than he had objected to the execution of Belgian civilians six years earlier. It was not that he was necessarily brutal or insensitive, but that such questions did not in his estimation fall under the prerogatives of an officer under orders. Besides, he may have been somewhat distracted during the latter portions of the campaign, having met a young *fraulein*, Herta Huyssen, in one of the houses in which he was quartered. The two were married soon after, a union that produced three children: Christa,

Hella, and Hansgeorg. On 1 October he was transferred to a line company in the 18th Infantry Regiment in Munich, receiving command of the regiment's machine-gun company the following year. After only a few months there, Model returned to staff duty under the artillery commander for the 6th Infantry Division, Major General Paul Hasse—the brother of the current *Chef des Truppenamt*. He remained there for four years.[16]

Model's next posting represented a significant advance in his career. In keeping with the tradition of alternating between staff and line, he was returned to company command in October 1925, taking over the ninth company in III Battalion, 8th Infantry Regiment, of the 3rd Infantry Division. The division was stationed in Wehrkreis III (Berlin), the battalion in Görlitz. Assignment to the 3rd Infantry Division placed Model not only near the center of the army's command structure but also in what came to be considered one of the Reichswehr's most elite formations. Heir to the traditions of the old Imperial III Corps, this division was one of the five major units deployed on or near the Polish border (three infantry and two cavalry divisions), which most senior officers of the Reichswehr—especially Prussians, Pomeranians, and Silesians—believed was the area in which Weimar Germany's reduced armed forces were most likely to be forced into battle. These divisions were therefore maintained in a consistently high state of readiness and also became laboratories for experiments with mechanized warfare. The cavalry divisions, for example, were constantly trying out new ways of mixing motorized and mounted units into a mobile breakthrough/exploitation corps; as Robert M. Citino notes, "The perceived challenge from Poland was the primary reason for the development of *Blitzkrieg* tactics."[17]

The 3rd Infantry Division's regiments were deeply involved in testing out new tactical innovations. The 9th Infantry Regiment was considered the de facto "training regiment" of the army, but in reality the whole division participated throughout the 1920s and early 1930s in maneuvers testing the potential of tanks (mock-ups, of course), armored cars, half-tracks, motorcycles, and antitank guns on the modern battlefield. Division elements participated in the 1928 army maneuvers that featured a fully motorized regimental *Kampfgruppe*, and again in 1929 in examinations of motorized infantry battalions, associated with officers like Josef Harpe, Werner Kempf, Oldwig von Natzmer, Walther Nehring, and Walther Wenck. It was Transport Battalion 3 that eventually became Major Heinz Guderian's prototype armored reconnaissance battalion, and the III Battalion, 3rd Artillery Regiment, that served as the training detachment for the Artillery School at Jüterbog. Model therefore found himself placed among the most innovative tactical and operational minds in the Reichswehr.[18]

It is sometimes erroneously assumed that Guderian and the other disciples of mechanized warfare provided the sparks of insight or even genius that attended the tactical innovations in the German army between the world wars. In fact, although it had its conservatives like any other military organization, the Reichswehr sustained an astonishing intensity of training at the division, corps, and army levels, combined with extensive experimentation with new weapons systems between 1923 and 1938. "Maneuvers were kept as realistic as possible," remarks James Corum in a recent study of the developing German tactical doctrine. Furthermore, despite the absence of heavy weapons, the Reichswehr envisioned tactics based on aggressive action, the tactical offensive, and slashing counterattacks. "The attack suits the soldier better than defense," wrote Wilhelm Ritter von Leeb—usually noted as one of the most conservative senior German officers—and the official training manuals agreed.[19] Von Seeckt's 1921 *Führung und Gefecht der verbunden Waffen* observed that

> Only when we preserve the knowledge of the employment of the forbidden weapon (airplanes, heavy artillery, armored vehicles, etc.), will we find the ways and means to hold our own without them against enemies with modern armaments. Their absence must

not cause us to be shy about attacking. Bolder maneuvers, better training, cleverness in the use of terrain, and frequent use of the cover of night offer part of their replacement. The troops must all learn to use camouflage skillfully to hide from enemy aerial observation. In exercises one side should frequently be denied modern equipment while the other employs it. It is of decisive importance to emphasize the cooperation of all weapons, especially the infantry and artillery, down to the smallest unit.[20]

Model's company consisted of two lieutenants and 161 NCOs and enlisted men, divided into three platoons of three squads, each of which was subdivided into a rifle team and a machine-gun team. There were three such companies in his battalion, as well as a machine-gun company with eight heavy machine guns—two of which were normally attached to Model's unit. The 8th Infantry Regiment contained three battalions as well as an organic infantry gun battery of three 75mm and one 105mm guns. The organization was surprisingly reminiscent of the *stoss* battalions of 1918, and the Germans trained them with the same intensity. Model fit right in. "The new company commander plunged himself with verve into this assignment," observes Walther Görlitz. "Training and more training was trumps."[21]

At the end of September 1928, Captain (Major in a few months) Walther Model left his company to become a staff officer at division headquarters. Serving in the training section under Lieutenant Colonel Hans-Georg Reinhardt, Model did double duty as a lecturer in tactics and war studies for the basic General Staff training course. From this phase of his career emerges some more early evidence of the qualities that would distinguish Model as an army commander. His grasp of strategic concepts and operational maneuver revealed itself in his 1929 study of Graf Niehardt von Gneisenau and his staff lectures on the Marne and Tannenberg campaigns. Among his students were future generals Adolf Heusinger, Ferdinand Jodl, Siegfried Rasp, Hans Speidel, and August Winter. Rasp later recalled Model as the best lecturer he had heard during his training. Both Speidel and Winter—each of whom later served as Model's chief of staff in 1944 and disliked him with a passion—admitted that what separated Model from other instructors was the fact that he not only could absorb and present tremendous amounts of technical and tactical details but always related those details to the overall concept of the campaign.

Perhaps the most important individual to be impressed with Model's talent was Major General Friedrich von Cochenhausen, who used his influence in one of his last acts prior to retiring from the army to have the young major transferred in 1930 to *Abteilung* 4 (Training) of the *Truppenamt*—known throughout the army as "T-4." This move brought Model for the first time into contact with the major figures who would be dominant during the German army's heady years of rearming, expanding, and overrunning Europe. His immediate superiors—in succession—were Colonels Wilhelm von List, Walther von Brauchitsch, and Walther Wever. Other officers with whom Model associated closely included Wilhelm Keitel, Friedrich Paulus (a frequent houseguest), and Franz Halder (who even in 1930 noted Model's obsession for his monocle). This assignment also included a six-week trip to Germany's secret training areas inside the Soviet Union. Model entered Russia with a group of officers including Walther von Brauchitsch, Wilhelm Keitel, and Erich Köstring; the delegation split up and inspected a variety of Red Army units and installations as well as their own covert installations. Model spent fourteen days observing the 9th Rifle Division in Rostov. As a result of this visit, he authored a technical paper on the current state of weapons technology in the Red Army.[22]

T-4 placed Model in the perfect position from which to watch the final pre–Hitler era maneuvers conducted by the Reichswehr in 1932. These exercises represented the culmination of a decade's worth of research and experimentation, as well as the vindication of the hard work of combined arms theorists. In the spring maneuvers at Grafenwöhr and Jüterbog, *Kraftfahrkampfabteilungen* (motorized combat battalions) configured as mechanized units with mock panzers practiced approach marches, moving into assembly areas, coordinating movement by radio, and setting up an antitank defense in cooperation with the regular infantry. The results of this exercise were reflected in the much larger fall maneuvers in Silesia in which Major General Karl Gerd von Rundstedt's 3rd Infantry Division (with one fully mechanized battalion and an infantry battalion motorized for the operation) was pitted against Major General Werner Freiherr von Fritsch's two-division cavalry corps (composed of a mixture of motorized and mounted units). "The 1932 maneuver was most impressive for its modernity," concludes historian Robert Citino, who also observes that this maneuver exemplified "the essence of what would come to be known as *Blitzkrieg* tactics." Model's section was responsible for helping to coordinate these exercises, umpiring them, digesting the technical results, and disseminating the results to the rest of the army.[23]

Several years later these experiences would stand Model in good stead when he played a significant role in the technical development of the panzer divisions, but for now his career and events required a return to troop command. Promoted to lieutenant colonel in 1932, Model received command of a battalion of the 2nd Infantry Regiment of the 1st Infantry Division, stationed in Allenstein, East Prussia, in November 1933. As the explosive expansion of the army began in the following year, each of the regiment's three battalions became the cadre for a new regiment, and Model became the commander of the new 2nd Infantry Regiment. Again the emphasis was on training and more training as the army strained to accommodate thousands of raw recruits, a horde composed of everyone from policemen to Hitler Youth.[24]

The significance of this period between 1932 and 1935, either to Walther Model or Germany, should not be dismissed lightly. When the Weimar Republic voluntarily swallowed the hemlock by appointing Adolph Hitler as chancellor, one naval officer recalled fifty years later that "very few suspected that the medicine taken on January 30, 1933, would turn out to be deadly poison which would ultimately destroy the Reich." Hitler's ascent to power revealed—at least in hindsight—that von Seeckt's apolitical army was a chimera; the rise of the Nazis revealed potential splits in the ranks of the officer corps from top to bottom. Among the most senior generals, the opportunistic Kurt von Schleicher saw Hitler as a pawn in his own games of power, the more conservative Kurt Freiherr von Hammerstein-Equord resisted Hitler's appointment, and the gullible Werner von Blomberg tied his own future unreservedly to that of the Führer. At the lower ranks, as F. L. Carsten notes, the Nazis and Hitler "were extremely attractive to young men who came from the same social groups as many young National Socialists and had the same basic ideas." In the celebrated 1929 trial of three lieutenants in Ulm who were charged with excessive propagandizing for the Nazis, one declared on the stand that "two-thirds of the young officers in the Reichswehr think as I do." The image of Hitler created by Josef Goebbels's publicity machine, the frustrations of long service with little potential for promotion, and the resentment of the restrictions of Versailles all combined to create such fertile ground for the National Socialist message that even the later archconspirator (then-Lieutenant) Henning von Tresckow was giving lectures on true Nazi principles to his peers in the 9th Infantry Regiment.[25]

But it was among the officers in the middle grades, from the field officers up through the junior generals, that there was the greatest potential for an almost schizophrenic dissonance. Schooled in the traditions of Prussian military honor, these were by and large the officers in whom von Seeckt and his successors had attempted to instill an inherently apolitical attitude, men who would proclaim, like Gerd von Rundstedt, "I have made it a guiding principle to confine myself to the military domain and to keep aloof from all political activity. I lack all talent for it." Yet in the trenches of France and the bloodstained streets of the postwar chaos, many of these officers had developed an instinctive, almost visceral fear of the political disorder into which they now saw Germany slipping. Hitler and the Nazis took great pains in the early 1930s to impress these men, and in many cases they succeeded; Albert Kesselring wrote in his memoirs that "I confess much of what I saw made a strong impression on me and that I admired their brilliant and smooth-running organisation," which made it possible for him "to ignore the less pleasing things." Others—like Walther von Reichenau—were far more impressed by Hitler himself, viewing him as the Bismarck-type strongman who could lead Germany back to the status of a major power; not coincidentally, this would be accompanied by the rapid expansion of the army, with promotions all around. Finally, as Hitler's fascination with technological innovation surfaced, the innovators among the officer corps naturally sought his patronage to overcome the resistance of their more conservative seniors.[26]

When he stopped to think about it, Walther Model would probably have classified himself as a monarchist who would have preferred, all things being equal, the restoration of the Kaiser to any other political arrangement. Short of that, however, everything in his personality, experience, and background argued for supporting Hitler; moreover, the circle of his closest associates and mentors included Walther von Brauchitsch, Wilhelm Keitel, and Friedrich Paulus, all of whom leaned quickly in the same direction. Furthermore, Model's fairly constant postings in Berlin and East Prussia during the mid-1930s brought him into close contact and eventually friendship with Josef Goebbels and Hermann Göring.[27]

Despite these connections, it was the traditionally minded Ludwig Beck, appointed chief of the Army General Staff in October 1933, who gave Model's career a critical boost. Although he would evolve into one of Hitler's most committed opponents, be lampooned by Guderian as a man with "no understanding for modern technical matters," and become "a paralyzing element wherever he appeared," Beck in the early 1930s was among the most insightful strategic thinkers in the army and had a strong appreciation for the potential of mechanized warfare. In October 1935, he inaugurated a new detachment, *Abteilung* 8, to analyze technical advances at home and abroad, under the direct supervision of the deputy chief of staff. To the great surprise of many other officers, Beck chose Model for the position.[28]

Beck appointed him, and the new commanding general of the army, von Fritsch, approved of Model's nomination, as did Gustav von Wietersheim, who would become his immediate superior, but it seems to have been Colonel Friedrich Hossbach, Hitler's adjutant, who was the driving force behind the choice. Hossbach knew that Model had, as Görlitz puts it, "no special affinity for technical details," being notable among his peers for the excellence of his horsemanship and the mediocrity of his driving. Yet Model did possess "a downright sixth sense for technical possibilities—for the general importance of technology in modern war and the role it would play in battle."[29]

The energy with which Model tackled his job made Hossbach look prescient. His staff spearheaded the development of assault guns as well as the motorized 240mm gun and advocated the expansion of the developing panzer formations into divisions and corps. He aligned himself with the likes of Guderian, Nehring, and von Manstein in pushing for fully mechanized units as the centerpiece of the army's offensive doctrine. Model personally conducted a detailed on-site study of the employment of armor and aircraft on the battlefield in Spain, and in the winter of 1937–1938 he traveled to the border of Czechoslovakia to examine the problem of utilizing heavy mortars and siege guns to overcome Czech defensive fortifications. He was successful enough in this endeavor to be slated as the potential chief of staff for the Seventh Army in the event of an invasion. Model's enthusiasm for innovation earned him the nickname "Armee Modernissimus" ("the army modernization fanatic") among his peers. In March 1938, he was promoted to major general.[30]

Unfortunately, the driving ferocity Walther Model brought to any assignment also earned him the enmity of Captain Hans Röttiger, his chief of staff, as well as any number of officers he steamrolled past. Erich von Manstein thought Model acted "like a pike in the carp pool of the officers of the ministry," and Franz Halder found him unnecessarily brusque and often intentionally impolite. Ironically, it was the increasing domination of Hitler over the army that led to Model's undoing. When Halder became chief of the Army General Staff in 1938, all of Model's protectors—Beck, von Fritsch, Hossbach, and von Manstein—had quit, been dismissed, retired, or transferred out of the Army High Command (*Oberkommando das Heer*—OKH). It was a time when massive personnel shifts were made to reduce the influence of anti-Nazi officers, and in the shuffle Halder managed to remove one minor pro-Hitler thorn from his side. On 10 November 1938, Walther Model found himself assigned as chief of staff to the IV Corps in Dresden, well removed from the center of power and influence for the first time in years.[31]

He was still there when Hitler declared war on Poland.

3

AS FUSSY AS
A FIELD MARSHAL

Chief of Staff, IV Corps
and Sixteenth Army

MODEL AND GENERAL OF INFANTRY VIKTOR VON SCHWEDLER had little in common except their exile to Dresden. Von Schwedler, the commander of the IV Corps, was six years older and tended to be an anti-Nazi. Since 1933 he had been chief of the Army Personnel Office, a position with powers and prerogatives in the German army so broad that since the middle of the eighteenth century the holder of that post had often been seen as a counterweight to the influence of the chief of the Army General Staff. For five years von Schwedler had held nearly undisputed sway over all but the most senior appointments to critical commands and key staff positions, and he had advanced in that time from a relatively junior colonel to being the eighteenth-highest-ranking officer in the army. The breaking of von Schwedler's power was one of the conditions that

Hitler placed on Walther von Brauchitsch when he replaced von Fritsch in February 1938.[1]

Von Schwedler, moreover, was a true conservative in military doctrine and a traditional Prussian gentleman in behavior. He belonged to that school of officers who still thought in terms of railroad mobilizations and marching infantry supported by horse-drawn guns as the backbone of the German war effort. He would have agreed completely with General Wilhelm von Ulex, who in 1938 informed Walther Nehring, after listening to an impassioned dissertation on panzer divisions and combined arms warfare: "What the colonel says may be well and true, but if we ever use these tanks in action, we will do so in the way *we* think fit" (emphasis added).[2] Now he found himself paired with a foul-mouthed, aggressive young chief of staff, brimming with ideas about tanks, assault guns, and dive bombers, whose motto was, "Can't it be done faster?"

It was not the recipe for a happy marriage. Worse, placed as the right-hand man to a commander with whom he would often find himself in vehement disagreement, Model soon discovered that in its rush toward expansion and innovation the German army seemed to have left the IV Corps without a single kindred spirit. His operations officer was the colorless Lieutenant Colonel Otto Beutler, a career infantryman from the same tradition as von Schwedler. The three infantry division commanders included the aging Lieutenant General Peter Weyer at the 14th Infantry and the technically rather than tactically minded Lieutenant General Friedrich Olbricht at the 24th. Only the much younger Major General Eric Hansen at the 4th Infantry, who would eventually become the head of the German Army Training Mission in Rumania, shared Model's progressive bent. Likewise, of the division operations officers, only Major Gerhard Feyerabend of the 24th could have been considered at all forward-thinking.[3]

Even though Walther Görlitz believes that, "in those stressful days General Model was right in his own element," it was no wonder then that the new chief of staff pushed as many noses out of joint and rubbed as many people the wrong way as he had in Berlin. Arriving soon after various IV Corps had returned from the bloodless occupation of the Sudetenland, Model took charge of his new office at a full gallop. Lieutenant Colonel Beutler quickly learned to fear his "athletic romps." Model turned up without warning during training exercises, and his proclivity for delivering tongue-lashings to those officers he felt had not put forth enough effort became legend. As would become a pattern for him during the next war, he became far more popular with the troops than with their leaders. In August 1944, when then-Field Marshal Model was transferred to France, he encountered an officer who had served under him at the IV Corps as the divisional adjutant of the 4th Infantry Division. When asked if he recalled his old chief of staff, the officer immediately responded in the affirmative, noting wryly that in 1938 Model "gave fussy orders like a Field Marshal even then."[4]

Training, however, was only one of Model's concerns. Technically he and von Schwedler were responsible for not only a corps headquarters that would control three infantry divisions and several smaller formations in the field but also a Wehrkreis—a military district headquarters. In this role he supervised a variety of military installations, oversaw recruiting and the mobilization of reserves, and took care of hundreds of other administrative details across Saxony, eastern Thuringia, and later part of the Sudetenland. Nearly eight million people lived in this area, including the major cities of Dresden, Leipzig, and Chemnitz. Allied intelligence in 1944 described Wehrkreis IV as "mostly hilly country with mountains in the south. Some mining of coal and ores. Mostly industrial, especially textiles around Chemnitz, chemicals in the Halle-Merselburg area, and small mechanical as well as automobile industries in various districts."[5]

Model had been on the job for only about three months when Adolph Hitler, unsatisfied with his gains at Munich, began ratcheting up the pressure for the dissolution of Czechoslovakia and the formal incorporation of Bohemia and Moravia into the Third Reich. As diplomatic communications heated up during February 1939, Model found himself immersed in frenzied preparations for war should the Czechs resist; the IV Corps bordered directly on northwestern Czechoslovakia and would play a key role in any advance on Prague. In early March, Model made a personal, clandestine reconnaissance to Prague to examine key march routes and possible Czech defensive positions. In reality, however, there was little or no prospect of serious military action, for the Munich accords of September 1938 had already stripped the Czechs of their border fortifications and quite thoroughly resolved in Germany's favor the question of whether Great Britain or France would be willing to commit their armies in the Czechs' defense. The German army marched into Czechoslovakia unopposed on 15 March 1939.[6]

Although war had been again avoided, the occupation of Bohemia and Moravia served as a pretext for further expansion of the German army. The pace of training among the regular divisions—if possible—increased. One young lieutenant in the 24th Infantry Division recalled years later that "we worked ten to twelve hours each day during the week. On Saturday, we worked until noon." Three camouflaged divisional staffs in Wehrkreis IV were now activated to control *Landwehr* divisions of older reservists, whose mission it was to be employed on security duties in the newly annexed territory in the event of war with Poland. *Landwehr-Kommandeur Dresden* became the 223rd *Landwehr* Infantry Division, while the 255th and 256th were formed around *Landwehr-Kommandeur Chemnitz* and *Heerendienstellen 5* (Army Installation 5). Additional plans were made to remove the artillery command staffs from the 4th and 24th Infantry Divisions to become the leadership cadres for two divisions of younger reservists—the 56th and 87th Infantry Divisions—which would be fleshed out only with the call to general mobilization. Finally, preparations were completed to organize Replacement Division Staffs 154 and 174 to take over recruitment, training, and the funneling of replacements to the front.[7]

As spring stretched into summer, war approached rapidly. Hitler's latest demand for territory involved the so-called Polish Corridor, which had been cut across West Prussia at the Versailles negotiations in order to guarantee Poland access to the Baltic Sea, and the "free city" of Danzig, which the same treaty prevented German armed forces from occupying. To the dictator's chagrin, however, the same British and French leaders who had backed down to him at Munich now concluded a military alliance with the Poles. He responded with what Hanson Baldwin characterizes as "the brass tongue of propaganda," including huge parades of military hardware (to convince the Poles that fighting Germany would be hopeless), warnings that the British could not be trusted (after selling out the Czechs at Munich), and broadcasts aimed at convincing the British that war with Germany would kill another generation of English youth for no good reason ("Is Danzig worth a war?"). The army Hitler ordered to be prepared to crush Poland quickly during the fall, "starting the war with sudden, heavy blows and . . . gaining rapid successes."[8]

Behind the scenes the Führer was taking even more concrete steps to ensure the destruction of Poland. Foreign Minister Joachim Ribbentrop had been ordered into secret negotiations with the Soviet Union, aimed at achieving a nonaggression pact that would not only delineate Soviet and German spheres of interest in Eastern Europe but also commit the Red Army to assisting in the defeat and dismemberment of an independent Poland. On 21 August, Josef Stalin assented to the idea, sending Hitler a personal letter in which he noted that "the conclusion of a non-aggression pact provides the foundation for eliminating political tension and for the re-establishment of peace and collaboration between our two countries." Receiving this message at a dinner party, Hitler banged loudly on the table and exclaimed, "I have them! I have them!" Albert Speer, who was sitting at the table, learned only then of the tense weeks of haggling and in his memoirs admitted that "to see Hitler and Stalin linked in friendship on a piece of paper was the most staggering, the most exciting turn of events I could possibly have imagined." Ever wary of potential future opponents, however, Hitler made sure to have a photographer accompany his official delegation to Moscow in order to get an up-to-date photo of Stalin—he wanted to be able to measure the shape and size of the Soviet leader's earlobes so that he could estimate the amount of Jewish blood running in his veins.[9]

Military preparations for the annihilation of Poland began in April, and active operational planning commenced in May. Colonel General Gerd von Rundstedt, who had been forcibly retired in 1938, was recalled to the colors to head *Arbeitstab von Rundstedt* (Working Staff von Rundstedt), which would become the command staff of Army Group South upon mobilization. For the first two months, however, this staff consisted of exactly three men—von Rundstedt, Lieutenant General Erich von Manstein, and Colonel Günther Blumentritt—and the initial stages of planning were a decidedly part-time endeavor. Until mid-August, von Rundstedt remained at home and out of uniform, communicating only infrequently, von Manstein continued to command the 18th Infantry Division, and OKH did not release Blumentritt from his duties in the Training Branch.[10]

OKH charged Army Group South with the conduct of operations from western Silesia, which included securing the south side of the so-called Poznan bulge between the Oder and Neisse Rivers, punching through Lodz directly for Warsaw, and advancing through the northern Carpathians and Slovakia into Galicia. For this ambitious set of objectives von Rundstedt disposed over three army headquarters: the Eighth (General of Infantry Johannes von Blaskowitz), Tenth (General of Artillery Walther von Reichenau), and the Fourteenth (Colonel General Wilhelm von List). The staff directed the Eighth Army, with only four infantry divisions and assorted *Grenzschutz* (Frontier Guard) units, to advance to the Warthe River and prevent General Rommel's Lodz Army from catching the main German attack in the northern flank. From the Carpathians the Fourteenth Army would employ a much stronger force across a broad front: five infantry, two mountain, two panzer, and one motorized infantry division plus a motorized SS regiment.[11]

The center of gravity of von Rundstedt's attack, however, was located with von Reichenau's Tenth Army in the Kreuzberg area. Von Reichenau received five corps headquarters, including all three peacetime headquarters created to control Germany's panzer, light, and motorized divisions. Commanding these corps were three of the army's foremost experts on mechanized warfare: Erich Hoepner, Hermann Hoth, and Gustav von Wietersheim. Between them were divided two panzer divisions, three light divisions, two motorized infantry divisions, and a motorized SS regiment. Considering that both the 1st and 2nd Light Divisions had been reinforced with an additional panzer regiment—bringing them up to a strength comparable to the regular panzer divisions—the Tenth Army contained 1,210 tanks (47 percent of the vehicles committed in Poland), of which 278 were the heavier Pzkw Mark IIIs and IVs (67.8 percent of the heavier tanks employed in the campaign). The Tenth Army was in fact, if not in name, the first "panzer army" deployed by the Wehrmacht. The IV and XI Corps were to provide the infantry support for the panzer drive.[12]

According to von Manstein, the "Tenth Army's tank formations, with its infantry divisions following as closely as possible behind, must make a concerted effort to over-run the enemy troop assemblies that would probably be taking place near the frontier, and that the tanks should if possible reach the Vistula crossings from Demblin to Warsaw ahead of the enemy." This meant that von Reichenau would be responsible for tearing through the front of the four infantry divisions and two cavalry brigades of the Lodz army. After forcing the Warthe River line, Manstein recalled, "Army Group H.Q. found it necessary to set Tenth Army two objectives," with a northern group of three corps (XI, XIV, and XVI) penetrating as quickly as possible toward Warsaw while a southern group (IV and XV Corps) pushed toward Radom. This divergence, leaving a weak center potentially exposed to an enemy counterattack, represented the greatest risk to be run by von Reichenau's army. Safeguarding that center would largely become the responsibility of the IV Corps.[13]

During the first phase of the attack the IV Corps would be sandwiched between the XVI and XV Corps, near Lublinitz on a direct axis between Oppeln on the Oder and Czestochova on the Warthe. Von Schwedler's infantry divisions had to push forward hard enough to attract the enemy's attention, but not so fast as to provoke a Polish retreat, while the 1st Panzer Division to the north and the 2nd Light Division to the south raced to envelop the Polish flanks and create a pocket near Czestochova. This was not a particularly complicated or risky operation, since the two Polish infantry divisions in the area were kept at only brigade strength during peacetime and would not be allowed enough time to mobilize their reserve components. Moreover, the Poles had insufficient numbers of antiquated French artillery pieces and no antitank guns worthy of the name, and the Polish air force would be destroyed on the ground in the first twelve hours of the conflict.[14]

The demands on von Schwedler and Model were severe nonetheless. OKH had avoided announcing a general mobilization so as not to tip Germany's hand to the Poles; when the final alert (postponed once for diplomatic reasons) took place on 28 August, the IV Corps staff had just under three days to accomplish several missions. Each of the corps' three regular divisions had to be moved to assembly areas outside the Wehrkreis, and it was probably only on 29 August that Model discovered that the 24th Infantry Division was being transferred to the Eighth Army. Before any of these divisions moved, however, every third battalion lost its commander, every third company lost its commander, and as many as 20 percent of the key NCOs and enlisted men were removed from each regiment to form cadres for the 56th and 87th Infantry Divisions, which had to be organized and deployed to the French border by 4 September. Moving these divisions not only required detailed staff work but left holes in the regular units that now had to be filled by reservists; undoubtedly, given the speed of the German movement to the border, there were still gaps in many of the lines.[15]

The detachment of the 24th Infantry Division served notice that in this war from the very beginning the corps would be considered a purely tactical headquarters, overseeing the operations of whatever divisions happened to be assigned to it rather than operating as the command element of an integral unit, as the corps of von Kluck's First Army had been in 1914. If the commander and chief of staff had any doubts on this point, they were dispelled on 30 August, when the 14th Infantry Division was removed from the IV Corps and replaced with the 46th Infantry Division out of Wehrkreis XIII. The same day the Tenth Army attached a gaggle of smaller, independent units to the corps, including engineer and construction troops, motorized bridging columns, army artillery battalions, security troops, flak batteries, and a Luftwaffe reconnaissance group. IV Corps absorbed these formations and made assignments without comment.[16]

One can almost imagine Walther Model's loud curses on 31 August, however, when his old friend Friedrich Paulus (now the Tenth Army chief of staff) called him up less than twenty-four hours before the beginning of the campaign to tell him that von Reichenau had decided that IV Corps possessed too many motorized assets for the nature of its mission. The motorized engineer battalion, two bridging columns, a flak battalion, and reconnaissance flights were all removed from his control as quickly as they had arrived. When Model asked just how IV Corps was to get its infantry and heavy weapons across the Warthe River without enough engineers and equipment to build a bridge, Paulus told him to capture one. Worse still, Paulus called again on the afternoon of 31 August with the news that the Tenth Army had also resolved to remove the 14th Infantry Division and attach it to the tank-heavy XVI Corps in order to get more weight on the army's main axis of attack. When Model protested—this time arguing that this move left his corps with only two infantry divisions in line and no reserves to repulse an enemy counterattack—Paulus quietly observed that Army Group South's reserve, the VII Corps, would be available in an emergency. Lieutenant Colonel Beutler's records suggest that Model made at least two additional telephone calls to Tenth Army headquarters on the evening of 31 August without convincing either von Reichenau or Paulus to reverse themselves. If the relatively mild-mannered Paulus took the calls, he undoubtedly attempted to reason with Model, but if von Reichenau answered the phone, he more than likely told the corps' chief of staff to shut up and carry out his mission with whatever resources he had been assigned.[17]

Thus, IV Corps' soldiers crossed the border in the predawn hours of 1 September 1939. If Walther Model had any glimmer of insight that Germany had just ignited a war that would engulf the world, he neither mentioned nor recorded it—not surprising given his lack of political interest and the demands of his position. Had he survived the war to record a set of memoirs, it is interesting to speculate on whether Model's normal bluntness would have allowed him to present himself as having been deeply disturbed by the thought of another world war, which was the course taken by most of his contemporaries. Guderian insisted that "we did not go light-heartedly to war and there was not one general who would not have advocated peace." Von Manstein spoke of Hitler's decision to invade Polad as "the decision we had not wanted to believe possible," while Albert Kesselring recalled "uncertainty and tension" at "the grim shadow of war," and Friedrich-Wilhelm von Mellenthin told his readers that "there was no trace of the jubilant crowds whom I had seen in 1914 as a boy of ten. Civilians or soldiers—nobody felt any elation or enthusiasm." Yet just how much of this was self-serving *apologia*? Guderian also detailed his immense pride in greeting Hitler after capturing Kulm—his birthplace—which had been German territory prior to 1919, and von Manstein waxed eloquent on the injustice of the post-Versailles borders: "That irrational demarcation of the frontier! That mutilation of our Fatherland!" Von Mellenthin prefaced his grimmer observations on the popular mood with a paragraph justifying Hitler's demands for the return of Danzig, while Kesselring went so far as to characterize the Germans as facing a "ruthlessly fanatical" enemy in the Poles.[18] The preserved diaries and letters of officers and soldiers from August and September 1939 that have not been modified to present what could be characterized as "post-Nazi politically correct" are far more in line with the sentiments of Wilhelm Prüller, a soldier in the 4th Light Division of the Tenth Army, on 39 August 1939:

> The situation is highly satisfactory for us, and it's unthinkable for us . . . as the greatest European power, to sit back and watch the persecution of the Voksdeutsche without doing something. It is our duty to rectify this wrong, which cries to Heaven. If we fight, then we know that we are serving a rightful cause.[19]

Given the few recorded comments Model made in later campaigns, it is difficult to doubt that he would have agreed.

The campaign, from the perspective of the IV Corps, lasted eleven days and consisted primarily of hard marching, punctuated at the very end by some bitter fighting. From 1 to 5 September the corps' primary mission was to secure the northern half of a division-sized pocket of Polish troops at Czestochova and push its fastest units toward the Warthe River. To Model's obvious relief, the Tenth Army transferred the 14th Infantry Division back to the IV Corps on 3 September; Schwedler and Model used it to hold the perimeter of the pocket while the 4th and 46th Infantry Divisions withdrew the bulk of their infantry toward the river, which they crossed on 5 September. On the same afternoon Paulus called Model to take away the 14th Infantry Division again and assign new operational objectives.[20]

The Tenth Army, reinforced by the VII Corps from Army Group South's reserve, had now entered the pursuit phase of the campaign on divergent axes. While the XI and XVI Corps followed the north bank of the Pilica River toward Warsaw, and the VII and half of the XV Corps turned south through the Lysa Gora Hills to link up with the Fourteenth Army, the IV, XIV, and other half of the XV Corps were given Radom as their next objective. Radom represented more than a geographic objective: Under constant bombardment from the Luftwaffe, five Polish infantry divisions and a cavalry brigade of the former General Reserve (3rd, 12th, 19th, 29th, and 36th Infantry and the Wilenska Cavalry) were frantically attempting to organize their reserves into an army that could support the defense of Warsaw. Again, with only the 4th and 46th Infantry Divisions, the IV Corps had to serve as the anvil to the twin hammers of the 1st and 2nd Light Divisions.[21]

Radom was surrounded on 9 September; even though subjected to heavy air attacks and concentrated artillery, some Polish units hung on and forced the Germans to dig them out in house-to-house fighting. This assignment was left primarily to the grenadiers of the 46th Infantry Division, and for them the next forty-eight hours were no blitzkrieg. Between them the 42nd, 72nd, and 97th Infantry Regiments took 1,871 casualties—more than twice the average casualties suffered by the other frontline infantry divisions in the campaign. The Poles surrendered on 11 September, and the IV Corps claimed 125 officers and 37,743 enlisted men as prisoners—a large enough haul, but their lack of armaments told much of the story of the campaign's outcome. Even though von Schwedler's men captured the bulk of four divisions, they only recorded taking 5,600 rifles, 20 antitank guns, 75 obsolete French artillery pieces, 47 mortars, and 261 machine guns.[22]

No sooner had Radom capitulated than the Tenth Army again removed the 46th Infantry Division from von Schwedler's control, leaving the corps headquarters with only the 4th Infantry Division and assorted artillery, engineer, and construction battalions under its supervision. The 4th Infantry Division was ordered to cross the Vistula River and capture Krasnik, while at the same time the IV Corps' area of responsibility was extended through most of the Tenth Army's rear area. Although Model chafed loudly but futilely at the implications of this move, after the seizure of Krasnik on 15 September the IV Corps was taken out of the line and assigned to coordinate the army's rear-area security. After all too brief a campaign, the chief of staff now found himself organizing transport columns, rebuilding bridges, shepherding prisoners, and attempting to mop up the bypassed remnants of the Polish Army.[23]

Eliminating small bands of soldiers who refused to surrender not only brought back grim memories from France in 1914 but presaged future "antipartisan" and "rear-area security" measures that would leave an indelible stain on the honor of the German army and ultimately be responsible for Walther Model being declared a war criminal. Hitler had insisted at the outset of the campaign that "we must all steel ourselves against humanitarian reasoning!" in dealing with the Poles, and this sentiment met with approbation among many senior officers. General Eduard Wagner, quartermaster general of the army (and therefore ultimately responsible for rear-area security during active operations), declared in his diary as early as 4 September: "Brutal guerilla war has broken out everywhere and we are ruthlessly stamping it out. We won't be reasoned with. We have already sent out emergency courts, and they are in continual session. The harder we strike, the quicker there will be peace again." General Halder accepted this premise as well, writing in his own diary that "whoever is found carrying arms will be put before a Court-martial," after authorizing such actions as the machine-gunning of refugees and the use of starvation to break the will of civilians to resist.[24]

The troops were in the mood to strike hard. Fed on a steady diet of inflammatory propaganda, the average *Landser* was more than willing to believe in large-scale guerrilla atrocities whose authors were Polish civilians as well as soldiers. "The Polish civilians are *franc-tireurs* and very good snipers," complained a XVI Corps soldier. "The regiment has lost several officers and NCOs to their unlawful activity." "We're lying ready in a wood. Banging of rifle shots," confided a member of the 10th Cavalry Rifle Regiment to his diary on 2 September. "We learn that there are five civilians behind our backs shooting at us. I go with two others, and in a few minutes these five civilians have had it." By the time the IV Corps took over rear-area security for the Tenth Army, the troops were literally willing to believe anything—even rumors as outrageous as, "Seven soldiers who were waiting for the signal to proceed in their car were attacked by the entire village population, they eyes gouged out and castrated," or, "A Red Cross convoy, doctors and assistants, wounded—180 men strong—not one of them armed, were murdered." Historians have often been willing to concentrate on the massacres perpetrated by the SS and rationalize the excesses of the army—Charles Messenger, for example, characterizes them as the product of "nervous tension arising from inexperience and traditional emnities"—but German soldiers and their officers proved even more willing to crack down violently than they had in Belgium a generation earlier. As Wilhelm Prüller of the 4th Light Division put it, "If an armed civilian crosses my path, I'll cut off his head with my own hands. I swear I will!"[25]

Within days the collapse of the organized resistance of the Polish army outside of Warsaw (hastened of course by the Red Army's invasion of eastern Poland) led to many units being freed from combat for assignment to security duty. On 16 September the IV Corps took control of the 2nd Light Division, 617th Engineer Regimental Staff (for special employment) and SS Engineer *Sturmbann* Dresden. These formations were split up into small security detachments throughout the Tenth Army rear area. Their orders were draconian: Possessing a weapon drew an immediate death penalty, and refugees were swiftly rounded up in concentration camps to await "screening" by the SS and *Polizei* (Police) prior to receiving forced-labor assignments. Although much attention has been drawn to the protests lodged by senior German officers later in the winter concerning SS atrocities against Polish civilians, the brief period of army control of the countryside was bloody enough to have brought a smile to Heinrich Himmler's face. Between 11 September and 25 October—after which the SS gained formal authority over the newly created "General Government"— the Germans burned 531 villages or towns and carried out 714 distinct reprisal executions, accounting for over 16,000 civilian deaths, at least 60 percent of which can be attributed to the Wehrmacht rather than the SS or the Police. Nor were these actions on the part of soldiers unrelated to the anti-Semitic policies of the Nazis. As Raul Hilberg points out, "Even during the first few weeks of the occupation, military and civilian officers seized the Jews in the streets and forced them to clear rubble, fill antitank ditches, shovel snow, and perform other emergency tasks."[26]

What was the extent of Model's knowledge of, or participation in, these events? Significantly, the IV Corps war diary indicates that on a daily basis subunits assigned to the corps reported their activities quite explicitly, including sweeps for suspected partisans, raids, burned villages, and reprisal executions. In addition, corps headquarters required thorough inventories of seizures of weapons, radios, horses, farm machinery, and other assorted booty. Several of these orders went out over Model's signature. By late September the war diary contains numerous references to SS and Police activities of the same type, although these entries are of a more general nature. As early as 28 September the IV Corps was designated as the controlling headquarters for the Lublin district of *Grenzabschnitte Mitte* of *Oberost* (Frontier Sector "Center" of Army High Command East), with the 4th and 228th Infantry and 2nd Panzer Divisions under its control. It was von

Schwedler's immediate superior, General Blaskowitz, who filed the first and most famous reports concerning SS misdeeds.[27]

Since the General Government area was intended to become the dumping ground for Jews forced out of other areas in the Reich and its annexed territories (with Lublin serving as one of the major ghettos), senior SS functionaries were appointed in early October to supervise the operations of the *Einsatzkommandos* (Special Commands—a code name for execution squads) and the Police. Appointed *Hohere SS und Polizei Führer Ost* (Higher SS and Police Leader East) was *Obergruppenführer* Friedrich-Wilhelm Krüger, who is described by Heinz Hohne as "a scandal-monger and a pedant, whose tales of supposedly deviationist comrades even Himmler found hard to stomach." During the first week in October, as had been mandated in an earlier agreement between the army and the SS, Krüger left his own headquarters at Krakow to visit the military-sector headquarters in his area. He met with von Schwedler, Model, and the senior staff of the IV Corps on either 3 or 4 September. No specific record of the agenda or outcome of the meeting has been unearthed, but during the heady days after the army's victory neither Hitler nor his SS offi-cers were mincing any words about their intent. "Whatever we can find in the shape of an upper class in Poland is to be liquidated; should anything take its place, it will be placed under guard and done away with at an appropriate time," Hitler had ordered in early September. OKH had already agreed to allow the SS and the Police access to all prisoners taken by the army, and in the Lublin area the execution of this directive began immediately following Krüger's meeting.[28]

Circumstantial evidence strongly supports the idea that Model—and many more German officers than is commonly believed—not only knew what was occurring in Poland but actually took part in carrying out what Halder himself described in October as "this devilish plan." Albert Seaton's verdict on the officer corps as a whole might as well have been written about Model as an individual: "It was in Poland that the generals and the officers and other ranks of the German Army were brought face to face with the stark realities of Hitler's racial policies, for the brutalities of the round-ups were there for all to see. By degrees all ranks became accustomed to them; and the generals, since they were no longer responsible for internal security in the occupied territories, came to believe that the atrocities were not their concern." Seaton, however, erred in asserting that "the time was not far off when the German Army itself was, on Hitler's order, to carry out the mass shootings of prisoners." As Model knew all too well, that practice had already begun.[29]

Model's awareness of and even participation in these activities did not make them any more personally palatable, even if he somehow rationalized them as unavoidable. Moreover, Model, in common with his peers, had no intention of sitting out the remainder of the war surrounded by Polish forests while the rest of the army redeployed west for the upcoming confrontation with the British and French armies. Thus, it came as quite a pleasurable surprise on 20 October when a telegraph arrived from Blaskowitz's headquarters announcing that "Major General Model on 22/10 becomes Chief of Staff to the 17th or 16th Army."[30]

Evidently a considerable amount of internal army politics lay behind this appointment, accounting in part for the confusing inability of OKH to specify exactly to which army Model had been posted. The Army Personnel Office's selection of Major General Herbert von Böckmann, chief of staff to Georg von Küchler's Third Army in Poland, for command of the 11th Infantry Division had raised the question of a successor. On 13 October, Halder proposed Major General Otto Stapf, the head of the Organization and Technical Branch of OKH and currently the senior army liaison officer to Hermann Göring. Stapf was a quiet, apolitical staff officer who was one of Halder's small group of protégés, and the chief of the Army General Staff apparently regarded it as his personal prerogative to nominate a candidate for

the position. The commanding general of the army, von Brauchitsch, however, had other ideas and surprised Halder by suggesting Model as an alternative candidate. Halder disliked Model
personally, but he could hardly discount the fact that Stapf's service record was far less impressive than Model's, and he could not
ignore the favorable opinions that von Reichenau and Paulus held
of the IV Corps' chief of staff. The two generals deferred a decision for five days, picking up the matter again on 19 October,
when it was decided that the position would go to Model, although Halder insisted on controlling the appointment of an operations officer who could "moderate" Model's "excessive
attachment to Göring"; Stapf, as an apparent consolation prize,
received command of the 111th Infantry Division early the next
year. It was the first time that von Brauchitsch, who had known
Model well since their trip to the Soviet Union a decade earlier, directly intervened in his behalf, but it would not be the last.[31]

Nonetheless, Model did not end up paired with Georg von
Küchler; on reporting to Berlin, he discovered that he would instead be working with General of Infantry Ernst Busch at the
newly formed Sixteenth Army. Busch, an "out-and-out Nazi" and
a "rabid supporter of Hitler," according to Samuel Mitcham, owed
a series of rapid promotions in the 1930s to his politics rather than
his professionalism. Before Hitler came to power, Busch had been
an obscure lieutenant colonel who stood 176th on the seniority
list; by 1939, however, following vocal support of the Führer at
every turn (even when it meant appearing as something of a toady
in the eyes of his fellows), he began the war as a general of infantry, commander of the VIII Corps, and the twentieth-most-
senior officer in the army. Although his record in command in
Poland while subordinated to the Fourteenth Army was at best
undistinguished, his politically correct stance garnered him the appointment at the head of the Sixteenth Army, ahead of several
more senior officers.[32]

Not by any means a Prussian, the fifty-four-year-old Busch had been born in Essen in the Ruhr; physically he was a large, phlegmatic man with bovine features and great physical endurance. He was no stranger to combat, having finished the First World War as a battalion commander in the 1918 offensives, and his bravery was not open to question either; he had won the coveted Pour le Mérite, the Second Reich's highest award for battlefield courage.[33] Busch's greatest failings as a commander would ultimately revolve around a lack of imagination, intellectual inflexibility, and insufficient resolution to resist Hitler's will at critical moments. But these inadequacies were not readily apparent in October 1939, when Busch seemed to be at least a solid if not inspired choice to command an army.

The greatest concern that von Brauchitsch and Halder had about Busch's capabilities after Poland was his total inexperience with the concept of mobile warfare and his almost stereotypical conservatism toward the role of tanks in battle. In a German army that had been revolutionized by the development of the panzer divisions and other mobile units, Busch remained a hidebound reactionary whose sole contribution to the professional debates of the mid-1930s had been an article entitled "Has the Decisive Battle Role of the Infantry Ended?" which was published in the 1937–1938 edition of the *Jahrbuch fur Wehrpolitik und Wehrwissenschaften*. In this short piece Busch made it quite clear that he had completely missed the strategic possibilities of Germany's panzers: "The basic idea behind the use of tanks is that by wiping out machine guns and artillery, hitherto so effective against infantry, the enemy forces can be annihilated." After cataloging what he considered to be the remote "possibility of real panzer battles with tanks fighting tanks" and likening the potential of "motorized and mechanized units" to that which "cavalry charges had in the past," Busch unsurprisingly concluded: "Nevertheless, the decisive role will remain with the infantry."[34] Nothing he witnessed in Poland had changed his mind.

Model, who had known his new superior for about ten years, seemed, in the best General Staff tradition, the perfect counterweight for Busch's weaknesses. Where the army commander was stolid and slow-moving, the chief of staff was mercurial and forever in frenzied action; where Busch conceived of warfare in terms of the slow maneuvers of marching infantry, Model had become an expert—at least in theory—on combined arms operations. On the other hand, the two men shared a number of characteristics that would allow them to work together effectively. Both came from petit bourgeois roots—Model the son of a teacher, Busch the offspring of an orphanage director. Both shared a love of horses and riding. And perhaps most importantly, Busch and Model were both among the ranks of the more pro-Hitler generals who found it possible to restrict their focus to the purely military aspects of the war and dismiss as regrettable but necessary the excesses of the current regime. There was no possibility that either man would raise discomforting moral issues that might sidetrack them from their mission or allow them to participate in the increasingly active anti-Hitler intrigues of the army's senior command.[35]

By the time Model arrived at Sixteenth Army headquarters in the Bitburg-Trier area of the Moselle Valley, OKH had already issued a second edition of *Fall Gelb*, the original plan of attack on France and the Low Countries worked out between Hitler, von Brauchitsch, and Halder. Model found himself still under von Rundstedt's general command (Army Group South having been redesignated "A") facing the Ardennes. Aside from the Sixteenth Army, the army group included only the Twelfth (the former Fourteenth under von List); the two armies consisted of only twenty-seven infantry divisions. Unlike Poland, where he had controlled the main strength of the German army, the strategic directive for the western campaign relegated von Rundstedt to conducting a subsidiary attack toward Sedan and through Luxembourg while von Bock's Army Group B made the primary assault through central Belgium and southern Holland with three armies and thirty-seven divisions, including virtually all the panzer and motorized units. The Sixteenth Army's specific mission was to serve as little more than a blocking force by occupying Luxembourg and the extreme southern tip of Belgium to prevent the French from catching the main effort in the flank with an attack out of the Maginot Line.[36]

Simple as this mission may have sounded, Model soon discovered that, given the troops and resources with which his army had to work, even a secondary defensive mission could be a challenge. To start, nearly all of the seven divisions assigned to the Sixteenth Army were those of mobilization waves 2 through 5, divisions raised since 1 September, consisting primarily of reservists who were either in their mid to late thirties or had almost no military training, leavened with fewer than 20 percent regular officers and NCOs. Two divisions had not even organized their third infantry regiments by mid-December. These divisions had been cobbled together in the first place with reduced scales of weapons, equipment, and transport—a large percentage of which was of Czech rather than German manufacture. Many of the guns and tanks were so old that Halder described the holdings of Busch's army as "a museum." Moreover, when he conducted his first inspections Model discovered that the army did not have a full ammunition load on hand; even light defensive operations would probably have depleted the available stocks in less than forty-eight hours. Conditions only deteriorated in early January, when OKH removed the training division that had been working overtime to bring Sixteenth Army's green troops up to combat standard and days later stripped nearly 70 percent of each division's trucks for use by units in Army Group B.[37]

Model barraged OKH for more of everything throughout November, December, and January, but the weather and an airplane crash had more to do with the sudden change in the fortunes of the Sixteenth Army that occurred in February. Foul weather played into the hands of those officers—from von Brauchitsch and Halder on down—who were convinced that Hitler's obsession

Stopping to brief the Sixteenth Army commander, General of Infantry Ernst Busch, was one of the few times that Model, as army chief of staff, was not a whirlwind of motion between October 1939 and June 1940.

with attacking the West as soon after completing the Polish campaign as possible would lead to disaster. Without air support, the invasion of France would have no chance, and the cloud cover over western Europe repeatedly kept Göring's planes grounded and several times required the cancellation of a planned attack. Like many other commanders, Busch and Model breathed a weary sigh of relief each time, knowing they had been granted a few more days for training and stockpiling supplies.

During the same period the dissatisfaction of a number of individuals with the OKH plan led to the development of an alternative approach. In what would commonly come to be called "the Manstein variant," the weight of the main attack was shifted south to Army Group A. A solid phalanx of panzer and motorized divisions would penetrate the Ardennes, force the Meuse, and race headlong for the Channel coast, ultimately cutting off more than seventy French and British divisions that were expected to plunge into Belgium as soon as the Germans crossed the border. Although the plan had several authors, including von Manstein, Guderian, and even Hitler himself, the German army did not irrevocably commit to it until after the Mechelen incident in late January, when a Luftwaffe officer crash-landed in Belgium, allowing a copy of the original plan to fall into enemy hands.[38]

This reorientation of the main effort required a whole new set of army and army group–level war games and materially enlarged the Sixteenth Army's task. The war games occurred at Koblenz on 7 and 14 February, with Model playing the role of the commander of the Sixteenth Army while Busch was assigned the part of General Maurice Gamelin, the French chief of staff and supreme commander for the upcoming battle. Most of the participants—including Halder, von Rundstedt, von List, and Guderian—focused on what they considered to be the critical issue of how quickly the panzer spearhead could force a crossing of the Meuse and a major breach in the French front. Guderian and von Wietersheim, commanding between them more than half of the panzer and motorized divisions committed to the main attack, argued for a rapid dash through the Ardennes and a hasty attack across the Meuse by their lead units on the fourth day of the offensive. Von Rundstedt and his senior staff officers, Blumentritt and Georg von Sodenstern, disagreed, being convinced that "there is no sense in the Armd. Corps attacking alone across the Meuse on A plus 4"; they held out for "a properly marshaled attack in mass" on the eighth day of the campaign, when sufficient infantry divisions and heavy artillery battalions had closed on the river to support the tanks. Guderian and von Wietersheim left the map maneuvers so angry about the general consensus to tie their mobile forces to the marching infantry that Halder recorded that the two panzer generals "plainly show lack of confidence in success. Guderian: Has lost confidence.—The whole tank operation is planned wrong!" As often occurred in his career, Guderian's pessimistic outburst cost him dearly: Originally slated to command the entire "armored wedge," Guderian was relegated by his superiors to corps command ten days later and was eventually replaced with General of Cavalry Ewald von Kleist.[39]

This disagreement about how fast the attack across the Meuse could be launched hinged on two misconceptions. Busch, as Gamelin, refused to plunge recklessly toward the Dyle River in Belgium with the bulk of the higher-quality French and British divisions (as the Allies actually did), finding such a maneuver foolhardy. Instead, he made a cautious advance into Belgium and as quickly as possible built a solid wall of nearly forty divisions along the Meuse during the first week of the battle. This left OKH and Army Group A convinced that the German army would be facing a defense in depth at the river. The second misconception stemmed from the fact that almost everyone present seriously underestimated the speed with which the nonmotorized infantry divisions could reach the river, concluding that the infantrymen could not be in position until the eighth or ninth day. If such was indeed the case, several generals openly wondered whether the decisive battle might actually have to be fought on the wrong side of the Meuse. Busch went so far in one meeting as to tell Guderian: "I don't think you'll cross the river in the first place!" More quietly, von Rundstedt himself confided to Halder that he had lost confidence in the idea of the panzer divisions leading the way through the Ardennes forest, and he suggested quite seriously that infantry divisions be placed in the vanguard of the attack until after the Meuse had been crossed.[40]

Gamelin would astound the Germans by recklessly leaving the Meuse River only lightly defended by second-rate troops, presenting them with the opportunity to tear a forty-mile breach in the Allied front. But even this blunder might not have been fatal had not the German infantry divisions confounded the experts by reaching the river in only four days. In a performance that has been most often ignored in favor of the dramatic maneuvers of the panzer divisions, those hard-marching *Landser*, by the fifth day of the offensive, managed to capture four bridgeheads without any assistance from Guderian's vaunted tanks. Furthermore, wave after successive wave of follow-up divisions moved so rapidly through the twisting roads of the Ardennes to cover the flanks of von Kleist's breakthrough that the French never had a realistic opportunity to stage a counterattack.[41]

Two of the men who were quietly responsible for this achievement were Model and Colonel General Güntherr von Kluge, commander of the Fourth Army. Since the best roads had been placed at the disposal of the panzer divisions, von Kluge consolidated virtually every vehicle in his infantry divisions under the control of regimental *kampfgruppen*. These ad hoc formations followed directly in the wake of the panzer divisions along the twisting network of secondary roads, fanning out as they hit the river. A typical group was exemplified by that built around the 83rd Infantry Regiment, which was supported by a motorized howitzer battalion, a platoon of 88mm flak, and a company of engineers; it seized a bridgehead at Rivierre on 14 May.[42]

Model, who was promoted to lieutenant general on 1 April, meanwhile busied himself with the logistical details of pushing forward the follow-up divisions. Under the revised plan, the Sixteenth Army now had to seize and occupy a much longer front of nearly seventy-five miles; after Army Group A's main effort had crossed the Meuse and turned due west, Busch's divisions were expected to make local spoiling attacks along the far western extension of the Maginot Line. Halder delineated this dual mission in a conference with Hitler on 18 February:

> *Sixteenth Army* to get to the border in southern Luxembourg with the utmost speed. Advance combat teams! *Mot. elements.* Obstacle Removal Detachments. Planes sowing mines, etc. Purpose: To seize the terrain needed for the defense as quickly as possible, and organize it for sustained defensive warfare.
>
> The enemy would be able to launch a strong counterattack in this sector after three to four days, covered by his fortress system (Camp of Chalons, etc.).
>
> It would thus be five or six days, before the main body of Sixteenth Army arrives and takes up positions, and the critical stages is overcome. Sixteenth Army will then be placed under AGp. C.

Considering the army's lack of motorized transport, the movement represented a huge challenge, but the prospect of even limited offensive action in the second phase of the campaign was chilling. At the moment that the overall plan changed, the Sixteenth Army contained still-incomplete divisions of minimally trained reservists with second-line weapons. Many of these units were among the ones that Colonel General Wilhelm Ritter von Leeb (commander of the western front during the Polish campaign) had characterized in October as "suitable for position warfare under quiet conditions" or even "suited for position warfare only after further training in defensive warfare."[43]

Fortunately for Model, he got help with both problems. Faced with a dire shortage of trucks, Halder decided to strip divisional truck columns from the waves 1, 2, and 4 infantry divisions, replacing them with horse-drawn supply columns and consolidating the motorized transport at army level. The Sixteenth Army was one of the few that actually benefited from this decision, since none of its divisions had a large number of trucks in the first place, and by early March, Busch and Model had received ten new truck columns. Furthermore, Hitler himself took an interest in the composition and execution of the obstacle removal teams that would precede the main body of the army through the forest and caused the Luftwaffe to set aside more than thirty Fieseler *Storch* liaison planes to be utilized in landing small detachments throughout Luxembourg before the enemy could react.[44]

During March and April the Sixteenth Army also underwent an almost continuous change in its composition that, while maddening from Model's point of view, left it much better off in terms of the quality and armaments of its infantry divisions. By 20 April Busch's command consisted of eleven divisions, five of which were Wave 1 units from the prewar army. In addition, Busch and Model controlled two of the German army's new assault gun batteries, six engineer battalions, fourteen construction battalions, and no fewer than fourteen army artillery battalions. The army had moreover been assigned three corps headquarters commanded by an exceptionally talented trio of officers: VII Corps (General of Infantry Eugen Ritter von Schobert), XII Corps (Lieutenant General Heinrich Freiherr von Vietinghoff gennant Scheel), and XXIII Corps (Lieutenant General Albrecht Schubert). By 5 May, however, further frantic changes had occurred, with the army gaining two more Wave 1 divisions at the cost of five artillery battalions, most of its construction battalions, and all of its assault guns. As in Poland, Model coped with these last-minute changes, though not without angry (and certainly profane) telephone calls to his superiors. Particularly with the reserved army group chief of staff, von Sodenstern, and his operations officer (Blumentritt), this behavior earned Model no points for either professionalism or congeniality and probably accounted for the fact that following the campaign he was one of the few army chiefs of staff not to receive either a decoration or a promotion.[45]

One also has to wonder at the impression that Model made on the Sixteenth Army's liaison officer, thirty-eight-year-old Major

Reinhard Gehlen, a Halder protégé who later achieved prominence as the head of the "Foreign Armies East." Von Brauchitsch and Halder dispatched liaison officers to all the major commands to function as the direct eyes and ears of the OKH and quickly (and confidentially) transmit their observations outside the formal channels of communication. Gehlen was ostensibly selected for the Sixteenth Army because he had until recently been chief of the Fortifications Group in OKH and was thus presumably as much of an expert on the Maginot Line as the Germans possessed. More likely, however, Gehlen's assignment was the result of Halder's persistent concern with Model's temperament and pro-Hitler political leanings.[46]

If later patterns of behavior held true in 1940, what Gehlen saw at Sixteenth Army headquarters in the predawn hours was a Walther Model consumed by nervous energy, pacing frantically, and snapping viciously at his subordinates while he waited for the first indications that his air-landed infantry had seized the border posts before the roads through the Ardennes could be obstructed. Just before dawn the reports began to filter back: Success had been achieved. Model immediately sent the orders for the advance *kampfgruppen* of the army's six leading divisions to jump off. Gehlen's late-night report to Halder on 11 May was positive enough for the chief of the Army General Staff to term the Sixteenth Army's successes on the first two days "gratifying."[47]

The Sixteenth Army's operations during the first decisive days of the campaign have not so much been overshadowed as eradicated from memory by the dramatic dash to the English Channel by Guderian's panzers and the drama surrounding the British evacuation of Dunkirk. In a very real sense the fact that Busch and Model earned not even the slightest mention by historians of the campaign is the best evidence of the success of their mission. The entries of Army Group A's war diary present the most accurate account—heretofore unavailable in English—from which an outline of the Sixteenth Army's operations can be extracted:

May 12: 16th Army, as from the evening of 11 May, continues to maneuver incessantly according to plan. The attack will go in against the critical terrain on the approaches of the Maginot Line.

May 13: 16th Army:

intends on 15 May for the attack to pass through Carignan.

XIII Corps has found itself in a stubborn battle along the line Virton—Longwy.

XXIII Corps has itself reached the proper line for the defense.

May 14: 16th Army has its right wing reach the assembly area for the attack past through the Chiers sector toward Carignan, while the center and left wing have driven the enemy into the Maginot Line and reached the line designated for the forward defense.

May 16: 16th Army:

Right wing improves its position and intends advancing on Margut. The remainder of the front is constructing defensive positions.

May 17: The 16th Army has been able to reach its line and managed to halt an obstinate counterattack.

The Army Group, even in these days, is appropriately interested in the first line of fortifications on the long southern flank. After all the impression exists that here in the next 2–3 days rather than on the right there may be strong enemy attacks. Yet the situation relaxes day by day. The division fartherest forward retains a continuous front running from the rear of the 16th Army, advancing La Fere and Rethel to the motorized formations of Group Kleist.

May 18: 16th Army:

VI Corps has taken 24 and 16 Infantry Divisions under control for defense. 36.Div. defends against an enemy armor attack on both sides of Beaumont.

VII Corps led the attack of the 16th Army with great bravery, assaulting at 19.30 against the tough French defensive Position 505 west of Margut.

At the beginning of the evening a single enemy tank attack
against Hill 311 (1200 m west of Olisy) was halted.

May 19: 3:30 A.M. telephone call from 16th Army that it is
preparing its VI Corps for an expected enemy tank attack.
They request that the Panzerjäger Battalion of the 10th Division be moved from south of Maasufer to a position in front
of Bulson and for Stuka support. Both moves have been made
by Army Group.

May 22: On the right flank of the 16th Army preparations have
been made for the set-piece attack early in the morning on
May 23 to isolate the improved positions between the Ardennes Canal and the Meuse. The army is constructing defensive positions on the rest of its front.

May 24: The 16th Army has carried out the attack on its right
flank (VI Corps) exactly according to plan, a set-piece and
more, with the counterattack made with tank support beaten
off.[48]

The following day von Rundstedt decided to call off the attack
because Busch and Model were tying up too many troops needed
near the Channel coast and also threatened to trespass across the
boundary into the territory of von Leeb's Army Group C. Halder's
diary also hints that the Sixteenth Army was intentionally diverting divisions earmarked by OKH simply to pass through its operational area. Moreover, army casualty figures had somehow
reached Hitler, who ordered the OKW operations officer, Major
General Alfred Jodl, to telephone Halder and insist that the army
"has too many casualties and is attacking needlessly." Halder, already frustrated by the Führer's personal interventions around

Dunkirk, scrawled an aggrieved "Pater Noster" after his record of the conversation. As a result of all these events, the Sixteenth Army went over to a strict defensive on 25 May, which it maintained until 9 June, when it attacked again as part of *Fall Rot* (Case Red), the post-Dunkirk phase of the Battle of France.[49]

The two-week interlude was hardly long enough for Model, who found the entire composition of his army changed once again. Because the Sixteenth Army's part in the upcoming offensive was merely another secondary attack, serving as the hinge between von Rundstedt and von Leeb, OKH utilized Busch's army as a source of replacements for other armies in more critical sectors. Thus, the army lost five of its seven Wave 1 divisions, which were replaced by lower-quality divisions raised after the Polish campaign and equipped with captured or Czech-manufactured weapons. Not only did nine of Busch's thirteen divisions therefore lack their heavy artillery battalions, but six either had only a bicycle squadron in place of a reconnaissance battalion or had no organic reconnaissance element at all. Nor could these deficiencies be made good from army troops: OKH had also snatched away six of the its fourteen independent artillery battalions. Furthermore, von Vietinghoff's XIII and Schubert's XXIII Corps headquarters were both transferred to the Twelfth Army and replaced by improvised Corps Commands (*Höherekommando*) XXXI and XXXVI. These headquarters were deficient in communications, transport, and trained staff; moreover, their respective commanders—General of Artillery Leonhard Kaupisch and Lieutenant General Hans Feige—were aging retirees recalled to the colors who could both be expected to need far more supervision than their predecessors. From Model's standpoint, the only possible redeeming feature of this reorganization was that he retained several excellent division commanders and senior staff officers. Among the former were Maximilian de Angelis, Hans Hube, and Georg Lindemann (all future army or army group commanders), while the latter included

Hans Krebs, a future chief of the Army General Staff who would serve out much of the war from early 1942 as Model's chief of staff.[50]

The Sixteenth Army's mission was to attack down the east bank of the Meuse, skirting the Meuse-Argonne forest of World War I fame, with an initial objective of Verdun. From there the army had to wheel almost directly east to force the Moselle River and seize Metz in cooperation with an attack through the Maginot Line by the First Army of Army Group C. During this final phase Busch's army would fall under von Leeb's control. The greatest danger associated with this operation was that significant French forces might concentrate in the Meuse-Argonne triangle, allow themselves to be bypassed, and then strike the Sixteenth Army in the flank and rear.[51]

Model received far more attention while planning this attack than he preferred; it must have seemed in fact that the entire command hierarchy of the German army was looking over his shoulder. On 1–2 June, Model and Busch were required to attend a Führer conference for senior officers at Charleville; two days later von Brauchitsch turned up at Sixteenth Army headquarters for a surprise visit, and Model had to entertain his patron. Model also had to reassure both Halder and von Rundstedt on 5 June that when he had drawn up his plan of attack he had taken into account French forces assumed to be massing on the army's right flank, and on the morning that the offensive opened it was necessary for Model likewise to calm down von Sodenstern, who was afraid that in the absence of air support Model's planned artillery barrage was too brief to be effective. A sure indication of Model's rising temper is that for several days in early June either Busch himself or Lieutenant Colonel Hans Boeckh-Behrends, the army operations officer, handled most of the routine communications with higher headquarters, presumably to spare everyone the experience of one of the chief of staff's now-notorious outbursts.[52]

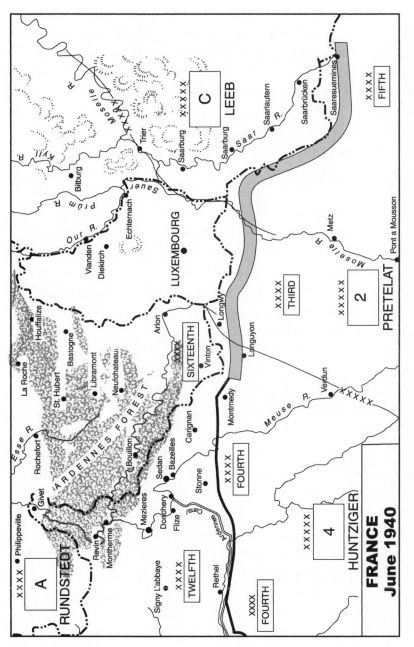

Busch's Sixteenth Army had only a limited role in the initial thrust through the Ardennes. After Dunkirk Busch and Model faced second-rate French troops, but also had to contend with the left flank of the Maginot Line.

In reality, most of these concerns were unnecessary, for as Model sensed, the French army was essentially defeated prior to the attack. Not only were the French divisions battered and demoralized by the debacle in the Low Countries and northern France, but there were now only about sixty of them left to face a German onslaught of nearly 150 divisions. To amass as much strength as possible against the dreaded panzer divisions, GHQ had left more than 150 miles of the Maginot Line garrisoned by only seventeen divisions (mostly Category B units—the oldest class of reservists). Concerning a possible concentration of enemy forces in the Meuse-Argonne triangle, Model rightly believed that they would be far more interested in attacking the flank of the Twelfth Army and Panzer Group Guderian rather than the Sixteenth Army. Nor was the Maginot Line the invulnerable line of fortifications that French propaganda attempted to make it. One divisional operations officer observed that "many of the French strongpoints were not proof against shells or bombs, and moreover, a large number of positions had not been sited for all-round defense and were easy to attack from the blind side with flamethrowers." He also noted that "the fortifications had only a moderate local value" and "were breached in a few hours by a normal infantry attack, without any tank support whatever."[53]

Busch and Model enjoyed one final advantage: Unlike the main line of armies in Army Groups A and B, their attack was scheduled to commence as much as forty-eight hours after many other formations had begun their assault. They could therefore hope that the meager French reserves would already have been drawn away from their sector. (This in fact turned out to be the case: By 9–10 June, Guderian's 1st Panzer Division had already drawn one French infantry and two armored divisions out of the Argonne forest.) The only concerns shared by the commander and his chief of staff were that the Twelfth Army might grow overzealous with its artillery support and target fires into the Sixteenth Army area or

that Guderian might advance so swiftly that he would comman-
deer the roads intended for their axis of advance toward Verdun.[54]

The attack, launched at 6:20 A.M. on 9 June, had been entrusted
to von Schobert's VII Corps, with the 24th and 36th Infantry Divisions (both regular units) spearheading the assault and the 58th
and 299th in reserve. The first day was frustrating; by 1:00 P.M., instead of breaking the French front, heavy, pre-registered enemy artillery fire and tenacious defensive fighting held von Schobert's
divisions to a minimal two-kilometer gain in the very center of the
front. Model had to grit his teeth and endure an evening telephone
call at army group from von Sodenstern, who chided him for the
army's failure to crack the French defenses, pointing out that the
Sixteenth Army was lagging behind the Twelfth and that this was
causing Guderian some hard fighting because Busch's attack had
not kept the full attention of the enemy forces in the Argonne.[55]

Most of 10 June appeared to be a repeat of the opening day.
Heavy French artillery fire continued to stymie the German advance, and at one point von Sodenstern called to suggest that it
might be necessary for the Twelfth Army (which had now broken
free on its front) to bend around and envelop the forces resisting
the VII Corps. Busch and Model both resisted this idea, and von
Schobert threw in his reserve divisions. Army Group A coughed up
an additional division, the 71st Infantry, to add still more weight to
the attack. By evening, Model was able to placate higher headquarters with a report that enemy resistance was "softening," implying that a breakthrough would be possible the following day.[56]

During the early morning hours of 11 June, Model began receiving reports that enemy artillery fire was slackening. Aerial reconnaissance confirmed around noon that large columns of
French vehicles were beginning to stream toward the rear. "The
enemy," Halder recorded in his journal, "who previously offered
stiff resistance to the west wing of Sixteenth Army now is falling
back." Von Schobert reported that his corps was on the verge of a

breakthrough by midafternoon, and Army Group A offered several flights of close-support aircraft to speed the process. Kaupisch and Feige on the army's flanks were told to prepare an attack for the morning of 12 June. The fight had gone out of the French; VII Corps scored its breakthrough soon after dawn, discovering that many of the pillboxes in its front had simply been abandoned during the night. While von Schobert's five divisions reoriented themselves from assault to pursuit mode, Kaupisch and Feige advanced in unspectacular but steady fashion on his flanks, widening the breach by several miles.[57]

Verdun fell to the VII Corps on 15 June, Toul and Epinal the next day. The Sixteenth Army began wheeling east (with Guderian's panzers describing a larger circle around Busch's right flank), in preparation for an assault on the rear of the upper Maginot Line, while the First Army of Army Group C attacked it from the front. For this purpose both the Sixteenth Army and Panzer Group Guderian came under von Leeb's authority on 17 June. Von Leeb's first orders, received on 18 June, required the army not to stop driving forces south even while it prepared to attack to the east. French disintegration had now become so pronounced that the primary objective of the campaign had switched from active combat operations to destroy the enemy to a head-over-heels pursuit to gobble up as much territory as possible before an armistice was announced. Thus, a scattering of French units operating in the army's rear area were simply to be ignored, left to the XVII Corps from Army Group A's reserve. Von Leeb's confidence was fully justified: By 22 June the First and Sixteenth Armies had made contact, pocketing two army commanders, four corps commanders, several divisions commanders, and an estimated 400,000 (later raised to 600,000) dispirited and totally defeated French soldiers. The armistice signed that day took effect on 25 June, ending one of the most remarkable campaigns in military history.[58]

The rewards passed out to German generals by Adolph Hitler were as grandiose as his plans for a "New Order" in Europe. Beginning with a ceremony on 19 July at Berlin's Kroll Opera House—impressive chiefly for glitter and gaud—the Führer created twelve new field marshals, advanced nineteen men to the rank of colonel general, and in short order promoted dozens more junior generals and field officers. Busch and all three of his original corps commanders—von Schobert, Schubert, and von Vietinghoff—moved up, as did most of the division commanders and a high percentage of the senior staff officers, and so did von Rundstedt and von Sodenstern at Army Group A.[59]

Conspicuously not a recipient of these laurels was Walther Model. The problem appears to have been the fact that his brusque and reckless style as chief of staff only cemented his existing image among other General Staff officers as something less than a gentleman and a member of the club. Model achieved results, certainly, but his frequent outbursts and rough language made no points with von Sodenstern, who undoubtedly reported his impression directly to Halder. Halder himself had already pushed Model aside once, and even though Hitler had now taken a much firmer grip on promotions among the senior commanders, the chief of the Army General Staff still controlled most staff advancements. The chiefs of staff rewarded in July and August—Kurt Felber, Eberhard von Mackensen, Hans von Salmuth, and Georg von Sodenstern—were all Halder protégés. Not for the first time in his career had Model's abrasive personality cost him dearly.[60]

Yet there was no time available for brooding, as Sixteenth Army headquarters was swiftly shifted in early July to Turcoing, on the coast of northern France, to be tasked as one of the three armies controlling forces in the projected cross-channel invasion of England. Just three days before the mass promotion ceremony in Berlin (punctuated by Hitler's last appeal for peace with Great Britain), Directive No. 16 for the Conduct of the War was issued. In it the Führer declared: "As England, in spite of the hopelessness of her military position, has so far shown herself unwilling to come to any compromise, I have therefore decided to begin to prepare for and, if necessary, to carry out an invasion of England." "During the ensuing nine weeks," observes historian Telford Taylor, "the preparations were not only begun but virtually completed, and by mid-September a makeshift armada of barges, tugs, and other small craft lay in the Channel harbors, ready to embark the assault troops and follow the course of Julius Caesar and William the Conquerer."[61]

Hitler had written Mussolini on 10 July that "the programme for the attack on England has been pursued and studied in the greatest detail for months past," and while this statement was technically true, it was also extremely disingenuous. Although both the German army and navy had begun feasibility studies and contingency plans for a cross-channel invasion in 1939, these activities had formed no part of Hitler's grand strategy. In fact, when first presented with information about the studies on 21 May, his response was less than lukewarm. Hitler preferred to pursue a strategy of using the Luftwaffe to batter the British into submission. Another two months would pass before the dictator reluctantly accepted the idea that Winston Churchill and his countrymen would not pull out of the war unless there were panzers in the suburbs of London.[62]

The original army plan, which viewed the English Channel as nothing more than a large river, envisioned thirteen divisions landing simultaneously along a 250-mile front that stretched from Cornwall to the mouth of the Thames. The complete invasion force, once ashore, was intended to include twenty-nine infantry, six panzer, three motorized, and two airborne divisions. Three armies—the Sixth, Ninth, and Sixteenth—would control the assault, with Busch's headquarters entrusted with the critical right flank. Three corps commanded by von Manstein, von Schobert, and von Vietinghoff, each with two infantry divisions, would secure beaches between Ramsgate and Hastings, while Reinhardt's XLI Motorized Corps (1st and 4th Panzer Divisions plus the SS *Totenkopf* Motorized Division) came ashore to punch through the British defenses.[63]

Walther Model had little or nothing to do with the greater arguments over strategy that convulsed the higher levels of command from mid-July through September as they constantly revised downward the scope of the landings because of the inability of the Luftwaffe to eliminate the Royal Air Force or the German navy's increasing disbelief in its ability to secure safe transport across the Channel in the face of the Royal Navy. During that time the initial assault force was reduced from thirteen to six divisions, the Sixth Army was dropped from the operation entirely, and the frontage of the invasion was reduced to little more than had been originally assigned to the Sixteenth Army under the original plan. In Busch's sector, von Manstein's XXXVIII Corps had been removed, leaving von Schobert's VII and von Vietinghoff's XIII Corps with the responsibility for establishing the beachhead. Reinhardt's XLI Motorized Corps had been reorganized to include the 8th and 10th Panzer Divisions, 29th Motorized Division, the *Grossdeutschland* Motorized Regiment, and the SS *Liebstandarte Adolph Hitler* Motorized Regiment; though significantly stronger than before, Reinhardt's corps would now take at least a week to cross the Channel and disembark.[64]

What did concern Model was the tactical planning for the assault, consolidation, and breakout. Army Group A's commander, the newly promoted Field Marshal von Rundstedt, had little confidence in the whole idea of a cross-channel invasion and therefore discouraged his own staff from active participation in the detailed planning. This left most of the tactical planning, by default, to Busch at the Sixteenth Army; given the rather obvious limits on Busch's intellectual capacities, this realistically meant that the work would be supervised by Model and his operations officer Boeckh-Behrends.[65]

This period of planning and training for an operation that never occurred is significant in the career of Walther Model because it highlights his superb grasp of logistics and his thorough understanding of the relationship of unit organization to tactical

missions. In later years, Model would become more and more famous for his tactical innovations and improvisations, first on the
Russian front and then in France again, and his techniques are too
often treated as if they had sprung whole-cloth from his imagination outside Moscow. In reality, as his experiences heretofore have
shown and as his preparations for the invasion of England so well
illustrate, Walther Model had long been a thorough student of
modern tactics—from panzer drives to beach landings.

The Sixteenth Army broke the problem of a beach landing into
three components: disembarking, assault, and consolidation.
Model and Busch had to assume (or there would be no invasion!)
that the navy could deliver its soldiers to the vicinity of the beach.
From that point the attack became the army's problem, with the
Luftwaffe and navy relegated to providing support fires. At Le
Touquet in early August Model had a special training center established to prepare key officers and NCOs to get their troops as
quickly as possible off the motley collection of barges expected to
serve as the invasion flotilla. More than 750 men passed through
an arduous course of instruction, then returned to their divisions
to lend their expertise to four full-scale divisional exercises in September. The results of this course revealed the need for more and
better ramps to allow the troops to exit the barges under fire. The
Sixteenth Army ordered 100 ramps specially built for the first wave
barges; unhappy with their design, Model offered a 3,000 *Reichs-
mark* reward for anyone who could come up with a significant improvement to them.[66]

The infantry divisions that would make the landings were
poorly organized for amphibious assault, primarily because the organization and tactics of the German army were built almost exclusively around ground combat in areas served by decent road
networks. Though OKH might conceptualize a cross-channel invasion as the equivalent of a river crossing, Model and his infantry
commanders knew better. Not only would naval gunfire and close

air support have to substitute completely for field artillery during the first critical hours, but a regiment making a landing at Folkestone or Dover would have to measure the time between initial contact with the enemy and substantial reinforcement quite differently than the divisions that had forced the Meuse. Follow-up forces could not paddle across from Calais in rubber assault boats or on makeshift rafts; given the shortage of invasion-equipped barges, this meant in practical terms that an assaulting regiment would have to wait up to eighteen hours for those unwieldy craft to make a road trip with the second wave.

Model met this challenge by restructuring the assault divisions— dividing each into first- and second-echelon components. The divisional first echelons consisted of two reinforced regiments, carrying all supplies necessary for a sustained assault. Both regiments had one specially organized battalion for advance penetration, and all first echelons were liberally supported by flamethrowing tanks, multiple rocket-launchers, and assault guns. The projected strength of a first-echelon *kampfgruppe* was to be 6,762 men, 372 machine guns, 226 mortars, 27 antitank guns, 22 artillery pieces, and 12 antiaircraft guns. In terms of mobility, these groups were equipped with 58 armored fighting vehicles, 127 trucks and cars, 181 motorcycles, and 1,908 bicycles. The second—or follow-up—echelon from each division consisted of the third regiment, the remainder of the divisional artillery and combat support units, and a reinforced transportation element: 12,376 men with 4,427 horses, 1,116 motor vehicles, and 876 motorcycles.[67]

All of this planning, however, was destined to come to naught. The Luftwaffe could not break the back of the Royal Air Force, the *Kriegsmarine* could not guarantee safe passage for the barges in the teeth of the Royal Navy, and without these prerequisites having been met, not even Adolph Hitler would risk the pride of the German army in what now appeared to be far more than a river crossing. Throughout late August and early September the invasion date was pushed back again and again, first to 6 September, then to 27 September, again to 8 October, and finally into infinity.[68] Though the pretext of a concentration for the invasion of England remained in place until March 1941, the fate of the army and Walther Model now lay far to the east.

4

GUDERIAN'S SPEARHEAD

3rd Panzer Division

THE EARLIEST INDICATIONS OF ADOLPH HITLER'S INTENTION TO
attack the Soviet Union in 1941 surfaced even before the futility of
a cross-channel invasion of the British Isles had become clear. The
Führer first raised the issue on 21 July 1940 and returned to the
subject with a more specific directive ten days later. By early August, while Walther Model was still deeply involved in considering
just how to get the infantrymen of the Sixteenth Army off their
waterlogged barges and onto the Folkstone beaches, his counterpart at Eighteenth Army headquarters—Major General Erich
Marcks—had already produced the first draft of what would gradually evolve into the plan behind Operation "Barbarossa."[1]

Yet even after the tacit cancellation of "Operation Sea Lion," it
seemed for several months that Walther Model's future lay in the
south rather than the east. Among the myriad strategic options offered to Hitler in the summer and fall of 1940 by such diverse authors as the commander-in-chief of the *Kriegsmarine* or the

National Defense Branch of OKW were plans for the siege and re-duction of Gibraltar, the occupation of Portugal, the seizure of northwest Africa, reinforcing the projected Italian invasion of Egypt, and intervening in Mussolini's rapidly disintegrating war with Greece. At one time or another, even the most farfetched of these undertakings came close enough to reality that force organi-zations were considered and commanders selected before the whole idea was scrapped or modified.[2]

A recurrent element in most of these plans was the participation of the 3rd Panzer Division. At various points throughout the fall of 1940, Halder's diary testifies to the fact that the 3rd Panzer was under serious consideration for deployment to Morocco, Ruma-nia, Greece, and Libya. The most likely destination for the Berlin division whose tactical emblem was a bear was Libya. In late Au-gust contingency plans surfaced to send a panzer corps of the 3rd and 5th Panzer Divisions as well as the 13th (Motorized) Infantry Division to North Africa. Both Hitler and the OKH, however, came to believe that the commitment of a full-scale panzer corps across the Mediterranean would strain Germany's logistical re-sources without providing decisive reinforcement for the Italians; thus, the potential force earmarked for the theater was repeatedly scaled down. By September the motorized division had been elim-inated, and the deployment of the 3rd and 11th Panzer Divisions was being considered. During October the force had been reduced again, to just the 3rd Panzer Division, and it would remain at this level through late December except for a brief flirtation with the idea of appending the SS *Liebstandarte Adolf Hitler* in late No-vember. Just before Christmas the orders for the 3rd Panzer Divi-sion were canceled as Hitler and Halder opted instead for an ad hoc *sperrverband* (blocking force) rather than a full-strength divi-sion to assist in the defense of Tripoli. But it should be noted that nearly one-third of the troops eventually included in the 5th Light Division had been pulled out of the 3rd Panzer.[3]

As the biographies of men like Erwin Rommel and Eduard Dietl would later attest, detached service—especially as one of the senior German officers supporting an allied army—could spur rapid career advancement. This fact made command of the 3rd Panzer Division during the fall of 1940 a potential plum assignment for a fast-moving officer. For a second time, therefore, von Brauchitsch intervened in favor of Walther Model, suggesting to Halder on 9 November, and again on 11 November, that the Sixteenth Army's chief of staff be given the position.[4] Even though it represented a normal career progression for an army chief of staff to receive a division command, several factors made this particular assignment unusual.

First, command of any panzer unit had acquired special prestige after the conquest of Poland, and the self-ordained clique of "panzer generals" jealously resisted incursions into its ranks. Erwin Rommel had required Hitler's personal intervention to receive the 7th Panzer Division, and even Erich von Manstein, the brightest star of the General Staff, had been forced to accept command of an infantry corps for several months before obtaining a transfer to a panzer corps. Model's credentials for a panzer command were relatively weak, resting entirely on staff work in the mid-1930s that was not only theoretical work without opportunities for leadership experience but a position created by Ludwig Beck, who had by now been demonized by the adherents of mobile warfare as the stereotype of the hidebound reactionary. It is safe to say that without von Brauchitsch's patronage, Walther Model would never have been considered for the 3rd Panzer.[5]

The other striking peculiarity about Model's new assignment was that von Brauchitsch had not waited for an opportune vacancy into which he could place his favorite but had insisted on creating one. Major General Horst Stumpff had been associated with the 3rd Panzer Division since its creation in 1935, leading the 3rd Panzer Brigade in Poland and succeeding Leo Freiherr Geyr von

Schweppenburg in command of the division in January 1940. Not only well known by and popular with the troops, Stumpff had compiled a strong record in the XVI Panzer Corps' duel with the French Cavalry Corps in northern Belgium. To make room for Model, von Brauchitsch and Halder had to have Stumpff transferred to the newly organizing 20th Panzer Division, a lateral move that was without precedent among panzer division commanders in 1940, and which essentially ended his career.[6]

The prospect of assuming command under such circumstances might have daunted many men, but not Walther Model. There was no indication of anxiety in his demeanor when Halder received him for the obligatory social call on the chief of the Army General Staff on 20 November, nor when he introduced himself to his staff and subordinate commanders over the next few days. Even at this point in his life, as the newest division commander in the German army, Model created anxious moments for others rather than suffering from them himself.[7]

The new commander's reputation preceded him. The division operations officer, Lieutenant Colonel Klaus von dem Borne, requested an immediate transfer—ironically, he ended up in North Africa with Rommel. Major Heinz Pomtow replaced von dem Borne and quickly learned to characterize Model as a "difficult boss" whose tongue was like a "sharp sword." Colonel Ulrich Kleemann, heading the 3rd (Motorized) Infantry Brigade, was an officer of the conservative school who found his new commander to be undignified in manner and fond of training methods so unorthodox as to be potentially dangerous.[8]

Model immediately instituted a crash training program that exemplified two hallmarks of what would become his tactical style: ruthless disregard for both the chain of command and formal tables of organization. He had already developed the disconcerting habit of appearing unannounced at battalion-, company-, and platoon-level training. Once on the ground, Model worked hard to establish a direct personal relationship with the *Landsers*, often at the expense of their officers. It was sometimes difficult to tell exactly which senior officers should be most concerned, since Model adamantly insisted on training in constantly changing *kampfgruppen* of all arms. A regimental commander like Lieutenant Colonel Günther von Mantueffel of Motorized Infantry Regiment 3 might find himself with one of his battalions farmed out to another headquarters and suddenly responsible for various companies of engineers, antitank gunners, artillerymen, and tankers. Remarkably, though within a few months such informal groupings would become the norm for the German army in Russia, even as late as the beginning of 1941 such was not uniformly the case.[9]

The reception accorded Model's ideas among the senior commanders varied widely. His more adaptable officers, such as Major General Hermann Breith (5th Panzer Brigade) and Lieutenant Colonel von Mantueffel (Motorized Infantry Regiment 3), quickly recognized the value of Model's organizational improvisations and the toughness he attempted to instill in their troops. On the other hand, Colonel Kleemann (3rd Motorized Infantry Brigade) and Lieutenant Colonel Oskar Audörsch found themselves continually upset by the pace and nature of the training. This dichotomy, however, represented more than a division in personal tastes or military philosophy. Both Breith and von Mantueffel had been commanding tanks or motorized infantry at their current level through two campaigns; they were more comfortable with their positions, presided over veteran units, and fully understood the need for combined arms integration in training and combat. But Kleemann and Audörsch were introduced to Model and his methods at a far more difficult time.[10]

Kleemann had been commanding his brigade since January 1940, but it had only included two battalions of motorized infantry and one of motorcyclists, all of which had been relegated to a supporting role in the march across northern Belgium. The decision to double the size of the motorized infantry component of the panzer divisions led to the assignment of the newly created Motorized

Infantry Regiment 394 to Kleemann's brigade. The regiment was literally patched together from all directions: staff from the 290th Infantry Division, one battalion from the 60th (Motorized) Infantry Division, and the other battalion from von Manteuffel's Motorized Infantry Regiment 3 (which had to raise four new companies to replace it). As commander for this assemblage, Kleemann received in Audörsch a man of modest ability who had spent the first year of the war in various technical offices at OKH—in other words, a man with no background in mechanized operations, no command experience, and no time in actual combat since 1918. Although Kleemann, Audörsch, and their soldiers had been together for several months when Model arrived, they had not yet managed to create a first-rate team, and their reaction to him was quite understandable.[11]

The staff officers' reactions to Walther Model were far less divided: To a man they hated him almost on sight. It was not so much his temper toward them (which was foul) or his language (which was frequently profane) that alienated them so much as it was the commander's penchant for ignoring their schedules, disdaining their advice, and holding them accountable when his own actions had hopelessly fouled up their plans. Possibly the best example of this sort of behavior could be found in the division's redeployment from Silesia into Poland during May 1941. Blithely disregarding the carefully constructed march tables that Major Pomtow and his officers had labored to complete, Model simply fired up his Opel command vehicle and set off down the highway to enforce his personal sense of "march discipline" on the troops, playing merry hell with route assignments, release points, and arrival dates while ingratiating himself with the common soldiers at the expense of the staff.[12]

Within a month of assuming command Model knew that his division was no longer earmarked for Africa, although he would lose a brigade headquarters, a panzer regiment, an artillery battalion, and an antitank battalion to the *Deutsche Afrika Korps*. Nor was the 3rd Panzer Division deployed in such a manner that it was likely to take part in any combat operations in Greece, Yugoslavia, or Rumania. Instead, Model's men took up a training position in Silesia, and the more senior officers were well aware that this meant a future commitment to the upcoming offensive against the Soviet Union. If Model pushed his regiments and battalions relentlessly in training, it was at least in part because he understood the vastness of the Russian steppes and the enormity of the risks entailed in any blitzkrieg to the east. Hitler expected to finish off the war in six weeks; Model was not so sanguine, but he opined privately that if the war began in the spring, it would be won by Christmas or not at all.[13]

Model's convictions about the imminent plunge into the Soviet Union, however, were driven by his personal experiences in Russia between the wars and his professional estimates of force and distance rather than any inside knowledge of the detailed plans of Operation Barbarossa. There were great map exercises and protracted disagreements over the ultimate objectives of the campaign, as there had been prior to the offensive in France, but having stepped down as army chief of staff, Model had, as von Manstein notes in another context, "naturally ceased to be informed of matters falling within the High Command's jurisdiction." Other General Staff officers in his place might have managed to utilize an informal network of friends to keep abreast of developments, but there is no indication that Model did so—nor is there any indication that he had any close friends privy to the process.[14]

He knew by mid-May, however, that the 3rd Panzer Division, along with the 4th Panzer, 1st Cavalry, 10th (Motorized) Infantry, and 267th Infantry Divisions, had been assigned to von Schweppenburg's XXIV Panzer Corps of Guderian's Panzer Group Two on the southern flank of von Bock's Army Group Center. Guderian's army-sized unit, which would assemble in the area just south of Brest-Litovsk, included five panzer divisions, three motorized infantry divisions, and the motorized Infantry Regiment

Grossdeutschland. To the immediate north of the panzer group was von Kluge's Fourth Army (seventeen infantry divisions) and Colonel General Adolph Strauss's Ninth Army (twelve infantry divisions). On the far northern flank of the army group, Guderian's counterpart, Hermann Hoth, commanded Panzer Group Three, composed of five panzer and two motorized infantry divisions. Of the 1,736 tanks employed in the two panzer groups, the 3rd Panzer Division entered the Soviet Union with 198 battleworthy panzers—58 Mark IIs, 108 Mark IIIs, and 32 Mark IVs—and 11 armored command vehicles, which was almost exactly the average strength of the other sixteen panzer divisions moving forward at the same time.[15]

Army Group Center's initial objective involved a double envelopment of the Third, Fourth, and Tenth Armies of the Soviet Western Special Military District in the Bialystock bend. The two panzer groups would slash through the frontier defenses and dash into the Red Army's rear somewhere in the vicinity of Novgorodok or Minsk while the infantry divisions marched in their wake to close the trap. The successful destruction of some forty divisions would presumably tear open a gigantic rent in the Russian front that, in concert with the advances of the smaller Army Groups North and South, would fulfill Hitler's intention that "the bulk of the Russian Army in Western Russia is to be annihilated in bold operations by deeply penetrating Panzer wedges, and the withdrawal of combat-capable units into the wide-open spaces of Russia to be prevented."[16] So far so good—at least in theory. This initial operation, while ambitious, was of the same scale as that carried out so successfully in France. While there were unknowns with which to contend, such as the question of the state of Russia's road net and the fighting qualities of the average Red Army soldier, such was the confidence level of the German army in early 1941 that no one seriously doubted the Wehrmacht's ability to achieve its first objective.

The rub lay in the fact that even by 22 June 1941, when the first shells burst, there was no consensus in the senior command structure of the German army with regard either to the strategy or tactics to be utilized in the second phase of the offensive. In strategic terms, men such as Halder, von Bock, Hoth, and Guderian believed fervently that the capture of Moscow was an essential prerequisite for victory. These generals insisted that the panzer divisions should be turned loose as soon as possible from the cauldron created around the Soviets in the Bialystock bend in order to breach the Dnepr River and secure jump-off positions for an advance on Moscow before the Red Army could mobilize its reserves. But Hitler and many of the staff officers responsible for the preliminary operational planning tended to emphasize the importance of seizing Leningrad and the Ukraine as the most important strategic goals of the invasion. They foresaw only Army Group Center's infantry marching across the Dnepr in the direction of Moscow and envisioned instead the diversion of Hoth's panzers toward Leningrad and Guderian's into the Ukraine. While Hitler's views were those embodied in the official operational directive, it would soon become apparent that the advocates of the Moscow option would go to great lengths to subvert his intentions.[17]

If profound differences over strategy would create a dysfunctional atmosphere of schizophrenia in the German command structure, fundamental disagreements over tactics would lead to shouting matches on the battlefield, charges of insubordination, wasted effort, and excessive, irreplaceable casualties. "Despite the very plain lessons of the Western Campaign," groused Guderian in his memoirs, "the supreme German command did not hold uniform views about the employment of armoured forces." Those generals who embraced the so-called *Blitzkrieg* concept believed that mechanized formations like the panzer and motorized divisions were being wasted if required to cooperate closely with the marching infantry in maintaining a solid ring around pocketed

Red Army units. They argued vociferously that the panzers should be cut free at the first opportunity to race deep into the heart of Russia, destroying communications, interrupting supplies, and striking at reservists in the midst of mobilization. Such surgical operations would destroy the Soviet command and control system so effectively that the infantry would be able to plow right through the chaos in pursuit of victory. Not surprisingly, this group of officers overlapped significantly with the pro-Moscow officers, including Guderian, Hoth, and von Bock. Halder, though his eyes were as firmly fixed on Moscow as theirs, was somewhat more conservative in his tactical views and vacillated between wanting to give the panzer generals free rein and holding them under close control. Even so, he was far closer in outlook to the panzer officers than men like von Schweppenburg, von Kluge, and even Hitler, who preferred a tight rein on German armor, with the penetration into Russia broken into a series of smaller tactical envelopments in which the mobile divisions were not allowed to get far enough separated from the infantry for either arm to get into trouble when unsupported.[18]

Ironically, had either group achieved a dominant position prior to the beginning of the invasion, the Germans might well have won the war in 1941. Instead, the command structure was sandwiched at every level with men seemingly more determined to work at cross-purposes with each other than to defeat the Russians, and this was a recipe for disaster. Only the case of Model's own chain of command need be considered to make this point. Model himself believed that either the Germans would reach Moscow by Christmas or they would not win the war, and in terms of tactics he sat firmly in the deep-thrusting panzer camp. His corps commander, von Schweppenburg, was a conservative who had already nearly come to blows over tactics with Guderian in Poland. The original proponent of daring panzer drives, Guderian found himself subordinated to the infantry-oriented von Kluge, who chafed in turn under the direction of von Bock, who would keep urging the panzers further east. Above Army Group Center, Halder and von Brauchitsch at OKH found themselves in a continual tug of war with Hitler and his cronies at OKW over the ultimate direction of the offensive.[19] Given this level of command disorganization, it is hardly surprising that, as shall soon become evident, the path of the 3rd Panzer Division across Russia sometimes more closely resembled the wandering of a drunken sailor than the purposeful maneuvers of a military unit.

There was an even more disquieting aspect to the German plans for the conquest of the Soviet Union, of which Model became aware at least by 30 March, when more than 250 senior generals were ordered to attend a personal briefing by Hitler himself. "After a lengthy harangue on the experience he had gained and the conclusions he had drawn," recalled Field Marshal Wilhelm Keitel of OKW, the dictator "finished with a declaration that war was a fight for survival and demanded that they dispense with all their outdated and traditional ideas about chivalry and the generally accepted rules of warfare; the Bolsheviks had long since dispensed with them." Halder's notes, penned later that day, were even more explicit than the *apologia* Keitel wrote while awaiting execution at Nuremburg. The chief of the Army General Staff recorded Hitler as delivering a "crushing denunciation of Bolshevism, identified with a social criminality. Communism is an enormous danger for our future. We must forget the concept of comradeship between soldiers. A Communist is no comrade before or after the battle. This is a war of extermination." Later in his speech Hitler returned to the theme of "extermination of the Bolshevist commissar and of the Communist intelligentsia. . . . Commissars and GPU men are criminals and must be dealt with as such." "The impression he had made with his speech upon his audience was not lost upon him, although nobody openly raised his voice in protest," Keitel observed. "He rounded off this unforgettable address with the memorable words: 'I do not expect my generals to understand me; but I shall expect them to obey my orders.'"[20]

This was not idle rhetoric. During the next several weeks senior officers from both OKW and OKH held high-level negotiations with the SS and SD to define spheres of responsibility in the upcoming campaign. Occupation zones were divided up between the army, the SS, and the newly created *Ostministerium*. Protocols for coordinating the activities of army security divisions with Himmler's SS and *Polizei* formations were drawn up with great formality. The *Einsatzgruppen*, organized to follow in the footsteps of the advancing army, were tasked with locating, segregating, and murdering Communists, Jews, and other undesirables; intelligence officers from every corps, army, and army group attended briefings on how these execution squads could help provide useful military information and control a potential partisan menace.[21]

Nor did the Wehrmacht take a back seat in implementing Hitler's intentions. Beginning with a draft document originally written in Lieutenant General Walther Warlimont's Section L of the OKW, a series of orders laid out the new ground rules of warfare for the German *Landser*. The infamous "Commissar Order" required that Red Army political officers not be accorded treatment as prisoners of war but should be shot out of hand when captured. The "Guidelines for the Conduct of the Troops in Russia," issued soon thereafter, insisted that "this struggle requires ruthless and energetic measures *against Bolshevik agitators, irregulars, saboteurs and Jews* and radical elimination of all active or passive resistance" (emphasis in original). This was followed by the even more specific "Decree Concerning the Implementation of Wartime Military Jurisdiction in the Area of Operation 'Barbarossa' and Specific Measures Undertaken by the Troops." The Decree exempted almost all conceivable crimes against Soviet citizens from the jurisdiction of military courts, owing to the necessity that "*the troops themselves*" must "relentlessly struggle against every threat posed by the civilian population." In a detailed listing of specific exemptions, the document flatly stated that "there exists *no obligation* to punish offences committed *by members of the Wehr-*

macht and its attendants against *hostile civilian persons*, even if
the act at the same time is a military crime or offense" (emphasis
in original). Halder himself approved standard operating procedures for combating partisan activity that went far beyond anything issued during World War I, authorizing drastic measures of
collective reprisal in the event of attacks on German rear areas.[22]

There has been a long-standing myth that the bulk of the officer
corps resisted these measures, at least passively. "For far too long
the memoirs of German generals, quickly translated into English
during the Cold War, shaped the public's image of the *Wehrmacht*'s record in the Second World War," argues historian Jürgen
Förster. "From Nuremberg onwards, the notion has existed of separating the Führer from his followers, the generals from their
supreme commander, and the *Wehrmacht* from the crimes of the
SS. Many a veteran still doggedly perpetuates the myth that the
soldiers had nothing to do with the ideological side of Barbarossa." Von Brauchitsch and Halder, former German officers
contended, went so far as to issue a supplementary order on
proper conduct designed to ameliorate the worst effects of the
"Commissar Order." Guderian even claimed in his memoirs that "I
forbade its forwarding to the divisions and ordered that it be returned to Berlin." Other commanders have made similar asser-
tions, leaving the impression that the entire German army simply
ignored Hitler's directives.[23]

This was far from the case. From von Brauchitsch all the way
down to the hard-marching grenadiers, the Wehrmacht was well
stocked with men who believed in Adolph Hitler, his ideology, and
his methods. Three days before Hitler's address to the senior generals, for example, von Brauchitsch had spoken with the staff officers of the Eighteenth Army, striking a very similar tone to that
of the Führer and warning that they must see the upcoming war
as a "struggle between two different races and act with the necessary severity." This message was received by many willing ears,
such as those of the III Corps chief of staff, Colonel Ernst Felix

Faeckenstadt, who had opined several months earlier that "the attitude of the German soldier towards the Jews is not under any discussion. Down to the last man, the standpoint has been taken that it is impossible to mix with this race and that it must be completely removed from the German living space one day." Senior commanders like Hermann Hoth, Erich von Manstein, Walther von Reichenau, and Karl-Heinrich von Stülpnagel would issue their own public orders supporting the Nazi ideological crusade and calling for draconian measures against Communists, partisans, and Jews; Hoth's order specifically contended that "the destruction of those same Jews who support Bolshevism and its organization for murder, the partisans, is a measure of self-preservation." This attitude could only percolate downward to the smaller unit commanders and the troops. The commander of the 12th Infantry Division encouraged his officers: "Prisoners behind the front-line . . . Shoot as a general principal [sic]!" The commander of XLVII Panzer Corps in Panzer Group Two witnessed firsthand "senseless shootings of both POWs and civilians" during the first weeks of the offensive, hardly a surprising consequence of the command emphasis, which created attitudes like that reflected in a letter home of a tank gunner in the 7th Panzer Division: "The battle against these sub-humans, who've been whipped into a frenzy by the Jews, was not only necessary but came in the nick of time. Our Führer has saved Europe from certain chaos."[24]

Again, Walther Model's silence and a dearth of surviving correspondence make it difficult to determine his precise attitude toward the ideological aspects of the war just prior to the invasion. The various OKW orders were disseminated to the regimental and battalion commanders of the 3rd Panzer Division, but without any particular emphasis. His record up to June 1941 suggests that Model had managed to achieve the contrived detachment of the apolitical *nur-soldat*, who convinces himself that what goes on behind the lines or out of his sight is none of his business. Model certainly did not concern himself with the moral question raised by suddenly turning on the country with which the Third Reich had observed a nonaggression pact for the past two years. On the eve of the invasion, a young lieutenant in Motorized Infantry Regiment 3 asked his division commander how he was supposed to justify the attack to his men. Model replied, "You say calmly that we need groceries for the long war against England, and we must fetch them now."[25]

The process of fetching the groceries began in earnest for the 3rd Panzer Division on the night of 21 June; as soon as dusk fell the troops loaded into their trucks, motorcycles, armored cars, and tanks for a twenty-kilometer approach march from their assembly area to a position on the west bank of the Bug River opposite Koden, just south of the Soviet fortress at Brest-Litovsk. The opening rounds of the artillery bombardment were scheduled to commence at 3:15 A.M. on 22 June, at which time the 3rd and 4th Panzer Divisions were to spring across the river, seize Koden, and drive northeast behind Brest toward the Brest-Kobryn road. The previous year Model's division had retained a small detachment of Mark III tanks modified for amphibious operations that were capable of fording the river if the Red Army bridge guards on the east bank succeeded in dynamiting the Koden Bridge. There were pontoon-bridge engineers on hand from corps and group reserves to throw emergency floating bridges across the river in that event, but Model preferred not to waste the time such an operation would entail. He therefore gained Guderian's approval to create a special assault detachment of infantry and combat engineers to slip across the bridge twenty minutes before the first shots were fired, quietly ambush the garrison, and remove the explosives. It was a tight timetable, but Model's men managed it: at 3:11 the operations officer of the XXIV Panzer Corps reported their success to Guderian's headquarters. As the roar of thousands of pieces of artillery split the night, the panzers of Model's division rolled across the Koden Bridge unopposed, having already won their first victory.[26] The first reports filtering back to headquarters indicated the extent to which complete operational surprise had been achieved:

> 0325 hours, *Kampfgruppe* Kleemann reports that enemy resistance is non-existent.
>
> 0330 hours, *Kampfgruppe* Audörsch reports that there is no enemy reaction in their sector.
>
> 0350 hours, Infantry Regt. 3 has already crossed [the Bug] as well as the first tanks of the Panzer Regiment.[27]

Even though the bridge had been secured and the available engineers quickly threw up additional spans a few kilometers up and down the river, a unit as large as the 3rd Panzer Division consumed many hours in crossing the Bug. Security teams fanned out along the eastern bank while the advance elements of the 1st Reconnaissance and 3rd Motorcycle Battalions pressed forward to locate the main body of the enemy. "These 'reconnaissance detachments,'" notes historian Alan Clark, "were mixed groups of motorcyclists with armoured cars and half-track infantry carriers towing anti-tank guns; sometimes they were supported by a sprinkling of light PzKw III medium tanks. On the road they moved at about twenty-five mph." As quickly as they could cross the river and reorganize, the larger *kampfgruppen* into which Model had organized his division formed up under the control of regimental and brigade staffs to follow in the wake of the scouting parties. There was an air of calm professionalism about these movements: Troops rode casually atop any moving vehicle, but the trained eye could not fail to observe that all eyes were scanning the road, the tree line, and the horizon, while every weapon was carried at the ready.[28]

It was midafternoon before the division support elements were ready to cross the river, and by that time the combat groups had already engaged the Russians, specifically disorganized bits and pieces of the 6th and 42nd Rifle Divisions of Major General V. S.

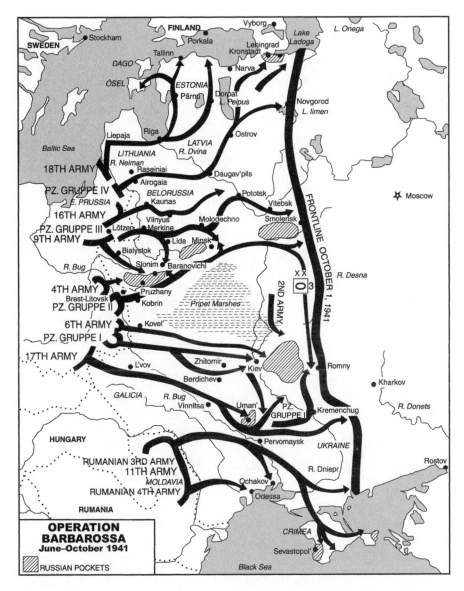

**OPERATION
BARBAROSSA**
June–October 1941

RUSSIAN POCKETS

Model's 3rd Panzer Division consistently performed as a spearhead division for Panzer group Guderian. Model's tenure in command ended soon after his division closed the final gap of the Kiev pocket.

Popov's XXVII Rifle Corps. Popov's men attempted to organize a defense under the worst possible conditions. Poorly trained to begin with, both divisions had been maintained at reduced manning levels and had recently been deprived of much of their field artillery. These men had not been at a high level of alert when the German bombardment started, and the efforts of their commanders to turn them out of their barracks into prepared defensive positions were hindered not only by enemy artillery but also by swarms of Luftwaffe fighter-bombers appearing with the dawn. When the main bodies of the divisions of the XXIV and XLVII Panzer Corps hit them, "the Russian defences might have been a row of glass houses," observed one German lieutenant.[29]

By midafternoon Model's division—led by *Gruppe* Lewinski, composed of the divisional reconnaissance battalion, one motorized infantry battalion, one panzer battalion, and two batteries of antitank guns—had cleared the frontier defenses and penetrated nearly a dozen miles toward Kobryn on the Mukhavets River. Both north and south of Brest, along with the other three panzer divisions of Guderian's command that made the initial assault across the Bug (the 4th, 17th, and 18th Panzer), the 3rd Panzer Division had torn a thirty-mile-wide hole in the front of Major General A. A. Korobkov's Fourth Army. In a desperate attempt to seal off this potentially fatal wound, General Dmitri Pavlov, commanding the Western Special Military District, directed Korobkov to commit the entire XIV Mechanized Corps to seal the breach.[30]

Major General S. I. Oborin's XIV Mechanized Corps was one of thirty created not quite a year earlier in the wake of the decisive German victory in France, when the Red Army experienced a sudden resurgence of faith in large tank and motorized formations. According to its table of organization, Oborin's corps by itself should have been nearly a match for Guderian's 750 panzers leading the assault: In its two tank (22nd, 30th) and one motorized rifle (205th) divisions, the XIV Mechanized Corps should have deployed 36,000 men, 1,031 tanks, 208 armored cars, and over 300 pieces of artillery. Nor were the Germans even aware that the Red Army deployed armored reserves immediately behind the frontier; intelligence assessments just prior to the invasion placed the five Soviet tank divisions believed to be the Western Special Military District reserve much farther back, in the vicinity of Minsk. Unfortunately for the Russians, however, the XIV Mechanized was far understrength (it contained only about 508 tanks, all of which were obsolete T-28s or BTs, and some of which were armed only with a machine gun), lacked a sufficient supply of armor-piercing ammunition, and suffered from a supply system that could provide few spare parts. Worse still, having been literally thrown together, the units of the corps moved out for battle on 22 June completely unprepared for the contest with veteran German panzers. Just twenty-four hours earlier the Fourth Army chief of staff had observed the field training exercise of Colonel Semen I. Bogdanov's 30th Tank Division near Pruzhany. "Even with a superficial acquaintance with the regiment," Major General Leonid M. Sandalov later wrote, "I was at once struck by the weakness of its preparedness. The battalions and companies operated with no coordination, tanks became confused on the course and often stopped to determine their location."[31]

The Luftwaffe quickly discovered the assembling Soviet tanks, and wave after wave of Ju87a *Stukas* screamed in, turning the corps' unwieldy march columns, which were unprotected by anti-aircraft guns, into long strings of blazing wrecks along the few roads immediately east of Brest. The 22nd Tank Division, which was to have opposed the XXIV Panzer Corps, was literally shot to pieces from the air before it could make contact with the Germans. The 3rd Panzer Division's lead elements did not so much engage the Red Army tanks as slice by them without slowing their pace. By the morning of 23 June, the division had destroyed 197 Soviet tanks, and *Gruppe* Lewinski was approaching Kobryn, where the headquarters of the Soviet Fourth Army was located. Model's men quickly secured the town, although the remnants of Bogdanov's

30th Tank Division—having retreated precipitously in front of the 18th Panzer Division—fought a tenacious enough rearguard action to allow Korobkov and his staff to escape. (This reprieve was short-lived: Korobkov, along with Pavlov and Oborin, was summarily shot when he finally made his way back to Moscow.)[32]

By midafternoon on 24 June, Model's division had forced a crossing of the Shchara River near Slonim. When XXIV Panzer Corps units captured the town, they cut off the only road over which the eight divisions of the Fourth Army could retreat, and in conjunction with Hoth's divisions they had almost completed the envelopment of the three Soviet armies in the Bialystock bend. Closing the pocket required Guderian's XLVI and Hoth's XXXIX Panzer Corps to link up at Minsk four days later, sealing the fate of nearly 300,000 Red Army soldiers and over 2,500 tanks.[33]

The Russians trapped within the pocket did not, however, lay down their arms and surrender, nor did they wait passively in defensive positions for the German infantry divisions marching through the dust of the panzer spearheads. Unit after unit of the Red Army marched resolutely out to attack its way out of the encirclement. There was little coordination or finesse involved in these attacks, but the Russians heavily outnumbered the handful of German divisions blockading their route to freedom. Along Guderian's portion of the cauldron particularly heavy casualties were sustained by the 29th Motorized, SS *Das Reich* Motorized, and 18th Panzer Divisions. At one point in late June in the 29th Motorized Division's sector, notes Paul Carell, "the divisional staff officers were lying in the infantry foxholes with carbines and machine pistols," so attenuated had the line become.[34]

Part of the reason for these casualties stemmed from the disagreement over tactics mentioned earlier. Guderian, contrary to the wishes of the OKH but with at least von Bock's tacit approval, had left only the thinnest possible screen around the eastern wall of the Minsk-Bialystock pocket in order to push substantial forces immediately toward the Dnepr. He detached von Schweppenburg's entire XXIV Panzer Corps on 26 June for a drive across the Berezina River, preparatory to a thrust for the Dnepr somewhere between Mogilev and Rogachev. Without missing a beat in its lightning dash, the 3rd Panzer Division seized Bobriusk on 28 June. Model ordered the exhausted II Battalion of Motorized Infantry Regiment 394 to capture a bridgehead over the Beresina without regard for the cost. Not having tanks on hand to support them, the infantrymen inflated rubber boats, crossed the river under heavy fire, and established a small enclave on the east bank. Only heavy artillery fire and close air support saved them from being wiped out over the next twenty-four hours. But Model's reconnaissance units were already probing further east when Guderian flew to XXIV Panzer Corps headquarters for a consultation with von Schweppenburg on 1 July. The corps commander confirmed Guderian's impression that "he was mainly opposed by units that had been hastily thrown together." On the other hand, "air reconnaissance during these days revealed clearly that the Russians were assembling fresh forces in the area Smolensk-Orsha-Mogilev." The panzer leader concluded that "if the line of the Dneiper was to be captured without waiting for the arrival of the infantry, which would mean the loss of weeks, we would have to hurry."[35]

Model was prepared to hurry. Even though his men had had little rest or sleep for eight days, the division commander urged them on. His French- and Czech-manufactured trucks began to break down, and Model ordered the immobilized vehicles pushed to the side of the road in order to clear a path for the advance. Tank strength in the three panzer battalions declined so rapidly that one armored vehicle status report indicated that by the end of the second week of the campaign the 3rd Panzer Division had 128 of 198 tanks at least temporarily out of action. (The culprit was dust more than it was the Red Army: Maneuvering down the primitive dirt roads of Belorussia, German tanks went through air filters at an ungodly rate, with the all-pervasive dust halving the life expectancy of the engines.) Even the sudden downpours on 2 and 3 July that turned the main road to Smolensk into a bottomless quagmire could not dissuade Model from ordering his weary division to lurch closer to the Dnepr. His more conservative commanders, especially Kleemann and Audörsch, began to balk, requesting a halt of at least twenty-four hours to rest, regroup, and refit. When their objections were brushed aside, Audörsch sent one of his battalion commanders to plead with Model, possibly reasoning that the division commander's well-known affinity for the more junior officers might cause him to listen to reason. Major Hans Kratzenberg presented his case at what passed for division headquarters, a small gathering of command vehicles backed together at a nameless crossroads. Model heard him out and then astounded the young battalion commander by agreeing with his technical arguments: "Kratzenberg, you are absolutely right." But then he explained why the division would nonetheless continue to push forward. "Every minute that we lose will cost us great losses later that we will not be able to afford," Model said. "We must push forward now, otherwise we risk everything. Hurry yourself with the technical aspects, a lot of time has already been lost."[36]

By 4 July, however, it was becoming evident that Guderian and Model might have pushed too far too fast. While his advance elements had actually closed to the Dnepr near Rogachev—even placing a battalion-sized bridgehead on the east bank—the remainder of the division was strung out on muddy roads all the way back to the Beresina. The rest of the XXIV Panzer Corps was in the same shape: The 4th Panzer Division was floundering down the Slutsk-Mogilev road, the 10th Motorized Division was spread out over a thirty-mile flank outside Zhlobin, and the 1st Cavalry Division was still struggling along the northern fringe of the Pripet Marshes. The nearest possible supporting units—the divisions of the XLVI Panzer Corps—were only now being relieved near Minsk by the infantry divisions of the Fourth Army. Guderian's spearhead stood poised on the brink of victory and disaster at the same moment, and not a few German officers began to realize viscerally just how large the Soviet Union was.[37]

Guderian's officers were also about to realize just how deep were Soviet reserves of manpower and equipment. Even as the divisions on the frontier underwent their tragic immolation, the Soviet high command (STAVKA) began the process of mobilizing its reserve forces into field armies and creating a second barrier between Army Group Center and Moscow—the Reserve Front, consisting of the Nineteenth, Twentieth, Twenty-first, and Twenty-second Armies. Contrary to the expectations of almost every level of the German command, the Red Army intended an active defense of the Dnepr River line and the vital Smolensk area.[38]

On 5 July Lieutenant General V. I. Gerasimenko's Twenty-first Army (headquarters at Gomel along Guderian's southeast flank) began a series of counterattacks that threw the XXIV Panzer Corps into its first major crisis of the campaign. Lieutenant General L. G. Petrovsky's LXIII Rifle Corps, employing elements of three divisions, attacked Model's small bridgehead on the Dnepr. At the same time, near Zhlobin, the two divisions of Major General F. Zubtsov's LXVI Rifle Corps, supported by tanks from the partly organized XXV Mechanized Corps, struck the 10th Motorized Division in a bid to retake Bobriusk. The attacks were poorly coordinated (albeit well supported by artillery), but von Schweppenburg's corps was deployed for pursuit, not a slugging match, and Gerasimenko had hit him at a moment when he lacked even a small tactical reserve.[39]

The 3rd Panzer Division went over to the defensive for the first time in two weeks. While attempting to hold his Dnepr bridgehead and keep pressure against Rogachev, Model simultaneously detached a *kampfgruppe* composed of at least half of his remaining seventy tanks and several batteries of antitank guns to reinforce the 10th Motorized Division. In a two-day fight the Germans managed to throw back the Russians around Zhlobin, but only at the cost of losing ground around Rogachev, the destruction of twenty-one tanks, and the evacuation under fire of Model's Dnepr bridgehead on 6 July. Small as it was, Gerasimenko's counterattack had delivered the first check to Guderian's impetuous plunge toward Moscow. The next day Russian forces farther north also scored tactical successes when the XLVI Panzer Corps' SS *Das Reich* Division failed to seize the bridges around Mogilev and the 17th Panzer Division of the XLVII Panzer Corps was unceremoniously ejected from Senna by the 1st Moscow Motorized Rifle Division.[40]

Guderian took stock of the situation and unsurprisingly concluded that the proper tactical solution was to push his Panzer Group across the Dnepr before the Soviets could mount even stronger attacks. In his memoirs Guderian wrote that "I had received no fresh instructions from my superiors and so I could only assume that the original intention by which Panzer Group 2 was to drive for the area Smolensk-Yelnya-Roslavl remained unaltered. Nor could I see any reason why this plan should be modified." This statement was disingenuous at best: Guderian had not received fresh instructions because he had carefully avoided remaining in one place long enough for them to be delivered. Somewhere, miles back in the vicinity of Minsk, von Kluge was frothing with anger over what he considered Guderian's reckless adventure. Von Kluge's Fourth Army headquarters had turned over its infantry divisions to the Second Army in order to assume (as the Fourth Panzer Army) coordinating control of both Panzer Groups Two and Three. Von Kluge had never countenanced the approach to the Dnepr prior to the liquidation of the Minsk-Bialystock pocket; he had no intention whatsoever of allowing Hoth and Guderian to fling themselves across that river while the nearest infantry division was still at least two weeks' worth of hard marching behind. Only fast talking, the taking of great liberties with the facts, and, again, the informal support of von Bock would allow Guderian to talk von Kluge into allowing him to continue.[41]

Nor was von Kluge the only one who needed convincing. Guderian planned to bypass the large Russian concentrations at Orsha, Mogilev, and Rogachev by forcing the Dnepr between the larger towns and cities. Waiting just long enough for his mobile divisions to concentrate on the river (but not, significantly, long enough for any infantry divisions to close the gap), from north to south he planned to throw the XLVII Panzer Corps across at Kopys, the XLVI at Shklov, and the XXIV at Staryy Bykhov. The northern and center elements of Panzer Group Two at least had their flanks covered, but von Schweppenburg's divisions were literally suspended in midair—and quite vulnerable to Soviet counterattacks, as the past few days had shown. Even more ominously, on 8 July one of von Schweppenburg's patrols captured a Russian map that appeared to detail plans for a major offensive from the Rogachev-Gomel area.[42]

Von Schweppenburg's concerns could best be summed up in a statement he wrote in 1952 in a slightly different context: "In military tactics it has never been disputed that when the main body has not yet arrived on the spot, the vanguard must fight a holding action only, and never on any account expose itself to the danger of complete defeat, in spite of its numerical inferiority, or occasional isolation." He asked Guderian to delay the attack until at least some infantry divisions reached the Dnepr line. But Guderian doubted the accuracy of the captured map and had no time in his calculations for generals who wanted to look toward their flanks. When von Schweppenburg approached him, he had only recently completed a briefing for all of his senior subordinates in which he admonished them: "All commanders of the panzer group and their troops must disregard threats to the flank and the rear. My divisions know only to press forward." This was quite probably his response to the commander of the XXIV Panzer Corps. The attack would go forward as ordered on 10 July; von Schweppenburg reluctantly assigned the Staryy Bykhov attack to Model's 3rd Panzer Division, shifting the 4th Panzer farther south to add weight to the 10th Motorized and 1st Cavalry along his extended flank.[43]

Model made good use of the forty-eight hours vouchsafed him for regrouping and preparation. To relieve all the major combat units of his division from the necessity of garrisoning his line of communications back through Bobriusk, he reached an informal arrangement with the LIII Corps to send back one of his own truck columns to transport forward a reinforced battalion of the 255th Infantry Division. This expedient was not reported to any higher headquarters.[44] Simultaneously, Model reorganized his division into three new *kampfgruppen*, specially designed to first place a strong infantry force on the east bank of the river and then to pass a heavily armored, mobile strike force through the bridgehead for immediate exploitation. Both groups, as well as Model's artillery command, were heavily augmented by corps troops and guns loaned from the 4th Panzer. The final divisional organization for the Starry Bykhov crossing was organized as follows:[45]

Gruppe Kleemann (3rd Motorized Brigade headquarters)
Motorized Infantry Regiment 3
Motorized Infantry Regiment 394 (I Battalion detached)
Motorcycle Battalion 3
III/Panzer Regiment 6
Panzerjäger Battalion 543
Panzerjäger Battalion 521 (attached from corps)
Engineer Battalion (motorized) 39 (3rd Company detached)
Engineer Battalion (motorized) 625 (attached from corps)

Gruppe Lewinski (Panzer Regiment 6 headquarters)
Panzer Regiment 6 (III Battalion detached)
I/Motorized Infantry Regiment 394
Reconnaissance Battalion 1
Staff, 2./Light Flak Battalion 91 (attached from corps)

3./Engineer Battalion (motorized)
Staff, 2./II. Artillery Regiment (motorized) 75

Artillery (headquarters, Artillery Commander 143 attached from corps)
Artillery Regiment (motorized) 75 (staff and 2nd Company of II Battalion detached)
Artillery Regiment (motorized) 103 (from 4th Panzer)
Artillery Regimental Staff 625 (attached from corps)
II/Artillery Regiment (motorized) 69
Heavy Mortar Battalion 604
Observation Battalion 1

Model's reinforced division thus deployed three times as many pieces of artillery, twice as many antitank guns, and twice as many engineers as usual. The greater weight of fire suppressed the Russian defenders so completely that Kleemann literally bounced his force across the Dnepr during the day on 10 July and had his first bridges operational that night. By midmorning of the next day *Gruppe* Lewinski had already passed through the bridgehead and resumed the advance eastward. Now that Model's men had drawn the bulk of Soviet attention in the XXIV Panzer Corps' sector, both the 4th Panzer and 10th Motorized managed virtually unopposed crossings south of Staryy Bykhov on 11 July. Ironically, the unwilling von Schweppenburg had managed to place his corps on the east bank of the Dnepr with far lighter losses than were suffered by his colleagues to the north. There was no time to savor this victory, however, for Model now had to swing Kleemann's infantry north to screen against enemy counterattacks from Mogilev, while Colonel G. von Lewinski's panzers pushed east, parallel to the main body of the 4th Panzer Division, toward Krichev at the confluence of the Sozh and Oster Rivers. The purpose of this deployment was to safeguard the flanks of the XLVI and XLVII

Panzer Corps while they linked up with Hoth's divisions to form another pocket in the Smolensk area and secured the area around Yelnya as the springboard for a subsequent offensive toward Moscow.[46]

Krichev fell on 15 July, but rather than the completion of a difficult tactical maneuver, this event represented the beginning of the most difficult and bloody week yet experienced by Model's men. With Guderian focused exclusively on the Smolensk-Yelnya area, the four divisions of the XXIV Panzer Corps were left without support to cover a twisting line of battle that masked Mogilev on both sides of the Dnepr and swept along a shallow arc of more than 140 miles from Lobkovitchi south to Krichev, along the Sozh to Propoisk, across the Dnepr to Staryy Bykhov, southwest toward Rogachev, and then west through Zhlobin to Bobriusk. Beginning on 16 July, the Soviet Twenty-first Army—now reinforced with newly raised divisions to a strength that gave it numerical superiority over its opponents in many places—launched a determined counterattack on the XXIV Panzer Corps that was part of Timoshenko's greater offensive to break open the Smolensk pocket, crush the German position at Yelnya, and smash the extended right flank of Army Group Center.[47]

Not only were Von Schweppenburg's divisions outnumbered and by now severely fatigued, but they were nearly out of fuel and ammunition as well. Despite Guderian's insistence that his panzer group desperately needed the Minsk-Bobriusk railroad repaired, the engineer and construction troops could only move forward behind the foot-slogging infantry because, as Army Group Center told Guderian, "this area was still too dangerous to work in." To make matters worse, the divisions of the Second Army's XII Corps had to be diverted northeast toward Smolensk and Yelnya rather than marched to the relief of the XXIV Panzer Corps. Not until 23 July would the lead elements of the XIII Corps arrive in Krichev to take some of the pressure off von Schweppenburg's hard-pressed units, and even then they would not be pulled out of the line, merely regrouped for a new offensive toward Roslavl.[48]

In that week of heavy battles, von Schweppenburg leaned heavily on Model and the 3rd Panzer Division. *Gruppe* Kleemann took over responsibility for the division's main line of defense, while the panzers of *Gruppe* Lewinski became a "fire-brigade" behind the hard-pressed 1st Cavalry and 10th Motorized Divisions. From 19 to 23 July, the entire 1st Cavalry Division was subordinated to the 3rd Panzer as *Gruppe* Model. As usual, Model himself was everywhere—except in division headquarters. He kept turning up, monocle in place and cursing, at every crisis point, whether it was the Soviet breakthrough southeast of Staryy Bykhov or the heavy tank attack at Propriusk—both on 19 July, but more than fifty kilometers apart![49]

As the weary divisions of the XIII and then the XII Corps began to take over responsibility for the southern flank of the German penetration at Smolensk-Yelnya, Model's men enjoyed their first few days out of the line since 22 June; parts of the division went into reserve as early as 23 July, while others had to fight on for five more days. It was hardly the ideal R&R for the 3rd Panzer Division, however, as the division still had responsibility for providing reaction forces known as *alarmeinheiten* to support the infantry against continuing Russian attacks. Moreover, there was a frantic effort on the part of the workshop companies to get as many tanks, trucks, and prime movers back into running order as possible, while Kleemann, Lewinksi, Audörsch, and von Manteuffel were reorganizing their units once again, consolidating depleted companies and platoons into combat-ready groups.[50]

On the afternoon of 28 July, a battered command vehicle carrying a large white "G" and a small escort of motorcyclists pulled up to division headquarters in Lobkovitchi. Out jumped the dusty figure of "Schnell Heinz" himself—Colonel General Guderian—to conduct a quick inspection and to present Model with the coveted

Knight's Cross. Model's conduct of divisional operations had actually won him the award on 9 July for the initial gallop from the Bug to the Dnepr, but the press of combat and Guderian's determination to present the medal personally had delayed the brief ceremony. Before he motored off to visit the 4th Panzer Division and confer with von Schweppenburg, Guderian told Model that his division's rest would necessarily be brief: The attack on Roslavl would jump off no later than 1 August.[51]

Eliminating the threatening Soviet concentrations around Roslavl (estimated by the Germans as at least fourteen infantry and four tank divisions) was considered by Guderian to be equally important to an eventual advance on Moscow as holding the Yelnya salient, if not more important. Thus, he not only committed the XXIV Panzer Corps—reinforced by the newly arrived VII Corps on the western prong of his attack—but pulled most of the XLVII Panzer Corps out of the ring around Smolensk and the IX Corps out of Yelnya. With as many as nine divisions attacking on 1 August, Guderian quickly returned to Model's area of operations: "I spent the afternoon with the leading units of the 3rd Panzer Division in the area immediately to the west of the Oster and south of Choronievo. General Model informed me that he had taken the bridges over the stream intact and had thus been able to capture an enemy battery. I expressed my thanks for the performance of their troops to a number of battalion commanders on the spot." After capturing Miloslavichi, the 3rd Panzer Division spread a thin screen of units west to Klimovichi; there Model's men relieved the 4th Panzer Division, which was to drive northeast behind the ground gained by the 3rd Panzer, 10th Motorized, and 78th Infantry Divisions in order to slice into Roslavl from the southwest. This was accomplished on 3 August.[52]

In the meantime, Model had orders to continue pressing south toward Rodnia, with an eye toward opening a potential future attack on either Gomel or Starodub. Threatening either of these towns would menace the already tenuous supply lines for the Soviet Fourth, Fifth, Thirteenth, and Twenty-first Armies, thus relieving pressure on the German Second Army, and the move might even pocket the last major Red Army forces of which the Germans were aware that could interfere with a drive on Moscow via Bryansk and Spas-Demensk. The fact that Model reported only light resistance south of Klimovichi supported Guderian's belief that he was on the verge of cracking the entire Soviet front wide open. It was at this point, however, that the tensions and disagreements in the upper levels of command exploded into full view, raising the question of whether Army Group Center should in fact take the offensive toward Moscow prior to assisting Army Group North in seizing Leningrad and Army Group South in defeating the Russians around Kiev. Model, who was obviously far too junior to be involved in such strategic squabbles, only experienced the first half of August as a frustrating set of tactical offensives and countermarches that further wore down his men without gaining appreciable ground.[53]

On 15 August, however, Guderian finally received authorization to commit the XXIV Panzer Corps to the Gomel-Starodub operation, and the following day Model's division lunged ahead, capturing the Mglin crossroads, cutting the Gomel-Bryansk railroad on 17 August, and entering Unecha on 18 August. This provoked a violent response from the Russians, who counterattacked the strung-out 3rd Panzer Division with everything at hand, including a handful of the dreaded T-34 tanks, against which German anti-tank guns were woefully inadequate. By the afternoon of 19 August, elements of the Soviet Fifth Army had interposed between Model's lead unit at Unecha—*Gruppe* Lewinski—and the main body of the division at Mglin. Having isolated the spearhead, the Russians assaulted the town with tanks and infantry, their T-34s shrugging off the 37mm and 50mm shells of Panzerjäger Battalion 524. Only the superior coordination of the outgunned Pzkw IIIs of Panzer Regiment 6 (supplemented at one point by the raw courage of a lieutenant of Motorized Infantry Regiment 394 who leapt on board the lead Soviet tank to deliver a grenade through an open hatch) allowed Colonel von Lewinski to hold on to Unecha. To reestablish communications with his advance, however, Model had to call off a planned attack on Novozybkhov.[54]

Russian attacks, albeit increasingly disorganized, continued in the vicinity of Unecha for the next few days, but Model again reorganized his division to be able to drive instantly in any direction. Audörsch, von Lewinski, and von Manteuffel now each commanded a *kampfgruppe* based on roughly the same organization: a regimental staff, two battalions of motorized infantry, one battalion of tanks, several batteries of antitank or antiaircraft guns, and small detachments of combat engineers, motorcyclists, and armored cars. The bulk of Engineer Battalion 39 was kept under Model's hand as a general emergency reserve, while the artillery was again consolidated under Artillery Commander 143 and supplemented by three battalions of corps artillery. With this deployment, Model managed to take Novozybkhov, defend Unecha, and even capture Major General Sostinki, artillery commander of the Soviet Fifth Army, replete with his entire staff.[55]

On 24 August, the same day that *Gruppe* Audörsch seized Novozybkhov, Model learned that the original intention of the Starodub-Gomel offensive—clearing the ground for an immediate advance toward Moscow—had been vetoed from above. Instead, Panzer Group Two, led by the XXIV Panzer Corps and spearheaded by the 3rd Panzer Division, had been dispatched due south, with the objective of slicing into the rear of the Soviet armies defending Kiev and the lower Dnepr. For Model and his men this would involve the most daring blitzkrieg yet, requiring them to traverse more than 275 kilometers of enemy territory, enjoying no flank protection whatsoever while crossing three major rivers and receiving virtually all supplies via airdrop. More amazing still, this had to be accomplished by a panzer division with only 41 tanks of the original complement of 198 in running order![56] Model's only advantages would be speed, the experience his men had gained in working in mixed *kampfgruppen,* and his own personal audacity.

Model's route of advance would lead his division first to force the Desna River at Novgorod-Severskii, in order to capture one of the 800-yard-long wooden bridges still arching across the river. On the afternoon of 25 August the division commander caught up with Lieutenant Colonel von Lewinski in a field overlooked by a windmill five hours drive south of Starodub. Von Lewinski spread out a captured map across a case of hand grenades.

"Where is this windmill?" Model demanded.

"Here, sir," responded the intelligence officer.

Model slid his pencil toward Novgorod-Severskii.

"How much farther?"

"Twenty-two miles, *Herr General.*"

Just then a radio operator handed Model the transcript of a signal from von Lewinski's forward detachment, reading: "Stubborn resistance at Novgorod. String enemy bridgehead on the western bank of the Desna to protect the two big bridges."

"The Russians want to hold the Desna line," Model said, and then looked directly at the commander of Panzer Regiment 6. "We must get one of those bridges intact, Lewinski. Otherwise it'll take us days, or even weeks, to get across this damn river."

"We'll do what we can, *Herr General.*"[57]

But the first attack, delivered in late afternoon, devolved into something of a fiasco. The Soviets were strongly dug in, and although the Red Army troops holding the town were older reservists, they were supported by a healthy contingent of 152mm guns, while the 3rd Panzer Division lacked the Luftwaffe support to make up the difference for its lighter artillery. In counterbattery fire the Soviets killed the commander of Artillery Regiment 75 and even managed to lodge a shell splinter in Model's hand. As the shadows began to grow longer, even Model was forced to admit that von Lewinski's men would have to regroup for an early morning attack, hoping against hope that during the night the Russians did not blow up both bridges.

Strangely enough, with the enemy before him in force, the local Soviet commander left both bridges intact, although thoroughly wired with explosives; perhaps it was not a failure of the intellect so much as the ingrained Red Army ethic that nothing so momentous could possibly be undertaken without orders. The cost of indecision, however, was high: At 5:00 A.M. von Lewinski sent a carefully selected combat team consisting of a company of motorized infantry, a platoon of tanks, and a section of engineers charging into Novgorod-Severskii without regard for anything but speed. Three lieutenants—Buchterkirch, Störck, and Vopal—led the detachment, which seized the bridge, slaughtered its guards, and defused the explosives while the remainder of the *kampf-gruppe* cleaned out enemy resistance in the center of town. Everything happened so fast that the Soviet artillery, so decisive the previous day, barely got off a shot. Lieutenant Störck, who had personally removed the detonator from the bomb planted in the center of the main bridge and then held off a Soviet counterattack, threw himself down in exhaustion as the first panzers and half-tracks sped across to secure the far bank. He was having a flesh wound on his left hand plastered when Model drove up in his command vehicle, waving his own bandaged hand and shouting, "This bridge is as good as a whole division, Störck."[58]

Without hesitation, Model ordered his entire division across the Desna, leaving the task of securing his rear to the 10th Motorized Division. In doing so, he expanded the bridgehead widely enough for von Schweppenburg to begin crossing the 10th Motorized and 4th Panzer Divisions, but he also placed his own division in the seam between three Soviet armies: the Thirteenth, Twenty-first, and Fortieth. Fortunately for Model, the Thirteenth and Twenty-first Armies belonged to two different Soviet fronts and therefore did not coordinate their attacks, and the Fortieth was actually a headquarters struggling to collect enough bits and pieces of mangled units to merit the title of an army. Otherwise, the 3rd Panzer Division, no matter how well schooled in operating deep in enemy territory, might well have become the first German division ignominiously gobbled up whole. As it was, the situation grew serious enough on 29 August, when strong Russian counterattacks south of the Desna halted the entire XXIV Panzer Corps in its tracks; the 10th Motorized Division even had to commit its Field Bakery Company to the fighting. Model himself was lightly wounded in fighting on 2 September. Even Guderian could see that his penetration into the Soviet rear had become more like a needle than a sword, and he ordered von Schweppenburg to spend a couple of days consolidating his position before attempting the next river, while simultaneously requesting reinforcements from von Bock.[59]

Yet these men—Guderian, von Schweppenburg, and Model— were too aggressive to think for long about anything but pushing forward. On 4 September Guderian arrived at von Schweppenburg's headquarters to discover that his corps commander had a much-appreciated present for him: a captured Soviet map detailing the disarray in the Red Army's front. Audacity, which had been momentarily lost, now returned, and Guderian immediately phoned the 3rd Panzer Division: "This is our chance, Model." Haunted by the possibility that the Russians might take advantage of his pause to slip their five armies out of the developing pocket at Kiev, Guderian again gave Model the green light. Model was more than willing, as Guderian noted in his memoirs: "General Model, too, had the impression that he had found a weak spot, if not an actual gap, in the enemy's defenses. I told Model to push on to the Konotop-Bielopolie railway as soon as he was over the Seim and to cut that line." The lead element of *Gruppe* Lewinski— Major Frank's 1st Reconnaissance Battalion—vaulted across the Seim River on 7 September, restoring both morale to the troops and momentum to the drive south.[60]

Yet morale and momentum could not negate the effects of the weather. Model's reckless plunge into the Ukraine was marked on any given day by either dust or mud. When the sun shone, notes Paul Carell, "the fine dust of the rough roads enveloped the columns in thick clouds, settled on the men's faces, got under their uniforms on to their skins." The dust covered men and vehicles alike "with an inch-thick layer of dirt. The dust was frightful—as fine as flour, impossible to keep out." Weapons jammed, and the absence of sufficiently fine filters on tanks, half-tracks, trucks, and prime movers severely reduced engine life; every mile the division advanced saw more and more precious vehicles abandoned by the side of the road. But the German soldiers came to hate the rain far worse than the dust, rain that whirled across the steppe in great thunderheads, suddenly dropping sheets of bone-chilling water that churned the inadequate Russian roads into quagmires that devoured trucks whole. "The roads and paths are completely soft," complained a soldier in the 9th Panzer Division, "so that the vehicles often slide into the ditch." Guderian noted that on 4 September his lone command vehicle required four and a half hours to traverse seventy-two kilometers, "so softened were the roads by the brief fall of rain," while a week later one motorized battalion required nearly twenty hours to cover barely sixty kilometers. "It's enough to make you desperate," wrote one NCO to his wife. The battle of Kiev was where Walther Model and thousands of other Germans first made the prolonged acquaintance of "General Mud," of whom they would be seeing much more in a few weeks.[61]

Of course the mud, as Alexander Werth observes, "affected the Russians as much as the Germans," and on 9 September the tenacity of the 3rd Panzer Division in driving forward despite all obstacles paid off again with a major strategic dividend. Colonel von Lewinski having been wounded, Model turned command of his group over to Lieutenant Colonel Oskar Munzel, commander of II Battalion, Panzer Regiment 6. Giving Munzel a chance to get oriented, Model leapfrogged both *Gruppe* Manteuffel and *Gruppe* Audörsch past Munzel, leaving immediate tactical supervision of the advance in the hands of Colonel Kleemann. Kleemann had orders to close on Konotop, but a column of enterprising motorcyclists under Captain Güntherr Pape soon discovered a gap in the Russian defenses between Konotop and Baturin—bogged down in the mud, the Soviets had committed the mistake of concentrating all their defenses along the main roads. Without waiting for approval from his superiors, Model bypassed Konotop completely, pushing his lead elements to Romny on the Ssula on 10 September.[62] Guderian's spearhead had now lodged very deeply into the Red Army's vitals.

The shaft of that spear had become dangerously long and thin, however. XXIV Panzer Corps' units were spread over more than 230 kilometers of mostly single-lane dirt roads that were often interdicted by Russian artillery, tanks, or even the remnants of the Soviet air force. Munzel had scarcely gotten himself situated at regimental headquarters when an emergency call required him to send a company-sized group north to save von Schweppenburg's forward command post from being overrun. Likewise Guderian, on one of his jaunts forward to peer over Model's shoulder, found that "on the Seim bridge we were attacked by Russian bombers," and "on the road we were shelled by Russian artillery." When Guderian finally located the headquarters of the 3rd Panzer Division at Chmeliov, he found no one there but an agitated Major Pomtow, the division operations officer, who was "tearing his hair" because his division was fighting in three different directions, Panzer Regiment 6 had only ten tanks still running, and nobody knew where Model was.[63]

Guderian spent the night in Chmeliov (possibly with the intent of calming Pomtow's nerves) but struck out again on the morning of 11 September in search of Model and the forward elements of his division. By midafternoon the panzer group commander had located the commander of the 3rd Panzer Division in Romny; in spite of the fact that his men had not completely cleared the town of enemy troops, Model had decided to keep moving south with *Gruppe* Manteuffel, leaving the cleanup operation to Kleemann.

As Guderian noted, Kleemann had no easy task: "The town was in his hands, but enemy stragglers were still at large in the gardens and it was therefore impossible to drive through except in armored vehicles." With Model impatient to cross the river and press on, Guderian wandered into Kleemann's command post at the north end of town, just as his staff was presenting their concerns about the mopping-up operation. "They were particularly worried about Russian air attacks, since our air force was incapable of offering adequate fighter cover; the reason for this was that the Russian air-fields were located in a fair-weather zone, while ours were in a bad-weather zone and the rain had made them unusable." As if to make the point for them, "we were at that moment attacked by three Russian machines firing their machine-guns; the bombs fell elsewhere." Model captured Lochvitsa the next morning.[64]

The trap had nearly closed on five Soviet armies. All that was required was the final lunge forward to close the fifty-kilometer gap between the 3rd Panzer Division and the 16th Panzer Division of Panzer Group One, advancing from the south. There was a final hesitation on 13 September. Von Schweppenburg, who had been rattled by his brush with death or capture, wanted more of his corps ferried across the Seim River before stretching his lines any farther. He told Guderian that he had reliable intelligence indicating that strong Russian forces—including tanks—were near Ssencha, moving to attack his flanks. Guderian again ventured forth to find Model and solicit his opinion. In his memoirs, Guderian presented this record of their meeting on 14 September:

I reached Model's headquarters, at Lochvitsa, just as darkness was falling. Up to then he had only managed to bring one of his regiments this far forward; the rest of his men were struggling along in the mud far to the rear. He informed me that the strong Russian concentration consisted primarily of supply troops. Only some of the units in question were equipped for combat. The Russian tanks that had been seen had probably been withdrawn from maintenance depots to cover the retreat.

What Guderian omitted from the pages of *Panzer Leader* was the fact that by the time he reached Model in Lochvitsa the division commander had already sent a small combat team with his last ten tanks forward to make contact with the 16th Panzer Division. This had been accomplished at 6:20 P.M.—about an hour before Guderian arrived. Without authorization (perhaps even against the orders of his corps commander, but neither Guderian nor von Schweppenburg were ready to argue with success), Walther Model had personally closed the Kiev trap.[65]

Keeping it closed required several more days of hard fighting, as tens of thousands of Russian soldiers made repeated attempts, often with locked arms and shouting "Urrah!," to break through the initially thin ring surrounding them to the east. Even a unit as weary as the 3rd Panzer Division could not be pulled out of the line for another week. In a peculiar way this was fitting, however, since on 20 September Model's Panzerjäger Battalion 543 concluded the operation by capturing the entire Soviet Fifth Army staff, including its commander, Major General M. I. Potapov, one of the more capable Red Army leaders in the first days of the war. Along with Potapov, the German tally for the battle of Kiev included 665,000 prisoners, 3,714 pieces of artillery, and 884 tanks; in tactical and operational terms, Kiev represented victorious German arms at their peak.[66]

Strategically speaking, the battle of Kiev had been a gigantic and costly detour on the road to Moscow. Success in the Ukraine convinced Hitler to order a resumption of the offensive toward Stalin's capital, but precious fair-weather campaigning days had been lost, soldiers had become more jaded, and engines more worn, by an additional month of fighting south rather than east, and with each passing hour Colonel General Georgi Zhukov dug in more divisions on the approaches to Moscow. Again Model was still too junior to be privy to the strategic arguments, though his soldier's instincts told him that each day saw the possibility of a German victory in 1941 slipping just a little further out of reach.

In practical terms, the approval of "Operation *Taifun*" meant another frantic regrouping and redeployment for the 3rd Panzer Division. As the division retraced its steps, marching back across the Ssula and the Seim nearly one hundred kilometers to Gluchov, Model's workshop companies miraculously managed, through cannibalization and the installation of a handful of replacement engines arrived from Germany, to coerce nearly one hundred of Panzer Regiment 6's tanks back into working order, along with a healthy number of armored personnel carriers. At the same time, Model again reshuffled his *kampfgruppen*, this time placing Kleemann in charge of the division assault group, giving von Mantueffel a blocking force heavy in infantry and antitank guns for flank protection, and assigning von Lewinski (returned from the hospital) his usual role as the leader of a balanced pursuit element of all arms. As usual, Model kept his engineer battalion available as the division reserve. The division arrived at Gluchov on 29 September and received orders that the attack in its sector would begin the following day.[67]

The tactics to be employed by the panzer divisions in this operation were more conservative than had heretofore been the case. Army Group Center would employ the Second, Fourth, and Ninth Armies as well as Panzer Groups Two, Three, and Four (transferred from the Leningrad front) in a massive double envelopment of more than a dozen Soviet armies concentrated in the Vyazma-Bryansk area. The panzer divisions would break the Red Army lines and then arc inward in much tighter pockets than formerly, and they would be required to hold those pockets tightly closed rather than racing ahead toward Moscow. From Hitler to von Bock there was rare agreement that these Russian armies should be thoroughly destroyed before pushing east. Though Guderian and Hoth might chafe at the new restrictions on their operational freedom, there were several compelling reasons for the change in tactics, including the shortage of trained replacements, extensive equipment losses, and worsening weather. Von Bock, moreover, was prepared to throw in everything, committing sixty-eight of his seventy divisions to the main attack. Guderian's task was to break open the Soviet front on the Sevsk-Orel axis and then turn north to link up with Panzer Group Four in the Bryansk area, encircling the Soviet Third and Thirteenth Armies. XXIV Panzer Corps again drew the responsibility for leading the attack, with both Sevsk and Orel lying in its sector, although this time the 4th Panzer Division would be the point of the spear, with Model's troops providing flank protection to the south.[68]

The operation opened with the usual tactical successes. Favored with a few days of dry weather and a sufficiency of close air support, von Schweppenburg grabbed Sevsk on the second day of the offensive and drove into Orel on 3 October. The following day the 4th Panzer and 10th Motorized Divisions turned north for Bryansk, while the 3rd and 18th Panzer Divisions were assigned to attack toward Karachev. But even though the two Russian armies were already doomed, several factors served notice on the Germans that the war was taking an even grimmer turn. The first was the deteriorating weather: On 6 October, Guderian noted, early rains were followed by the first snow of the season: "It did not lie for long and, as usual, the roads rapidly became nothing but canals of bottomless mud, along which our vehicles could only advance at a snail's pace and with great wear to the engines."[69]

About the same time, Model's division encountered the first T-34s since the disjointed Soviet counterattack at Unecha two months earlier. At Bryansk the Red Army not only committed the heavier tanks en masse but also deployed some of its best operational commanders in a desperate attempt to blunt the German thrust. Major General Dmitri D. Lelyushenko's hastily assembled I Guards Rifle Corps included the 5th and 6th Guards Rifle Divisions, the 4th and 11th

Tank Brigades (both equipped with T-34s), several brigades of the V Parachute Corps, the 36th Motorcycle Regiment, artillery from the Tula Military School, and a regiment of Katusha multiple rocket-launchers. Stalin personally made the decision to support Lely-ushenko with two fighter, one ground attack, and one light bomber regiment from the Soviet air force's meager holdings. Lelyushenko was one of the few Russian commanders who had at least held his own in tank battles against the Germans at Dvinsk and Ostrov, and he was ably supported by Colonel Mikhail E. Katukov at the head of the 4th Tank Brigade. As soon as each element of his corps arrived, Lelyushenko threw it into battle; in heavy fighting around Mtensk on the Zusha River from 5 to 11 October, he succeeded in fighting the XXIV Panzer Corps to a virtual standstill. Even though the 4th Panzer Division finally managed to close the Bryansk pocket, the tenacious Soviet defenders of Mtensk held on to the town until 22 October, repulsing at least three heavy attacks in which the 3rd Panzer took part.[70]

The battle of Bryansk officially ended on 25 October with another tactical windfall: Between Bryansk and Vyazma, another 700,000 Soviet soldiers marched into German captivity. For Model and his men it had been a frustrating three weeks of contending with rain, mud, snow, and growing Red Army strength and slogging through territory defended by bunkers and camouflaged tanks rather than racing into an unprotected rear area. Yet morale remained high as the division regrouped one last time prior to the last heave toward Moscow. Panzer Group Two would launch itself in the direction of Tula during the last days of October, this time given a final objective east of Moscow.

Walther Model would not lead the 3rd Panzer Division in this offensive. On 26 October he received word that he had been nominated as the new commander of the XLI Panzer Corps in Panzer Group Three, *vice* General of Panzer Troops Georg-Hans Reinhardt, who was himself replacing Hoth in command of the panzer group. Model's promotion to general of Panzer Troops quickly followed, retroactively dated to 1 October. After a final parting with his staff and subordinate commanders, Model left Bolchow for Kalinin on 28 October. Major General Hermann Breith, transferred from a staff position at OKH, took over the 3rd Panzer Division.[71]

During Model's tenure as a division commander, many of the characteristics had already emerged that would later distinguish him as an army and army group commander. He was considered impossible to work with by his staff and overly demanding by his subordinate commanders. Willing to take the most outrageous risks if the potential gain was high enough, Model's operations often rode the thin edge between victory and disaster, but he consistently retained a strong confidence in his own improvisational ability to meet any crisis. His methods of constantly regrouping divisional assets into tailor-made *kampfgruppen* were well established and would stand him in good stead at higher levels. All in all, during five months on incessant campaigning, Walther Model had justifiably earned a reputation as one of the finest panzer division commanders in the German army.

5

ADVANCE AND RETREAT

XLI Panzer Corps

WHEN WALTHER MODEL ARRIVED IN KALININ ON THE EVENING of 14 November, he was met by Colonel Hans Röttiger, XLI Panzer Corps chief of staff. The two men knew each other from their work together in the Technical Branch in the mid-1930s, and on Röttiger's part at least there was no love lost. Aside from disliking Model, Röttiger was a fervent admirer of his former chief, Georg-Hans Reinhardt, and would have been cool toward almost any successor; he and several other senior staff officers had been denied transfers for which they applied just after learning the identity of their new commander.[1]

There was also apparently some resentment over an issue of seniority. Röttiger and other officers may have assumed that Lieutenant General Friedrich Kirchner of the 1st Panzer Division would automatically have been in line for the corps command, and—given von Brauchitsch's well-known interventions on Model's behalf in the past—Model's promotion smacked of favoritism. This was especially true since both Kirchner and Model had been promoted to lieutenant general and even major general on exactly the same day. Yet in reality the fall 1941 promotions of panzer division commanders followed very closely the rules of seniority and General Staff training. The five senior panzer division commanders in Russia were, in order, Rudolf Veiel, Ferdinand Schaal, Hans-Jürgen von Arnim, Walther Model, and Friedrich Kirchner (the last distinction based on Model's seniority as a colonel). Veiel was a holdover from the mid-1930s who had never been in competition for a higher position and who would soon be removed from operational command. Schaal received the LVI Panzer Corps on 13 September—well ahead of Model. Von Arnim was not appointed to command of the XXXIX Panzer Corps until 11 November, but he had been fairly severely wounded in September and the Army Personnel Office took care to see that his eventual promotion to general of Panzer Troops maintained his seniority vis-à-vis Model. Nor was Kirchner slighted; the day after Model arrived in Kalinin he was selected to lead the LVII Panzer Corps. (Kirchner's promotion came as a distinct relief to Model, who was quite aware of the tenuous nature of his own seniority and was embarrassed to have been placed over him.)[2] Of course these details were not available to the officers of the XLI Panzer Corps, and even if they had been, Model's growing reputation of being grating, overbearing, and uncouth would probably have rendered such a technical explanation unsatisfying.

For Model this was nothing new; by now he was becoming used to a frosty greeting. He responded to the reception as he usually did—by treating his staff in his patented brusque manner and making no attempts at all to be diplomatic or to develop a sense of camaraderie. What was novel for Model was the assumption of a new assignment in the midst of an operation—heretofore he had always had the luxury of several months to become accustomed to new responsibilities prior to active campaigning. Now his position resembled that of a rider thrown suddenly atop a flagging horse he had never before ridden, struggling to maintain momentum against the pack in the final curve.[3]

At roughly the same time in early October that the 3rd Panzer Division had jumped off from Gluchov for the drive toward Orel, the XLI Panzer Corps had also launched an assault as the left flank of Panzer Group Three, which, along with the Ninth Army, formed the northernmost element of Army Group Center's offensive aimed at Moscow. Between 2 and 12 October, the 1st Panzer and 36th Motorized Divisions had blitzed through Belyi, Sychevka, Zubsov, and Staritza. Reinforced by the motorized *Lehr* Brigade 900, Reinhardt's corps had then sliced through disjointed Soviet opposition to reach Kalinin on 14 October, 350 kilometers northwest of Moscow. Despite civilian resistance in the streets, *Vorausabteilung* (advance detachment) Eckinger, based on I Battalion, Motorized Infantry Regiment 113 of the 1st Panzer Division, seized the Volga River bridge by a *coup de main*.[4]

"The question arose now," reported Röttiger, "in which direction the Corps was to continue its advance and exploit its unexpected success." Colonel General Adolf Strauss, commanding the Ninth Army to which Panzer Group Three was subordinated, wanted Reinhardt's divisions to turn northwest and march on Torzhok in order to relieve enemy pressure on his left-flank infantry divisions. Reinhardt, Röttiger, and Hoth all pointed to their inability to keep those Russians from slipping through their fingers, cited logistical difficulties, and argued vehemently for both corps of Panzer Group Three to turn southeast—directly toward Moscow. Strauss overruled them and committed the XLI Panzer Corps to a pointless but costly advance on Torzhok on 17 October. Five days of heavy fighting in the Mjednoye area stymied the spearheads of the 1st Panzer Division, while heavy Red Army pressure against Kalinin forced its recall to that city on 22 October.[5]

From the Soviet perspective, the German penetration across the Volga at Kalinin represented a potentially disastrous development:

If Panzer Group Three managed to cross significant mobile forces and drive down the east bank of the river, the Germans could threaten Moscow from its lightly defended rear. Even if the panzer divisions merely turned due south, they would outflank the critical Mozhaisk line, the last major fortified position outside the Soviet capital. Thus, the day after Reinhardt took Kalinin, STAVKA created a special force of five rifle divisions, two cavalry divisions, and two tank brigades to seal this breach and push the Germans back. On 17 October the Kalinin Front was established under Colonel General Ivan S. Konev, and the Russians began reinforcing the "Kalinin Operational Group" with the Twenty-second, Twenty-ninth, Thirtieth, and Thirtieth-first Armies, deploying at least twenty rifle divisions between them.[6]

All that the XLI Panzer Corps had at hand with which to defend Kalinin was the battle-weary 1st Panzer Division (nine tanks remaining after the Torzhok attack), the equally jaded 36th Motorized Division, *Lehr* Brigade 900, and the advance elements of the 6th Panzer and 129th Infantry Divisions. Not only were the soldiers in all these units exhausted and their vehicles on their last legs, but air support had petered out and ammunition supplies hovered perilously close to nonexistent. Far from recognizing any immediate necessity for reinforcing Reinhardt's hard-pressed grenadiers, Strauss diverted the 6th Infantry Division away from Kalinin for another useless attack on Torzhok. It was a measure of the XLI Panzer Corps' weakness that in early November it could not prevent Major General V. A. Yuskevich's Thirty-first Army from establishing its own bridgehead southwest of Kalinin in a position to interdict the Staritza-Kalinin highway intermittently. "As a result, the supply shipments to Kalinin continued to be at a standstill during this period," noted Röttiger, "and could only be carried out under very heavy convoy guard."[7]

This was the situation when Model arrived, after struggling up through Sychevka and Staritza along roads that the Army Group Center chief of staff described in grim terms: "Bad weather, a mixture of snow, thaw, and rain transformed the overused roads within a short time into streaks of mire. Entire stretches of road were passable only with the help of prime movers; the motor vehicles of the artillery and antitank units bogged down." The new commander immediately set to work reorganizing the defenses to his own satisfaction, as usual ignoring all niceties of chain of command and formal unit organization. All workshop companies from whatever division were ruthlessly conglomerated into one unit and ordered to begin repairing tanks—any tanks, friendly or enemy—around the clock. Support troops were dragooned into the Kalinin textile mill to begin producing makeshift winter parkas for the frontline combat soldiers. In the absence of white paint for winter vehicle camouflage, chalk from the city's chalk factory was mixed with mud and smeared over tanks and half-tracks. Lacking antifreeze, Model ordered combat vehicles to be kept idling all night, regardless of the fuel supply; if a tank would not start, he reasoned, then it did not matter how short the fuel supply was. More than once he gave these orders without any reference to Röttiger, leaving his chief of staff increasingly embittered about his commander's unwillingness to respect his prerogatives.[8]

Nor did he rely on staff reports, preferring to make personal reconnaissances to the front. One day Model marched for several hours with an infantry battalion being deployed across the Volga. The following morning he stood beside an antitank battery fending off a Soviet tank attack, shouting aiming instructions at the top of his lungs. Very quickly the word spread throughout his divisions that even lowly company commanders should always be prepared to have the corps commander materialize at their elbows. Unfortunately, he rarely briefed his staff concerning his itinerary and was often out of communication for hours.[9]

Even though the XLI Panzer Corps was hanging on to Kalinin by the slimmest of margins, within twenty-four hours Model learned that neither OKH nor Army Group Center considered the offensive against Moscow to be over. New directives had been

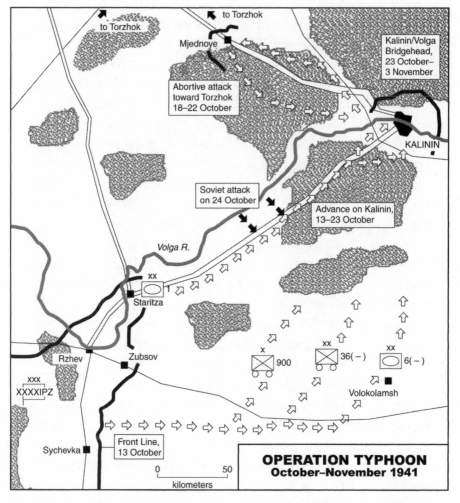

Model took command of XLI Panzer Corps soon after the capture of Kalinin.

issued requiring an attack down the west bank of the Volga toward the Volga Reservoir. Model and Röttiger examined their maps and proposed that the XLI Panzer Corps be tasked with this attack. Outrageous as this sounded, there was method in their madness. Both men agreed that the Russian units around the reservoir were weaker than those currently battering their lines, and an essential component of their plan was the immediate assumption of the defense of Kalinin by one of the Ninth Army's infantry corps. In other words, Model jumped at the chance to attack his way out of a tight spot.[10]

Unfortunately, Strauss did not accept the plan. One of the more conservative senior generals in the army, he grew uncomfortable at any thought of panzers racing ahead of his infantry, and thus his preferred solution was an infantry attack toward the Volga Reservoir. He assigned the task to a middle-aged mediocrity, General of Infantry Albert Wäger, whose XXVI Corps moved so tentatively that nearly all the Russians escaped across the Volga, burning their bridges behind them. Worse still, Wäger did not assume responsibility for Kalinin and free the XLI Panzer Corps to join Schaal's LVI Panzer Corps in an attack toward the key crossroads town of Klin until 20 November.[11]

By that time Schaal's offensive had been under way for four days and had reached the road between Reshetnikovo and the reservoir crossing. Model—much to his disgust—was assigned to follow in his wake and provide security for his rear. Schaal's attack made good headway. Klin fell to the 6th Panzer Division on 23 November, and Major Hans von Luck's Reconnaissance Battalion 3 of the 7th Panzer Division pushed across the Volga at Yahkroma, just twenty-five kilometers from Moscow, on 28 November—the battalion was so close that, according to one tank driver, "at night we could see the Moscow flak shooting at our planes." When the attack stalled at Dmitov, however, Reinhardt shifted Schaal's and Model's areas of responsibility. The LVI Panzer Corps was given responsibility for the extended flank from

Yahkroma through Rogachev to the Moscow Reservoir, for which it had assigned the 7th Panzer and the 14th and 36th Motorized Divisions. The XLI Panzer Corps took over the 1st and 6th Panzer Divisions, to which was later added the 23rd Infantry Division, for the last push into Moscow.[12]

Troop morale remained fairly high, even though the veterans who had overrun Poland and France were hard-bitten realists who understood quite clearly that they were dangling at the end of a tenuous supply line and fighting a desperate enemy on his home ground. By all accounts, the German *Landser* remained confident in his own abilities and focused on his goal. "Despite all difficulties, command and troops continued to do everything in their power to reach the prize, objective 'Moscow,' in front of them," observed Röttiger. And the most determined man in Panzer Group Three appeared to be Walther Model. Model was firmly convinced that the Russians were on their last legs and that, as in his drive into the Ukraine, victory would go to the side that kept pressing relentlessly forward. He tried to be everywhere, praising, urging, cursing; his presence was unsettling, for Model accepted no excuses for failure. If an officer pointed out to him that the combined tank strength of his two panzer divisions was only forty-one tanks, Model shot back that forty-one was four times as many operational tanks as he had available at Kiev. During these last few days of the German advance Model earned another of his many nicknames, being called "the wild optimist" (*Zweckoptimisimus*), and it was an accurate designation.[13]

Model was also learning a key difference between corps and division command. In the 3rd Panzer Division he knew every regimental and battalion commander and recognized even his most junior lieutenants by sight. He knew who needed to receive detailed instructions and who could be entrusted with general objectives, who to pick for a daring foray against a mined and guarded bridge and who to send to defend a key line of supply. In a corps command the units under his control were constantly changing, however, and he found himself forced to practice tactics with officers whom he did not know and who had been trained by others. Since it was impossible for Model ever to become as familiar as he would like with his subordinates on the battle line below the level of division and regimental commanders, he had to learn to work through his division commanders and their staffs.

This led to Model's first experience of working with the 6th Panzer Division's new commander, Major General Erhard Raus, the beginning of a collaboration and friendship that would dramatically affect both men's careers and the course of the war in Russia. Raus, a fifty-two-year-old Austrian absorbed into the German army in 1938, was Model's opposite in many ways. Model was mercurial, Raus phlegmatic, and where Model was notoriously unpopular with his own staff officers, Raus was "Papa" to most of his. Model was unfailingly and brazenly optimistic, while Raus was so thoughtful and reflective that he was sometimes called "the far-sighted thinker" (*der Nachdenker*). But between these two men there quickly developed a mutual confidence and a chemistry that allowed them to work hand in glove over many a battlefield.[14]

Within hours of the 6th Panzer's assignment to the XLI Panzer Corps, Raus was entrusted not only with his own division but also *Kampfgruppe* Westhoven of the 1st Panzer Division and Infantry Regiment 68 of the 23rd Infantry Division. Raus adopted the same conservative but effective approach to the advance that he had pioneered during the 6th Panzer Division's summer dash through the Baltic countries to the gates of Leningrad. Each day his spearheads would force their way forward as aggressively as possible until about two hours before dark. Then they selected a farm or village and dug into a hedgehog defense. Raus described the process in detail after the war:

> Several hay barns in a major clearing were selected as the location for the divisional command post. Covered by thick underbrush, the tanks were placed in a wide circle around the barns with their guns

ready to fire at the edge of the woods. In front of the tanks was an outer ring of infantry in foxholes and ditches and behind embankments which enable the tanks to fire over their heads. Security patrols and outposts formed an outer cordon. The Russians recognized the strength of these protective measures . . . and resigned themselves to harassing the hedgehog area with tank and machine gun fire and a few rounds of artillery shells.

For at least a few days the Raus-Model combination kept the offensive moving. In hard fighting, *Kampfgruppe* Koll of the 6th Panzer Division took Iohnca and was slugging its way into Yakroma on 5 December.[15]

Then the real winter hit. All the snow, ice, and subzero temperatures that had come before had been mild prologue. On 4 December the mercury plummeted to -25°F. On the few tanks left to the 1st, 6th, and 7th Panzer Divisions, "our breath condensed on the metal, so that everything you touched inside the tank was covered with ice," recalled NCO Karl Rupp. Raus later detailed the consequences of the sudden deep freeze: "Paralyzed by cold, the German troops could not aim their rifle fire, and bolt mechanisms jammed or strikers shattered in the bitter winter weather. Machine guns became encrusted with ice, recoil liquid froze in guns, ammunition supply failed. Mortar shells detonated in deep snow with a hollow, harmless thud, and mines were no longer reliable." The following morning Reinhardt tersely called an end to Panzer Group Three's last lunge for Stalin's capital, radioing Army Group Center that "a fight for greater objectives [is] impossible. The decision to capture a line which can be held in the winter will have to be taken."[16]

Reinhardt need not have bothered, for General of the Army Georgi K. Zhukov had called off the German offensive himself—by launching the first blows in the great Soviet winter counteroffensive designed to envelop and crush Army Group Center. Some of Zhukov's strongest blows were aimed directly at Panzer Group

Three, precisely because Schaal's offensive had been initially successful. The LVI Panzer Corps had hit a seam between the Russian Sixteenth and Thirtieth Armies, and von Luck's venture across the Volga into Yahkroma had so unnerved Josef Stalin that he had immediately hauled Zhukov to his headquarters and demanded, "Are you sure we'll be able to hold Moscow?"[17]

Zhukov did not hesitate to reassure the Soviet dictator ("We'll hold Moscow by all means") or to angle for more reinforcements from the STAVKA reserves ("But we'll need at least two more armies and another two hundred tanks"). Of the two armies that Stalin then transferred to the Western Front, Zhukov placed Lieutenant General F. I. Kuznetsov's First Shock Army of ten rifle brigades opposite the single *kampfgruppe* of the 7th Panzer Division at Yahkroma. This allowed General Lelyushenko's Thirtieth Army to concentrate ten rifle divisions, one cavalry division, two tank brigades, and assorted units opposite the remainder of the LVI Panzer Corps, while Lieutenant General Andrei A. Vlasov's Twentieth Army threw six rifle divisions, one cavalry division, and several small independent tank units against the XLI Panzer Corps. Even allowing for the depleted state of divisions on both sides, the three armies that Zhukov placed for a concentric attack toward Klin outnumbered Panzer Group Three by at least three-to-one in manpower and two-to-one in tanks. Those Soviet soldiers, moreover, were warmly clad in quilted parkas and snow boots, while many of the tanks were the formidable T-34s that not only were capable of shrugging off the lighter German antitank shells but had such wide tracks that they could traverse soft terrain that would immobilize Pzkw IIIs and IVs. The only real advantages favoring the Germans were greater experience and cohesion in their combat units, better communications, and a slight edge in field artillery that might make itself felt if the front could be stabilized.[18]

The heaviest blow initially fell on the 36th Motorized Division, north of Klin in the LVI Panzer Corps sector; the overstretched German lines there buckled in less than thirty-six hours, with Soviet troops on snowshoes and skis breaking through between Rogachev and Borshchevo on 7 December. A morning attack on Schaal's corps headquarters at Bolshoye-Shchapovo on 8 December was barely beaten back, and "the general himself was lying behind a lorry with his carbine firing aimed single rounds," according to Paul Carell. About noon the same day the Red Army retook Spas-Zaulok and Yamuga, just five miles north of Klin. The only major road through which Panzer Group Three could hope to retreat out of danger ran directly through Klin. The Soviets were now well within artillery range, although the relative weakness of the Red Army's artillery park around Moscow ruled out effective interdiction fire. To bag Reinhardt's two corps, Kuznetsov, Lelyushenko, and Vlasov would have to push their way into the town itself.[19]

For several days it seemed like this might happen, but Reinhardt read the situation correctly and made the only choice that could possibly stave off disaster. He immediately took the 1st Panzer Division away from Model, pulled the 14th Motorized out of its defensive positions opposite Dmitov, as well as the 7th Panzer out of Yahkroma, and combined all these divisions with the 2nd Panzer Division (released by Panzer Group Four) under Schaal's command to hold Klin at least long enough for an orderly retreat. Model was left with only the 6th Panzer and 23rd Infantry Divisions to defend a line that had been extended from Dmitov to Iohnca—nearly fifty kilometers. The XLI Panzer Corps now controlled exactly four tanks.[20]

Chaos very nearly devoured Panzer Group Three in the blinding snowstorms of that Russian December. The retreat had to be strictly limited to the main roads, since only there had tracked vehicles pushed clear lanes for traffic; the resulting drifts on either side of the road were often ten and twelve feet high and far too icy to climb. "It was a grisly sight," recalled Hans von Luck. "Alongside dead horses lay dead and wounded infantrymen. 'Take us with you or else shoot us,' they begged. As far as space allowed, we took them on our supply vehicles."[21] General Schaal, desperately attempting to organize spoiling attacks to keep the Russians off balance, felt control of the situation slipping away:

> Discipline began to crack. There were more and more soldiers making their own way back to the west, without any weapons, leading a calf on a rope, or drawing a sledge with potatoes behind them— just trudging westward with no one in command. Men killed by aerial bombardment were no longer buried. . . . The entire supply train—except where units were firmly led—was streaming back in wild flight. Supply units were in the grip of psychosis, almost of panic, probably because in the past they had only been used to headlong advances. Without food, shivering in the cold, in utter confusion, the men moved west. Among them were wounded whom it had been impossible to send back to base in time. Crews of motor vehicles unwilling to wait in the open for the traffic jams to clear just went into the nearest villages.[22]

For Model there was a haunting parallel between this retreat and the near rout of the German army in front of Paris twenty-seven years earlier. This time, however, as a corps commander instead of a battalion adjutant, he was well placed to make a difference, and his temperament and previous experiences now stood him in good stead. This is the first opportunity we have to glimpse the Walther Model whose defensive skills would become a mainstay of the Russian front. In his initial assignment to fight a holding action on the panzer group's eastern front and organize his support units for retreat while Schaal fought the battle for Klin, Model immediately started reorganizing his divisions into the same sort of *kampfgruppen* he had employed at the 3rd Panzer Division. Where possible, Model kept the infantry of the 23rd Infantry Division in the main battle line, reinforced with motorized antitank guns from the 6th Panzer, while the main combat units of Raus's division were held back as mobile reserves. At the same time he fought vigorously against the sort of rear-area disorganization described by General Schaal. "All headquarters and traffic control units which could somehow be spared had to be committed for the purpose of restoring good order again, and reprimanding the troops to keep calm." On more than one occasion at some congested crossroads that reprimand was delivered by Model himself with a drawn pistol. Even the staff officers who had smarted under his verbal lash now admitted that Model's direct relationship with the men and barely harnessed brutality paid great dividends during the retreat. This did not necessarily endear him to them, however, for many of his exhortations to the troops included the necessity of having faith in Adolph Hitler's leadership and the staying power of good National Socialists. His performance earned him yet another nickname (one that would follow him through the rest of his career): *Frontschwein*—"the Frontline Pig."[23]

Meanwhile, on 9 December, Schaal launched a determined counterattack with two *kampfgruppen* of the 1st Panzer Division—Westhoven and von Wietersheim—against Birevo and Yamuga. These attacks were unsuccessful in terms of recapturing the villages in question, but they diverted Russian attention long enough for all of the LIV Panzer Corps' remaining tanks to be concentrated into one group commanded by Colonel Eduard Hauser of the 7th Panzer Division's Panzer Regiment 25. Hauser's orders, says Paul Carell, were "to break out of the switchline east of Klin, mop up enemy divisional headquarters identified and located by radio reconnaissance between Yamuga, Spas-Zaulock, and Birevo, attack the Soviet artillery from the rear and put the guns out of action, and then, having spread chaos and confusion, to return inside the German defensive ring." Unfortunately, before *Gruppe* Hauser could be committed, the First Shock Army broke through the seam between the 23rd Infantry Division and Panzer Group Four. Pressure along the rest of the 23rd Infantry's front was so heavy that Model had already been forced to commit all of his slender reserves, and thus on 12 December Reinhardt reluctantly ordered Schaal to cancel the spoiling attack north of Klin in order to switch *Gruppe* Hauser rapidly to the threatened flank. Reinhardt also switched the command responsibilities of his two corps at the same time. Schaal now took over the eastern flank in the Krasnaya Polyana area, while Model and Röttiger inherited responsibility for the defense of Klin.[24]

Major General Franz Landgraf, commander of the 1st Panzer Division, and Lieutenant Colonel Walther Wenck, his operations officer, reported that the situation around the town was growing increasingly critical. Lelyushenko's Thirtieth Army had recovered from the minor check delivered on 9 December and was now attacking hard in a final attempt to cut off the panzer group's retreat. The last handful of operational tanks in Panzer Regiment 1 had been dispatched with Colonel Hauser. Of the division's two motorized infantry regiments, only a battalion-sized *kampfgruppe* in armored personnel carriers under Lieutenant Colonel Wend von Wietersheim retained the tactical mobility usually attributed to a mechanized unit. The rest of the formerly motorized infantry, along with the crews from burnt-out and broken-down tanks, mechanics, and cooks, was formed into an improvised two-battalion regiment of marching infantry under Lieutenant Colonel Franz Westhoven. Panzer Engineer Battalion 37 had been forced to haul its remaining equipment on horse-drawn *panje* sleds, while Panzer Artillery Regiment 73 had been reduced to using not only horses but sometimes columns of Russian prisoners harnessed together with rope to move its guns. The "trench" strength of the division had been whittled down to fewer than two thousand men, and there were nearly one thousand wounded in a makeshift hospital in the center of town. Under these conditions, Landgraf and Wenck told Model that they might be able to hold the town for another thirty-six to forty-eight hours, but that to do so would risk the division being cut off by Red Army divisions moving around their flanks.[25]

Model, having no choice, told them to hold Klin at all hazards, because if they did not, the entire eastern wing of Panzer Group Three—a force of more than five divisions—would lose its last line of retreat. By continuing to enforce draconian traffic discipline, Model funneled the major elements of the 2nd and 6th Panzer, 14th and 36th Motorized, and 23rd Infantry Divisions past the Klin bottleneck between 12 and 14 December. Often directing traffic himself, Model grimly ordered that any vehicle that stalled or died on the main road would simply be pushed to the side of the road and abandoned. But even with measures as stern as these being employed, time ran out for the defenders of Klin: Just as the last jumbled trains of the 23rd Infantry shuffled down the road toward Nekrasino, the Soviet Thirtieth Army slipped in behind them, isolating the 1st Panzer Division. With the bulk of Panzer Group Three scrambling to get back to an improvised defensive line on the Lama River, neither Reinhardt nor Model had anything available with which to help extract the encircled division.[26]

Left to their own devices, Landgraf and Wenck did not panic. Instead, after rejecting a Soviet surrender ultimatum, they calmly instructed von Wietersheim, with his battalion of armored infantry, to attack northwest toward Golyadi on the night of 14 December. Von Wietersheim and his men were allowed to believe that they were the spearhead of the real breakout attempt, which was attempting to pass around the flank of the Russians between Klin and Nekrasino. In reality, however, this attack was a feint, and at a designated moment the fires of the divisional artillery were suddenly shifted south, where *Kampfgruppe* Westhoven made an old-fashioned infantry assault along the shortest route to Nekrasino. The Soviets, having thinned their lines to oppose von Wietersheim, were caught off guard and easily pushed aside. Westhoven's men opened up a narrow corridor to safety through which the wounded, the engineers, the artillery, and—last of all—von Wietersheim's battalion all passed. At 7:00 A.M. on 15 December,

Wenck triumphantly radioed Model, "All fighting men behind cover forces of rearguard 1st Panzer Division!"[27]

Wounded but still fighting, Panzer Group Three had slipped out of the Russian trap. Now the question became one of finding a place to halt the retreat in order to avoid piecemeal destruction in the open. The line that Army Group Center directed Reinhardt to occupy ran roughly along the Lama River; if held it would secure the right flank of the equally hard-pressed Ninth Army. Even a frozen river represented an obstacle to the advancing Red Army, since the boggy ground around it was too soft to allow tanks, vehicles, or heavy weapons to approach cross-country, and therefore it allowed the Germans to concentrate on defending roads and major crossings. Of equal importance was the fact that during their retreat in November the Russians had begun fortifying both banks of the river, digging in rudimentary positions for infantry and artillery. Poorly situated and incomplete, these positions were nonetheless a gigantic boon for the Germans, since the ground had already frozen solid to a depth of well over a meter. By 16 December, as the first units began occupying the Lama River line, the temperature had dropped to -40°F.[28]

While he superintended the retreat of his trailing elements from Nekrasino, Model delegated to Raus the improvement of the defensive line in the XLI Panzer Corps sector. Finding the ground impervious to picks and shovels, Raus consolidated all the divisional and corps engineers he could find—about 150 men from three different battalions—and set them to work with their remaining explosives to blow holes into the frozen earth. "Three craters," reported Raus, "were to be echeloned in width and depth and were to hold three to five men each. The engineers were also to mine certain areas and build tank obstacles in three places. The reserves and service troops were ordered to pack down paths between the craters and the rear. They were to use readily available lumber to cover the craters." To back up this line all the available armored personnel carriers left in the 2nd and 6th Panzer Divisions were consolidated into one battalion controlled by Motorized Infantry Regiment 4, while the remainder of Raus's division wryly redesignated itself "the 6th Panzer Division of Foot." By the time Model arrived with the bulk of the corps—now the 1st Panzer and 23rd Infantry Divisions—a rough defensive position was in place.[29]

Russian attacks followed quickly, most often employing a predictable pattern. "The Russians usually attacked along existing roads or on paths beaten down by their tanks," Raus said. "Frequently, the infantry followed close behind their tanks, using the trail made by the tank tracks. . . . In mass attacks the Russians usually debouched from woods and burrowed their way through the deep snow as quickly as possible." The Germans met these attacks with machine guns and hand grenades, but even when they were successful, "the first wave would be followed by a second attack, which moved forward a short distance over the bodies of the dead before coming to a standstill. This was repeated by as many as ten waves, until the Russians bogged down from heavy losses and exhaustion or until the German defences were penetrated." The Red Army generally enjoyed its greatest successes when the Germans adopted a strongpoint defense rather than a continuous line (either from shortages of manpower or succumbing to the natural tendency to clump together for warmth). Model recognized this reality and resorted to every measure at his disposal to keep his troops spread out in an uninterrupted line; this allowed the corps to take advantage of its artillery advantage over the Soviets when their attacks stalled.[30]

Regardless of the grousing incurred among the frontline troops by this decision, Model held firm, and the result was that there were very few breakthroughs on the XLI Panzer Corps line over the next ten days, and those that did occur were quickly sealed off by small mechanized *kampfgruppen* or *alarmeinheiten* (literally "alarm units") organized from support troops. The most dangerous enemy penetration took place on Christmas Eve, when the Soviets hit the newly arrived and badly depleted 106th Infantry Division west of Volokolamsk and blew a hole in the front nearly a kilometer wide. The strange thing about winter combat in 1941 was that after the initial counterattack in early December, events seemed to move in slow motion. Not even the warmly clad Russians could survive outside shelter at night when the mercury dived as low as -50°F. Nor did the Red Army have a logistical system up to providing support for a fast-moving offensive; many of Lelyushenko's soldiers were poorly fed and low on ammunition. As a result, while a large gap in the front represented a crisis, there was no threat that it would immediately be exploited with fast-moving tanks or cavalry, as would be the case in 1943–1945; this was particularly the case on Christmas morning, when a blinding snowstorm struck and paralyzed the entire front.[31]

Twelve miles away in Shakhovskaya the armored personnel carrier battalion of Motorized Infantry Regiment 4 was alerted, and Model ordered it to throw back the Russians. No movement was possible that day; in fact, the battalion required forty-eight hours filled with repeated halts in villages along the way to cover the twelve miles. Along with a regiment from the 23rd Infantry Division, the battalion caught the Soviets by surprise on the evening of 28 December and by noon the following day had the enemy surrounded. Unfortunately, the surrounded Russians were inside a small village, which gave them someplace to crouch during the night, while the Germans were caught in the open. Model reluctantly ordered a withdrawal and was forced to bend his line in around the breakthrough. Even though the greatest danger for the moment had been mastered, the cost was high. By the end of December the mechanized battalion of Motorized Infantry Regiment 4 had been reduced to a strength of seventy-seven men and three artillery pieces; the entire 6th Panzer Division could deploy only one thousand men, counting every engineer, cook, clerk, and medic.[32]

Nonetheless, Panzer Group Three held the Lama River for nearly two weeks, after which the deterioration of the Ninth

Army's position further to the west caused Army Group Center to order a withdrawal to the Staritza area. Model ironically became one of the only commanders along the entire front in the winter of 1941 to protest a decision to retreat. Not only had he fought hard to maintain his position, but early reconnaissance of the new defensive zone also indicated that XLI Panzer Corps would be assigned a sector of dense woods with little time to prepare even hasty fighting positions. In a masterpiece of understatement that only hinted at his commander's response to this development, Röttiger described Model as "not very happy" about his new orders. Of course there was nothing optional about those orders, and Model resolutely sent advance parties to begin preparing his new line. Nor did anyone listen to his complaints when, in short order, both the 1st and 6th Panzer Divisions were taken from him, leaving the XLI Panzer Corps with only the 2nd Panzer, 14th Motorized, and 36th Motorized Divisions, which were by this time almost completely bereft of tanks, trucks, and experienced infantry. No one listened to Walther Model because he was, after all, only one of twenty-three corps commanders spread across the six armies of Army Group Center, all of whom were currently screaming for more fuel, more ammunition, and more reinforcements, and most of whom were in worse straits than he.[33]

This relative anonymity, however, was about to end. On 16 January orders came down from Panzer Group Three headquarters for Model to fly immediately to Hitler's headquarters in Rastenburg, East Prussia. He had just been appointed commander of the Ninth Army.

PART TWO

The Ninth Army

6

WHO COMMANDS
THE NINTH ARMY?

The Ninth Army:
January to March 1942

BECAUSE OF HITLER'S LATER DEVOTION TO WALTHER MODEL, and because in January he was abruptly plucked from relative obscurity ahead of several dozen other officers for a critical posting, Model's selection as Ninth Army commander has always been the subject of special scrutiny. Paul Carell speaks of "surprised faces all around" when the appointment was announced to the army's staff and characterizes Model's rise in rank as "meteoric," which Samuel Mitcham echoes. Both authors manage to include an imputation that Model, like such men as Ernst Busch or Eugen Ritter von Schobert before him, approached army command after only three months as a corps commander owing to his Nazi sympathies and Hitler's personal favor. Albert Seaton is even more explicit: "Model's personality and methods were to bring him to the notice and favor of the Führer and, under Hitler's patronage, he was to be promoted two ranks from lieutenant-general to colonel-general in the space of three months." Seaton portrays Model as "the first of a new school of senior German generals, a hard-bitten, narrow-minded little company, blindly loyal to the dictator, who were to fight so tenaciously to the very end in Hitler's forlorn cause."[1]

Like Model's earlier promotions, this one deserves closer examination. To this point it could hardly be argued that Hitler had displayed any personal interest in Model's career. Then to what influence could his sudden vaulting past at least fifteen corps commanders of greater seniority in Army Group Center alone be attributed? Model's primary patron in two earlier promotions had been Walther von Brauchitsch, and his fiercest partisan since the Russian campaign opened had been Heinz Guderian. But von Brauchitsch had been forced into retirement in December, and while Guderian had not yet been relieved of his own command, his prestige and influence at Hitler's headquarters were rapidly waning. So much for Model's obvious supporters. He also had his share of detractors, primarily General Staff officers, whose sensibilities he had offended over the past few years, all the way up to and including Franz Halder. Then again, it could hardly be argued that either Halder or the rest of the General Staff stood too highly in Adolph Hitler's estimation in January 1942. Thus, there were no obvious candidates to have intervened either in or against Model's promotion.

The question then becomes one of what brought Model to Hitler's attention. While there is only circumstantial evidence on this point, some of it is quite compelling. Model's pro-Hitler, pro-Nazi sentiments certainly played a part, though this should not be overestimated. It was more likely the tenacity and improvisational skills Model displayed in the retreat through Klin and his vocal resistance to a retreat from the Lama River (when virtually every other officer was calling for lengthy withdrawals) that put the spotlight on the commander of the XLI Panzer Corps.

An examination of the other officers elevated to army command between December 1941 and February 1942 reveals something about the criteria Hitler employed in selecting officers for promotion. During that period there were changes of command at the Eighteenth Army in Army Group North; the Second Panzer, Fourth, Fourth Panzer, and Ninth Armies in Army Group Center; and the Sixth Army in Army Group South. In three of these cases (Second Panzer, Fourth Panzer, and Eighteenth), command passed to the senior corps commander in the army. Field Marshal von Reichenau, who left the Sixth Army by promotion to Army Group Command, was essentially allowed to name his own successor, and he specified General of Panzer Troops Friedrich von Paulus, his former chief of staff. At Fourth Army the choice initially fell on the Austrian general of Mountain Troops, Ludwig Kübler, one of the early favorites in the mountain troops. This may well have happened because the former Fourth Army commander, Field Marshal von Kluge (who had also advanced to Army Group Command, though he represented a far more reluctant choice for Hitler than did von Reichenau), either declined to suggest his own successor or was not offered the opportunity. But when Kübler declared himself unequal to the job after a month, the permanent promotion went to General of Infantry Gotthard Heinrici—again to the senior corps commander in the army. Thus, the rule seems generally to have been to select the ranking corps commander in the army.[2]

In the Ninth Army, however, the ranking corps commander was General of Infantry Albrecht Schubert of the XXIII Corps (who had been corps commander in the Sixteenth Army when Model was Busch's chief of staff). Under other conditions, von Schubert might well have been chosen for the post, but in mid-January his corps and a few attached units were isolated in a pocket around Olenino, where they were fighting for their lives against three Russian armies. It was not German practice under such conditions to pull a commander out of a pocket, at least not until the tactical situation had stabilized. The Ninth Army's VI Corps was temporarily under the direction of a Luftwaffe officer, General of Flyers Wolfram von Richthofen, because Hitler and Halder, in agreement that General of Engineers Otto-Wilhelm Förster had lost his nerve, had relieved him. Lieutenant General Eccard Freiherr von Gablenz held only temporary command of the XXVII Corps (after Wäger had been relieved just before Christmas) and so was not a candidate for advancement. Simply put, the senior command of the Ninth Army was in a shambles, a situation made all the worse by the fact that Colonel Kurt Weckmann, the army's chief of staff, had also been relieved, owing to ill health, at the same time as Strauss, effectively leaving all three corps under the authority of a headquarters controlled only by the operations officer, Lieutenant Colonel Edmund Blaurock.[3]

Speed in getting a new commander and chief of staff into harness was therefore a critical consideration, and waiting three weeks for them to arrive (as Fourth Army had been obliged to do before Kübler could assume command) was out of the question. Also, because it was vital that the new command team already have an appreciation of the tactical conditions around Moscow, the available candidates were limited to those in the adjacent armies. Narrowing the field in such a fashion restricted the possible choices to corps commanders in the Third Panzer, Fourth, and Fourth Panzer Armies. Of those twelve officers, most were senior to Model, but the tactical situations of most of the corps in the Fourth Army ruled out those officers for the same reason that selecting von Schubert was impossible. Over the remainder one important factor gave Walther Model the edge: General Staff experience. One of the great ironies of the war is that Model, who was quickly becoming as much the bane of the officers bearing the red trouser-stripe as Hitler, probably received his shot at army command because he was the only immediately available officer who had commanded a division and a corps and served as chief of staff to both a corps and an army. As his new chief of staff he received Colonel Hans Krebs of the VII Corps in the Fourth Army.

Whatever the reasons for his promotion, Model quickly enough discovered that he had once more fallen into the midst of a crisis, and this particular crisis was so severe that failure to master it could lead to the loss not only of his own army but of Army Group Center in its entirety. The Soviet Twenty-ninth and Thirty-ninth Armies of the Kalinin Front, as well as the XI Cavalry Corps, had broken through the Ninth Army's thin line of defenses near the Volga between Rzhev and Olenino at the boundary of the VI and XXIII Corps. As a result, more than three divisions were isolated in the Olenino-Karpov-Motowaja area. The remainder of the Ninth Army fought with the limited resources at its disposal to maintain its grip on Rzhev, Sychevka, and the rail line running between them back to Vyazma.[4]

Far more was at stake than the survival of a single corps: The primary supply line for the northern wing of Army Group Center—the Third Panzer, Fourth, Fourth Panzer, and Ninth Armies—ran along that single, tenuous axis from Smolensk to Vyazma to Sychevka to Rzhev. South of Vyazma the Fourth Army was just managing to keep the Russian Tenth Army and I Guards Cavalry Corps off the main rail line from Smolensk, while from Yukhnov north through Gzhatsk to Staritza the battered Third and Fourth Panzer Armies were barely holding their own against five enemy armies. Although there were daily emergencies on each of these fronts, a coherent defensive line was slowly emerging. But in the Ninth Army's sector the situation had deteriorated so precipitously that there were Russians attacking the Sychevka switching station just a few kilometers from army headquarters. Telephone and telegraph communications had been lost with the encircled XXIII Corps at Olenino, while the VI and XXVII Corps were facing sixteen Soviet divisions in the Rzhev area. Of the Ninth Army's assigned strength of 262,215 men, 864 guns, and 165 armored fighting vehicles, there remained only 59,582 men,

369 guns, four assault guns, and a single Pzkw III. On 13 January Strauss ordered most of his staff to evacuate Sychevka and set up shop in Vyazma. The Rzhev-Sychevka area, Halder insisted, was "the most decisive spot on the Eastern front," and he argued that the adjacent armies must give up troops to reinforce the Ninth Army, even if doing so required immediate tactical withdrawals, with their inherent losses in equipment and munitions, and even at the risk of exposing Vyazma to assault from the east. If the Russians shattered what was left of the Ninth Army, they would be in position to roll down through the rear of the Third Panzer, Fourth, and Fourth Panzer Armies. Preventing this from happening would become Model's job.[5]

There is a widely repeated anecdote concerning Model's arrival at army headquarters in Sychevka. According to it, Model appeared on 18 January, swept into the room without ceremony, and examined the situation map while polishing his monocle. Moments later he pronounced the army's predicament to be "rather a mess." When informed by Lieutenant Colonel Blaurock that his current plans extended no further than pushing the Russians away from the rail line, Model suddenly added, "And then the first thing to do will be to close the gap up here," pointing at the Rzhev-Olenino breakthrough. "We've got to turn off the supply tap of those Russian divisions which have broken through. And from down here"—now indicating Sychevka—"we shall then strike at the Russian flank and catch them in a strangle-hold." The astounded Blaurock inquired, "And what, *Herr General*, have you brought us for this operation?" Model, as the story goes, looked at him severely and responded, "Myself!" before bursting into laughter.[6]

While somewhat consistent with Model's character, this narrative is almost certainly apocryphal. Just prior to his departure for the front the new army commander had held lengthy consultations with both Hitler and Halder in which, with rare accord, the dictator-turned-general-in-chief and the chief of the Army General Staff had both portrayed the Ninth Army command organization as one that had lost its nerve. They impressed upon Model that great firmness would be necessary to save the army from destruction, and his vehemence in return had so impressed Hitler that upon the general's departure he remarked: "Did you see that eye?," meaning *the look* in Model's eye. "I trust that man to do it, but I wouldn't want to serve under him." Later that evening, relaxing with his cronies, Hitler made an obvious reference to Model's personality and demeanor: "Generals must be tough, pitiless men, as crabbed as mastiffs—cross-grained men, such as I have in the Party." Obviously, the mood in which Walther Model arrived at Sychevka was hardly one of levity.[7]

More importantly, Model had in fact brought far more than himself to the Ninth Army. Finally alive to the danger of a completely inflexible no-retreat policy, Hitler had grudgingly accepted Halder's strategic assessment and decided to permit the other three armies to conduct a short retreat to the so-called *Königsberg* position in order to free enough troops to retrieve the situation around Rzhev. This decision had been taken prior to Model's appointment and had already resulted in the transfer from the Third Panzer Army of the 1st Panzer Division (admittedly only as strong as a motorized regimental *kampfgruppe* with no tanks and little artillery) to secure the Sychevka area; this was to be followed in days by the reassignment of the equally depleted 6th Panzer and, at the end of January, of the somewhat stronger 7th Panzer—both from the Third Panzer Army. The Fourth Panzer Army had received orders to release the XLVII Panzer Corps headquarters, along with the 5th Panzer (one of the strongest panzer divisions left to Army Group Center) and the SS *Das Reich* Motorized Division. Heinrici's Fourth Army had been required to relinquish the 403rd Security Division and elements of the 219th Infantry Division, while Army Group Center coughed up a regiment of the 339th Infantry Division from its own meager reserves, as well as allocating Model the 246th Infantry Division, which was arriving by rail from garrison duty in southwestern France. Moreover, the Luftwaffe provided Flak Regiment Staff 125 and the equivalent of five battalions of heavy antiaircraft guns. Even though it should be readily granted that almost all of these units were far understrength and arrived in bits and pieces over the course of two and a half weeks, it must be admitted that Model brought far more than himself to the Ninth Army.[8]

As they got down to business, Model and Blaurock discussed the army's options. Blaurock told his new commander that Strauss had assembled modest forces in the east end of the XXIII Corps pocket and the western flank of the VI Corps position for a proposed attack between 20 and 22 January to close the Rzhev-Olenino gap. Model asked what forces were available, and Blaurock quickly detailed them. It was not an impressive accumulation. Schubert's XXIII Corps would spearhead its attack with the SS Cavalry Brigade, a unit whose only "combat" experience heretofore had been massacring Jews and other Russian civilians in army group rear areas, supported by a weak *Kampfgruppe* from the 206th Infantry Division and the last four *Sturmgeschutze* IIIs belonging to Assault Gun Battalion 189. For its part in the attack, von Richthofen's VI Corps could spare only ten worn-out infantry battalions from five different divisions, controlled by the staff and signal troops of yet a sixth division. The operations officer suggested that, in light of the reinforcements en route, it might be more prudent to delay the attack for a few days.[9]

Model shook his head. Not only did he refuse to consider delaying the attack (he set its opening day as 21 January), but he expanded its scope. To strengthen the VI Corps' attack he would pull one of the 1st Panzer Division's precious motorized battalions away from Sychevka and disengage the entire 251st Infantry Division from the battered XXVII Corps. Moreover, the remainder of the 1st Panzer was ordered to provide a third wing for the attack, assaulting northwest from the Sychevka area toward Olenino; for this purpose it would be reinforced by the Reconnaissance and

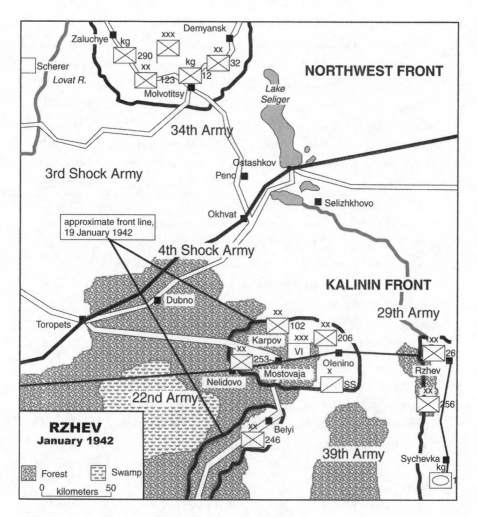

The situation at Rzhev when Model assumed command of the Ninth Army in late January 1942 had deteriorated to the point that the army no longer possessed any semblance of a continuous front.

Motorcycle Battalions of *Das Reich*, which had already reached Sychevka. As the 1st Panzer Division attack got going, Model intended to throw in each additional battalion of *Das Reich* as it arrived, and he ordered Blaurock to seize every single truck, bus, and engineer vehicle left in the army rear area to bring them forward faster. Behind the SS division would come the 5th Panzer Division and General of Panzer Troops Heinrich von Vietinghoff gennant Scheel's XLVII Panzer Corps headquarters, which would take control of the southern part of the battle as soon as it was in position.

Model also issued a strict order limiting the little air support available from the VII *Flieger* Corps—an average of just thirty-eight planes operational on a given day—to direct support of the main attack; he specifically forbade calling in planes to assist in the defense of the rail line from Sychevka south to Vyazma. The defense of Sychevka would be turned over to Raus's 6th Panzer Division headquarters. The single battalion of motorized troops the division had remaining, however, would be sent to reinforce the 1st Panzer Division. To secure the army's long supply line Raus would be given plenipotentiary authority to latch on to any service or support unit he could find, but he would have to improvise his defense without any first-line combat units at all—Model was committing everything he had to the three-pronged attack. It is hardly to be wondered that the overwhelmed Lieutenant Colonel Blaurock confided to the army war diary later in the evening that, whatever else might happen, the army had suddenly received "an infusion of fresh nerves." As soon as their conference was over, Model left for Rzhev to supervise VI Corps' preparations personally.

What Model had instinctively grasped was the fact that the divisions of Lieutenant General V. I. Shvetsov's Twenty-ninth Army, Lieutenant General I. I. Maslennikov's Thirty-ninth Army, and the XI Cavalry Corps he intended to attack were in almost as dire straits, logistically speaking, as the German divisions cut off at Olenino. Although they were far better clothed for the arctic temperatures, the Russians had no supply route from the Volga that was secure from German artillery, few vehicles were available to them, and they had almost no artillery or antitank ammunition. They had been issued three days' rations at the beginning of the attack and then been told to capture whatever additional food they needed from the Germans. Their training had been brief, and their officers were almost completely inexperienced. Having failed to capture Sychevka, Rzhev, or Olenino in the first thrust of the offensive, they were now only in position to dig in and hold their ground while awaiting reinforcements. Every hour Model gave them was another hour in which necessary supplies could trickle down to them.[10]

Before he could launch his attack, however, Model had to deal for the first time with an attempt by Adolph Hitler to interfere with his arrangements. A telephone call from Army Group Center's chief of staff on 19 January informed Model that Hitler, having become nervous about the direct Soviet threat against Vyazma, had decided that the XLVII Panzer Corps, SS *Das Reich*, and the 5th Panzer Division were not to be employed in the Sychevka-Olenino operation but reserved for use in the Gzhatsk area. Aghast at the idea of his army being forced to attack in two different directions, Model drove back from Rzhev to Vyazma on 19 January in a raging blizzard and boarded a plane for East Prussia. Bypassing von Kluge, his immediate superior, Model sought a personal confrontation with Hitler. At first he attempted to lay out his reasons in the best, dispassionate General Staff manner, only to find the Führer unmoved by logic. Finally, desperate and disgusted, Model uttered the words that would cement his moral ascendancy over his commander-in-chief. Glaring at Hitler through his monocle, Model brusquely demanded to know:

"*Mein Führer*, who commands Ninth Army, you or I?"

Hitler, shocked at this show of open defiance from his newest army commander, attempted to cut the discussion short by issuing a direct order to employ von Vietinghoff's troops toward Gzhatsk.

Model shook his head: "That must not stand for me."

"Good, Model," the dictator finally responded, exasperated. "You do it as you please, but it will be your head at risk."[11]

It was the first time that a German general had so bluntly confronted his *Führer*, and the lesson was not lost on Walther Model: Hitler respected only strength and determination, and he could be intimidated. Again, Hitler's "table talk" later that night provides some insight into the impact that Model's performance had on him: "I distrust officers who have exaggeratedly theoretical minds. I'd like to know what becomes of their theories at the moment of action." But when an officer "is worthy of command" (and timing suggests that Hitler was here referring to Model), the dictator told *Reichsführer* Heinrich Himmler, "he must be given the prerogatives corresponding to his functions."[12]

(Halder, who had dismissed the seriousness of the immediate threat to Vyazma, also appeared satisfied with the results of Model's confrontation with Hitler. What he would discover in only a few weeks, however, was that Model could argue just as obstinately against positions held by the chief of the Army General Staff as he had against the Führer. When that happened, Halder would complain bitterly to his diary about the unfortunate influence of "strong-willed army commanders."[13])

The VI and XXIII Corps both attacked on schedule at 10:30 A.M. on 21 January, with the mercury reading -42°F. German soldiers advanced with their uniforms stuffed with newspapers in an attempt to insulate their summer-weight clothing against temperatures so severe that men froze to death on short watches in their foxholes even during daylight hours. Infantry officers had remonstrated with Model to postpone the operation until there was a break in the weather, but the Ninth Army commander brushed their objections aside: "Why, gentlemen? Tomorrow or the day after won't be any warmer. The Russians aren't stopping their operations." From Olenino dismounted SS cavalrymen of *Kampfgruppe* Zehender followed in the wake of Assault Gun Battalion

189's four remaining StG IIIs, rolling through Russian positions that lacked armor-piercing shells for their guns. *Gruppe* Recke, created to control the hodgepodge of battalions pushing out of Rzhev, had no tanks or assault guns but enjoyed close air support. Nearly frozen themselves, the Russians failed to react quickly enough to this counteroffensive, and in little more than forty-eight hours contact had been reestablished with the isolated XXIII Corps. Model had reason to be pleased, as his assault elements together reported the capture of twenty-one pieces of artillery, twenty antitank guns, ten mortars, seventeen heavy machine guns, and sixty-four vehicles. Better still, the tables had been turned on the Soviets, with all of Maslennikov's army and about one-third of Shvetsov's now cut off from their own sources of supply.[14]

This tactical victory, however, did not end the Ninth Army's problems or even completely close the bag around the Russians. Avoiding the trap was the bulk of the Twenty-ninth Army, which, along with Lelyushenko's Thirtieth Army, was sure to make a serious attempt to reopen communications. The 1st Panzer Division's assault northwest from Sychevka had run out of steam fairly quickly—it had, after all, been started with a force of only three battalions. Nor was Maslennikov without an escape route, should he care to use it: There remained to his west a fifteen-kilometer-wide gap between Olenino and Belyi, which neither the XXIII Corps nor the newly arrived 246th Infantry Division yet had the strength to close. Of equal concern was the fact that, isolated or not, both the Thirty-ninth Army and the XI Cavalry Corps retained positions from which to threaten Sychevka and Vyazma, the defenses of which Model had stripped for his attack.

Model now had to reorient his forces. Because the 1st Panzer Division attack was not making headway, he decided to break off the action long enough to assemble the bulk of the XLVII Panzer Corps. Those portions of SS *Das Reich* already attached to the panzer division were left there (chiefly the Motorcycle and Reconnaissance Battalions and the *Deutschland* Motorized Regiment), but the SS division's other motorized regiment—*Der Führer*—was diverted into the VI Corps area of responsibility. *Gruppe* Recke had exhausted itself in closing the Rzhev-Olenino gap; in order to keep it closed fresh forces were required. "Hold on at all costs," Model instructed *Standartenführer* Otto Kumm when he placed the regiment along the Volga. "At all costs," he repeated before leaving.[15]

Meanwhile, von Vietinghoff was laboriously concentrating his forces for a larger-scale attack out of Sychevka, the objective of which would be to seal up all possible escape routes that Maslennikov might try. For this purpose he deployed elements of three divisions. Krüger's 1st Panzer Division was represented by *Kampfgruppe* von Wietersheim, now composed of the 338th Infantry Division's Infantry Regiment 309 (minus one battalion); three batteries from Panzer Artillery Regiment 109; and Heavy Artillery Battalion 620. *Das Reich* contributed *Kampfgruppe* Ostendorff, containing the *Deutschland* Motorized Regiment (consolidated into two small battalions); the Motorcycle and Reconnaissance Battalions (returned by the 1st Panzer); and four heavy weapons companies (infantry howitzers and antitank guns). The main striking power of von Vietinghoff's corps, however, would be provided by Major General Gustav Fehn's 5th Panzer Division. Withheld from the early stages of Operation Barbarossa for refitting after its participation in the Balkan campaign, Fehn's division had taken considerably less wear and tear in Russia than almost any other panzer division. Thus, even in late January 1942 the 5th Panzer Division still boasted over 1,500 motorized infantrymen, its artillery regiment retained 27 functioning guns, and Panzer Regiment 31 could put 70 operational tanks into battle. By the standards of midwinter, therefore, von Vietinghoff's corps represented a potent striking force.[16]

Establishing his headquarters at Sychevka on 25 January, von Vietinghoff immediately received orders to attack three days later. The reserved fifty-four-year-old Prussian certainly remembered from his experience in France (where his XIII Corps had briefly been assigned to the Sixteenth Army) that when Model specified a jump-off date, he intended it to be met. Thus, XLVII Panzer Corps' headquarters staff filed no protests but set to work to make the attack happen, even though many corps elements (including the lead battalion of Panzer Regiment 31) could not possibly arrive prior to 1 February. As temperatures dropped even lower and isolated Russian divisions engaged in local counterattacks, however, even the impatient Model had to agree to postpone the attack for twenty-four hours, simply because von Vietinghoff needed the extra day to get his troops into position.[17]

Attacking through snowdrifts that often loomed above the soldiers' heads, XLVII Panzer Corps pushed slowly but relentlessly into the defensive positions of the Soviet Twenty-ninth and Thirty-ninth Armies. Initially the only tanks available were a handful of obsolete Pzkw IIs and some captured T-34s (with German swastikas incongruously mounted on all sides of the turrets to avoid misidentification), controlled by the 2nd Company, Panzer Regiment 1 of the 1st Panzer Division. By 2 February, roughly twenty more tanks from Panzer Regiment 31 had been committed. This attack was no blitzkrieg: Detachments of two or three tanks spearheaded company-sized *Kampfgruppen*, composed of whatever mix of armored cars, half-tracks, motorcycles, marching infantry, and combat engineers could be assembled. Many of the "infantrymen" were learning dismounted combat tactics on the job. *Das Reich*, after the loss of its last assault gun, had drafted the surviving gunners into the *Der Führer* Regiment, while the 1st Panzer Division issued skis to the panzer crews who had lost their vehicles.[18]

Red Army troops defended their village strongpoints tenaciously, but fought at a critical disadvantage. Soviet artillery lacked the ammunition for anything other than sporadic shelling, and antitank munitions were practically nonexistent. The Germans seized Cherdino on 5 February, cutting off communications between the two Russian armies and their front headquarters on the east bank of the Volga and effectively reversing the tactical situation Model had faced when he took command. The price had not been cheap: Less than two weeks of fighting cost the Ninth Army nearly 5,000 casualties (almost 10 percent of the army's combat strength on 19 January), but the results had been worth it. Model's officers counted over 26,000 dead Russians on the battlefield, processed nearly 5,000 prisoners, knocked out 187 enemy tanks, and captured 343 artillery pieces. The magnitude of this accomplishment had become evident to Hitler and Halder even before the XLVII Panzer Corps' offensive had reached its objective, and they summoned Model to East Prussia on 31 January to receive the oak-leaf cluster to his Knight's Cross and a promotion to colonel general.[19]

Concentrating the XLVII Panzer Corps and reinforcing the VI Corps consumed almost every combat unit the Ninth Army possessed, since both the 246th Infantry and 403rd Security Divisions had their hands full defending Belyi long enough for the main counterattack to encircle Maslennikov's army. What this meant was that nothing in the way of line units had been left to Raus's 6th Panzer Division headquarters to defend the sixty-five-kilometer-long Sychevka-Vyazma supply line from the still-numerous Siberian infantry and Russian cavalry threatening it. But Raus had not been idle. Moving his headquarters to Novo-Dugino (halfway between Sychevka and Vyazma), he distributed his staff officers across the entire rear area of the Ninth Army, "intercepting every available officer and man in their respective areas and forming emergency alert units of varied strength and composition. . . . The newly formed units had to be committed without delay wherever the danger was greatest. Frequently this baptism occurred on the very day of their initial organization."[20]

Had the Russians opposite his front not been suffering from severe supply shortages, Raus might not have been able to secure his line, for the list of units under his control in late January was hardly impressive, consisting primarily of construction troops, bridging columns, and Luftwaffe service units, all of which had been stripped of vehicles and heavy weapons to reinforce one of the major attacks. All told, however, between these units and individual stragglers impressed into service, Raus had managed to assemble nearly 35,000 men by the start of von Vietinghoff's attack. By 31 January he had even collected sufficient motorcycles and armored cars to outfit a full reconnaissance company, which he assembled by the expedient of waylaying every panzer division soldier returning from the hospital or furlough who passed his collection points. Other than a few towed antiaircraft guns surrounding the airfield, he had no artillery available whatsoever until the middle of the first week of February, but fortunately the nearby Red Army soldiers had no shells for their own guns.[21]

Raus's contribution to Model's initial successes should neither be forgotten nor minimized; without his ready willingness to accept the thankless responsibility for the rear area and his innate ability to improvise, none of the Ninth Army's attacks could have been carried out at the same strength. Model was quite aware of this and, as we shall see, made a point throughout his tenure in army command to identify men like Raus, to give them all the responsibility they could handle, and to agitate when necessary for their advancement. This careful and continuous cultivation of like-minded subordinates would result slightly more than two years later in Model and his protégés being simultaneously in charge of three army groups and four armies across the breadth of the Russian front.

Another important supporting character should also be introduced: Colonel Hans Krebs (Major General Krebs as of 1 February), the new Ninth Army chief of staff, arrived at Sychevka two days later than his boss. A forty-three-year-old West Prussian, Krebs had solid credentials for his new post, including a General Staff background, two years' experience as a corps chief of staff, and a fluent command of the Russian language. But it was his personality rather than any of his military accomplishments that made him the perfect partner for Walther Model. Krebs had not been cut from the cloth of the stiff-necked, iron-willed staff officer who saw it as his duty to counterbalance his commander's initiative with cold reasoning. Described by some as sycophantic and by Stalin as "a smooth, surviving type," Krebs saw his role as divining his commander's intentions and finding some way to carry them out. Having been a corps chief of staff under Model at the Sixteenth Army, Krebs knew never to question Model's rash commitments to this attack or that maneuver, but to simply pick up the telephone and start demanding action from the Ninth Army's constituent units. A certain sense of intellectual shallowness emerges when Krebs's record is studied closely. Model might demand the impossible from his troops in order to stimulate them to perform the improbable; Krebs never seems to have realized that Model's demands were often just that—impossible—and simply parroted them, embellished with dire threats for noncompliance. One thing Krebs did realize almost immediately, however, was that Model represented a rapidly rising star to whom he would attach himself as completely as possible.[22]

From late January through early March, Krebs's impact on Ninth Army operations was minimal, primarily because he did have enough good sense to realize on his arrival that Lieutenant Colonel Blaurock was better prepared than he to coordinate the army's various attacks. Krebs therefore essentially removed himself from the operational staff and assumed responsibility for expediting the army's logistics. Thus, the senior command structure of the Ninth Army almost resembled the picture of individual molecules bouncing around in near-vacuum: Model floating between Rzhev, Olenino, and Sychevka, and Krebs circulating from Sychevka to Vyazma and occasionally Belyi, with only Blaurock remaining stationary at the command post. Strangely enough, it worked.

The Russians, predictably, had no intention of allowing the bulk of two armies to remain isolated in their pocket, and throughout

February the Kalinin Front launched a series of fierce, although generally uncoordinated attacks to reopen communications. Repeatedly the Red Army attempted to break through the Ninth Army's northernmost front, which still ran along the frozen Volga. To muster the troops for von Vietinghoff's offensive and the long, meandering front held by his understrength divisions, Model had to rely, even for this critical sector, on an improvised blocking force (*sperrverband*) to hold the line. Designated *Gruppe* Recke—for Major General Heinrich Recke, commander of the 161st Infantry Division—this unit consisted primarily of *Kampfgruppe* de Monteton (built around Infantry Regiment 169) and *Kampfgruppe* Kumm (centering on the *Der Führer* Regiment).[23]

Standartenführer Otto Kumm's *Der Führer* had entered the Soviet Union with nearly 2,000 men but seven months later barely mustered 650, and many of these men had begun the campaign in other divisional units, only to be transferred into the ever-diminishing ranks of the infantry companies as losses in men and machines mounted. Initially supported only by its own infantry guns and a scattering of 37mm antitank guns, the regiment deployed along a four-mile front that wound back and forth across the Volga River, running through village strongpoints at Solomino, Klepenino, Opjachtino, and Kokosch. Opposite Kumm's thinly held line lay the bulk of the Soviet Thirtieth Army, which Ninth Army intelligence rated at seven rifle divisions and six tank brigades; even if those units were understrength and poorly supplied, the Red Army's overwhelming numbers on the ground meant that the SS troops faced odds as high as thirty-to-one in some attacks. "Maybe Ivan has swindled us," Model told Kumm with a smile, implying that perhaps Zhukov would not throw everything into his attacks.[24]

Zhukov had not swindled his enemies: From 26 January until 17 February, the Soviets threw every man, tank, and shell available into a nearly continuous attempt to breach Kumm's outpost line on the Volga. "Everything depended on the heavy weapons," recalled one young SS officer, "because the front was only thinly held. We sat in snow bunkers and during the day lay in heavy artillery fire. A pause in the artillery bombardment meant that the Russian attack was coming." Kumm himself reported: "Every attack is broken [only] at the cost of fearful casualties, often in close combat with grenades and side arms. Mounds of enemy dead pile up in front of the company positions. Most horrible of all are the attacks by enemy tanks."[25]

Der Führer's stand became the stuff of legend, first in the Ninth Army, then among the soldiers of the Waffen SS, and finally among military history enthusiasts across six decades after the war. Stories of hand-to-hand fighting ("I'm the only one left from the company. They're all dead"), improvised antitank tactics (Kumm himself was credited with participation in nearly two dozen kills), and harsh winter conditions (foxholes that could only be dug with satchel charges) have combined to etch an aura of myth around the three-week struggle. Inevitably such recountings end on 18 February, with Kumm reporting back to Model near Ninth Army headquarters.

"I know what your regiment went through, Kumm," Model is quoted as saying. "But I still can't do without it. How strong is it now?"

Kumm then gestured for his army commander to look out the window at no more than thirty-five exhausted soldiers collapsed in the street. "*Herr Generaloberst*, my regiment is on parade outside."[26]

This rendition of events has tended to obscure some of the tactical realities of the situation. *Der Führer*'s 650 men never held that four-mile line on the Volga unsupported: On 26 January *Gruppe* Kumm included the equivalent of two companies of Infantry Regiment 471; elements of Flak Battalion II/4; at least one platoon from the 3rd Company, Engineer Battalion 185; and a battalion of Artillery Regiment 251. Over the next three weeks the following units were added to the mix:

29 January: elements of Panzerjäger Battalion 561

30 January: I Battalion, Infantry Regiment 471; 2nd Battery, Assault Gun Battalion 189

31 January: two companies from the 256th Infantry Division

 1 February: 3rd Company, Engineer Battalion 256

 2 February: additional elements of Panzerjäger Battalion 561; draft of 200 men from SS Artillery Regiment *Das Reich* (serving as infantry)

 3 February: at least four companies of construction troops

 4 February: two companies, I Battalion, Infantry Regiment 456

 6 February: Reconnaissance Battalion 256

 7 February: main body of II Battalion, Infantry Regiment 252 and at least one company of Engineer Battalion 251

 8 February: 200 SS replacements from a march battalion

 9 February: I Battalion, SS Regiment *Deutschland*

10 February: Headquarters, Motorcycle Battalion, and at least two artillery battalions from SS Division *Das Reich* begin arriving.[27]

Even considering that all of these units entered the battle seriously below their authorized strength, the Ninth Army's sketchy records indicate that *Gruppe* Kumm began with nearly 1,100 men and by the time SS Division *Das Reich* headquarters took control of the sector on 10 February had received at least 1,500 reinforcements. Moreover, Model committed at least five StG III assault guns, four 88mm flak guns, and about thirty pieces of artillery to the battle. In effect, *Gruppe* Kumm deployed troops at about twice the level of density of any other section of the Ninth Army's meandering front line. Granted, the SS troops from *Das Reich* formed the backbone of the defense and lost grievously in fighting that often became house to house and hand to hand, but Model never left them standing alone and unsupported on the Volga. Instead, personally visiting the sector almost every day (sometimes on horseback if no vehicles were available), the army commander coldly calculated the minimum number of reinforcements he could send Kumm to hold off the Russian attack while von Vietinghoff and Raus liquidated the Red Army forces encircled behind the Ninth Army's front line. Moreover, Ninth Army records suggest that on two occasions when it appeared Kumm's line was about to buckle, Model had a *Kampfgruppe* from 1st Panzer Division alerted to intervene.[28]

By mid-February Zhukov's attacks had tailed off, and within another few weeks the last Soviet troops behind Model's lines had been contained or eliminated.

It was now apparent to everyone exactly who commanded the Ninth Army.

7

WE MUST NOT BREAK

The Ninth Army:
April 1942 to January 1943

A COLD DAY IN THE RZHEV SALIENT, IN THE SECTOR HELD BY THE 195th Infantry Division. Men from a battery of Panzerjäger Battalion 95 were huddled not around their 37mm PAK but around a large bonfire. "There were six or seven of us standing around the fire with men from other units, including a sergeant and a corporal," recalled Bernhard Averback, but when a party of high-ranking officers approached, the gunner abruptly discovered that "before I knew it most of the men around the fire had disappeared." The officers strode closer, so Averback reluctantly tossed his cigarette into the flames, squared his shoulders, and saluted, reporting his name, company, and orders of the day. One monocled general ("somewhat smaller than the others") "took my report and asked questions on several details concerning the defenses we were constructing." Averback answered to the best of his ability, and to the apparent satisfaction of the general, who "told me to go back to the fire and warm myself"; then he walked off with a bemused chuckle. His hands still trembling when his comrades returned, Averback realized that he had just met Walther Model.[1]

Between January 1942 and March 1943, Model's Ninth Army held the Rzhev salient against repeated Red Army offensives. It was this tenacious defense even more than his grim January counterattack that cemented Model's capabilities in Hitler's mind. There "the Lion of the Defense" also developed among his peers and subordinates the reputation of an unusually talented tactician as well as an exceptionally coldhearted commander. Given the Germany army's circumstances during the second year of the war in Russia and Model's personality, neither he nor his army could have survived any other way.

Even as Army Group Center's long, meandering front line was stabilized as the spring mud set in, the extent of the crippling wounds inflicted on the German army outside Moscow could not be disguised. Losses in men and materiel simply could not be made good, as evidenced by Hitler's decisions in rebuilding a new strike force for his projected summer campaign in southern Russia. To refurbish the panzer divisions for that offensive, those panzer divisions left along the northern and central fronts found their armored strength permanently cut to a single battalion. The southern concentration also required stripping Army Groups North and Center of hundreds of precious motor vehicles, rendering most infantry divisions functionally immobile. So many pieces of field artillery and prime movers had been lost that the batteries of the infantry divisions in Army Groups North and Center suffered a reduction from four guns each to three.[2]

Manpower shortages affected the long-suffering infantry divisions most of all. Intent upon raising new formations as Army Group South divisions were refitted, Hitler essentially cut off all but a trickle of replacements to the regiments in the trenches. Commanders—from Model down to his division commanders—took drastic measures to reinforce their frontline strength. Rear-area units were "combed out" to find men fit for combat, often by replacing cooks, drivers, and other support personnel with indigenous Russian volunteers known as *Hiwis*. Reconnaissance, engineer, antitank, and replacement battalions dwindled to company size (and sometimes disappeared completely) as more men found themselves drafted into the infantry regiments. Helmut Hörner, a machine-gunner in Infantry Regiment 109 who returned to the front that spring from an extended convalescent leave, discovered the extent of these changes: "I was assigned to the 4th Machine Gun Company. My company leader was Paul Nagel, whom I had known since 1938. After a short private talk he sent me with a runner to my position. There I found only four grenade launchers; two of them were Russian. There were none of the old crowd among the young men. They were all glad that I had experience at the front."[3]

None of these expedients, however, could halt the steady decline in the Ninth Army's infantry strength. By 10 May the army controlled thirteen infantry divisions, two motorized divisions, one panzer division, and several improvised *Kampfgruppen* ranging from regimental to brigade strength. The authorized strength of Model's infantry divisions called for 117 infantry battalions, each of which should have mustered between 400 and 500 men. He could actually deploy along the front only 97 such battalions, most of which contained only 250 to 300 men. The reported infantry shortfall in those divisions during May approached 28,400, leaving him at about 46 percent of his authorized infantry strength. Some divisions had shrunk to mere skeletons. The 256th Infantry Division was reduced from nine to four infantry battalions, its artillery regiment was cut from twelve to six batteries, and its engineer, antitank, and reconnaissance elements were consolidated into a four-company fusilier battalion. Nonetheless, with a single attached infantry battalion from another division, Colonel Friedrich Weber's depleted division remained responsible for an eleven-mile defensive sector.[4]

The Ninth Army's lone armored unit, the 1st Panzer Division, hardly resembled the tracked legions that had overrun most of European Russia the previous summer. Major General Walther Krüger's organic division assets had been reduced to Motorized Infantry Regiment 443 (two battalions), one battalion of Artillery Regiment 73, and one company of Antitank Battalion 37. Former tank crews had been dragooned into the line with rifles; most of the division's artillery and all of its supply transport was now horse-drawn rather than motorized. Neither the 14th nor the 36th Motorized Divisions looked much better. Virtually all of the Ninth Army's tiny supply of armored fighting vehicles had been concentrated in two units—Panzer Battalion Herschel and Assault Gun Battalion 189—which were farmed out in platoon and company-sized packets to the infantry divisions. (The definition of "armored fighting vehicle" at the front lines near Moscow had, by May 1942, come to include everything from captured Soviet T-26s and T-34s to armored cars, obsolete French tanks hastily imported from the West, and weaponless command vehicles placed ostentatiously near the front for a deterrent effect.)[5]

Logic therefore dictated that the Ninth Army's bulging front around Rzhev, which marked the closest German outpost to Moscow, be significantly shortened. Both Model and von Kluge recommended this on several occasions, but Hitler consistently overruled them. The Führer argued that such a withdrawal would hurt Germany's international prestige and that the Ninth Army's mere continued existence so near Stalin's capital would force the Russians to maintain large troop concentrations around the city— troops therefore unavailable to resist the summer drive toward the Caucasus and the oil fields. In May 1942 Hitler's arguments had merit: Turkey remained open to German influence, but only so long as the Soviets appeared to be losing the fight, while subsequent events south of Kharkov would prove that Stalin's generals had in fact kept too many troops near Moscow. The downside to the Führer's argument lay in the fact that those Red Army troops around Moscow might not be available to counter the Germans in the south, but they could certainly make life hell for the soldiers of the Ninth Army.

Faced with those constraints (an overextended line and no replacements in the offing), as well as the need to clean out surviving fragments of Red Army units lodged in his own rear area, Model and his subordinates developed a different approach to defensive warfare than their contemporaries who would fight the highly mobile panzer battles across the Ukrainian steppes. Never formally named, Model's defensive doctrine was not quite an "elastic" defense; nor was it a "defense in depth." It embodied several key principles:

- Relying heavily on frontline intelligence gathering rather than depending on the reports churned out by *Fremd Heer Ost* (Foreign Armies East)
- Manning a continuous front rather than outposts, no matter how thinly this spread infantry strength on the ground
- Relying on tactical rather than operational reserves
- Centralizing artillery command and control
- Constructing multiple switchlines (far in excess of that normally required by German doctrine)

The German army placed a high premium on conducting operational reconnaissance, making wireless intercepts, and sending out patrols to capture prisoners. The Ninth Army took this concept to even greater depth because Model insisted that his 1c (intelligence officer), Colonel Georg Buntrock, not simply use locally generated materials to supplement what was received from *Fremd Heer Ost* but develop his own independent appraisals. As historian David Glantz notes, even though "Buntrock lacked the resources and broad perspective available to higher commands . . . his information tended to be fresher." In support of Buntrock's activities, Model stripped away all mounted reconnaissance assets from his infantry divisions and converted them into Cavalry Brigade Model, which performed dually as a reconnaissance and antipartisan force. Such intelligence gathering also demanded a higher level of patrolling—especially at night—than the Ninth Army's soldiers would have preferred. Of these unwelcome excursions one *Landser* recalled, "We had to maneuver on stomachs past mined obstacles and uncollected dead until we could sneak through the Russian line and into their rear." Yet such patrols were undeniably valuable. On several occasions (most notably the November 1942 offensive against Rzhev) Buntrock's analysis gave Model extra days or even weeks to prepare for major attacks. Model came to rely on his own army's assessments more heavily than on those generated through OKH.[6]

The official German defensive doctrine for infantry remained, even in 1942, nearly unchanged from that employed during the Great War. A key component of that doctrine was that front lines should not be held in strength most of the time, but by small detachments. Given that most attacks were preceded by heavy bombardments, this tactic usually spared the defensive force unnecessary casualties. When the bombardment lifted during the enemy's final approach, the main body of the defending regiments would race to their posts to lay down a wall of machine-gun fire in the hopes of turning back the attack. As well as this had worked from 1914 to 1918, and as fervently as many officers still subscribed to it (Model would have prolonged, bitter arguments about the subject with Hermann Balck in 1944), conditions in Russia had rendered it obsolete. As Lieutenant General Otto Schellert, commanding the 253rd Infantry Division, recalled:

> It was a question whether a continuous line or individual strong-points were to be established. The system of strong-points would afford closer concentration and better control over the troops, as well as closer cooperation with heavy weapons, and a small echeloning in depth. A continuous line, on the other hand, would pro-

vide better observation and the possibility of shelling the intermediate area, and it would make it more difficult for the enemy to in-
filtrate behind German lines; it would also reduce German losses
from heavy enemy fire.

The division ordered the establishment of a continuous line.[7]

Likewise, Hans Röttiger, chief of staff for the XLI Panzer
Corps, noted, "The Russians usually noticed very soon the gaps
which thus formed along this line consisting solely of strong
points. Taking advantage of this condition, they carried out
thrusts into the depth and rear of the position. Rigorous training
was necessary to convince the troops of the necessity of occupying
as uninterrupted a front line as possible, in spite of the cold
weather."[8]

The distinction between tactical and operational reserves was
also critical to Model's success at holding his line. In this case,
"tactical reserves" referred to those reserves immediately available
to the commander responsible for a particular stretch of the line;
at the battalion level this might have consisted of a company or a
platoon, while at the division level such a reserve might have been
a mixed, battalion-size *Kampfgruppe*. "Operational reserves" existed at the corps level and higher and tended to be entire units (or
large subunits capable of acting independently) that could be rapidly switched from sector to sector on the orders of the commander at least one echelon above the officer commanding the
front line. The purpose of these reserves was to deliver a bigger
punch than tactical reserves and also to be available to deal with
any large-scale ruptures of the main battle line.

Panzer and motorized units, with their ability to maneuver and
respond quickly, obviously represented the "fire brigades" of
choice in the German army, but the reality of the Ninth Army's
tactical situation usually rendered the operational use of such
units in defense impractical. Throughout most of his tenure defending Rzhev, Model counted himself lucky if he had more than

a single, understrength panzer division in army reserve. Given that the peninsular shape of the Ninth Army's front rendered it vulnerable to multiple, simultaneous attacks, there would often be more emergencies than his operational reserves could meet. So Model in large measure did away with operational reserves and committed the forces that would otherwise have been used for them to stiffen and strengthen the tactical reserves along his entire line. This meant, for example, that in May 1942, when the Ninth Army deployed no more than sixty armored fighting vehicles, they were farmed out in platoon and company strength to corps and divisions rather than being retained as whole battalions under army command. Such a deployment enraged the panzer officers, who had been trained to view this kind of thinking as sacrilegious, and they often lodged vigorous protests with army headquarters. Model ignored them, having reasoned that if his panzer reserves were too small to deal with a sizable breakthrough, he would be better off deploying them to prevent that breakthrough in the first place. On one occasion, during the summer of 1942, XXIII Corps commander Johannes Freissner returned from leave in Germany at the height of a Soviet attack to discover that virtually every tactical reserve his corps possessed had already been thrown into the battle. Without reserves, Freissner argued, his line was sure to break somewhere, but an unrepentant Model snapped back: "No, that's just it, we must not break *anywhere*."[9]

Of course, as the two major defensive battles the Ninth Army waged during the summer and fall of 1942 would prove, even this expedient could not guarantee that the Red Army would not sometimes rip open the front. In those cases Model became an expert at pleading his case with Army Group Center for the release of its operational reserves to restore the Ninth Army's line. He could, after all, point to the fact that every unit he had available had already been committed. What Model did with these "borrowed" operational reserves is also instructive. To conserve the strength of the Ninth Army's long-serving divisions, Model quite coldly or-

dered divisions like *Grossdeutschland* into situations he knew
would generate high casualties. He reasoned, however, that the
elite unit would eventually be withdrawn, replenished, and refitted
somewhere in the rear, an option not open to his frontline divisions. Thus, he preferred to blood the army group's "fire brigades"
in order to save his own men. This tendency, which was quickly noticed by the officers and men of *Grossdeutschland* and the Waffen
SS, did not endear Model to them.

For example, *Grossdeutschland*—having recently been reorganized into a fully motorized infantry division with an assigned
panzer battalion—received orders transferring it from Army
Group Center's reserve to the Ninth Army in late August 1942. As
one officer at division headquarters noted, "Orders from the highest levels of command forbade committing the division in anything
less than full strength." Model began chipping away at this directive when the division entered active operations on 10 September.
He detached both the reconnaissance and engineer battalions as
tactical reserves for his VI Corps, while simultaneously ordering
Artillery Regiment *Grossdeutschland* subordinated to Artillery
Commander (ARKO) 122, along with the guns of the 129th and
172nd Infantry Divisions.[10]

Over the following month the Ninth Army threw the bulk of
Grossdeutschland's infantry first into the teeth of the strongest Soviet attacks and then into a series of bloody, head-on counterattacks with minimal support from other divisions. On 30 September
the officers and men of this elite division had come dangerously
close to mutiny: Infantry Regiment GD 2, commanded by Colonel
Eugen Garski, received a directive from army headquarters to
launch a full-scale counterattack in the face of heavy Russian artillery superiority. The attack's objective was to regain a 400- to
600-meter-square piece of forest from which the regiment had been
ejected three days earlier. Garski barraged his division commander—Major General Walther Hörnlein—with daunting statistics about high casualties and low morale, along with biting

commentaries on the tactical inconsequence of this particular strip of woods. Hörnlein took these arguments to Model, along with the observation that additional heavy casualties might render his division incapable of defending its current line. Model, according to Helmuth Später, "rejected these concerns, commenting that the Fuehrer had ordered the attack and that he expected *Grossdeutschland* to do its duty." Garski, several of his company commanders, and hundreds more soldiers fell attempting to perform that duty. By the time Hörnlein's division was finally relieved on 10 October, Infantry Regiment GD 1 had suffered nearly 1,400 casualties; the division's total loss probably exceeded 4,500.[11]

Even then, however, with *Grossdeutschland* technically remanded to OKH reserve for rehabilitation, Model continued to request the employment of division subunits as tactical reserves for his hard-pressed corps commanders. He was so successful in this piecemeal endeavor that, by late November (when Colonel Buntrock believed the next Red Army offensive would begin), various *Grossdeutschland* elements had been dispersed to at least six different organizations across a front line 110 kilometers wide:

Under control of XLI Panzer Corps:
Fusilier Regiment GD (four infantry battalions)
Reconnaissance Battalion GD
Assault Gun Battalion GD
I Battalion, Artillery Regiment GD
2nd Company, Panzerjäger Battalion GD
2nd Medical Company
3rd Ambulance Platoon

Under control of XXIII Corps:
3rd Battery, Flak Battalion GD

Under control of 253rd Infantry Division:
III Battalion, Grenadier Regiment GD
Armored Observation Battery GD

Under control of 206th Infantry Division:
2nd Company, Panzer Battalion GD
II Battalion, Artillery Regiment GD
2nd Battery, Flak Battalion GD

Under control of 14th Motorized Division:
3rd Company, Panzer Battalion GD
3rd Company, Engineer Battalion GD

Under control of Supply Battalion 692:
GD supply columns 4, 6, 9, 10, 12, 13, 17

These deployments left Hörnlein in control of only three battalions of infantry, one panzerjäger company, one artillery battalion, and the remains of the division's flak and engineer battalions. Because the division's "main body," however, had still been assigned to a full defensive sector under XXIII Corps, the Ninth Army also attached back to *Grossdeutschland* the equivalent of three infantry battalions, two engineer companies, and one reinforced artillery battalion from the 86th and 110th Infantry Divisions. Clearly, as heavy fighting again developed in December, the Ninth Army intended the detached *Grossdeutschland* units to bleed themselves white in the counterattacks necessary to restore the line so that Model's long-serving divisions would be spared as much as possible. By mid-December Model had even begun raiding Hörnlein's "main body" for company-strength emergency response units (*alarmeinheiten*) to send into adjacent divisional sectors.[12]

These decisions, noted the divisional historian, contributed to "an increasing alienation between the I.D. GD and XXIII Corps as well as Ninth Army." Regarding Model, Helmuth Später wrote with a candor unusual in postwar unit histories, criticizing "the false optimism of the Ninth Army which, in order to give a positive picture of the situation to those above, made unrealistic demands which failed to take into account the actual condition of

the fighting units." Später also pointed out that Model repeatedly voiced pointed criticisms about *Grossdeutschland* to Army
Group Center and OKH when Hörnlein's attacks in the Luchesa
Valley failed to throw the Russians back, but cynically omitted
the fact that over half of the division had been tasked out to
other missions. By the time Hörnlein's battalions finally escaped
the Ninth Army in early January 1943, of the 18,000 men who
had entered the Rzhev salient in September, nearly 10,000 had
been killed or wounded. From Model's perspective, this was a
positive outcome, however, since these represented 10,000 fallen
soldiers whose loss did not come out of divisions he considered
organic to the Ninth Army.

Another innovation upon which Model insisted was the central-
ization of artillery command. The structure of German infantry
divisions worked against the creation of large concentrations of
fire. As a holdover from the *stoss* battalions of the previous war,
which had needed light artillery pieces that could be hauled over
shell-torn ground to support their advances, the 1939 infantry division organization placed a significant amount of divisional firepower in the so-called infantry guns that were organically assigned
to each regiment. Moreover, each of the three battalions of the divisional artillery regiment was often assigned—more or less permanently—to support a specific regiment. Thus, every regimental
commander could count on always having *some* dedicated artillery
support available, but only at the cost of making it difficult for the
division commander to organize heavier concentrations of fire
when needed. The expedient that evolved to close this gap was the
ad hoc assignment of independent "army" artillery battalions
under either an "Artillery Regiment Special Staff" or an "Artillery
Commander" (ARKO) for special assignments.

Model effectively reversed this relationship by pushing forward
these artillery commanders and regimental staffs and giving them
semipermanent control not only of certain army artillery battalions but also of organic division assets. For example, to Lieutenant

The fatigue now evident on his lined face, Colonel General Walther Model faces a Soviet offensive against Rzhev in October 1942.

General Josef Harpe's XLI Panzer Corps in May 1942 Model attached Artillery Regiment Special Staffs 74 and 78 to the organic staff of Artillery Commander (ARKO) 30. Artillery Regimental Staff 74 was attached to the 161st Infantry Division with one army artillery battalion and five independent batteries, to which the division's own Artillery Regiment 241 was also subordinated. The usual informal but long-standing relationships between the individual battalions of Artillery Regiment 241 and each of Major

General Heinrich Recke's three infantry regiments were severed, requiring infantry commanders to call in all requests for fire to a centralized command post. Again, these measures were unpopular—at least initially—but they worked.[13]

Model also capitalized on his earlier experience in the trenches in France and forced his divisions to dig a far more extensive series of alternate firing positions and defensive switchlines than German doctrine required. Troops rotated off the front line found themselves assigned to fatigue duty (although more often supervising the excavations of Soviet prisoners of *Ostruppen*—literally "Eastern troops," Russian volunteers placed in service battalions). As one grenadier recalled, "There were days when we didn't see a single Russian. Every day we dug more trenches and eventually bunkers, all during daylight. There wasn't a shot fired from a rifle or artillery for weeks." Model required not only that such lines be created, but that fields of fire be registered and minefields laid out (with all appropriate documentation) so that when a battalion or a regiment fell back into such a position, there would be only minimal disruption before the unit was ready to defend it.[14]

This expedient might not seem anything close to a stroke of genius, unless it is remembered that from December 1941 onward Hitler had often expressly forbidden such construction, fearing that the frontline soldiers would begin "looking over the shoulder" rather than fight for their current line. Model's innovation was therefore political as much as tactical: He simply ignored such prohibitions and failed to report his army's activities. Defensive maps forwarded by the Ninth Army's engineers to Army Group Center often looked far different from those possessed by Model's corps commanders. If staff officers at von Kluge's headquarters noticed these discrepancies (and it is a near-certainty that they did), they never drew anyone's attention to them.

During the twelve months following March 1942 the Red Army launched major offensives against the Ninth Army from 30 July to 23 September and from 25 November to 16 December, as well as a number of minor attacks conducted in the course of routine attrition warfare. In both of the strategic offensives Model's chief opponents were Georgi Zhukov and Ivan Konev. In late July Model was absent on convalescent leave, having been wounded by a chance rifle shot that hit him when he was flying over the front several weeks earlier. The Ninth Army's acting commander—Heinrich Freiherr von Vietinghoff gennant Scheel—found his front torn open in several places within the first seventy-two hours and informed Army Group Center that without substantial reinforcements he could not hold the army's 175-mile front and might in fact lose several divisions if he tried to withdraw. For once, Hitler and OKH responded quickly, canceling a minor offensive in the Second Panzer Army's sector and rushing 1st, 2nd, and 5th Panzer Divisions, as well as the 78th and 102nd Infantry Divisions, to the scene of the unfolding disaster. Unfortunately, the situation had unraveled so quickly that the five divisions could not be used as a coherent counterattacking force but had to be fed directly into the defensive line. By 17 August (roughly when Model arrived at the front), the Ninth Army had suffered 21,000 casualties.[15]

Model immediately presented von Kluge with a demand for at least three or four more divisions; if he did not receive them, he insisted that Army Group Center "provide detailed instructions as to how the battle is to be continued." Von Kluge had only the 72nd Infantry Division available, but promised Model he would work on additional reinforcements, including *Grossdeutschland*. By 1 September, however, having absorbed another 21,000 casualties, Model argued vehemently that the Rzhev salient would have to be surrendered if more divisions were not forthcoming. *Grossdeutschland* finally arrived, along with promises of the 95th Infantry Division and the 9th Panzer Division during the next two weeks. "Someone must collapse," Hitler insisted. "It will not be us!" Eventually, in the third week of September, the Red Army offensive ground to a halt amid the early fall rain and mud, after having cost the Ninth Army nearly 60,000 casualties.[16]

This "victory" could be attributed, objectively speaking, more to Model's ability to wrangle nine additional divisions (along with probably another two divisions' worth of independent regiments and battalions) out of Adolph Hitler than to the army commander's tactical acumen. Freissner recalled that Model's ability to speak to the Führer "like an old soldier" rather than as a staff officer proved decisive here.[17] His coarse demeanor impressed Hitler, as did his cold-blooded willingness to order division after division into headlong counterattacks to stave off disaster. The battle also solidified Model's unequal relationship with von Kluge. Repeatedly the field marshal had given Model orders that the army commander circumvented or manipulated Hitler to countermand. By late September it almost seemed that the Ninth Army had been unofficially detached from Army Group Center to operate under the direct control of OKH.

The second major offensive—the Red Army's "Operation Mars"—kicked off on 24 November. STAVKA intended Mars as the companion piece to "Operation Uranus" at Stalingrad and charged Zhukov with lopping off the Ninth Army at Rzhev while Marshal Andrei A. Vasilievsky encircled the Sixth Army on the Volga. Operating from the assumption that Stalingrad would consume all available German theater-level reserves, Zhukov committed seven armies, 2,352 tanks, and over 10,000 guns and mortars in a three-pronged offensive designed to collapse the Rzhev salient in less than a week. To meet this challenge Model deployed fourteen infantry divisions, two panzer divisions, two motorized divisions, and the SS Cavalry Division, all of which were seriously understrength and many of which had not had the opportunity to make good their losses in the previous campaign. Fragmentary returns from the Ninth Army suggest an initial combat strength of fewer than 90,000 soldiers, no more than 200 panzers, and perhaps 1,800 guns.[18]

Nonetheless, in a monthlong slugging match Model's Ninth Army denied Stalin a second, simultaneous strategic victory and handed Zhukov the worst defeat he suffered during the course of the war. The Red Army lost at least 335,000 men and over 1,600 tanks without cracking Model's line. The defeat was so embarrassing and so costly that the Soviets literally refused to admit the existence and purpose of the offensive for several decades. The fighting again proved fierce and costly to both sides. Model's advanced intelligence about the attack, which had allowed him to forecast the approximate timing of the assault, and his ability to influence the high command to send reinforcements both proved critical, but more fundamental issues affected the battle's outcome. Zhukov's forces conducted poor reconnaissance; the cooperation between infantry, tanks, and artillery often broke down; and local Red Army commanders proved hesitant to exploit local breakthroughs. As a result, the offensive's momentum usually foundered against Model's second, third, or fourth line of defenses.

Even so, the battle validated what Model and von Kluge had both been saying for months: The Rzhev salient could not be held indefinitely. Had Army Group Center been allowed to straighten its line in late September or early October, as many as twelve to fourteen divisions could have been pulled out of the line. With such a reserve available to be shifted south toward Stalingrad in November and December, the Sixth Army might well have been relieved before that disaster played itself out. As it was, Hitler continued to refuse to countenance the evacuation of the salient until the Sixth Army surrendered at the end of January 1943.[19] The irony of Model's yearlong defense of Rzhev was that his tactical successes constituted a strategic defeat for the German army. Zhukov never managed to penetrate the Ninth Army's lines, and hundreds of thousands of Red Army soldiers died as a result of those efforts, but the cost of that prestige victory was too high. Between 30 July and 24 December the Ninth Army sustained over 100,000 casualties to defend ground that would ultimately be surrendered voluntarily.

Model's ability to hold his ground, however, had understandably caused his stock to rise with Hitler, and he was already marked down as a future army group commander. Model had also developed a cadre of talented corps commanders whose careers spiraled upward along with his own. Of the men commanding corps and divisions in the Ninth Army during 1942, four (Hans-Jürgen von Arnim, Johannes Freissner, Josef Harpe, and Heinrich von Vietinghoff) ultimately rose to become army group commanders, and four more (Hans Jordan, Joachim Lemelsen, Erhard Raus, and Hans Zorn) would eventually lead armies. This represented—especially during the latter half of the war—unprecedented influence among Hitler's senior generals. When the Army Personnel Office began, in late June 1944, to compile formal lists of potential successors to command at all levels from division up, with a mandate to "ignore considerations of current rank," the reports submitted to OKH make it abundantly clear that Model's headquarters had generally been the first office consulted.[20]

8

CRIMINAL BUFFALOES AND IMAGINARY PANTHERS

The Ninth Army: February to June 1943

ON 21 MARCH 1943 WALTHER MODEL UNWITTINGLY ALMOST assisted in the assassination of Adolph Hitler. Deputizing for Field Marshal von Kluge, Model flew to Berlin with Colonel Rudolf Freiherr von Gersdorff of Army Group Center's staff to attend the annual "Heroes' Memorial Day." That Model appeared in place of von Kluge not only indicated his rising stock with the Führer but also suggested that the dictator wished to thank the Ninth Army's commander personally for the safe extrication of his divisions from the Rzhev salient. What neither Model nor Hitler knew, however, was that von Gersdorff arrived in Berlin with two small bombs in his pocket that he was determined to detonate when the Führer paused long enough. Ironically, Model aided von Gersdorff in this endeavor by several times attempting to convince Hitler to stop and take a long look at some captured weapons on display. Hitler, however, rushed through the whole procedure; historian Peter Hoffmann remarks that, "if anyone says that Hitler must have had some presentiment or 'smell' of danger, this need not be brushed aside as ridiculous. . . . The possibility that Hitler sensed Gersdorff's nervousness and took warning from it is not so far-fetched." Model, on the other hand, noticed nothing—not even von Gersdorff's dejected attitude as the two men returned to Russia.[1]

That March represented an unusual lull in the German-Soviet conflict. Field Marshal Erich von Manstein's famous "backhand blow" in the Donets region during late February and early March had not only recaptured Kharkov and ended Stalin's dreams of converting his Stalingrad victory into a war-winning campaign but also inflicted so many casualties on the Red Army that (along with the onset of the muddy season) active operations came to a halt. Meanwhile, in early February Hitler had finally relented concerning the retention of the Rzhev salient, allowing Model to execute "Operation Buffalo" (*Bueffel*)—a phased withdrawal that simultaneously shortened Army Group Center's front by nearly two hundred miles and allowed twenty divisions to form a new strategic reserve.

The Ninth Army's operations staff had been planning such a withdrawal for months. Both Hans Krebs and his successor as chief of staff, Rudolph Freiherr von Elverfeldt, had always recognized the dangers inherent in Model's tenacious defense of the salient. At any moment a tactical misfortune or the simple weight of numbers could have rendered the army's position untenable; prudence therefore dictated that the staff be ready to save as much as possible on short notice. (As with many of the Ninth Army's other tactical procedures, this planning did not of course get reported either to von Kluge's staff or to OKH.) Thus, when the surprising news that Hitler had sanctioned the withdrawal even without a current Soviet offensive, Model and his subordinates responded with a master-

This April 1943 photograph is one of the more famous images of Walther Model, taken during the lull prior to Operation Citadel, but also one that fails to capture his trademark intensity.

piece of careful logistical and tactical planning in the best German General Staff tradition.

Although his twenty-four divisions were all seriously under-strength, Model's army represented a huge force to slip out from under the watchful eyes of his opponents: 8,691 officers, 2,325 civilian employees, 57,083 NCOs, 256,825 German troops, and probably an additional 40,000 Russian volunteers. The army's artillery and antitank gun park exceeded 400 weapons, and the 2nd and 9th Panzer Divisions (plus various smaller units) deployed about 100 armored fighting vehicles between them. In addition, to prevent retreat from degenerating into rout, a new fortified position had to be constructed along the base of the salient—and it had to be essentially completed in three weeks![2]

On 4 February the Ninth Army created a special staff (*Erkundungsstaebe*) to take charge of the entire operation. Operations Order 800/43 subordinated all army engineer, construction, and POW labor units to the army's senior engineer, whose first order of business was the basic work on the new main battle line position (*Hauptkampflinie*) between Velizh and Kirov. Within that zone, the primary infantry, antitank, and artillery positions were to be surveyed and excavated, with lines of approach and fields of fire sketched out. At the end of that period each division was to send back a liaison team under the control of one senior staff officer and one engineer to examine its new assigned sector. Small work parties for each division were to be organized by pulling a few key elements out of the line and stopping all returning convalescents and furloughed soldiers to provide the bulk of the manpower. Each division and corps artillery commander was tasked to create a new defensive fire plan to be forwarded to army headquarters no later than 1 March.[3]

As the divisional working parties took over responsibility for the new line, the army's engineers moved back into the salient to begin laying minefields, constructing major switchlines for temporary stops during the retreat, erecting new bridges, and placing a complete secondary telephone network into operation. This net was a critical component of operational security for the withdrawal: Model had personally forbidden the mention of Operation Buffalo in any radio traffic, and the actual retreat was to be conducted—as much as possible—only through telephonic orders.

Simultaneously, the Ninth Army stepped up antipartisan operations. As crowded with German units as the Rzhev area appeared when looking at the tactical maps, in reality partisans and Red Army soldiers cut off from their units inhabited large sections of forest and swamp during the various Soviet offensives. A February Ninth Army intelligence report suggested that as many as 12,000 armed Soviets might be lurking to ambush German retreating columns. Thus, XXXIX Panzer Corps supervised a two-week antipartisan operation that employed the SS Cavalry Division, elements of four other divisions, and an unsavory array of smaller SS, Police, and Russian volunteer units. Final reports claimed the "elimination" of 3,000 "partisans," a figure of speech that almost always referred to the number of corpses counted at the end of the fighting. The reports also tacitly admitted that most of the partisans had been unarmed: the 3,000 Russian casualties had between them just 277 rifles, 41 pistols, 61 machine guns, 17 mortars, 9 antitank rifles, and 16 small artillery pieces of various makes and calibers. Typical rather than exceptional were descriptions like that of Corporal Hans Waigel, 4th Panzer Division:

> The other day, our patrol caught an old man and a six-year-old sprog with a supply of salt and potatoes. They claimed they were using it to catch fish, but they had something else in mind entirely [passing on the food to partisans]. We didn't keep them prisoner long, but set them free—through death. I personally haven't had the pleasure of shooting anyone yet, but would do so with joy.[4]

Such brutality was hardly unusual for German antipartisan operations, but in Operation Buffalo there was a new twist. Probably thinking back to his World War I experiences when the German army retired to the Hindenburg Line, Model personally ordered all male inhabitants evacuated from the salient (lest they be immediately conscripted into the Red Army), all foodstuffs confiscated, all wells poisoned, and at least two dozen villages burnt to the ground. Combined with the bloody nature of the antipartisan operations, these orders would eventually be responsible for the Soviet Union labeling Model as a war criminal.[5]

As the withdrawal approached, the special staff divided the Ninth Army's rear area into three main sectors and then subdivided the *Erkundungsstaebe* into Sector Staffs A, B, and C to control all vehicular and foot movements once the army commenced its retrograde. Each sector staff was placed under an infantry regiment commander and consisted of artillery, antitank, engineer, and signals officers, each responsible for a specific facet of the move. Corps and division commanders received a sternly worded letter of instructions notifying them that they modified or failed to comply with the directives of these officers at their peril. Meanwhile, each corps commander also received instructions to assign all smaller independent units in their areas to the supervision of the nearest division commander, and division commanders were told to prepare mobile, company-sized assault troops (*Stosstruppen*) to deal with any Soviet incursions during the march.[6]

The movement, which began on 1 March, obviously caught the Soviets by surprise. Nothing more serious than tentative probes disrupted any division's movement, each switchline was occupied and then abandoned with serious enemy pressure, and the final line was reached and manned within two weeks. By the time Model and von Gersdorff visited Berlin, the Ninth Army had lumbered backward in some sectors more than sixty miles, taking no serious casualties and losing virtually no equipment. The forces freed by Operation Buffalo, in combination with the divisions transferred to Russia from France during the past two months, in large measure compensated for the loss of the Sixth Army at Stalingrad and made it possible (for the final time during the war) for Hitler and OKH to contemplate a choice between retaking the initiative with an offensive or awaiting the next Soviet attack with a substantial reserve to thwart it. Hitler wasted little time in deciding which course to pursue: The preliminary operations order for "Operation Citadel" (*Zitadelle*), which envisioned a two-pronged offensive by Army Groups Center and South to wipe out the Soviet concentration of troops and tanks in the Kursk salient, was dated 13 March.

Before considering the Kursk offensive, however, it is important to place Operation Buffalo in perspective. Walther Model is most frequently limned as a master of tactical improvisation, and that reputation is well deserved. What separated Model from some of his peers, however, was his equal capability in supervising and conducting detailed operations and logistical planning. Nothing about Operation Buffalo was improvised; the Ninth Army's timetables and march route designations would have won the approval of Field Marshal von Schlieffen several decades earlier. While it can be argued that much of the credit for this logically rests with the operations staff rather than the army commander, such an assertion ignores the impact that any army commander has on the selection and training of his staff. In February and March 1943 the Ninth Army had a first-rate staff because Model had built one. This is not to say that he was beloved (his foul tongue and irate temperament prohibited that response) or that he did not often drive the staff to distraction with his long absences from headquarters. What Operation Buffalo underscores is the often forgotten truth that, first and foremost, Model had been trained as a General Staff officer.

As either a staff officer or a frontline tactician, Model read Hitler's final Operation Citadel directive on 15 April with considerable skepticism. The order opened with these fateful words:

> I have decided to conduct Citadel, the first offensive of the year, as soon as the weather permits. This attack is of the utmost importance. It must be executed quickly. It must seize the initiative for us in the spring and summer. Therefore, all preparations must be conducted with great circumspection and enterprise. The best

formations, the best weapons, the best commanders, and great stocks of ammunition must be committed in the main efforts. Each commander and man must be impressed with the decisive significance of this operation. The victory at Kursk must be a signal to all the world.[7]

The Ninth Army's headquarters would be shifted to the Orel sector and inserted on the northern face of the Kursk bulge, between the Second Panzer and Second Armies. For his attack south toward Kursk, Model would control fourteen infantry divisions, six panzer divisions, and one panzergrenadier division, to be supplemented by the new PzKw V Panthers, PzKw VI Tigers, Ferdinand heavy assault guns, radio-controlled tanks, hundreds of pieces of heavy artillery, and hundreds of aircraft. OKH promised that manpower and equipment shortfalls would be addressed in short order and that Model would have at least two weeks to integrate replacement soldiers and vehicles into his formations. The attack would take place on 15 May.

Model balked. Lieutenant Colonel Buntrock's intelligence-gathering operations and Luftwaffe photographic reconnaissance convinced him within days that neither Hitler nor the operations staff at OKH understood the depth of the Soviet defenses he faced, nor the extent to which Army General Konstantin K. Rokossovsky's Central Front had been reinforced. Buntrock's reports placed Rokossovsky's strength in mid-May at 31 rifle divisions, 1,200 guns, 200 multiple rocket-launchers, and 1,500 tanks—a two-to-one superiority over the Ninth Army in nearly every category. Worse still, the promised replacements and reinforcements arrived in a trickle rather than a flood. By 16 May only an average of 378 new soldiers or returning convalescents had reached each of Model's divisions, his artillery park was 35 percent below authorized strength, his infantry divisions were 2,000 vehicles below establishment, and several of his so-called panzergrenadier battalions could move only by foot or horse-drawn wagon. The Ninth Army had received sufficient tanks to bring its total strength up to roughly 800 AFVs, but not more than half a dozen of these vehicles were the new, heavy Tigers, and promises of Panthers remained just that: empty promises.[8]

These grim realities caused Model to present Hitler with an extremely gloomy report of his army's chances on 3 May. Buttressed by aerial photographs of prepared Soviet antitank positions and trench lines, Model advanced a direct argument that the offensive should be postponed by at least a month, during which time his army would have to receive the reinforcements thus far lacking. His assessment became the centerpiece for discussion in a critical meeting between Hitler and his senior commanders. Present were Kurt Zeitzler (chief of the Army General Staff), Albert Speer (armaments minister), Heinz Guderian (inspector general of panzer troops), and the two affected army group commanders, Hans von Kluge and Erich von Manstein. Neither Zeitzler, von Kluge, nor von Manstein agreed with the idea of a postponement, but Model's arguments were, in the final analysis, impossible to refute. Reluctantly, Hitler ordered the offensive postponed until mid-June.[9]

Although Model's position was based on thorough research and sound reasoning, delaying Citadel into mid-June (which eventually became early July) was a fatal error. What the Germans failed to factor into their decision was the unpalatable reality that Soviet strength in the Kursk salient was growing much faster than the Wehrmacht could muster the forces to attack it. In April Rokossovsky's Central Front had deployed only 538,480 men, 920 tanks, 7,860 guns, and 660 aircraft; by mid-May the figures in these categories had increased at least to the numbers Model cited in his report. Unfortunately for the Germans, in early July Rokossovsky deployed 711,575 men (not counting STAVKA reserves), 1,785 AFVs, 12,453 guns, and 1,050 aircraft. Model had gained an additional 200 AFVs, but his strength relative to that of the Red Army had actually declined by 500 vehicles. Likewise, in the time it took OKH to reinforce Model with an additional 362 guns between 15 May and 1 July, STAVKA sent Rokossovsky nearly 6,000. A similar situation existed on Army Group South's front.[10]

Army Group Center's operations officer, Colonel Peter von der Groeben, argued immediately after the war that Model had not intended his report to delay the offensive but to scuttle it. Von der Groeben suggested that Model was attempting to manipulate Hitler into a series of delays that would put off the attack for so long that the Soviets would lose patience and launch their own offensive. This would give von Kluge, von Manstein, and Model the opportunity they all wanted to fight a defensive battle rather than an offensive one. To support this contention von der Groeben noted that Model had a series of defensive switchlines built throughout the Orel region, even in the rear area of the neighboring Second Panzer Army. Such positions, the operations officer argued, would only become necessary in the event of repelling a Soviet offensive. Such an interpretation remains speculative, though imminently plausible.[11]

Model conducted most of his detailed tactical planning for Operation Citadel during the last two weeks of June. (Another potential supporting argument for von der Groeben's position is that Model did not commence such planning until convinced he could not argue Hitler out of the attack.) Part of the reason for this delay was that Model took personal leave in May after having held temporary command of Army Group South while von Manstein did the same during March. In Model's absence, command of the Ninth Army (under a variety of alternate designations designed to fool Soviet military intelligence) usually fell to General of Infantry Walther Weiss, who assumed responsibility for a large-scale antipartisan sweep through Army Group Center's rear areas. Partisan activity had grown so bold, conceded von der Groeben, that "the main supply route from Bryansk to Orel could be traveled intermittently and in convoys only." On 16 March, therefore, the Ninth

Army (as *Gruppe* Weiss) kicked off "Operation Gypsy Baron" (*Zigeuner Baron*), a three-week antipartisan sweep that employed the 4th and 18th Panzer Divisions, the 10th Panzergrenadier Division, the 7th and 292nd Infantry Divisions, and the 102nd Hungarian Light Infantry Division. Successfully rounding up (and executing) several thousand partisans and Jews (but capturing relatively few weapons), Army Group Center announced the operation as a success, but von der Groeben himself was less pleased:

> Unfortunately, the anti-partisan operation consumed time and resulted in considerable losses, especially in motor vehicles. Although it can be argued that the spearhead divisions participating in this operation did receive valuable training while engaging in "brush warfare," this experience could by no means be considered sufficient to prepare them for the kind of fighting they would have to do in open terrain, assaulting prepared Soviet positions.[12]

This last point was the key to Model's tactical problem. Soviet defenses along the north face of the Kursk salient had become so deep that he did not believe that the typical "blitz" attack by his panzer divisions would carry them through into open country—at least not without sustaining losses so heavy as to render effective exploitation impossible. Thus, Model intended to breach Rokossovsky's lines with an infantry attack, heavily supported by heavy tanks, assault guns, artillery, and aircraft. Of the eight mobile divisions potentially available to the Ninth Army, only the weakest—the 20th Panzer Division—would be committed in the initial assault; instead, the brunt would fall on eight infantry divisions. (This approach was precisely the reverse of that employed in Army Group South by von Manstein, who threw all of his panzer divisions into battle on the first day, risking heavy tank casualties in exchange for a potential quick breakthrough.)[13]

The main effort of the Ninth Army's attack would therefore fall in the XLVII Panzer Corps' sector between the villages of Gnilez and Butyrki—where lay the boundary line, Buntrock's intelligence suggested, separating the Soviet Thirteenth and Seventieth Armies. The XLVII Panzer Corps (led by General of Panzer Troops Joachim Lemelsen, a relative newcomer to Model and his methods) would attack on the first day with the 6th Infantry and 20th Panzer Divisions, holding in reserve the much stronger 2nd and 9th Panzer Divisions to enter the battle when Rokossovsky's defenses had been penetrated. In a supporting attack on Lemelsen's left flank, the XLI Panzer Corps (led by General of Panzer Troops Josef Harpe) would throw the 86th and 292nd Infantry Divisions forward against the high ground near Ponyriy, while holding the 18th Panzer Division in reserve. On Harpe's immediate left, the XXIII Corps (led by General of Infantry Johannes Freissner) would conduct a secondary attack against Malo-Archangelsk with the 78th Sturm and 216th Infantry Divisions. On the right of Lemelsen's main effort (*Schwerpunkt*), the XLVI Panzer Corps (led by General of Infantry Hans Zorn) would push forward with the 7th, 31st, 102nd, and 258th Infantry Divisions. Three divisions— the 10th Panzergrenadier and the 4th and 12th Panzer—remained under army group control as the decisive exploitation force. In the preliminary planning von Kluge did not expect to release them to Model until after his own panzer divisions had gained freedom of maneuver behind Central Front's defensive line.[14]

Model's plan was logical but risky. Even by 5 July his infantry divisions remained far below established strength: Exactly one infantry division in the Ninth Army was rated at the highest offensive level, and only four were deemed suitable "for limited offensive action." Moreover, the Ninth Army's infantry—even the veterans—lacked experience in conducting set-piece attacks against prepared positions. Worse still, if Model centered the attack on his infantry and took prohibitive losses during the first two days of battle, he might find himself forced to fall back on the panzer divisions anyway.[15]

What Model and his staff devoutly hoped was that the lumbering 82-ton Ferdinands, the Tigers mounting their 88mm guns, and swarms of StG III assault guns would provide his assault parties with enough of an advantage to offset their slender numbers. That was why Ninth Army headquarters watched tank and assault gun deliveries so closely as summer approached. The results were disappointing: Between 12 and 27 June, 118 PzKw IVs and 11 Tigers arrived, but of these 60 had to be assigned to the 5th Panzer Division, which formed the Second Panzer Army's reserve and was not participating in the offensive. By 6 July another 30 PzKw IVs had reached Orel, yet again they went to the 8th Panzer Division, held in army group reserve. Despite repeated promises, every single Panther was diverted at the last minute to Army Group South.[16]

Model continued to argue his case against the attack as structured to anyone who would listen. Unfortunately, beyond a sympathetic (but hardly influential) Guderian, Model had so infuriated other key players during the May conclave that neither Zeitzler nor von Kluge had any particular interest in acting as his audience, and Hitler—though willing repeatedly to postpone the offensive—remained committed to launching it eventually. That being the case, the Ninth Army's commander reverted to his traditional pattern of making life miserable for those around him. He rose before dawn and fell asleep around midnight, only after consuming several glasses of wine. During the long days Model continually harassed Elverfeldt and the army operations staff, demanding detailed technical reports on a whim or changing his entire attack lineup when sudden inspiration hit during one of his many visits to the front.

At other times his wrath fell upon the field commanders, as General of Panzer Troops Joachim Lemelsen, commanding the XLVII Panzer Corps and therefore the spearhead attack, discovered in late June. Having had problems with the new, heavy tanks and assault guns getting bogged down crossing muddy streambeds, Lemelsen's staff conceived the idea of removing the turrets from two or three

of the older PzKw IIIs and IVs in order to convert them into improvised recovery vehicles. Extraordinarily sensitive to his deficiency in
armored strength vis-à-vis the Russians, Model blew up, demanding that Lemelsen replace the turrets immediately. What should
have been handled quietly between staff officers instead became a
semiofficial public reprimand of a key officer just days before the
offensive opened.[17] Such was life in the Ninth Army when its commander was disgruntled; small wonder then that his staff and subordinates longed for the final attack orders so that Model would
finally concentrate his fury on the Russians.

They had to wait until 5 July.

9

CONFLAGRATION AT
KURSK AND OREL

The Ninth Army:
July to December 1943

IN THE TRADITIONAL, LACONIC FASHION OF GERMAN WAR diaries, an anonymous officer in Lieutenant General Güntherr von Kluge's 292nd Infantry Division recorded the start of Operation Citadel:

0110 [5 July 1943]—Artillery fire began to range a steady and heavy barrage against the main enemy battle line in the woodline, and the enemy rear areas along the line of Glebovo-Kamenka for two hours. . . . From deserter statements we knew that the Russians were expecting the attack, and were observing as our engineers went out to clear the minefields. . . . At 0330 the main barrage began raining down fire on the enemy trench system—sadly, this later turned out to have been ineffective because the Russians were

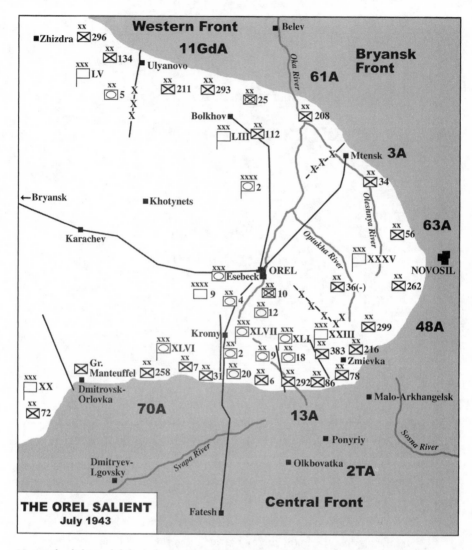

Not only did Model face the prospect of breaking open formidable Soviet defenses in front of Kursk, but in July 1943 the Orel salient—his rear area—could hardly have been said to be secure.

so deeply dug in. . . . Nonetheless, our infantry and engineers went
forward confident of victory.[1]

This entry captures several elements critical for understanding
the battle of Kursk. First, it is important to recognize that the artillery noted by the staff officer at 1:10 A.M. (0110) was not in fact
the preliminary German ranging fire but a preemptive Soviet barrage ordered by General Konstantin K. Rokossovsky to disrupt his
enemies during the final minutes of their attack preparation. That
the Russian counterpreparation could be mistaken in the sector
immediately adjacent to Model's *Schwerpunkt* for outgoing
friendly fire suggests that even officers at division headquarters in
the XLI Panzer Corps were not familiar with the fire plans of
neighboring corps and divisions. It also suggests that the conclusions reached by the Red Army General Staff the following year—
that "the primary mass of artillery fire was directed at suppressing
enemy batteries, and this was achieved," with the result that "the
enemy offensive was delayed for almost two hours"—is highly suspect.[2] In other words, at Kursk (perhaps even more so than in other
battles) even primary sources and eyewitness accounts have to be
examined as carefully as those German assault engineers crawling
through the dark scrutinized every suspicious mound of dirt.
Quite literally, combatants at Kursk—up to the highest levels—did
not always know what they were seeing.

This observation should be supplemented by the fact that the
vast majority of research and writing—from both German and Soviet perspectives—has focused on the southern front of the Kursk
salient, to the continued detriment of our understanding of the nu-
ances of the battle that matched Model's Ninth Army against
Rokossovsky's Central Front from 5 to 10 July.[3] The definitive narrative of this fighting has yet to be published for a variety of reasons, chief among them the capture and/or destruction of most of
the Ninth Army's headquarters records by the Red Army during
the summer of 1944. The Ninth Army war diary and many parallel

documents at corps level are not among those held by the German *Bundesarchiv* or the U.S. National Archives. This has left historians seeking to re-create the battle heavily dependent on fragmentary records at OKH and division level, situation maps, and postwar narratives.

Fortunately for the purpose of better understanding Walther Model's personal role in the battle, a key document has survived: the rough "notes for the war diary" (*Notz fur Kriegtagebuch*) kept in penciled longhand at army headquarters, which detail the army commander's movements and decisions during the first two days of the offensive. Some portions, such as the entries for the earliest hours of 5 July 1943, are either so smeared or so faint as to be virtually undecipherable, but what remains—when supplemented by other sources—provides an unprecedented look at the hour-by-hour activities of a German army commander in the midst of a critical battle, as well as incredible insight into Model's idiosyncratic command style.[4]

Model appears to have left his headquarters around 5:30 A.M. on 5 July—or just as soon as the main artillery preparation began to wind down. Accompanied by his personal aide, a small guard, and a single radio truck, he first visited the headquarters of Joachim Lemelsen's XLVI Panzer Corps for a report on the progress made by the 20th Panzer and 6th Infantry Divisions in the main attack toward Kashara. Following that briefing, he drove east to XLI Panzer Corps headquarters, where the 292nd Infantry Division had gone forward to secure the 6th Infantry's flank and ultimately widen the breach.[5]

The early indications appeared cautiously favorable. Though sustaining heavier casualties than expected, Lieutenant General Heinz Grossmann's 6th Infantry scored critical tactical successes with both attacking regiments against the 47th Rifle Regiment of Colonel V. N. Dzhandzhgava's 15th Rifle Division. Supported by the heavy Ferdinand tanks of Panzerjäger Regiment 656, massive Luftwaffe sorties, and other reinforcements, Grenadier Regiment 18 crossed the Oka

River and seized the village of Jasnaya Polyana by 7:00 A.M. Grenadier Regiment 58, similarly supported, also traversed the Oka and captured Novi Chutor. Further to the right, Major General Mortimer von Kessel's 20th Panzer Division waded into a complex tangle of minefields, antitank positions, and concealed Russian fighting positions, but reported to corps headquarters that by 6:30 A.M. Panzergrenadier Regiments 59 and 112 had forced their way two kilometers into the 47th Rifle Regiment's defenses.[6]

At the headquarters of Josef Harpe's XLI Panzer Corps, Model also received what appeared to be positive news. Grenadier Regiment 508 of the 292nd Infantry Division had overrun its first objective, but then bogged down in a previously undiscovered minefield. By 9:00 A.M. the regiments of I Battalion had come under heavy counterattack by reserve elements of Colonel A. B. Barinov's 81st Rifle Division. What pleased Model about this increasingly bitter fighting, however, was that Harpe had already acted on his own initiative to order Panzer Regiment 101 of the 18th Panzer Division out of his second-line units to reinforce the drive toward Oserki. This represented the kind of decisionmaking that Model liked to see in his subordinates.[7]

By 10:30 A.M., however, when Model arrived back at army headquarters, the map briefing by his own staff painted a far less optimistic picture. In the 6th Infantry Division's sector, the 322nd Rifle Regiment had already moved up from its reserve position to launch a series of bloody counterattacks supported by heavy mortar fire against both Grenadier Regiments 18 and 58, while the 20th Panzer Division's attack had completely stalled. Reinforcements could not be fed quickly into the fighting because the engineers had lagged behind schedule in clearing safe approaches through the enemy minefields. At this point Model appeared—for the first time but not the last—unhappy with Lemelsen's performance, for the corps commander had neither issued revised tactical orders to his spearhead division, committed any reserves, nor modified his artillery fire support plan.[8]

Model as usual took matters into his own hands prior to driving off for a personal visit to his other corps headquarters. He telephoned the army's senior artillery commander, ruthlessly diverting almost every available army artillery battalion away from supporting the subsidiary attacks by XXIII and XLVI Panzer Corps to lay additional fire into the contested sectors on Harpe's and Lemelsen's front. Next he ordered the Ninth Army's senior engineer to advance several additional companies of combat engineers into the XLVII Panzer Corps sector to speed up the mine-clearing process behind the 6th Infantry Division.

Two hours of driving were required to reach the headquarters of General of Infantry Hans Zorn's XLVI Panzer Corps. Arriving at 2:00 P.M., Model waved off a corps-level briefing and demanded to be escorted forward for a personal view of the supporting attacks by the 7th and 31st Infantry Divisions on the right flank of the 20th Panzer Division. This turned out to be impossible, for these assaults had also bogged down in Russian minefields, and the corps staff could not guarantee a safe passage to the front. Before leaving after thirty minutes, however, Model pointedly reminded Zorn that he was responsible for keeping the Soviet Seventieth Army from hitting the XLVII Panzer Corps flank.[9]

Ninety more minutes passed as Model motored laterally back across the entire front to General of Infantry Johannes Freissner's XXIII Corps, where he discovered that the attack toward Malo-Archangelsk by the 78th Sturm and 216th Infantry Divisions had also failed to reach their initial tactical objectives. Freissner warned his army commander that, given Model's decision to remove most of his artillery support, no further progress could be expected the rest of the day.[10]

Disgruntled but unable to argue the point, Model then left for a second visit to Harpe's XLI Panzer Corps, arriving at 4:30 P.M. Thanks to Model's commitment of additional tanks, Harpe had made progress toward Oserki, but admitted that he would not reach the town before dusk. The two men spent twenty minutes poring over the situation maps to analyze the prospects for a continuation of the attack on 6 July. Harpe proposed that since he had already fed the 18th Panzer's tanks into the battle, Model should consider reinforcing the rapidly depleting infantry of the 6th and 292nd Infantry Divisions with Panzergrenadier Regiments 51 and 101, respectively, on 6 July. Granting that this would essentially dismember the 18th Panzer, Harpe argued that the division's lack of motorized transport made it the least useful panzer division for exploiting any breakthroughs, while its dismounted infantry could perform a critical service by assisting in cracking the second line of Rokossovsky's defenses. Neither agreeing nor disagreeing, Model took the issue under advisement, promising a decision in time to move the troops up if necessary.[11]

No such ambiguity existed when the army commander had his second conversation at XLVII Panzer Corps at 5:00 P.M., and the contrast between Model's handling of Lemelsen and Harpe was stark. Model informed rather than consulted Lemelsen about his decision (reached somewhere during his day of long drives) to commit the 2nd and 9th Panzer Divisions to the battle the next day despite the fact that these two units had been intended for use only when a complete break in the Soviet defenses had been achieved. He then read Lemelsen's proposed battle orders for 6 July and directed multiple changes without discussion. This took Model only half an hour, but before he left XLVII Panzer Corps headquarters he also issued a series of armywide orders about assuming the defensive for the night, including details about artillery blocking fires and the security lines to be employed by panzer battalions. Later notations in the record make clear, significantly, that the only staff not to receive these orders were at Model's own headquarters.[12]

Finally back at army headquarters around 7:00 P.M., an exhausted Model spent an hour closeted with his chief of staff, Colonel Harald Freiherr von Elverfeldt, and the operations staff, specifically covering the issue of whether to devote the bulk of available Luftwaffe support the next day exclusively to XLVII

Panzer Corps or split the sorties between Harpe and Lemelsen. As much as Model would probably have preferred by this point that the main attack be under Harpe's command, he could not overcome his staff's insistence that the best prospect of a quick breakthrough remained in Lemelsen's sector. Thus, the air support went to XLVII Panzer Corps, but almost as an afterthought Model approved Harpe's proposal to split up the elements of the 18th Panzer Division between two infantry divisions.[13]

Model's final act of the day occurred at 8:40 P.M., when his harried operations officers interrupted him after a brief conversation with Field Marshal von Kluge at Army Group Center as he was having a few drinks and preparing for bed. They had just discovered Model's long spate of orders issued at XLVII Panzer Corps headquarters three hours earlier and found themselves forced either to ask their commander to repeat them or to admit to the rest of the army that they had been left in the dark. With his usual taciturn grunt, Model enlightened them.

Thus ended Model's first day at Kursk. Though he remained pessimistic about the overall chances for a strategic success from Operation Citadel, he still believed that he had secured a reasonably deep lodgment in the Russian defensive system, that he had forced Rokossovsky to commit his reserves early in the battle, and that a breakthrough to operational freedom for his panzer divisions would be possible on 6 July. He was wrong on all three counts. Only the 6th and 292nd Infantry Divisions had even made it completely through the first of Central Front's three defensive lines, and those penetrations were narrow. The Soviets had not yet felt themselves forced to send all of the front's strategic reserves into action, though the Second Tank Army and several artillery divisions had been moved up. Finally, as Model would discover over the next four days, adding more tanks to the battlefield would not come close to guaranteeing a breakout.

The question of armor on the northern front is crucial, for that has remained one of the main criticisms of Model's conduct of the offensive. At midday Grossmann had felt that his 6th Infantry Division was on the verge of cracking the Soviet defenses, as he explained after the war: "If, at that point, one additional Panzer-Division had rolled through, we would probably have reached the objective of Kursk, for the enemy was totally surprised and locally weak. Valuable time was lost which the enemy used to throw in his reserves." Walther Nehring among others picked up this argument after the war; in his history of the German panzer forces Guderian's former chief of staff observed, "Of the six mechanized divisions in the northern army, five were in reserve. That already gave a decisive advantage to the Red Army. It would have been expedient to have placed two armored divisions forward."[14]

Though Model's assault plan arguably had its faults, failure to send sufficient armor forward on the first day was not one of them. According to reports on 1 July, the Ninth Army controlled 920 tanks and assault guns. Admittedly, in using the 20th Panzer Division from the start and allowing Panzer Regiment 101 of the 18th Panzer to be funneled forward during the day, Model employed his two weakest panzer divisions in the assault. The 20th Panzer Division at best contained fifty tanks; the 18th Panzer Division boasted only sixty-nine. But Model also engaged Panzerjäger Regiment 656 as well as Assault Gun Battalions 177 and 244 in the XLI Panzer Corps sector; these units totaled 233 tanks and assault guns. To support the XLVII Panzer Corps attack, Model used two companies (all available) of Tiger Battalion 505, plus Assault Gun Battalions 245 and 904; these three battalions deployed 93 armored fighting vehicles. The supporting attack by XLVI Panzer Corps included 40 tanks and assault guns, while the XXIII Corps controlled 62 assault guns. In total then the Ninth Army placed 542 armored fighting vehicles (57.7 percent of the total available strength) into the fight on 5 July. At the *Schwerpunkt* in Lemelsen's sector, this meant an AFV density of 18 vehicles per kilometer of front, and in Harpe's case the theoretical density reached 25 vehicles per kilometer after the commitment of Panzer Regiment 101.[15]

Several hundred additional panzers would enter the battle between 6 and 8 July, but the stark reality was that all this accomplished was jammed traffic on the German side—a target-rich environment for Soviet antitank gunners and ground-attack aircraft. The attack front was simply too narrow to allow the employment of regular panzer tactics. Put in different terms, the Soviets effectively neutralized the German advantage in tactical movement, leaving success on the field dependent almost entirely on the weight of fire that could be delivered, and that was a game the Wehrmacht could not win. An officer from I Battalion, Panzer Regiment 35 (4th Panzer Division), explained the situation in stark tactical detail in his after-action report:

> The Russians had prepared defensive positions on all commanding and tactically important terrain features which tanks only had to be driven into in order to be used as armored machine gun and cannon nests. . . . Silencing the dug-in tanks was difficult because they were very well camouflaged and their guns were very close to the ground. The long width of the position didn't allow it to be enveloped and attacked from the rear with the available forces. The Russian tanks, especially the T34, KW-1 and KW-2, are very well suited for such employment because of their thick armor and good weapons. When it isn't possible to attack from the rear, they can be destroyed only with the cooperation of heavy artillery and Stukas.[16]

Could other tactics have produced better results? That seems highly unlikely given the fixed parameters of time and attack frontage with which Model had to work. If the Ninth Army was to batter its way through to the high ground it was necessary to secure as the prerequisite for a panzer thrust toward Kursk, a tank-supported infantry assault with plenty of artillery fire and sustained Luftwaffe sorties represented the best chance. That such chances were slim indeed can be charged at least partly against Model, who—like Adolph Hitler and Army Chief of Staff Kurt

Zeitzler—consistently underestimated the strength of the Red Army buildup in the Kursk salient. On the other hand, a number of witnesses testify to the fact that even in July Model did not want to attack at all. Like Erich von Manstein in the south, Model appears to have believed that the best course for the Germans in the summer of 1943 consisted of waiting for the inevitable Soviet attack and defeating it. The man who had held the Rzhev salient for over a year with understrength infantry divisions backed only by a handful of tanks would hardly have found it difficult to defend the Orel salient with nearly one thousand armored vehicles at his disposal.

Of the fighting on 6 July historian Franz Kurowski has commented, "This second day of major combat was so filled with confusing battle impressions that it is scarcely possible to come up with a coherent account." Much of the fighting can be summed up in statements from the War Diaries of the units at the sharp end of the Ninth Army's assault wedge. "Enemy resistance today strengthened hour by hour," reported an officer of the 292nd Infantry Division, while the war diary of Panzer Battalion 21 (20th Panzer Division) mentioned harassing artillery fire before dawn, strong antitank fire from fixed positions, and multiple tanks lost to mines, all occurring before "the Russian counter-strike set in with strong forces. Flashes from many artillery batteries could be seen far off on the horizon. . . . At the same time, several waves of enemy tanks, with infantry riding on them, charged toward our attack point."[17]

By 3:30 A.M. Lemelsen's heavily reinforced XLVII Panzer Corps units, now deploying over six hundred armored fighting vehicles, began moving forward to attack. On the left Grossmann's 6th Infantry Division, now supported by a panzergrenadier regiment from the 18th Panzer and the eighty-nine tanks of Lieutenant General Walther Scheller's 9th Panzer Division, had the assignment of swinging past Saburovka to drive toward Hill 274 and Olkovatka. (Their left flank would be secured by the advance of the XLI

Panzer Corps' 292nd and 86th Infantry Divisions pushing toward Ponyriy.) In the center one of the strongest units available to the Ninth Army, Lieutenant General Vollrath Luebbe's 2nd Panzer Division (with 140 organic tanks and 150 attached assault guns), would drive directly past Gnilez and Bobrik toward Hill 272 and Teploye. Von Kessel's 20th Panzer Division and the 31st Infantry Division (XLVI Panzer Corps) were to advance along Luebbe's right flank. The subsidiary attacks by XLVI Panzer Corps toward Nikolskoye and XXIII Corps toward Malo-Archangelsk had been scaled back to little more than demonstrations in order to concentrate artillery and air support behind the main effort. Thus, on 6 July Model had narrowed his attack frontage by one-third, while increasing his commitment of armor by 50 percent.[18]

Model began his day at 4:20 A.M. with a map orientation at army headquarters in which his operations staff outlined the reorganization and reconcentration of assault units in the XXIII, XLI Panzer, and XLVI Panzer Corps sectors. Having only managed about three hours of sleep, Model appeared more surly than usual, brusquely demanding several last-minute changes in the lineup for several battalions in Harpe's XLI Panzer Corps. As these alterations were being telephoned directly to Harpe, Model then examined the morning fire plan with his army's senior artillery officer, again making significant changes in the barrages ordered in support of the XXIII Corps' 292nd Infantry Division. At 5:20 A.M. Lemelsen telephoned Model with concerns about the weak armored strength of the 20th Panzer Division, specifically requesting that at least one company of Tiger Battalion 505 be transferred from XXIII Corps to him. Model approved the idea, but told his staff to move two companies instead of one. (Unfortunately, the lateness of this interchange meant that even in the best possible scenario the Ferdinands in question would be out of the battle transiting behind the front lines until nearly midday.)[19]

The army commander then began examining the number of replacements—both officers and enlisted men—available to be funneled into the assault divisions to make good the losses on 5 July. There appear to have been only 200 to 300 men per division in the replacement pools. Model insisted on personally reviewing all of the officer assignments down to battalion and company level, much to the chagrin of his personnel officers, who had apparently already dispatched the men in question to their collection points. Ten minutes later, however, at about 5:30, the XLI Panzer Corps operations officer interrupted this process with a telephone call to army headquarters. He expressed Harpe's concern that Luftwaffe reconnaissance and his own forward observers had picked up signs of a potential large-scale counterattack by the Soviet Thirteenth Army. If this attack commenced prior to the German assault, XLI Panzer Corps argued, it would prevent the 292nd Infantry Division from protecting XLVI Panzer Corps' left flank. What Harpe apparently wanted—and got—was for Model to shift some artillery assets back to XLI Panzer Corps and to ensure that the bulk of the 18th Panzer Division would remain in his sector rather than being attached to the 6th Infantry Division, as Harpe himself had suggested the previous afternoon. Again Model agreed.[20]

At 5:40 Model picked up the telephone to call Field Marshal von Kluge at Army Group Center. He rehearsed his attack plan for the army group commander, confidently predicting that he would end the day by seizing the high ground around Ponyriy, Olkovatka, Kashara, and Teploye. Such success would, Model believed, take him through the crust of Rokossovsky's prepared defenses and place the Ninth Army in position to launch the main attack toward Kursk. Model's problem was that sending the 2nd and 9th Panzer Divisions to make the breach almost certainly guaranteed that these two units would be too chewed up for an immediate exploitation into the Soviet rear, leaving only the 4th Panzer Division unblooded for the advance toward Kursk. Plainly, Model told von Kluge, this was not a large enough force, so he asked the army group commander to release the 10th Panzergrenadier and 12th Panzer Divisions from his own reserve to be placed with 4th Panzer in a special exploitation group under direct control of Lieutenant General Hans-Karl Freiherr von Esebeck.[21]

For the moment von Kluge balked. The field marshal had to consider not only the Ninth Army's offensive toward Kursk but also the dangerous position of the Second Panzer Army, holding the long, winding front of the Orel salient, which secured Model's far left flank and rear. These divisions had been earmarked for the dual purpose of reinforcing Model's exploitation group and serving as an emergency strategic reserve behind both armies. Despite its name, the Second Panzer Army consisted almost exclusively of infantry divisions, except for the 5th Panzer Division (ninety-three tanks) and the 25th Panzergrenadier Division (despite the name lacking any tanks), and there were already indications that the Soviet Western and Bryansk Fronts had been massing large forces along the eastern face of the salient. If von Kluge approved the movement of these two divisions toward the Ninth Army, there would literally be no armored reserve behind the Second Panzer Army until the one hundred AFVs of the 8th Panzer Division reached his area of operations. Since the 8th Panzer was not due until 12 July, Model's request entailed substantial risk.

There was another consideration. Colonel General Rudolf Schmidt, commander of the Second Panzer Army since December 1941, had just been relieved of his command on suspicion of antigovernment sentiments. Technically—by seniority—this left General of Infantry Heinrich Clössner (LIII Corps) in command of the army. A fifty-four-year-old mediocrity, Clössner had seriously disappointed his superiors in 1941 as commander of the 25th Motorized Infantry Division, whose regiments never seemed to gel into a coherent fighting force. Unfortunately, Clössner was also senior to Model's corps commanders, which kept von Kluge from supplanting him by swapping headquarters. What the field marshal therefore appears to have told the Ninth Army commander was that he would let him have the two divisions on the condition that if the Soviets mounted a large-scale attack on the Orel salient,

Model would assume responsibility for both armies. Anxious to get the 10th Panzergrenadier and 12th Panzer started toward the front, Model instantly agreed. Before the conversation ended, von Kluge also advised the army commander that he would be coming forward to visit the front lines in XLVII Panzer Corps that morning, his undertone suggesting that he would make his final decision based upon what he saw on the ground. Hanging up, Model immediately telephoned Lemelsen's staff to make the necessary preparations to introduce another three divisions into the battle over the next twenty-four hours; almost as an afterthought, he alerted them to the field marshal's impending arrival.[22]

Breakfast was served after this last call. At 8:30 A.M. Model demanded that XLVI Panzer Corps provide updated strength reports for the 2nd, 9th, and 20th Panzer Divisions. During this telephone call Lemelsen's operations officer passed along the good news that von Kessel's 20th Panzer Division had just about fought its way into Gnilez (which in fact was cleared of Red Army forces by 9:00). Delighted, Model expressed his confidence that the day's fighting would finally see the breakthrough that had been denied on 5 July. What the XLVI Panzer Corps operations officer forgot to tell the army commander, however, was that his intelligence officer had determined that both the XVI and XIX Tank Corps of Lieutenant General A. G. Rodin's Second Tank Army had already moved into position immediately behind the hard-pressed Soviet front.[23]

Unaware of the impending Russian armored counterattack that was about to hit his spearhead units, Model made a final telephone call to the Ninth Army's chief engineer to discuss bridging the Oka River; he then hopped into his command vehicle at 8:45 for a tour of the front lines. The army commander intended to place himself much closer to the front lines, so he ordered his driver to bypass Lemelsen's headquarters and head directly to the command post of the 2nd Panzer Division. He reached Luebbe's headquarters around 10:00 A.M., just in time to witness the division commander performing part of his own final map orientation for regiment and battalion commanders. Luebbe's timing was bad, since Model, who apparently arrived just after Luebbe had briefed his subordinates on the intelligence regarding the arrival of Rodin's Second Tank Army, did not understand the context of the division commander's orders and considered them excessively cautious.[24]

Instead of raising this issue with Luebbe then, Model got back in his vehicle and motored to the headquarters of the 6th Infantry Division, where he found part of the XLVI Panzer Corps operations staff assisting in a similar map orientation. The primary difference was that General Grossmann's briefing was attended not only by Model but also by Lemelsen and von Kluge. It was here, about 10:20, that the Ninth Army commander finally found out what his own corps and division commanders had known for at least two hours about the presence of the Soviet Second Tank Army. His reaction to this news was not recorded in the notes. Plainly, however, the army group commander was impressed by the seriousness of the situation, for he gave his final approval to releasing the 10th Panzergrenadier and 12th Panzer Divisions.[25]

Owing probably to the threat of Russian aircraft, which had now begun appearing over the battlefield in significant numbers, Model's four-kilometer drive to the forward headquarters of von Kessel's 20th Panzer Division consumed at least one hour. There the army commander congratulated the division staff for capturing Gnilez and the apparently imminent fall of Bobrik. As this discussion continued the first reports of heavy Soviet tank attacks began to arrive from the front lines: As many as 150 T-34s were sighted lumbering toward German positions. As he began to direct defensive operations von Kessel pointedly asked his army commander when he could expect the promised Ferdinands from Tiger Battalion 505 to start arriving. Model did not have an answer; nor did a quick telephone call to army headquarters succeed in locating the heavy tanks.[26]

Leaving von Kessel to fight his battle, Model now headed back for the 2nd Panzer Division. His concerns appear to have been twofold. First, given what Model thought he knew about the strength of Rokossovsky's reserves, if large tank forces had concentrated against the 20th Panzer Division, this might well have created a corresponding weakness in front of the 2nd Panzer Division. If von Kessel could parry the tank attack with his own resources, Luebbe's division might be able to crack through the last defensive belt more easily. Conversely, Model also reasoned that excessive caution might keep the 2nd Panzer's commander from taking full advantage of the situation and that an extra pair of eyes looking over his shoulder might motivate Luebbe to act more aggressively.[27]

The army commander arrived at the forward command post of the 2nd Panzer Division at 1:00 P.M., where he remained for the next six hours. Later Model would have sharp words for Lemelsen with regard to Luebbe's conduct of operations, but the record uncharacteristically does not record him as having delivered these rebukes to the division commander in person.[28] There are two possible reasons for this. First, such information may in fact have been recorded in the finalized version of the Ninth Army's war diary; we shall know for sure when the Russians finally release it for the scrutiny of researchers. It is also conceivable, however, that Model became severely disenchanted with Luebbe's performance only in hindsight, when he began looking for scapegoats for the army's ultimate failure to break open the Soviet defenses.

This alternative explanation appears especially feasible in light of what the Ninth Army accomplished—or failed to accomplish—on 6 July. The 2nd Panzer Division could not force its way south to Olkovatka that afternoon; the best that Luebbe's panzers and panzergrenadiers could do was to repulse continuing attacks by the Second Tank Army while gaining about two kilometers and capturing Ssnova. Across the rest of XLVII Panzer Corps' front neither the 9th Panzer, 20th Panzer, nor 6th Infantry Divisions did any better. Moreover, the tenor of the fighting had changed in twenty-four hours. On 5 July the Ninth Army conducted an infantry attack supported by armor, gaining up to fourteen kilometers in some areas while losing 7,223 casualties; the following day the tanks and assault guns took the lead, meeting the Red Army counterattacks head to head and inching toward the day's tactical objectives. Gains on 6 July (except in XLI Panzer Corps' sector) were limited to roughly two kilometers, but total army casualties—2,996—dropped to less than half those sustained the previous day.[29] What was the connection between these two figures?

First consider the anomaly that Harpe's XLI Panzer Corps, which had reinforced the 292nd and 86th Infantry Divisions with additional ground troops rather than more AFVs, made better progress on 6 July than did Lemelsen's tank-heavy corps. Why? The war diary of the 292nd Infantry Division suggests strongly that the vulnerability of tanks and assault guns to the prepared Soviet antitank positions could be ameliorated only by accompanying each vehicle with at least a squad and sometimes a platoon of infantrymen. Further, all extant German reports indicate that when the Soviets threw tanks into the battle, they were always followed by large numbers of infantry. The simple fact of armored warfare was that tanks might surge ahead and seize an objective, but without infantry they could not hold it.

This explains a lot about the futile efforts of the 2nd, 9th, and 20th Panzer Divisions to push deeper into the Soviet defenses that afternoon. The war diary of Panzer Battalion 21 (20th Panzer Division) notes in passing that the tanks had fewer panzergrenadiers available in support during the second day of the offensive. From a panzer battalion's point of view, the day was a tactical success: The Red Army lost at least four tanks for every German vehicle hit or damaged, and without adequate infantry support, the Russians could not gain ground. (And it was a successful tank battle on the part of all three divisions: The Second Tank Army officially ad-

mitted to losing over ninety vehicles, sixty-nine of which were destroyed beyond recovery and repair. Irrevocable German tank and
assault gun losses in the XLVII Panzer Corps sector on 6 July are
difficult to isolate because of the vagaries of the reporting system
but appear to have been roughly twenty AFVs, with perhaps half
of those being write-offs.)[30]

Certainly Model, the former panzer division commander, understood the inherent paradox that in such a slugging match his armor
could not gain ground without infantry support. But if so, why did
he feed additional tanks rather than significantly more infantry
into the battle zone? The reason is relatively simple: The Ninth
Army possessed a sufficiency of panzers for Operation Citadel, but
nowhere near enough infantrymen. This was one of the reasons
that Model had repeatedly pressed Hitler and Zeitzler for a postponement of the offensive: He needed time to rebuild his shattered
infantry regiments and battalions. Discounting the four divisions of
the XX Corps (which had no role in the offensive), the Ninth Army
entered the battle for Kursk with only 68,747 combat troops. Each
of Model's infantry divisions averaged a "ration" strength of
11,134 and a "trench" strength of 3,296, as compared to the infantry divisions of Army Group South taking part in the offensive,
which boasted an average ration strength of 17,369 and a trench
strength of 6,344. Simply put, Model's infantry regiments (most of
which possessed only six battalions) jumped off into the battle at
little more than half the strength of their comrades to the south.[31]

Given that Model recognized the necessity for a strong infantry
attack on 5 July, this meant that he placed every available infantry
division in the front line, leaving only mobile divisions (which had
much smaller infantry components) in reserve. The 7,223 casualties suffered on 5 July on a statistical basis eliminated over 20 percent of the available infantry in the main attack sectors. Because
the Ninth Army had no infantry reserves worth mentioning,
Model had to change tactics on 6 July whether he wanted to do so
or not. The army having exceeded 10,000 casualties by dawn on 7

July, Model found himself in the unusual tactical situation of being better able to afford tank losses than dead or wounded grenadiers.

Further complicating the conduct of the battle on 6 July was Model's decision to remain at the 2nd Panzer Division throughout the afternoon. It is debatable exactly when his own army operations staff figured out the location of its wayward commander, but even knowing where Model had finally landed did little good. The forward command post of a division—even a panzer division—did not possess adequate signals equipment for an army commander to supervise fighting on a front now over thirty kilometers wide. This arrangement guaranteed that Model would receive critical information too late to act upon it and that any decisions he did make would be based on far less information than that available to his own headquarters. For example, word reached army headquarters at roughly 3:30 P.M. that the 20th Panzer Division had taken Bobrik and begun an advance out of Gnilez toward Podolyan. Had the 2nd or 9th Panzer Division been immediately ordered to lunge west instead of south—therefore attracting the attention of the XVI Tank Corps at a critical moment—von Kessel's attack might have gained ground fairly quickly. Unfortunately, the Ninth Army's operations staff lacked the authority to change either division's tactical objectives, and Lemelsen—after having been micromanaged by Model the previous day—seemed intent on not making any independent decisions. This information did not reach Model until after 4:00 because all the incoming telephone lines to the 2nd Panzer Division appear to have been tied up in the legitimate business of running the division. When alerted, Model realized that the moment had passed to divert any panzers toward the west, but he unwisely attempted at 4:30 to redirect the Ninth Army's artillery fire plan to provide greater support for von Kessel's attack. All this achieved was frustration and confusion as both the 6th Infantry and 9th Panzer Divisions briefly lost their artillery support without the 20th Panzer Division gaining it.[32]

Two hours later (about 6:30) Model telephoned his own headquarters for a report on the deployment plans for Lieutenant General Dietrich von Saucken's 4th Panzer Division, which was to enter the battle on 7 July. Apparently Model had decided from the front lines that von Saucken's division, which he had originally wanted to reinforce the 9th Panzer Division's axis of attack, would be better employed by passing through the 2nd Panzer Division's line. He also demanded to know the location of the errant Ferdinands from the XXIII Corps, whose presence he had suddenly decided would lead to an immediate breakthrough. The operations staff dutifully diverted the 4th Panzer Division's approach march but could not discover the whereabouts of the heavy tanks. (Later in the evening it would become apparent that they had never actually left the XXIII Corps' front, Freissner having declared them indispensable.)[33]

Sometime around 7:00 P.M. Model started back toward army headquarters but did not arrive for at least two hours, during which time nobody knew precisely where to find him. It turned out that Model had made an unscheduled stop at the headquarters of Lieutenant General Ernst Buffa's 12th Flak Division to discuss reinforcing XLVII Panzer Corps spearheads the next morning with the heavy antiaircraft guns of Flak Regiment 12. Unfortunately, because Buffa's communications ran directly through the 1st Flieger Division and Luftflotte Six rather than army headquarters, for the duration of this conference Model appeared to his own operations staff to have dropped off the map.[34]

Reaching Ninth Army headquarters about 9:30 P.M., Model finally received a comprehensive briefing on the day's attacks. The army commander again overruled his own operations staff, who reiterated the case for placing the 4th Panzer Division behind the 9th Panzer on the Olkovatka front. Instead, Model envisioned having the 18th Panzer Division reassembled from its constituent units to allow that division and the 9th Panzer to assume blocking positions near Ssnova, where Luftwaffe reconnaissance flights indicated that the XIX Tank Corps had massed. He would then shift the main focus of the attack farther west to the 2nd and 4th Panzer Divisions. Model's idea appears to have been to attack in an unexpected direction, at least to the extent that one could do so in such a constricted battlefield. The potential flaw in his design was that this left his two offensive groupings for 7 July (the 2nd and 4th Panzer Divisions attacking toward Teploye and the 292nd and 86th Infantry Divisions attempting to capture Ponyriy) striking out in opposite directions, with the connecting force between them ordered into a static defense. If the Soviets—especially Rodin at the Second Tank Army—figured out Model's tactic early enough in the day, they would enjoy almost unhindered lateral movement across the front to concentrate forces against the Ninth Army's assault elements either simultaneously or in succession.[35]

At 10:00 P.M. Model telephoned Army Group Center; von Kluge being unavailable, he discussed the situation with the field marshal's adjutant. About half an hour later he sat down with his chief of staff, Colonel Harald Freiherr von Elverfeldt, to hash out air support for the next morning. In keeping with his concept of diverging attacks toward Teploye and Ponyriy, Model directed a staggered commitment by the 1st Flieger Division. Sorties would support the 2nd and 4th Panzer Divisions in Lemelsen's sector from 5:00 to 7:00 A.M., then shift abruptly to support the 292nd and 86th Infantry Divisions in Harpe's sector from 7:00 to 12:00. After that, throughout the afternoon, available sorties would be placed at the disposal of Freissner's XXIII Corps for a renewed assault toward Malo-Archangelsk. This complicated arrangement required yet another reordering of the army's artillery plan, a process that took until well after midnight. (It was apparently then that Model also found out what had happened to the two companies of Ferdinands, which he now decided to leave with Freissner.) Model's final recorded order during 6 July was given at 10:45, when he reiterated his instructions to von Elverfeldt about placing the 9th and 18th Panzer Divisions in their blocking positions near Ssnova. He then finished the last of several glasses of wine and turned in for what again would be only about three hours of sleep.[36]

The anonymous notes detailing Model's travels end on 7 July, though the pattern is well established. The Ninth Army commander generally left his headquarters early in the morning and spent the bulk of his day driving back and forth between division and corps command posts. His operations staff understood that he would neither advise them of his proposed itinerary nor reappear until early evening. At least by 8 July the harassed staff officers could rely on Model spending most of his day somewhere in the XLVII Panzer Corps sector, and the surviving telephone logs for the Ninth Army during the first few days of Operation Citadel suggest that almost as many calls were made to track down the army commander as to inquire about conditions at the front. Although German command doctrine placed a high premium on officers "leading from the front," Model—like Heinz Guderian and Erwin Rommel, to name only two famous practitioners of the art—probably did not accrue sufficient advantage from his freewheeling tactics to offset the lack of efficiency that resulted from them.

The fighting on 7 July had cost the Ninth Army another 2,861 casualties, bringing the three-day total up to 13,080—plainly a loss rate that could not be sustained for very long (although losses in tanks and assault guns—still under fifty—and aircraft—only seventeen machines!—were much more modest). Conversely, Central Front had also sustained heavy losses. Even the best Soviet records tended to minimize losses, as Niklas Zetterling and Anders Frankson (the premier statistical researchers of the battle) have taken great pains to illustrate. Nonetheless, a legitimate estimate can be made that Rokossovsky's forces had suffered over 30,000 troop casualties, combined with the loss of more than 150 tanks and 185 aircraft.[37]

More importantly, the Germans *believed* that the Red Army had taken far more grievous wounds over the first seventy-two hours of the battle. Army headquarters estimated on the morning of 8 July that the Russians had lost more than 60,000 men, over 300 tanks, and at least as many aircraft. Matching these presumed losses against the Ninth Army's working estimate of Central Front's strength at the beginning of the offensive, the reason for Model's guarded optimism becomes clear: He thought that he had chewed up nearly half of the Soviet frontline infantry strength and over 20 percent of Rokossovsky's precious armored reserve.[38]

As Model had intended, two battles developed that day: XLVII Panzer Corps' attack toward Teploye and XLI Panzer Corps' continuing assault on Soviet positions at Ponyriy. The grim fighting at Ponyriy, which so recalls the bloody, indecisive fighting of the Great War, has captured the imagination of participants and historians to the point that the events of 7 to 10 July are often presented as *the* story of the Ninth Army's assault toward Kursk. The official Soviet General Staff study of the battle devotes the bulk of its coverage of Central Front's fight to the battle for the village, noting, "Understanding the significance of this center, the Germans decided to capture it at all costs . . . so that they could freely advance to the south." The Soviet General Staff attributed the XLVII Panzer Corps' attacks on 7 and 8 July to the Germans' "having failed to achieve success in the Ponyri region."[39]

The Soviet perspective has merit: Panzer divisions thrusting toward Kursk after a breakthrough at Teploye or Olkovatka would have found their line of communication under enemy observation and artillery fire from key points like Hills 253.5 and 239.8. Yet it is not difficult to infer that Model would have had von Esebeck's group use the 10th Panzergrenadier Division to widen the breach, presumably taking the Ponyriy bastion under fire from the rear. Moreover, while Ponyriy controlled access to critical high ground, terrain analysis suggests strongly that the preferred path for exploiting panzers would have been found several kilometers farther west. So to Model, while the continuing assault against Ponyriy was important, it was less essential than ramming his tanks and assault guns through the final Soviet defensive system in the Teploye-Olkovatka area. Thus, the comment by a staff officer at army headquarters (probably paraphrasing Model himself) early on 8 July becomes explicable: "The morning attack of the 4. Panzer-Division, attacking fresh and forming part of the *Schwerpunkt*, can open the way for the breakthrough to the south."[40]

Model, his operations officer, Lemelsen, and Lieutenant General Dietrich von Saucken (commander of the 4th Panzer Division) held a telephone conference call at 8:30 A.M. on 8 July regarding the division's strength and the axis of attack. The 4th Panzer, one of the German army's crack divisions, had been reduced during heavy fighting from January to March 1943 to a shadow of its former self, suffering over 2,500 casualties. The motor transport situation of the division had been so depleted that Army Group Center assigned Panzergrenadier Regiments 12 and 33 over 2,500 horses to take the place of lost vehicles. On 13 March the 4th Panzer deployed only 36 battered tanks. Rebuilt behind the front lines between April and June, von Saucken's division prepared to enter Operation Citadel with 13,166 men and 96 tanks, supported by relatively full complements of trucks, half-tracks, and self-propelled artillery. Although newly promoted to division command, von Saucken had the gritty reputation of a frontline fighter (*Frontkampfer*) that Model preferred in his subordinates rather than the more detached, orthodox command style he had seen displayed the previous afternoon by Vollrath Luebbe.[41]

What Model—again cut off from a steady stream of information from army headquarters by his incessant travels hither and yon—did not know was that Lemelsen had his own ideas about how to use the 4th Panzer Division. The XLVII Panzer Corps commander detached von Saucken's entire Panzer Regiment 35 to be consolidated with the available tanks from the 2nd Panzer Division and Tiger Battalion 503 into Panzer Brigade Burmeister, led by

Major General Arnold Burmeister of the 2nd Panzer Division. The ad hoc brigade was subordinated directly to corps headquarters rather than being placed under either Luebbe or von Saucken (although it operated in the 2nd Panzer Division's sector and by midafternoon Luebbe had taken de facto control of the unit). By way of compensation, von Saucken received Assault Gun Battalion 904 to accompany his panzergrenadier regiments. Essentially, therefore, Lemelsen had converted the 4th Panzer Division into a weak, four-battalion infantry division supported by a handful of assault guns, while redirecting his main attack into the 2nd Panzer Division's area.[42]

Model discovered this change around 12:30 P.M. when he arrived at the 4th Panzer Division's forward command post, where he had to be briefed by the assistant operations officer, since no one else was present. The operations officer had just been killed in a Soviet air raid; von Saucken and the commander of Panzergrenadier Regiment 33 (both of them wounded) were at the very front lines and unavailable for comment. After four hours of combat, the staff officer told his army commander that the division's final reserve (a panzerjäger battery) had just been thrown into the line to halt a Soviet counterattack. The panzergrenadier companies had been bled down to strengths of fifteen to twenty soldiers, while the detachment of Panzer Regiment 35 had led to the bizarre (and disheartening) spectacle of "tanks idle for hours in front of the Russian hill positions," under attack by German infantry. At the cost of hundreds of panzergrenadier casualties in von Saucken's regiments, the village of Teploye had finally fallen, but not several of the critical hills surrounding it; no breakthrough appeared imminent or even possible.[43]

Model exploded. Lemelsen, he said, "usually did not have any exact picture of the situation," while XLVII Panzer Corps staff "too often . . . led from the map board without any factual knowledge." A few telephone calls determined that the 2nd Panzer Division's attack was not succeeding either, even though supported by over two hundred tanks. "The removal of various officers, particularly the leadership of the 2nd Panzer Division and the brigade commander of Panzer Brigade 12 [Burmeister], must be investigated," Model groused. He immediately ordered all tanks returned to their parent divisions, not to be detached again without explicit permission from army headquarters. Unfortunately for the Ninth Army's breakthrough chances, this order could not feasibly be carried out until evening.[44]

Understanding that his division would have to bear the brunt of a resumed offensive, the combative von Saucken nonetheless wanted to resume the attack the next morning once he had been assured his panzer regiment would be returned. Model initially agreed, only to be convinced otherwise by his operations staff during the evening of 8 July. Colonel von Elverfeldt pointed out that another 3,220 German soldiers had become casualties that day (about evenly divided between the two major offensive actions) for gains measured in dozens or hundreds of meters rather than kilometers. Many officers and soldiers—especially in the 18th and 20th Panzer Divisions, as well as in the 6th, 86th, and 292nd Infantry Divisions—had gone virtually without sleep for up to ninety-six hours; even the unwounded teetered on the brink of physical collapse. Between them the 2nd, 4th, and 9th Panzer Divisions had lost nearly 50 percent of their infantry, and while German total losses among AFVs remained low, dozens if not hundreds of vehicles were under repair. The much-vaunted Ferdinands had not only proven vulnerable to Russian infantry (owing to the lack of any machine guns to supplement the main gun) but had also turned out to be prone to broken tracks, either through malfunction or enemy fire. Worse still, the Ninth Army's intelligence section had confirmed that Rokossovsky had moved two complete artillery divisions into supporting position behind his front line, adding enormously to his ability to rain down fire on assaulting Germans.[45]

When Model reluctantly agreed to set aside major offensive action on 9 July in favor of reorganizing the spearhead divisions in both the XLI and XLVII Panzer Corps sectors, he recognized that this decision was nearly tantamount to calling off the entire northern segment of Operation Citadel. At Army Group Center, von Kluge instantly reached the same conclusion, but both men knew that neither Hitler nor Zeitzler would countenance such a unilateral decision, especially since the southern prong of the offensive (Army Group South's Fourth Panzer Army, led by the II SS Panzer Corps) had broken through Voronezh Front's defenses and continued to push north toward Oboyan and Kursk. Thus, von Kluge instructed Model, along with Harpe and Lemelsen, to meet him at XLVII Panzer Corps headquarters the following morning to hash out the Ninth Army's next moves.

It was not an optimistic meeting. Harpe admitted that, especially given the additional artillery Rokossovsky had moved into position, he would probably run out of infantry long before he managed to take Ponyriy. Lemelsen's corps still retained some offensive potential, but when given the limited objective of seizing several hills just beyond Teploye on 10 July, the XLVII Panzer Corps commander and his staff could only assemble a brigade-sized armored assault contingent by combining assets from the 2nd, 4th, and 20th Panzer Divisions. Model acknowledged formally to von Kluge that the Ninth Army could not reasonably expect to create the necessary breakthrough, a position he maintained even when the field marshal offered not just the 10th Panzergrenadier and 12th Panzer Divisions but the 36th Infantry Division (Motorized) as well. All that Model would promise was a series of tactical attacks, designed as "a rolling battle of attrition" (*rollende Materielschlacht*) that might at least continue to attract Soviet reserves away from the southern half of the Kursk salient. To this von Kluge immediately agreed.[46]

Given that both Model and von Kluge expected a Soviet counteroffensive any day against the weakly held northern and eastern faces of the Orel salient, there are strong indications that the two men were knowingly engaged in misleading OKH and Hitler. No message left Army Group Center for East Prussia that morning detailing the fact that the Ninth Army's participation in Operation Citadel had effectively ended; instead, von Kluge portrayed 9 July as a brief moment of respite before a renewal of the breakthrough effort. Yet Lieutenant General August Schmidt's 10th Panzergrenadier Division moved up to the front so slowly that it did not reach the battlefield until the morning of 12 July, while Major General Erpo Freiherr von Bodenhausen's 12th Panzer and Major General Hans Gollnik's 36th Infantry lagged twenty-four hours behind. Moreover, when the Russians did attack east of Orel on 12 July, both the Ninth Army and Army Group Center reoriented themselves with suspicious rapidity. Harpe's corps headquarters was pulled out of the battle line almost instantly, the 12th Panzer and 36th Infantry (Motorized) Divisions were diverted, and preplanned withdrawals were ordered for the 18th and 20th Panzer Divisions as well as for the Ferdinands of Panzerjäger Battalions 653 and 654 and the heavy guns of Army Artillery Battalion 848. Model, in a Fieseler *Storch* liaison aircraft, preceded these units to Orel, where the Second Panzer Army's headquarters staff had already been briefed to expect him to assume command by 5:45 P.M. on 12 July.[47]

Historian Franz Kurowski suggests that all of this was the work of Model: "Without consulting *Generalfeldmarschall* von Kluge, Model called a halt to all attack operations." Such an interpretation is consistent with Model's popular image for independent decisionmaking but overlooks the dynamic of the army commander's relationship with the field marshal. Just as when Model constructed illicit (by OKH standards) defensive fallback positions at Rzhev and Orel with Army Group Center's tacit (though always unwritten) approval, the sheer number of telephone calls and personal meetings between Model and von Kluge makes it highly unlikely that the Ninth Army acted against the wishes of its immediate superior command. What Model did provide von Kluge was an aura of what today would be called "plausible deniability."

The army group commander could steadfastly maintain to OKH that he had given the Ninth Army no orders contravening Hitler's wishes; if Model often seemed to react to changing situations with almost unnatural reflexes, von Kluge could then simply refer to his well-known talent as a tactical improviser. That the staff of Army Group Center would be willing to play such a dangerous double game is hardly unthinkable: The chief of staff was Model's old crony Hans Krebs, and the operations officer was Colonel Henning von Tresckow, who spent his free time plotting to assassinate Hitler and overthrow the Nazi regime.[48]

None of these behind-the-scenes maneuvers changed the fact that on 10 and 11 July German soldiers in the XLI and XLVII Panzer Corps continued to fall as Model coldheartedly ordered them forward in attacks that no longer served any rational purpose beyond protective coloration. By midnight on 11 July, total Ninth Army casualties had risen to 22,273, with the five panzer divisions assigned to XLI and XLVII Panzer Corps (the 2nd, 4th, 9th, 18th, and 20th) accounting for over 6,500—chiefly among their depleted panzergrenadier regiments. Conversely, Model's losses in tanks and assault guns (except for the unwieldy and unreliable Ferdinands) had been relatively light, and Luftflotte Six had suffered only 94 aircraft losses in flying more than 10,000 sorties.[49] The postwar conclusion reached by Theodor Busse, chief of staff to von Manstein's Army Group South, applied equally to the northern attack:

> To force the enemy into an open battle by means of a breakthrough was an erroneous decision considering our limited forces, and in particular our inadequate number of infantry divisions. One did not have to wait for the experiences of this war to appreciate the drain on military strength that attends any breakthrough of well-fortified positions even if vast amounts of supplies are available. . . . The [available] panzer and panzergrenadier divisions . . . would

have sufficed to gain a major victory—but only if they succeeded in reaching open terrain.[50]

Had Model and von Kluge been waiting for Hitler and Zeitzler to reach this conclusion on their own, the Ninth Army might have been forced to continue bleeding itself white against prepared Soviet positions for at least another four or five days as the great, roiling tank battle near Prokhorovka in the south kept alive the illusion of possible victory. Fortunately, the Red Army helped out Army Group Center in this regard. After another lull in the fighting on 12 July, Dietrich von Saucken prepared to throw his exhausted 4th Panzer Division into the teeth of the Soviet defenses yet again on the morning of 13 July. Roughly an hour before the scheduled artillery preparation, however, Lemelsen appeared personally at the division command post, announcing, "The enemy attacked yesterday in the Orel salient in various places. He has achieved a deep penetration with strong armored forces." The corps commander then instructed von Saucken to go over to defensive operations, extending his lines to cover the 20th Panzer Division's sector as von Kessel's unit pulled out for immediate redeployment. Model himself flew to the Second Panzer Army's headquarters at Orel, taking control of both armies, as he and von Kluge had earlier agreed. The next morning Model issued his first order of the day to his combined command: "The Red Army is attacking on the entire front of the Orel salient. In front of us are battles that can decide everything. In this hour that demands superhuman exertion, I have taken over command of the battle-proven 2. Panzer-Armee."[51]

The three-week battle for the Orel salient, while less well known than the week of the Ninth Army's Citadel offensive, dwarfed the earlier battle in terms of men, tanks, guns, and aircraft, not to mention the casualties incurred by both the Wehrmacht and Red Army during the struggle. With the addition of the 5th and 8th

Panzer Divisions (the Second Panzer Army's reserve), the *Gross-deutschland* Panzergrenadier Division (transferred from Army Group South in mid-July), and a small but steady stream of additional tanks and assault guns delivered from Germany while the battle raged, Model controlled over 1,200 AFVs and more than 30 divisions. Luftflotte Six also received additional aircraft from Luftflotte Four in the Kharkov area.

Nor did the Red Army stint on the resources it committed to crushing two German armies. To Rokossovsky's Central Front (still well over 600,000 troops, with at least 1,200 AFVs, 10,000 guns, and over 800 aircraft) could now be added Colonel General Markian M. Popov's Bryansk Front (433,000 men, 1,500 AFVs, 7,500 guns, and 1,000 aircraft), as well as Lieutenant General Ivan Kh. Bagramyan's Eleventh Guards Army (135,000 men, 280 AFVs, 2,700 guns, and the potential support of several hundred aircraft) of the Western Front. This appeared to be such a crushing superiority of strength that STAVKA expected to collapse both flanks of Clössner's LIII Corps and penetrate the center of General of Infantry Lothar Dr. Rendulic's XXXV Corps during the first day of the attack and to reach Orel (thereby fragmenting the German forces into at least three parts) within forty-eight hours.[52]

That the ensuing battle for the Orel salient ended three weeks later with a German defensive victory, as Army Group Center extricated its two armies step by step from the box prepared for them while inflicting heavy casualties on three Soviet fronts, represented one of the most significant strategic achievements in Walther Model's career. Unfortunately, as with the northern wing of the Kursk offensive, this operation continues to languish in relative obscurity. It is usually swept aside in a paragraph or two before the historian returns to von Manstein's battles for Kharkov and the lower Dnepr. Often the only representation of the battle is a misleading graphic that shows the Soviets sweeping through the Orel salient, implying that Model's defense there amounted to nothing more than another failed effort to halt the inexorable Red tide.

Nor does the context of a biography allow a blow-by-blow recounting of the fighting. It is possible, however, to analyze with broad strokes the critical decisions that Model made that snatched survival (if not outright victory) from the jaws of destruction. First, it will be recalled that the Ninth Army's commander quietly ignored the OKH orders prior to Operation Citadel that no intermediate defensive lines should be constructed within the salient. The Ninth Army's organic rear-area command—Korueck 582—had been detached after the withdrawal from Rzhev, leaving rear-area security in the Orel salient fragmented. Theoretically, the Second Panzer Army's Korueck 532—overseeing the 707th (Static) Infantry Division; thirty assorted battalions of security troops, Russian volunteers, and German disciplinary troops; and three dozen engineer or construction battalions—would have controlled the major lines of communication and been responsible for building fixed defenses. Model, however, had Division Staff 442, the 203rd Security Division, the 221st Security Division, and another half-dozen engineer and construction units directly assigned to his command. What appears to have happened is that Model's senior security division commander, Lieutenant General Karl Bornemann, very quietly took de facto control of nearly all the rear-area assets in the Orel salient during late May and early June. By 5 July at least four major defensive switchlines of the type Model employed at Rzhev had been surveyed and construction had begun. As at Rzhev, during the Orel fighting these phase lines served their purpose: temporarily halting the Soviet onrush just long enough to feed new reserves into the most critical parts of the battle.[53]

Model's second—and in many ways his most important—decision regarded command organization. When Operation Citadel began, the Ninth Army held responsibility only for roughly one-quarter of the Orel salient, into which had been squeezed all the resources devoted to the Kursk offensive. The Second Panzer Army, conversely, deployed only twelve understrength divisions in the remainder of an arc stretching nearly 140 miles. Recognizing instantly that massive reinforcement would have to be withdrawn from the Ninth Army to prevent this long, convex front from collapsing, Model restructured his command to fight three separate battles. Freissner's XXIII Corps headquarters, Harpe's XLI Panzer Corps headquarters, and the headquarters staff assembled as *Gruppe* Esebeck were all removed from the Ninth Army's line by 14 July; the sectors of XX Corps, XLVI Panzer Corps, and XLVII Panzer Corps were expanded to control the line. For this purely defensive battle Model was content to leave Lemelsen in as overall tactical commander. The XLVII Panzer Corps commander may have disappointed Model as an offensive general, but on defensive (as he would also prove as an army commander in Italy) his stolid temperament and stubborn reluctance to give up ground made him the perfect choice to conduct operations on what quickly became the Orel salient's quietest point.

To control the sector ranging from Ulyamovo to Bolkhov (where the attenuated German line faced not just the Eleventh Guards Army but also eventually the Eleventh Army and the Fourth Tank Army) Model upgraded Josef Harpe's XLI Panzer Corps to *Gruppe* Harpe and entrusted the Austrian with fully one-third of the available troops. At its peak, around 23 July, *Gruppe* Harpe would include the following major units:

XLI Panzer Corps
    2nd Panzer Division
    8th Panzer Division
    9th Panzer Division
    Grossdeutschland Panzergrenadier Division

LIII Corps
    25th Panzergrenadier Division
    26th Infantry Division
    34th Infantry Division
    253rd Infantry Division

Security Regiment 350 (221st Security Division)
Gruppe Wuethmann
208th Infantry Division
112th Infantry Division
12th Panzer Division
Assault Gun Battalion 270

XXIII Corps
10th Panzergrenadier Division
129th Infantry Division
134th Infantry Division
183rd Infantry Division
Gruppe Esebeck
18th Panzer Division
20th Panzer Division

This was, in terms of the number and type of divisions, a larger force than the Ninth Army had been at the opening of Operation Citadel.[54]

Harpe fully justified Model's confidence, fighting a three-week running battle that not only blunted Bagramyan's thrust south toward Orel but held together the remnants of Clössner's LIII Corps around Bolkhov. Where appropriate, he engaged in the "elastic defense" tactics preferred by panzer officers, but like his mentor, Harpe did not hesitate to lure the Russians into trackless patches of forest and swamp, where his own infantry absorbed dreadful casualties stopping the forward momentum of the Soviet surge.[55]

East of Orel, facing the Forty-eighth and Sixty-third Armies, later reinforced by the Third Tank Army, Model relied on another Austrian, General of Infantry Lothar Dr. Rendulic, commander of XXXV Corps. A committed Nazi and a virulent anti-Communist, Rendulic was nonetheless an excellent tactician. At the outset his four depleted infantry divisions stretched to cover more than eighty miles of front, with only 196 pieces of field artillery, roughly 70 antitank guns, and no infantry reserve larger than a battalion. "On 11 July," Rendulic recalled (overstating his case only slightly), "the Soviets disposed over sixteen rifle divisions and one tank army (composed of three corps), further reinforced by an additional tank corps and six independent heavy tank brigades. . . . All together the enemy had concentrated 1,400 heavy tanks in the area. His artillery buildup consisted of more than 100 new batteries."[56]

Rendulic had a daunting yet critical assignment. If his corps collapsed, the Soviets would reach Orel in less than two days, seizing the main line of communication for the Ninth Army. On the other hand, Bagramyan's thrust west of Bolkhov threatened an even larger strategic defeat with the encirclement of both German armies, a circumstance that severely limited the reinforcements Model could send in XXXV Corps' direction. Rendulic met the initial Red Army attack by gambling on the accuracy of his front-line intelligence gathering to pinpoint the sector of the main Soviet attack, which he believed would fall on the six-mile-wide front of Infantry Regiment 431 (262nd Infantry Division). Personally directing the defensive dispositions, Rendulic took advantage of a deep stream in the area to funnel advancing Soviet tanks into a pre-planned kill zone. He then reinforced Infantry Regiment 431 with four additional infantry battalions, twenty-six antitank guns, and more than seventy pieces of field artillery. Rendulic admitted that "the great danger existed that the rest of the front had been left so weak that it could not even have resisted even small-scale operations. I had to take this calculated risk, however, if the enemy was to be engaged at all in the main-effort zone."[57]

The gamble paid off: On 12 and 13 July, XXXV Corps held its ground against a determined Russian attack. When Model flew to meet Rendulic for the first time on 13 July, he was impressed by the Austrian's cool demeanor and bold willingness to risk everything in order to meet the Soviet offensive on relatively equal terms. This was the kind of tactical approach Model appreciated. When Rendulic admitted that he could not maintain his front for more than another twenty-four hours without major reinforcements, Model agreed, but detailed for Rendulic the equally desperate situation for Harpe to the north. What he intended to do, Model explained, was commit most of his available forces to *Gruppe* Harpe and feed Rendulic only what XXXV Corps absolutely required to avoid a decisive enemy penetration. This would require Rendulic to be just as ruthless as Model himself, asking for nothing more than the bare minimum reinforcements necessary. Either a miscalculation or a failure of nerve could doom all the German forces in the salient.

Over the next week Soviet attacks intensified, and Rendulic's infantry repeatedly came close to the breaking point. Model, however, visited the front on an almost daily basis, and at each crisis he lived up to his promise to send forward just sufficient troops to stave off disaster. Thus, on 13 July Rendulic received two assault gun battalions and a battery of self-propelled antitank guns; on 15 July the 36th Infantry Division (Motorized) arrived; on 16 July the 8th Panzer Division reached the front; and on 17 July the 2nd and 12th Panzer Divisions checked in. Rarely did Rendulic get to keep any of these divisions longer than two days (most of them eventually ended up in *Gruppe* Harpe), but the steady if modest stream of troops, tanks, and guns passing through the sector provided him exactly what Model had promised.[58]

Beyond Model's delegation of the three sectors of the defensive battle to Lemelsen, Harpe, and Rendulic, one final factor played an important role in saving the German forces in the Orel salient. Midway through Operation Citadel, OKH decided (unwisely, as it turned out) to divert additional Luftwaffe assets from Army Group South to Army Group Center. The intent of this redeployment appears to have been to jump-start the Ninth Army's ineffective offensive with additional airpower. The timing of the move, however, guaranteed that Army Group South would lose the aircraft at a critical moment (just as II SS Panzer Corps was

approaching Prokhorovka), while the Ninth Army would not receive the extra support until after von Kluge and Model had
called off the offensive.[59]

As a result, for the only time in his career as an army or army
group commander Model fought the battle of the Orel salient with
air parity, if not air superiority, throughout the struggle. German
interceptors prevented the Soviet Air Force (VVS) from providing
effective ground support to either the Eleventh Guards Army or
the Soviet armies opposite XXXV Corps. More significantly,
Model instinctively grasped the tactical use of airpower in this
kind of multifront battle. On a day-by-day, even hour-by-hour,
basis he shifted the bulk of his air support from one sector to the
next, employing his planes en masse rather than distributing them
across the front. Thus, on 14 July, when no ground reinforcements
could reach Rendulic's front, Model committed several squadrons
of Ju87a Stuka dive-bombers to blunt the Soviet armored spearheads. Just as quickly, when one of the Eleventh Guards Army's independent tank brigades broke through Harpe's line a few days
later, Model sent wave after wave of aircraft against it until emergency blocking forces could be found to surround and destroy it.[60]

When Model finally received approval from OKH to evacuate
the Orel salient and move into the so-called Hagen position at the
end of July, the butcher's bill was high. During the main period of
Operation Citadel (1 to 10 July) the combined losses of the Ninth
and Second Panzer Armies had amounted to 21,248; the fight for
the Orel salient (11 to 31 July) cost an additional 62,305 men.[61]
Total losses in tanks and assault guns for the month appear to have
exceeded 400. Yet not only did Model frustrate the Red Army's attempt to conduct what might almost be considered "Operation
Citadel Reversed," but he managed to so shorten the front as the
Ninth and Second Panzer Armies retired behind the Dnepr River in
early fall that one army headquarters, two corps headquarters, and
at least one dozen divisions could be released for service elsewhere.

Model himself was also soon destined for service elsewhere.

PART THREE

The Fireman on
the Eastern Front

10

THE SWINE OF THE BALTIC

Army Group North: January to March 1944

AFTER SPENDING THE EARLY FALL SUCCESSFULLY DEFENDING THE upper Dnepr River line, Model applied for leave at the end of September. Hitler instead directed that Model relinquish command of the Ninth Army and enter the "Leader's Reserve" (*Führerreserv*). Normally this move would have been tantamount to being placed on the shelf, but toward the end of 1943 Hitler, Zeitzler, and General of Infantry Rudolf Schmundt (head of the Army Personnel Office) had developed the idea that they should prepare a cadre of younger commanders ready to step in and replace army group commanders like von Kluge and von Manstein should the older men become "fatigued"—essentially a euphemism for losing Hitler's confidence. Model's name, followed by that of Ferdinand Schörner, topped the list, and OKH wanted him well rested when the critical moment came.[1]

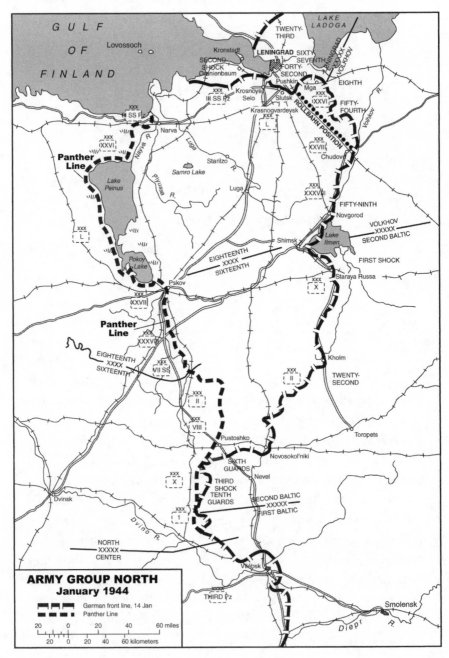

ARMY GROUP NORTH
January 1944

German front line, 14 Jan
Panther Line

20 — 0 — 20 — 40 — 60 miles
20 — 0 — 20 — 40 — 60 kilometers

The best that Model could achieve against overwhelming odds in facing the Soviet offensive that finally relieved Leningrad in January 1944 was to convince Hitler to allow a withdrawal to the shorter, more defensible Panther Line.

Three months' leave in Dresden allowed Model to see his family for the last Christmas he would ever spend at home. His wife rejoiced in the opportunity to show off her highly decorated husband at various cultural and social events around the city. Hans-Georg told his father of his plans to volunteer for officer training during the upcoming year.[2]

This familial interlude ended abruptly on 28 January 1944 with a preemptory summons to East Prussia. Two weeks earlier a well-conceived Soviet offensive had shattered the front of Army Group North's Sixteenth and Eighteenth Armies, which for two years had held an effectively static front in a convex arc extending from Leningrad south to Velikie Luki. The siege of Leningrad had been broken in the first hours, after which the floodgates had opened. Historian David Glantz summarizes the situation:

At the end of January, the Leningrad Front's 2d Shock and 42d Armies were poised along the Luga River, prepared to advance on Narva, the gateway to the Baltic region, from the east, and the *front's* 67th Army had advanced halfway from Leningrad toward Luga from the north and northwest. The Volkhov Front's 59th and 8th Armies were threatening Luga from the east, and its 54th Army was advancing on Oredezh and Luga from the northeast. A genuine opportunity existed for the two *fronts* to encircle and destroy the bulk of the Eighteenth Army north and northeast of Luga.[3]

With Hitler and OKH demanding that he close the gaps in his front and reestablish a coherent north-south defensive line (despite the fact that the Eighteenth Army had suffered over 40,000 casualties), Field Marshal Georg von Küchler had been reduced to pleading with his superiors in East Prussia for permission at least to fall back to the Luga Defensive Line, if not the halfway completed Panther Line at the Estonia border. Hitler finally agreed to the lesser step (albeit couched with other impossible tactical demands) on 30 January, but both the dictator and the chief of the Army

General Staff had become convinced that von Küchler's nerves had broken more thoroughly than his front line.[4]

Model arrived at the Führer's headquarters in a foul mood, asking few questions during situation reports and grunting mono-syllabic replies when directly addressed. The tenor of his mood could be gauged by a single interchange: When Model entered the room, Hitler and his senior generals had been poring over maps of western Europe, speculating on the likely focus of the Anglo-American invasion they expected in late spring or early summer. Hitler already favored Normandy, while many of the officers at OKH and OKW believed that the enemy would come ashore at Pas de Calais. When Hitler asked Model if he had any thoughts about a potential Allied landing site, the general answered sarcas-tically, "Yes. Portugal."[5]

Model's orders upon assuming command of Army Group North sounded familiar: He was to take charge of a desperate tac-tical situation, stabilize the front without retreating, and regain the ground his predecessor had lost. Reinforcements were promised and assurances tendered by confident OKH staffers that the situa-tion was not as bleak as von Küchler had painted it. Model un-doubtedly knew that if he received any additional troops, they would be less than the grandiose promises made in East Prussia and that the frontline officers really did understand the situation better than the headquarters types, but he also knew that it was worse than useless to point out such unpopular realities. Instead, he appeared to accept his briefing as substantially accurate and even sent an optimistic message ahead to army group headquar-ters: "Not a single step backward will be taken without my express permission. I am flying to Eighteenth Army this afternoon. Tell General Lindemann [the army commander] that I beg his trust in me. We have worked together before."[6]

General Georg Lindemann and Model might have had some limited mutual experience, but most of the commanders and sen-ior staff officers of Army Group North were strangers to their new leader. Model therefore asked for at least one dependable (and familiar) officer from his old Ninth Army stable. Zeitzler approved the immediate transfer of XXIII Corps commander Johannes Freissner to the Leningrad sector, giving Model authority to place him in any command position other than at the head of either army. Bringing along a personal favorite would not endear Model to his new command, but little he did that week made him any friends at Army Group North. Leaving East Prussia, for example, Model happened to comment at Führer headquarters that, having been on extended leave, he lacked a personal adjutant. When Hitler's SS liaison, Hermann Fegelein, heard this, he immediately offered Model a young Waffen SS officer for the post. Asking only about the officer's field experience, Model accepted him without ever considering how such a selection might jar the sensitivities of his new staff.[7]

Ironically, the Waffen SS adjutant did not become the first bone of contention between Model and his new chief of staff, Major General Eberhard Kinzel. The plane carrying Model to the front arrived at Army Group North's headquarters several hours after midnight, and Kinzel had to be awakened to meet his new boss. Guessing incorrectly that time would be more important than uniform, Kinzel appeared unshaven and wearing pajamas. Furious, Model delivered a blistering tongue-lashing and then spent most of the flight toward Luga dictating new uniform policies for his command that specifically ruled out pajamas. From the point at which the SS adjutant delivered these orders to the chief of staff, relations had nowhere to go except down.[8]

At Luga, Model found what he had expected: a situation far worse than Hitler and Zeitzler believed. The Eighteenth Army's XXXVIII Corps had been reduced from five infantry divisions and the Spanish Legion to six regiment-strength *Kampfgruppen* totaling no more than 5,516 combat troops assigned to defend a forty-mile front. The XXVIII Corps still possessed—for the most part—intact division organizations but could put only

6,660 infantrymen in the trenches. In the worst condition of Lindemann's three corps, L Corps retained a trench strength of only about 4,500 men in two shattered divisions and one regimental *Kampfgruppe*. All contact had been lost between army headquarters and III SS Panzer Corps, which was fighting its own separate battle around Narva; Lindemann could not even estimate that corps' strength. Reported equipment losses during the first two weeks of the Soviet offensive included 2,173 machine guns, 249 antitank guns, 62 infantry guns, 307 pieces of field artillery, and 51 *Nebelwerfer* multiple mortars. More than 52,000 wounded men clogged the medical evacuation channels and the field hospitals.[9]

For Model, walking across the airfield in the frigid wind, it might have been Rzhev all over again. But two years had seen a marked deterioration in the Wehrmacht's resources to redeem such a potential catastrophe. Whereas in January 1942 he had come to the Ninth Army ahead of at least five divisions of reinforcements (no matter how understrength), at Army Group North only the 12th Panzer Division (forty-three tanks) and Panzergrenadier Division *Feldherrnhalle* (twenty-five assault guns)—neither exceptionally strong—were being rushed to the front. *Feldherrnhalle* had already been earmarked for the Narva front because a Soviet breakthrough there would guarantee not only the complete destruction of the Eighteenth Army but also the immediate loss of Latvia, Lithuania, and Estonia.[10]

Yet Model did possess some tactical advantages. Soviet losses had also been high, and as David Glantz points out, the initial combined strength of the Leningrad and Volkhov Fronts did not greatly exceed that of Model's Sixteenth and Eighteenth Armies— at least by German standards in early 1944. The two Russian fronts had entered the battle with roughly 800,000 men, 650 tanks, and 3,680 guns and mortars against a German strength of about 500,000 men, 146 tanks, and 2,389 guns and mortars. That the Red Army had so completely torn open the Eighteenth Army's front had more to do with effective concentration of force in selected attack zones than overwhelming weight of numbers. In addition, Soviet transport assets still being fairly primitive, many of the heaviest guns could not be brought forward as quickly as the Eighteenth Army had fallen back, and supplies remained problematic.[11]

A second factor was Model's understanding of just how many men were actually available for combat, as opposed to those carried as "trench strength." Aside from the fact that he could be sure that Army Group North—like every other command in the East— had systematically reported the lowest possible strength in order to avoid having units ordered away to other parts of the front, Model knew that thousands of artillerymen whose weapons had been lost, headquarters staffs, and support personnel still inhabited the rear areas of the Eighteenth Army. If they could be quickly mobilized into emergency units (*alarmeinheiten*) to be thrown into the defensive line, he would be able to free what was left of his veteran infantry for necessary counterattacks.

Finally, there remained the Sixteenth Army, holding the southern flank of the front that connected to Army Group Center. This army had not yet been targeted by the Soviets, although everyone expected that circumstance to change very quickly. Drawing out entire divisions from the Sixteenth Army to reinforce the Eighteenth was a desperate expedient that Army Group North had thus far avoided. Nor was Model interested in doing so. He could, however, divert all the field replacements and returning convalescents destined for the Sixteenth Army and direct them toward Lindemann's hard-pressed command. This maneuver, his staff assured him, would send an additional five thousand combat troops into the lines within ten days.[12]

None of these advantages would matter, however, if the Eighteenth Army remained tied by *Führerdirectiv* to the defense of Luga, because Lindemann simply did not have the forces necessary to secure his right flank. The Soviet Second Shock and Forty-second Armies were pouring troops into a seventy-mile-wide gap separating the Eighteenth Army's main body from III SS Panzer Corps at Narva. Either that gap had to be closed or the army had to retreat. Model knew that the safest "school solution" would entail a retreat to the Panther Line, which would pull both armies out of harm's way and shorten the front à la Operation Buffalo to allow him to draw several divisions out of the line as reserves. He also knew that Hitler would not sanction even the loss of Luga, much less a sixty-mile retrograde.

Model met the challenge by consciously manipulating everyone: Hitler, his own staff, and the troops in the line. Capitalizing on his well-publicized reputation as "the Lion of the Defense," Model darted around the front in his patented fashion, appearing on the front lines, at division command posts, and even in the reception stations for returning soldiers. His message remained consistent throughout: Reinforcements are on the way, the crisis will be mastered, every man must do his duty. A young SS lieutenant commanding a panzer company at Narva recalled Model's exact words: "You are personally responsible to me to ensure that no Russian tanks break through. None of your Tigers will be knocked out due to enemy fire. We need every gun tube."[13]

To his staff he was as foul-mouthed and uncompromising as usual. He told Kinzel that no one was allowed to report to him with problems unless they also brought with them at least two potential solutions. When his Luftwaffe liaison told him that no air support was available for the hard-pressed 121st Infantry Division on 5 February because it was not "*Stuka* weather," Model exploded. "*Stuka* weather? It's not *Stuka* weather?" He shouted. "It's always infantry weather!" The planes flew. Within hours the local Luftwaffe commander also discovered that on the strength of orders from East Prussia, Model had commandeered literally every available battalion of light and heavy flak for direct infantry support.[14]

To Hitler and Zeitzler, Model appeared to be exactly the tonic that Army Group North required. He forbade any mention of the

Panther Line in army communications, telling his superiors that he even wanted the designation abolished so that the men would not fight "looking over the shoulder," planning to pull back to the next fortified position rather than holding their ground. He also created a new tactical theory: "Shield and Sword" (*Schild und Schwert*). The idea, as Model explained it to Hitler, was that ground would only be temporarily ceded in order to concentrate the troops necessary for an immediate counterattack that would not only reduce Soviet pressure on another part of the front but also allow the surrendered terrain to be recaptured in short order. Given that OKH had no substantial reinforcements to send him, this aggressive-sounding policy won over his superiors.

Both of these moves—silencing talk about the Panther Line and the *Schild und Schwert*—have been misinterpreted by most historians. Earl F. Ziemke believes that the Panther Line orders represented a genuine attempt by Model "to dissipate what he called the PANTHER psychosis"; suggesting that *Schild und Schwert* was actually "Hitler's latest brainchild," Ziemke asserts: "That Model placed overly much faith in the theory may be doubted."[15]

These are reasonable conclusions—unless measured against Model's record at the Ninth Army, where he consistently created, maintained, and occupied fortified defensive lines whose existence he rarely revealed to his own army group, let alone OKH. Model's real motive in prohibiting mention of the Panther Line was to move preparations for its occupation out of the sight of OKH's prying eyes. Internal records of Army Group North's chief engineer indicate that in fact one of Model's first orders was to detach divisional engineer assets from the Sixteenth Army to speed up the completion of the fortifications formerly known as the Panther Line. Model understood that in the long run Army Group North could not survive without those fortifications, but that in the meantime Hitler and Zeitzler had to stop hearing about them.[16]

As for *Schild und Schwert*, the term's first appearance in communications from Army Group North to OKH resolves the question of origination. Discerning Model's actual thinking again requires recourse to his preferred tactical methods. Throughout February Model repeatedly ordered limited withdrawals to concentrate troops for what turned out to be unsuccessful counterattacks. The 12th Panzer Division lost two dozen tanks and nearly one thousand men in a three-day running fight with the Forty-second Army that failed to throw the Soviets back. Likewise, several other infantry divisions were further blooded in attacks that, without exception, failed to recover a foot of ground. The best estimate is that Model sustained at least an additional ten thousand to twelve thousand casualties in these attacks, losses that led his own staff (and that of the Eighteenth Army) to see him as simply a Hitler sycophant willing to butcher his troops at the Führer's whim.[17]

Other evidence suggests that Model had different ends in mind. Had he continued simply to hold the defensive position around Luga with the usual linear tactics, as was Hitler's original intent, he could have been assured of suffering far more than twelve thousand casualties. Instead, what Model did was contract his lines into more defensible positions, replace the bulk of his veterans with the hastily organized emergency units, and then meet the most dangerous Soviet spearheads head on. If the badly depleted German units could not throw the Russians back, they did inflict heavy casualties and halt the enemy advance. In the meantime, Model's apparent aggressiveness and often misleading communications with OKH won him sufficient political capital with Hitler and Zeitzler to turn each of his "temporary" retreats into permanent ones. Thus, the Eighteenth Army's front crept slowly backward at the reasonable cost, Model thought, of twelve thousand casualties he would have certainly suffered anyway.

Simultaneously, Model placed Freissner in command of an operational group of two (later three) corps at the juncture between the Eighteenth and Sixteenth Armies, where he was well positioned to resist the Soviet attack on the Sixteenth Army's northern flank. Freissner understood Model's methods from prolonged exposure: The rhetoric of his dispatches was inflammatory, but his tactics were conservative and almost always yielded ground rather than risk losing large numbers of troops. Given that the Narva front had also been set up as a functionally independent command (*Gruppe* Sponheimer), Model achieved the same sort of improvised command organization he had employed in the Orel salient. The de jure Eighteenth and Sixteenth Army commanders found their forces pared down and their purview reduced to that of grand tactical commanders, while the forces at the most critical positions answered directly to Model.

Luga fell to the Soviets on 12 February, by which time Model had succeeded in erecting (without OKH noticing) several defensive switchlines between that city and the Panther Line. While the Eighteenth Army fought its way slowly back, the speed of the Soviet advance noticeably slowed as mounting casualties and logistical difficulties dogged the Red Army's operations. The Second Baltic Front, for example, lost over twenty-nine thousand men between 10 February and 1 March; the Leningrad Front's losses were comparable. STAVKA continued to demand further advances despite these casualties, but by the end of February Model had most of his army group within the Panther Line along a solid front running south from Narva to Ostrov.[18] It had been a near-catastrophe at times, with fighting as desperate as that required at Rzhev or Orel, yet Army Group North had been saved.

On 28 March Model sat in his headquarters completing an estimate of the number of divisions that might be released now that Army Group North held the Panther Line. He concluded that his armies "might" be able to release two infantry divisions to reinforce Army Group South after the latest round of Soviet attacks had been repulsed. Before this message could be sent, Schmundt appeared in his office, fresh from a courier flight from

East Prussia. Schmundt informed him that Hitler had now decided the time was right for Model to replace von Manstein; the two men would fly back to the Führer's headquarters the next day. In one of his least honorable (but perhaps most revealing) actions of the war, Model quickly revised his estimate of the forces Army Group North might yield to his new command. The version actually telegraphed to OKH then said that not two but six divisions could be spared and that these could be joined by the 12th Panzer Division as soon as two new assault gun brigades arrived to replace it. When Zeitzler balked at this idea, Model disingenuously used his lame-duck authority over army group on 29 March to order the transfer, telling his staff that Hitler had approved it. Zeitzler again managed, albeit with some difficulty, to block this maneuver.[19]

Model's tenure at Army Group North had been marked by such poisonous relations with his own staff that, even before he attempted to raid their reserve divisions, Kinzel and his operations officers felt nothing but relief upon his departure. A single officer was dispatched to accompany Model and his SS aide to the airfield, and when that officer saw the Ju52 transport leap into the air, he walked to the nearest telephone. Ringing army headquarters, he identified himself and uttered the code word Kinzel had designated to report Model's exit: "Schweinfuhrt." This could have been merely a reference to the German city, but it was not. In its literal sense, "Schweinfuhrt" expressed the true feelings of Model's subordinates at Army Group North:

"The swine has flown."[20]

11

INTERLUDE IN
THE CARPATHIANS

Army Group North Ukraine:
March to June 1944

OBLIVIOUS TO HIS STAFF'S DISDAIN, MODEL FLEW ON 30 MARCH to East Prussia, where, along with General of Mountain Troops Ferdinand Schörner, he cooled his heels in a waiting room as Hitler decorated Field Marshals von Manstein and von Kleist with the swords to their Knight's Crosses as a prelude to firing both men. "I hope for your sake your decision today turns out right for you," von Manstein told Hitler while shaking the Führer's hand for the last time. As two of the army's most venerated officers were shuffled out the door, Hitler greeted Model and Schörner, promoted both men, and assigned them, respectively, to command of Army Groups South (now redesignated "North Ukraine") and A (similarly renamed "South Ukraine"). Such a tawdry scene would have given pause to any officer endowed with the smallest fragment of introspection, but neither Model nor Schörner possessed sufficient perspective to draw any conclusions from this macabre piece of theater. Nor did a personal meeting with von Manstein at Lvov three days later do anything to temper Model's outlook.[1]

Thanks to spring mud, Soviet exhaustion, and von Manstein's successful extrication of the First Panzer Army from its recent encirclement, Model inherited a less calamitous tactical situation than those to which he had become accustomed. The army group's front had essentially stabilized along a reasonably straight 285-mile line east of the Carpathian Mountains running from Kovel in the north toward Stanislav (just west of the Dnestr River) down to the Hungarian-Romanian border. To defend this sector Model had the First and Fourth Panzer Armies (437,000 men, 811 tanks, 426 assault guns, and 1,100 guns) as well as the newly mobilized First Hungarian Army. Although badly battered in the late winter battles, the two dozen infantry and ten panzer divisions making up these armies included some of the best units in the Wehrmacht, including: the 1st and 72nd Infantry; the 28th Jäger; the 1st, 4th, 5th, and 8th Panzer; the 5th SS *Wiking* Panzer; and—at least temporarily—the inexperienced but well-equipped 9th and 10th SS Panzer Divisions of the II SS Panzer Corps. Both Foreign Armies East (*Fremde Heer Ost*) and the army group intelligence officers rated the Red Army formations opposite them as understrength and lacking serious offensive capability.[2]

Nor did Model have grounds to complain about the quality of his subordinates. General of Panzer Troops Hans Hube, who commanded the First Panzer Army, not only had been associated with Model since his cadet days but had won a reputation for courageous and effective tactical leadership that had already caused Hitler and OKH to place him on the list to receive his own army group command in the near future. The Fourth Panzer Army fell under the quietly competent Erhard Raus (now a general of panzer troops), upon whom Model had learned to rely implicitly during the dark days of the 1941–1942 Soviet winter counteroffensive.

Among the corps commanders were Model's favorite deputy, Josef Harpe, as well as veterans like Hermann Balck, Hermann Breith, and Walther Nehring.

Model also profited from the conclusion drawn by Hitler and OKH during the winter of 1943–1944 that STAVKA would continue in the upcoming months to focus the main Soviet offensive effort on the southern half of the Russian front. The Führer's reading of the situation convinced him that the next major Red Army attack would be a massive assault by the First Belorussian and First Ukrainian Fronts against Army Group North Ukraine, with the intent of smashing open Model's line before wheeling north toward the Baltic Sea to trap Army Groups North and Center in a gigantic cauldron. Thus, in early May Model managed to convince OKH to transfer LVI Panzer Corps from Army Group Center to Army Group North Ukraine, despite the fact that Field Marshal Ernst Busch's front was nearly three times longer. Whether Model genuinely believed in an upcoming Ukrainian offensive or cynically agreed with Hitler's appreciation in order to increase his own forces is impossible to determine.[3]

Lvov, roughly fifty miles west of Army Group North Ukraine's center, represented the key to the entire position, because the vast majority of the region's main transportation lines funneled through the city. From two standpoints—logistics and lateral mobility—the loss of Lvov would render it impossible for the Germans to maintain an army group west of the junction of the Carpathians and the Vistula River. On the other hand, seizing Lvov would provide the Soviets with multiple strategic options: turning north toward the Baltic, as Hitler feared; driving west into Hungary; or attacking south to peel back the German flank in Romania.[4]

This reality—that Army Group North Ukraine had no choice other than to tie all of its operational planning to an unyielding defense of Lvov—set up an unusually divisive dynamic between Model and some of his army and corps commanders. Officers like

Balck, Breith, Hube, and Nehring (all of whom based their beliefs primarily on combat experience in the south) favored the concept of elastic defense that von Manstein had made the linchpin of his strategy during his entire tenure in army group command. The premise was best summarized by Friedrich-Wilhelm von Mellenthin (then chief of staff of XLVIII Panzer Corps) in his exceptionally popular postwar memoir *Panzer Battles*:

> On the whole, the defensive battles in the Western Ukraine were successful because there was no rigid defense line, but an elastic one, which was allowed to bend but not to break. For this reason the enemy was never able to wipe out German formations. The junior commanders took advantage of every opportunity to counterattack, with a view toward destroying as many Russians as possible.
>
> On the other hand, a rigid defense system . . . usually broke to pieces in a very short time. Such dispositions must be blamed on local commanders. Armor employed en masse and in surprise attacks pierced almost any front, as in the vast spaces of Russia every defensive line was more or less a screen. The secret of a successful defense depended on the dispositions of the reserves, and the weight and vigor of counterattacks.[5]

By contrast, Model, Harpe, and Raus—all of whom brought to the situation experience gained much farther north, between Rzhev and Orel—believed that the German army no longer had the ability to surrender "vast spaces of Russia" without immediately disastrous consequences. Moreover, all three men subscribed to the idea that a carefully planned defense could not only blunt Red Army tank attacks but hold ground at the same time. This was to be accomplished through a deep system of alternate battle positions, heavily mined lines of communications, flexible artillery concentrations with multiple firing points, and sharp local counterattacks with carefully organized panzer *kampfgruppen*. Fundamental to this defense-in-depth approach was the idea that

German infantry should hold the front lines in strength right up to the moment of the opening of the Red Army's pre-assault artillery barrage, withdrawing a few miles at the last moment to allow the shells to be wasted on empty trenches. Thus, the Soviets would advance directly into an intact, prepared defense, where they could be repulsed and the little ground relinquished might be recovered almost instantly.[6]

This conviction, it must be noted, was a far cry from Hitler's rigid insistence that "not a step back" be taken, nor "an inch of ground" yielded, an approach that, Raus correctly observed, "could never prevent Soviet breakthroughs, let alone lead to victory." After the war, however, Balck, Guderian, and von Mellenthin would successfully conflate the two in the public mind. In part this occurred because Model had adopted such tactics at Army Group North under cover of Hitler's *Schild und Schwert* rhetoric, allowing the Führer to believe whatever was necessary to achieve a tactical free hand. Raus spoke more accurately of "zone defense tactics" (*Grosskampfzonie*), and he appears to have been the primary architect of the doctrine's technical details.

"The task of indoctrinating our unit commanders in all the essential zone defensive measures was far from easy," Raus later admitted. At the First Panzer Army Hube was reluctant to adopt the new strategy, and Balck was adamantly opposed to it. On 21 April, however, Hube died in an airplane accident; ironically, he was returning from East Prussia, where he had just received the oak-leaf cluster to his Knight's Cross and promotion to colonel general. Model wanted Harpe selected as Hube's replacement, but there were issues of relative seniority among the army's corps commanders, so OKH instead transferred Raus from the Fourth to the First Panzer Army and named Harpe to command the Fourth. This arrangement gave Model like-minded subordinates at both army headquarters, but it also set up a more direct conflict with Balck at XLVIII Panzer Corps, which controlled the 1st and 8th Panzer Divisions. Raus and Balck had been paired before—during the fighting at Zhitomir and Kiev the previous year—and both Balck and the corps chief of staff, von Mellenthin, considered the Austrian too conservative for a panzer commander. Relying in part on von Mellenthin's friendship with Karl Wagener (Raus's chief of staff), the two campaigned incessantly throughout late April and early May against the zone defense concept.[7]

Instead of seeking to reconcile these differences, Model applied his usual heavy hand. "Although a soldier of great driving power and energy," von Mellenthin later argued, Model "could hardly be regarded as an adequate substitute for Manstein." Model first ordered Balck to follow directives from Raus and then showed up unannounced at key points to ensure that his directives had been followed. This was what von Mellenthin characterized as being "too prone to interfere in matters of detail and to tell his corps and army commanders exactly where they should dispose their troops. General Balck found this very irritating."

When Balck dragged his feet about breaking his divisions into the smaller *kampfgruppen* required for zone defense tactics, he apparently had several blazing arguments with his army group commander. "In my diary I had noted: 'to work with Model is in no respect simple,'" Balck recalled, and he castigated the Prussian not only for interference and bad manners but also for the supposedly inappropriate comments of his SS aide. His inherently short patience exhausted, Model responded by having Raus transfer the two panzer divisions to the more compliant Hermann Breith (III Panzer Corps), and he put XLVIII Panzer Corps in charge of four understrength infantry divisions in the army's front line. Balck and von Mellenthin continued to quarrel with Raus over everything from the placement of minefields to alternative firing positions for their field artillery, but their ability to influence the army group's overall strategy had been effectively eliminated.[8]

(Model would leave Army Group North Ukraine before the Soviets seriously tested his defensive scheme, but the outcome of

First Ukrainian Front's mid-July attack is instructive. In the First Panzer Army sector Raus enjoyed significant success in minimizing Red Army tank penetrations and holding a cohesive line. Lvov fell anyway, however, when the Fourth Panzer Army's defenses collapsed—primarily because Model in his new capacity as commander of Army Group Center had ordered away Harpe's panzer reserve, the 4th and 5th Panzer Divisions, reducing the army's tank strength by at least 40 percent. Ironically, in August Balck succeeded Harpe as commander of the Fourth Panzer Army. Again, this outcome illustrated Model's inability to visualize the Eastern Front as a whole; he remained interested only in acquiring resources for his current command, no matter what the cost elsewhere.)

The most significant combat action to play out during Model's brief tenure in western Galicia was the tragic loss of the Ternopol garrison. The action had begun several weeks earlier during the last lunge of Marshal Zhikov's First Ukrainian Front toward the critical rail junction at Proskurov. Ternopol, with a scratch garrison of 4,600 men (a large percentage of whom were eighteen-year-olds with no combat experience) under Major General Egon von Neindorff, was first encircled on 9 March but tenuously reconnected with the main front two days later. In the interim, the city became the first "fortified place" (*Festungplatz*) so designated by Führer Directive No. 11. This order represented Hitler's decision to saddle his commanders with the imperative to create breakwaters in the face of Russian offensives that would be held to the last extremity even if surrounded. Unfortunately for Neindorff and his men, the city's selection did not include the defensive emplacements, heavy weapons, or ammunition to turn the honorific into reality.[9]

On 23 March the Soviet advance again engulfed Ternopol, leaving the city surrounded about twelve miles from XLVIII Panzer Corps' main line of resistance (*Hauptkampflinie*). Two days later a strong *kampfgruppe* of the 8th Panzer Division thrust close to the city, only to reel back with heavy casualties short of its goal. Even had the maneuver been successful, it would have been pointless: Hitler had not authorized a breakout, only a replenishment of supply. The dictator later chided Model that his army group was "honor-bound" to reestablish a permanent link with the beleaguered garrison. Before Model had even arrived at his new command, however, the Soviets unleashed a thirty-one-hour artillery barrage, collapsed von Neindorff's outer defenses, and drove the desperate defenders back into the city proper. On 1 April the army group operations officer handed the field marshal the transcript of a radio message that read in part, "Despite bitter resistance unable to hold any longer. Request Führer's permission for a breakout attempt."[10]

Model had long since proven himself impervious to Hitler's verbal barbs—as well as hard-hearted enough to accept the sacrifice of 4,600 troops as a tactical necessity—yet he also recognized the damage to his soldiers' morale if the army group did not mount a serious relief attempt. So while he did not take a personal hand in planning the attack, Model did authorize Raus to reinforce the 8th Panzer Division's *Kampfgruppe* Friebe with a heavy contingent from the 9th SS Panzer Division. The attack went forward through rain and mud on 11 April, but despite sustaining heavy casualties, the two divisions managed to drive forward only half the distance separating them from Ternopol. Von Neindorff died in the fighting on 15 April, and organized resistance quickly collapsed; only fifty-five fugitives reached the 9th SS Panzer the next day as the relief column prepared to withdraw. The official Wehrmacht communiqué cynically inflated this number on 18 April, announcing, "Near Ternopol further elements of the garrison fought their way through the advancing units of the Army and Waffen-SS."[11]

The debacle—which Hitler's tactical inflexibility had made inevitable—cost Army Group North Ukraine 5,800 casualties in the garrison and relief force. Model, in ordering the relief, had not argued the point with the Führer, as other commanders often did, but he had not merely acquiesced either. Instead, the field marshal deftly manipulated the dictator by expressing willingness to concentrate forces for the attempt *if* Hitler authorized the Fourth Panzer Army to give up its vulnerable positions east of the Seret River. As cold-blooded and cynical as this linkage seems, Model would have argued that attaining permission to pull the Fourth Panzer Army away from the Seret ultimately saved the army many more thousands of fallen soldiers.

Before Model's defensive strategy for blunting the next Soviet offensive could be tested in extremis, a telephone call from OKH on 28 June whisked him off to an even greater challenge.

12

MORE HOLE THAN FRONT

*Army Group Center:
June to August 1944*

THE MIDDAY TELEPHONE CALL ON 28 JUNE APPOINTING WALTHER Model commander of Army Group Center (without relieving him of his current position at Army Group North Ukraine) could hardly have been a surprise. The Red Army's "Operation Bagration," which had commenced six days earlier, had torn gaping holes in the overextended fronts of three of Field Marshal Ernst Busch's four armies. What must, however, have shocked even Model was the magnitude of the disaster that had engulfed his old army group in less than a week.

On the army group's northern flank the Third Panzer Army had lost virtually the entire LIII Corps in a cauldron at Vitebsk; that its remaining six divisions—understrength, battered, and possessing just forty-four artillery pieces in total—had managed to avoid a further encirclement could only be attributed to the outstanding tactical abilities of Colonel General Hans-Georg Reinhardt. Yet

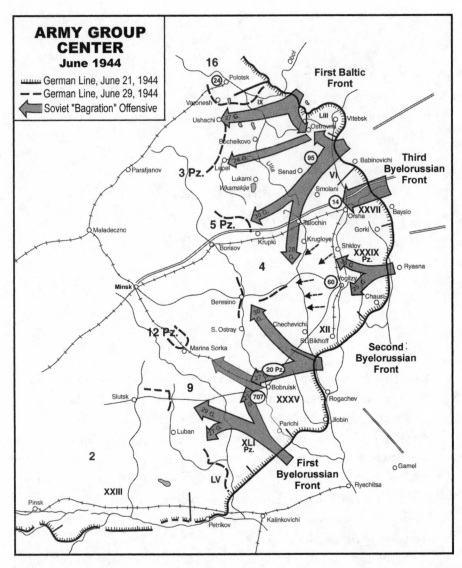

The first week of the Soviet "Bagration" Offensive in late June 1944 had truly left Army Group Center with "more hole than front," and presented Model with an almost insurmountable challenge.

with yawning gaps of up to forty miles on each flank—patrolled only by Soviet tanks and infantry riding American lend-lease trucks—Reinhardt's army could not hope to survive more than a few additional days without immediate reinforcement. "These aren't just penetrations," Reinhardt told OKH that day. "There's a full-blown gap in the north, and another big hole southwest of Lepel."[1]

General of Infantry Kurt von Tippelskirch's Fourth Army had been tied by Hitler's stand-fast orders to defensive positions around Mogilev and Orsha as heavy Soviet columns ripped around its flanks, creating the conditions necessary for cutting off whole army corps. Under constant air attack, with communications intermittently interrupted at all levels, von Tippelskirch and his subordinates recognized that only a timely retreat behind the Berezina River offered the badly wounded army any chance of survival. Again, however, Hitler had flatly refused, chanting the mantra of "fortified places" to Busch when he advocated the withdrawal. Not until midafternoon on 28 June did Busch manage to wrangle permission for the retreat, and his order that afternoon "for the speedy continuation of the rearward movement, in the first place to River Berezina," was probably the last issued on his authority. Reading the teleprinter message, von Tippelskirch thought bitterly, "Now the order is on its way—too late." Nonetheless, he instantly forwarded the directive to his corps commanders: "Get to the Berezina. No time constraints."[2]

The same day General of Panzer Troops Nikolaus von Vormann (an old associate from Model's tenure in command) assumed command of the Ninth Army—or what was left of it. The daily entry in the army's war diary starkly recorded, "Army has virtually ceased to exist as a fighting force. It has not a single battleworthy formation left." The entire XLI Panzer Corps had been cut off in Bobriusk, and even when von Vormann received belated approval for a breakout about 12:45 P.M., he could not be sure that General of Artillery Karl Weidling even received the order for several hours.

A midnight escape was quickly organized, at the agonizing expense of leaving behind 3,600 wounded soldiers for whom evacuation transport could not be found. Unfortunately, while rearguard elements still fought within the city itself, XLI Panzer Corps discovered that the Berezina River bridge at Shatkovo had been rendered unusable, forcing the bulk of the now-moving pocket to seek sanctuary in the forests near Sychkovo. The nearest relief force—*Kampfgruppe* Lindig—was thirty-five miles distant and hardly a force to slice through the Soviets like a knife: "People ran as soon as they heard tanks coming," the army war diary acidly observed.[3]

Holding the southern flank of the army group along the Pripet Marshes (and incidentally connecting to Army Group North Ukraine), the Second Army had come under heavy pressure but thus far had not been the subject of a major Soviet attack. The 35th Infantry Division had been mauled and the army's left flank separated from the Fourth Army, but for the moment Colonel General Walther Weiss had fewer problems than his contemporaries. Yet no one looking at a large-scale map of the entire Russian front could be sanguine about that army's long-term prospects. The Fourth Army's nearly inevitable collapse would expose Weiss's communications, and even OKH had to admit that the Soviets had mounted their frontal assault on Army Group Center without weakening their offensive concentration near Kovel.[4]

Other than promises, the only significant reinforcements to reach the battle area from other fronts were the 4th, 5th, and 12th Panzer Divisions, all battle-tested veteran units but hardly a force capable of stemming the Soviet tide, even if employed as a single, unified panzer corps. Tactical circumstances, however, had forced all three divisions to be committed piecemeal (even battalion by battalion on arrival) in different critical areas of the front. Worse still, what was needed—and not available—to reestablish a coherent line was infantry. Even Adolph Hitler later admitted that on 28 June, "when Field Marshal Model came, Army Group Center was in fact only a hole."[5]

The opinions of historians regarding Model's prospects for re-trieving the situation have been nearly unanimous: The profane, monocled Prussian faced an impossible task. Alex Buchner con-cludes that "Model could not change what was taking place or save the army group; all he could do was try and slow down the enemy advance with the few new divisions he was sent." "Even Model could not raise armies from nothing," remarks Paul Carell. "Without an effective Luftwaffe, without adequate anti-tank weapons, without a minimum of mobile reserves and infantry, even a general as bold and favoured by the fortunes of war as Model could not stand up to the Soviet onslaught." Samuel Mitcham suggests that, as a tactical realist, Model did not even at-tempt to create a new defensive line: "With Army Group Center in remnants, Model's strategy was simple: give ground rapidly and save what was left, until the Soviets outran their supply lines and he could be reinforced with divisions then forming in Germany."[6]

Model would not have agreed with these assessments. By 28 June he believed that Army Group Center had suffered a defeat, but not one that had to become a disaster. With the proper coordi-nation of forces between Army Groups North, Center, and North Ukraine, a front might be rebuilt as far east as Minsk. That evening Model and Colonel General Kurt Zeitzler agreed in prin-ciple that the situation might be retrieved if four actions were taken. First, the army group had to place its highest priority on getting the bulk of the Fourth Army back into the Minsk area. This would require the assembly of a relief group (one panzer, one infantry, and one jäger division) in the Baranovichi area to attack south toward von Tippelskirch's retreating divisions. To accom-plish this Model proposed that a tidying of the Second Army's line would release some troops, while others could be shifted from re-serve positions behind the First Panzer Army in Army Group North Ukraine. Succoring Reinhardt's Third Panzer Army would require Army Group North to withdraw to the Dvina River line (placing its right flank at Polotsk), a movement that would allow the gap to be closed with Reinhardt's army while also freeing two infantry divisions for transfer to Minsk.[7]

The strongest belief in Model's ability to salvage the situation resided at Ninth Army headquarters, where the war diarist took the time to write on 28 June: "The news of Field Marshal Model's arrival is noted with satisfaction and confidence." Unfortunately—although Model would never have admitted it— he had already written off the Ninth Army as lost, beyond any forces that could fight their way back to German lines essentially unassisted. The historian of the 45th Infantry Division chronicled one such desperate venture: "Despite all efforts the 133rd Regiment's battle group was completely encircled northeast of Bobriusk on June 27. Even though the discipline of the men and their officers had not weakened for a moment, here and there the first signs of despair were beginning to show in this almost hopeless situation, evidenced by the first suicides." In the 6th Infantry Division's hegira toward safety, "the wounded had been taken along under the leadership of the division's medical officer, *Oberstabsarzt* Dr. Lorenz. It was not his fault that the horse-drawn wagons sank in the swamps. Dr. Lorenz shot himself after being wounded in the pelvis, *Oberstabsarzt* Dr. Schulz likewise after being shot in the stomach."[8]

Realism forced the conclusion that what was left of the Ninth Army had to be sacrificed to have any chance of saving the rest of the army group; the following day Model even opposed the commitment of the 12th Panzer Division in the gap between the Fourth and Ninth Armies. Within forty-eight more hours the army would be reduced in designation to *Gruppe* von Vormann and subordinated to the Second Army, as too many communications and support units had been lost to control even the remnants of its fighting formations. The loss of the army that he first commanded, and which had held fast throughout the dark year at Rzhev, must have gnawed at Model, and it may have been one of the reasons, as his staff noticed, that his nightly drinking increased.

Could Model's solution have worked? Even initiated with vigor from OKH down, it remains doubtful that Model's battered army group could have fought the Soviets to a halt at Minsk. Soviet tank armies had already begun the maneuvers necessary to encircle the Fourth Army between the Berezina River and Minsk, and German armored reinforcements were arriving too slowly to be able to frustrate them. On the other hand, had Army Group North begun an immediate withdrawal toward Polotsk (as Colonel General Georg Lindemann himself had advocated), the Third Panzer Army's prospects would have dramatically improved. Moreover, with two divisions from the Baltic and three from Galicia converging on Minsk-Baranovichi (along with the three panzer divisions already present or en route), there would have been assembled the nucleus of an intact, army-sized force capable of at least establishing a continuous screen in front of the Red Army spearheads and giving ground without shattering to pieces. At best then, Model's plan could reasonably have reduced the 300,000 casualties (and attendant losses in weapons, equipment, and supplies) that Army Group Center suffered between 22 June and 15 July to a figure perhaps half as large.

Hitler, however, denied Model the chance to achieve even that modest accomplishment, because there were two elements of this plan that the Führer could not accept. Several critical days passed as the dictator refused to allow Army Group North's withdrawal to Polotsk; instead, he insisted that Lindemann close the gap between himself and Reinhardt with an attack southwest through the rear of the advancing Soviet armies. Hitler's motivations appear to have been in large measure political (reluctance to give up Estonia) and naval (his admirals carped about the necessity of holding the Baltic ports), but the effect was to leave the Third Panzer Army in a dangerous limbo, place Army Group North in an increasingly vulnerable strategic position, and deny Model the two infantry divisions he badly needed at Minsk. (The belated withdrawal finally took place when Zeitzler effectively demanded that Hitler accede to the maneuver or dismiss him as chief of the Army General Staff. "I bear the responsibility, not you," groused the Führer as he acquiesced without firing Zeitzler—yet.)[9]

Secondly, Hitler could not accept the fact that only a hasty retreat toward (if not beyond) Minsk offered any chance of saving the Fourth Army. He reiterated through the OKH operations staff that intermediate lines had to be established and if possible held. By this juncture, Hitler literally did not understand the state of affairs at the front, partly because few coherent communications could be picked up from the Fourth Army's isolated elements. Thus, instead of viewing the Berezina as an obstacle to be crossed under enemy pressure, he saw the river as a potential defensive line upon which the Russian onslaught might be halted. That misunderstanding (from which neither Zeitzler, Model, nor von Tippelskirch could shake him) would doom the Fourth Army.[10]

Model coped with this dissonance between what he knew needed to be done and what Hitler would allow by continuing to press for a different decision while simultaneously avoiding complete compliance with the Führer's unending stream of tactically inane directives. For example, it became clear very quickly to the commanders of the 4th, 5th, and 12th Panzer Divisions that army group expected them to fight a mobile battle in which they would give ground when necessary to avoid being themselves encircled. This was the kind of fighting at which German panzer troops excelled, as exemplified by the 5th Panzer's conduct of operations against the entire Fifth Guards Tank Army on the Orsha-Borsiov-Minsk axis between 27 June and 9 July. Reinforced by Tiger Battalion 505, the 5th Panzer entered the battle with twenty Tigers, seventy Panthers, and fifty Pzkw IVs sporting the long 75mm main gun. In nearly two weeks of continuous combat the division destroyed 486 Russian tanks, 11 assault guns, 119 antitank guns, and more than 100 American-made trucks. "We fought by camouflaging ourselves, firing everything we had, withdrawing and then attacking again from a different direction," recalled the commander of Panzergrenadier Regiment 13. "Sleep was totally out of the question." A radio intercept from the Fifth Guards Tank Army ironically testified to the success of Major General Karl Decker's soldiers: "If you meet 5th Panzer, try to go round them!"[11]

Even though Model never stopped trying (along with Zeitzler at OKH) to change Hitler's mind regarding necessary retreats, he also pursued the dangerous course of undermining the Führer's orders. He could not of course overtly defy the dictator's commandments, but he could encourage a certain elasticity in their execution while nonetheless creating a paper record of apparent compliance. This becomes especially evident when considering the many interchanges between the army group's chief of staff—Model's old deputy Hans Krebs—and the commanders of chiefs of staff in the various armies. Krebs would always begin the conversation with a straight reiteration of the formal orders and then essentially allow himself to be browbeaten into sanctioning near-outright disobedience. The following excerpts illustrate this stratagem:

4:35 P.M., 1 July:

KREBS: The Field Marshal's orders are these. 9 Army is to establish Stolbtsy as a strongpoint by using all service support elements which are there or can be got there. Report name of commandant.

STÄDKE (CHIEF OF STAFF, NINTH ARMY): Where and when will 28 Light Division with its anti-tank weapons get in?

KREBS: Probably in the morning.

STÄDKE: That's too late.

KREBS: We still don't know for sure whether the enemy column from Bobovnya is headed for Stolbtsy.

STÄDKE: Sure as eggs is eggs it is.

KREBS: Look at the map, and you'll see they're going for Nesvizh.

STÄDKE: I've nothing more to say.[12]

Midnight, 9 July:

KREBS: 3 Pz Army, while continuing to defend "firm position" Vilnius and IX Corps' present positions, is to concentrate an offensive group of newly arriving formations in the area Kaunas-Yanovo-Ukmerge, and employ it to re-establish contact with IX Army Corps' right and "firm position" Vilnius. Until concentration is completed, the enemy advance round and north of Vilnius is to be delayed by mobile forces.

REINHARDT (TO MODEL): I must come back at you about Vilnius. Surely it's nonsense to make troops which aren't suited to it fight this way. Holding firm at Vilnius will merely produce yet another gap, with serious operational consequences. There are no troops to plug it. . . . This business of "too late" has gradually become such a habit that one can't go along with it any more. I reserve the right to decide for myself. Constantly acting against my better judgment is more than I can do.

2:35 A.M., 10 July:

KREBS: You must hold firm at Byten.

VON TRESCKOW (CHIEF OF STAFF, SECOND ARMY): If the Army Group's last remaining Army isn't to be cut to pieces, that's simply not on. Brave words don't win battles, proper command decisions do! Hanging on stolidly is no good; you can't give 2 Army an impossible task. We must have freedom of action. . . . One thing's for sure, we can only hold the Shchara line for a limited time. The Army Commander must be free to pull back to the Zel'byanka line. . . .

KREBS: Just give your orders as if you really mean it!

7:50 A.M., 10 July:

VON TRESCKOW: The Army Commander must have freedom of action and not be tied to the [Shchara] line.

KREBS: He's not tied to it. The main thing is to try and hold firm at all.

VON TRESCKOW: Does that mean he has freedom of action?
KREBS: Well, no, not exactly.[13]

Normally, as most officers who ever served below Model discovered in short order, such defiant language would have been met with instant fireworks from his headquarters, probably followed in hours by the relief of the commander in question. Not so at Army Group Center that summer. Instead, Model and Krebs consistently represented their corps and army commanders to OKH as striving to carry out even the most nonsensical orders to the letter.

Model had personally given up any hope of holding Minsk by 1 July, though this conviction was not communicated to OKH for another twenty-four hours, when the Soviet Third Army had already begun probing the city's defenses. The field marshal held Minsk for one more day, in reality to evacuate nearly 15,000 wounded soldiers, but in his portrayals to Hitler Model's rationale again resembled the *Schild und Schwert*: He had given up the city in order to re-create a firm line to the west that would allow him to concentrate counterattack forces capable of rescuing the Fourth Army and reclaiming the ground lost. A prima facie case could be made for this idea, as Army Group Center now had the three panzer divisions—the 28th Jäger Division and the 50th and 170th Infantry Divisions—in the Minsk area. (What Zeitzler could have told the Führer—but declined to—was that six divisions had no chance of halting the Russian onslaught by themselves. Instead, the chief of the Army General Staff again tacitly aligned himself with Model in hopes that by subterfuge the proper tactic of elastic defense might finally be initiated. Both men realized, however, that the cost of stabilizing the front in that manner was writing off tens of thousands of Fourth Army soldiers still struggling toward the west in small, fragmented groups.)[14]

Meanwhile, the Red Army prepared to expand its summer offensive. On 14 July the moment of truth arrived for the Second Army when the First Belorussian Front struck the army's now-exposed left flank. Marshal Konstantin Rokossovsky's immediate operational objective was Brest-Litovsk, the fortress on the edge of the Pripet Marshes, but in reality the Red Army had now taken aim at Warsaw in central Poland. Conceivably the resources still existed to counter this threat if Army Group North received authorization for a withdrawal from Estonia, which would make several relatively fresh divisions available. In an attempt to force just that decision, Model had flown to Rastenburg, East Prussia, on 10 July for a face-to-face meeting with Hitler. Along with Zeitzler, Model's old Ninth Army stalwart Johannes Freissner (now commanding Army Group North) also attended. Given Model's simultaneous control of two army groups, this meant that the leadership of three-quarters of the Eastern Front's armies had now been concentrated in the hands of Model or his protégé. Even von Manstein at the peak of his influence had not enjoyed such an advantage.

Whatever confidence Model had felt upon boarding his plane, however, quickly proved to be misplaced. Hitler had buttressed himself for the conference with the presence of Grand Admiral Karl Dönitz, commander of the German navy. At the appropriate moment in the discussion the admiral ponderously allowed that the loss of Estonia would cripple the *Kriegsmarine* by denying his U-boat crews their only safe training area, torpedoing the plan advocated by Model, Zeitzler, and Freissner. When Freissner raised the potential disaster that would occur if the Russians menaced Riga (in Latvia) while substantial German forces remained in Estonia, Dönitz admitted that "it might be advisable at once to take appropriate measures," but exactly what he meant by this comment was unclear. Before Model or Zeitzler could react to the statement, Hitler effectively ended the matter by declaring an immediate evacuation of Estonia out of the question.[15]

Within a week the Soviet Second Tank Army had penetrated to within twenty-five miles of Warsaw. Stunned, Hitler finally relented, agreeing to the Estonian withdrawal and the release of several elite divisions refitting in the interior. The 3rd SS *Totenkopf*,

5th SS *Wiking, Hermann Göring,* and *Grossdeutschland* Panzer Divisions then rushed into combat, belatedly bringing the Russian advance to a halt along the Vistula River (though arguably the exhaustion of the Red Army's supply system had just as much to do with this result). The damage, however, had been done in the Baltic, where Army Group North barely managed to execute a fighting pullout from Estonia and funnel thousands of troops through the bottleneck at Riga, only to be isolated against the Courland coast later that summer.[16]

Meanwhile, on 20 July, Colonel Klaus von Stauffenburg placed a bomb at Hitler's feet during the daily military conference. Accidentally shielded from the worst of the blast by a heavy oaken table leg, the Führer survived the explosion, but the assassination attempt led to a horrifying series of arrests, torture, show trials, and executions as the dictator ruthlessly pursued his vengeance— primarily directed against army officers of doubtful loyalty to the now-tottering regime. Model himself was hardly a suspect (despite having been unwittingly surrounded by conspiring officers at various points in his career), and indeed he became the first senior commander to transmit a message to East Prussia reaffirming his loyalty to Hitler. Nonetheless, the incident had important consequences that directly affected Model.

In the wake of the assassination attempt the Führer finally sacked Zeitzler as chief of the Army General Staff, replacing him with Heinz Guderian. Given their past association at Panzer Group Two in 1941, this might have seemed to Model to be a favorable change, but outward appearances were deceiving. Guderian belonged to the same school of "elastic defense" and large-scale panzer tactics with which Model had so rudely clashed in Galicia. Indeed, "Fast Heinz" had by this time begun to associate Model with the same practices he had long condemned in von Kluge:

> Herr von Kluge was a hard-working soldier, his knowledge of small-scale tactics was good, but he was totally ignorant concerning the

employment of armoured formations in mobile operations. His influence on the command of armour was invariably, so far as I ever came across it, restrictive. He was an expert at breaking up units. It is therefore hardly surprising that the command in the West continued to try to cure each symptom that appeared instead of attacking the root of the disease, and going over to mobile warfare with what still remained of its armoured strength. What did remain was squandered in further frontal attacks with limited objectives made under fire of the enemy's naval guns.[17]

Given that Model had been a successful panzer division commander, Guderian would not have labeled Model "totally ignorant" of mobile operations. On the other hand, reports from Hermann Balck and Walther Nehring (both Guderian protégés) from Army Group North Ukraine would have alerted the new chief of the Army General Staff that Model now pursued a different tactical model. As such, although he praised Model's "courageous example" in restoring Army Group Center's front line in Poland, Guderian had no intention of allowing the field marshal to retain command of what he considered the critical sector defending his own East Prussian homeland.[18]

Hardly the apolitical career soldier that he painted himself in his memoirs, Guderian launched a Machiavellian campaign against both von Kluge and Model even before Hitler had left his hospital bed. To understand the nature of his maneuver, one must first realize that, to Heinz Guderian, the war had been irrevocably lost, but "the Eastern Front was tottering on the edge of an abyss from which it was necessary to save millions of German soldiers and civilians. I should have regarded myself as a shabby coward if I had refused to attempt to save the eastern armies and my homeland, eastern Germany." Whatever occurred in France or along Germany's western frontier was in fact of little interest to Guderian from this point forward, except as that front competed with him for a share of the Reich's dwindling resources of manpower, weapons, and fuel. Thus, during his 21 July conversation with the Führer, Guderian made several unsubtle references to von Kluge's complicity in the bomb plot, as well as damning his conduct of operations with faint praise. The unspoken message was clear: Von Kluge should be relieved of his command. Guderian could hardly have been unaware that Model represented the most probable successor to the position of *Oberbefehlshaber* West (OB West), which would then clear the path for his own preferred candidate to take over Army Group Center: Hans-Georg Reinhardt of the Third Panzer Army. Hitler initially resisted this idea, but within three weeks the disintegration of the Normandy front, combined with even clearer indications that von Kluge might be trying to negotiate his own terms with the Allies, led to exactly the scenario Guderian desired.[19]

On 1 August, meanwhile, Model's tactical situation became even more convoluted. In late July the field marshal had unilaterally ordered the abandonment of the last "fortified positions" east of the 1939 German-Soviet line partitioning Poland, thus freeing sufficient forces to contain the most advanced Soviet spearheads. Another evacuation, however, was taking place behind his own lines as German police, administration, and even military garrison units began a hasty (and equally unauthorized) withdrawal from Warsaw. Guderian countermanded this panicky movement on 26 July, but a dangerous vacuum had been created, along with the local perception that Red Army tanks were only hours away from rolling into the Polish capital. Thus, while Model labored to piece together a coherent front east of Warsaw, within that city the Polish Home Army emerged from the shadows to inaugurate an uprising against the German garrison.

Model apparently had advance warning about the uprising but chose to consider the problem primarily one for rear-area commanders to sort out as best they could. Because critical supply lines ran through the Warsaw suburbs of Praga and Saska-Kepa east of the Vistula, the field marshal quickly committed regular troops to crushing the rebellion there and maintaining control of the four large bridges across which his supplies flowed. Beyond that, he was coldly content to see the fight carried on in the city proper by a motley collection of police, minor SS units, and foreign "volunteers" whose tactics became so draconian that they shocked even members of Hitler's inner circle. Model, who ignored rather than condoned these atrocities, had once again become associated with operations that would later rise to the level of war crimes.[20]

The doomed rebellion still raged on 15 August when Hitler again summoned Model to Rastenburg and announced his second transfer in less than two months. Awarding him the diamonds to his Knight's Cross, Hitler thanked Model for stabilizing the front and rewarded him with an even more difficult assignment: supreme command in France. In the background hovered Guderian, smiling triumphantly.

PART FOUR

The Fireman
Heads West

13

WITH BLASTING HATRED
AND UNCEASING COURAGE

Army Group B:
August to November 1944

WALTHER MODEL ARRIVED AT THE HEADQUARTERS OF OB
West/Army Group B at La Roche Guyon during the evening of 17
August, bearing with him the order relieving von Kluge. That
OKW relied upon Model's abrupt appearance with written orders
rather than notifying von Kluge ahead of time (the usual procedure) suggests that Hitler had some rather strong suspicions
about the level of defiance—to say nothing of potential treason—
brewing at the upper echelons of the western army. Hitler's letter
to von Kluge transferred him to the "Führer Reserve" (*Führerreserv*) for "recuperation," which by the late summer of 1944 could
mean anything from retirement in obscurity to a noose of piano
wire after condemnation by the so-called People's Court. Given
the rumor that OKW's wireless intercept section had picked up a

signal "from Kluge to Patton concerning the possibility of a truce" during his last trip to the front, Model's old commander undoubtedly had some idea of what awaited him as he read the final line of his orders: "Field Marshal von Kluge is to state to which part of Germany he is going."[1]

(Some accounts suggest that Hitler had informed Model, upon assigning him to the command, that von Kluge had been branded a traitor and conspirator in the 20 July assassination attempt in the coerced confession of Lieutenant Colonel Cesar von Hofacker. Hitler then charged Model with rooting out all other subversive elements in his command. This information Model is supposed to have communicated to von Kluge during their final private dinner. Without adequate documentation, it is difficult to accept this story as more than apocrypha.)[2]

Such was von Kluge's stolid demeanor, however, that no one noticed either agitation or fear when the two field marshals spoke that evening; observers like Chief of Staff Hans Speidel and Operations Officer Bodo Zimmermann noted that "Kluge took his dismissal quite calmly." There are no records of the private conversation between von Kluge and Model, but neither the atmosphere nor the essentials of the discussion are difficult to reconstruct. Though they had worked together for more than a year at Army Group Center, their relationship was not warm. Model had either bypassed his army group commander with direct communications to Hitler or simply evaded, ignored, or disobeyed von Kluge's orders on multiple occasions. Moreover, von Kluge had knowingly (if uncomfortably) presided over the coterie of anti-Hitler conspirators at Army Group Center's headquarters and now had drifted fully into the camp of those who believed the war had been lost, with a negotiated peace in the West being Germany's only chance to avoid being overrun by the Red Army.[3]

What von Kluge told his successor, therefore, certainly echoed what he had written to Hitler not two weeks earlier: "I arrived here with the firm intention of carrying out your orders to hold fast at all costs. But . . . the price which must be paid consists of the slow but steady annihilation of our troops." Between 6 June and 14 August, even the fragmentary casualty reports available at headquarters document that Army Group B had lost nearly 160,000 men. Even before the breakout attack at Avranches by George Patton's U.S. Third Army, von Kluge had warned that "once the enemy has penetrated into open country, organized operations will no longer be possible to control owing to our troops' lack of mobility." This was the situation he sketched for Model on the maps: the Seventh Army, the Fifth Panzer Army, four corps headquarters, and elements of at least thirteen divisions had been all but isolated in the Falaise pocket, with the only remaining route of escape already susceptible to Allied artillery fire. The invasion of southern France, which had occurred forty-eight hours earlier, represented only the latest in a string of seemingly unending disasters.[4]

Summarizing one final time his views for Hitler, von Kluge wrote on 18 August, "I do not know whether Field Marshal Model, a man of proved ability, can still save the situation. I wish him success with all my heart. But if he does not succeed, . . . I appeal to you to end this war." For himself, the dejected field marshal claimed that "I cannot bear the accusation of having brought about the fate of our armies in the West by mistaken measures, and I have no means of defending myself." Secreted within the briefcase von Kluge placed on the seat of his departing staff car was a capsule of potassium cyanide, which he swallowed in the vicinity of Metz: "I am therefore taking the only action I can, and shall go where thousands of my compatriots have preceded me." The Gestapo arrested both his son and son-in-law (both serving officers), while dark rumors circulated that an SS officer had executed him in cold blood.[5]

Model of course had yet to reach the point where he admitted to himself that Germany's cause was hopeless (although his increasingly heavy drinking belied his overt optimism). Zimmermann noted that "Model, who had hitherto seen action only on the Eastern front, did not immediately grasp the full gravity of the situation in France and hoped that he might yet restore it." While Model would have agreed that the tactical situation was grim, his experience in Russia seemed to have left him with the firm—to the point of being unrealistic—conviction that he could master any crisis. Thus, his usual abrupt manner with staff and subordinates degenerated within hours into an uncouth gruffness unusual even by his own draconian standards. "He began his work, just as von Kluge had done," recalled Speidel, "with preconceived notions and accusations against his new staff and army commanders. The first orders that he gave were for continued resistance south of the Seine in the Falaise pocket." Model's directives, Speidel insisted, "embodied the unimaginative idea that every inch of ground must be defended without hope of relief or even escape."[6]

These recollections cannot be accepted at face value; they were initially collected by American interrogators after the war. During the period 1945 to 1948 the American military history project concentrated heavily on debriefing men like Fritz Bayerlein, Günther Blumentritt, Speidel, Walther Warlimont, and Zimmermann regarding operations on the Western Front between D-Day and the Battle of the Bulge. The German officers answering the questions had two primary personal objectives: avoiding culpability for war crimes and blaming Hitler for virtually all errors of military judgment. Model—both dead and closely associated with the Nazi regime—made an excellent target and was often presented as little more than the Führer's abusive "boy marshal."

The truth is that Model followed the same course of action he had pursued at Army Groups North and Center: publicly issuing the orders that Hitler demanded while quietly suborning them. He specified a new defensive line on the Seine River, not because he had any illusions that it might be held, but because Hitler had specifically ordered him to "build up a new western front as far forward of the Seine-Yonne line as possible, using the divisions which will be gradually evacuated from southern France." Given that the Allied invasion of southern France had already rendered part of his orders irrelevant, Model capitalized on Hitler's mention of the Seine as de facto authority to save the troops in the Falaise pocket. Even as his headquarters at La Roche Guyon came under fire from Allied patrols and had to be evacuated on 19 August, Model commanded that the troops and staffs of the Seventh and Fifth Panzer Armies begin an immediate withdrawal via the last partly open escape route, leaving behind all heavy equipment if necessary. This decision probably succored nearly 130,000 men. (Model missed the attack on his headquarters because he had gone as far forward as the headquarters of II SS Panzer Corps to examine the situation personally.)[7]

The fully motorized American and British armies, however, lunged forward with a speed unexpected by even the most pessimistic German officers. Patton in rapid succession took Dreux, Chateaudun, and Orleans (17 August); Versailles (18 August); Mantes Grassicourt (19 August); and Fontainebleau (20 August). The U.S. XV Corps forced the first bridgehead across the Seine on 20 August; two days later the French resistance staged a massive uprising in Paris. Hitler and OKW maintained the fantastical conviction that by transferring three nonmotorized infantry divisions from the Fifteenth Army (in the Pas de Calais area) to the Seine, Paris might be held and the front stabilized. In the event that Paris could not be held, the city commandant, Lieutenant General Dieter von Choltitz, received instructions to destroy the city's military installations and Seine River bridges, "even if residential areas and artistic monuments are destroyed thereby."[8]

Model countered by informing Hitler that he could hold Paris and the river line, but only with 200,000 additional troops and several hundred tanks. Speidel represented this request as "naive," never realizing that this interchange represented yet another variation of Model's *Schild und Schwert* maneuver: promising Hitler what he wanted if an impossible condition could be met. In reality, Model had no intention of defending Paris or even committing troops to crush the Maqui uprising, any more than he had been willing to intervene against the Polish Home Army. He certainly was not unhappy when von Choltitz disobeyed orders, allowing the 4th French Armored Division to enter a largely intact Paris on 25 August, although he acceded to Hitler's demand for an in absentia condemnation of the garrison commander.[9]

By this time the designation of Model as *Oberbefehlshaber* West had become essentially academic, as contact had been lost with General Johannes von Blaskowitz's Army Group G in southern France, freeing the field marshal to concentrate on saving the remnants of Army Group B. *Oberstgruppenführer* Sepp Dietrich's Fifth Panzer Army had been decimated, but his mobile divisions—both SS and army—had managed to organize *Kampfgruppen* around their few remaining vehicles and tanks that were capable of weak but organized resistance along both banks of the Oise River. The Seventh Army had nearly disintegrated while running the gauntlet out of Falaise, losing its commander, several division headquarters, and virtually all transport and heavy weapons. When the army's chief of staff, Lieutenant General Rudolf Freiherr von Gersdorff (the same officer who had used an unwitting Model to cover his March 1943 attempt to assassinate Hitler), managed to reach headquarters, he and the newly appointed army commander, General Erich Brandenberger, faced the unenviable task of sorting out what little remained while fleeing across central France.

Model's only intact army—General Gustav von Zangen's Fifteenth Army—had been stripped piecemeal of most of its transportation during the two-month-long battle for Normandy; nearly a dozen divisions had been left immobile along the coast of northwestern France. For a few days it looked like the British 21st Army Group and the U.S. First Army might not duplicate Patton's advance and there might be an opportunity to extract von Zangen's command as the nucleus of a new defensive line along the Somme and Marne Rivers. By 27 August, however, British and American armored divisions had also forced the lower Seine, and in a mad dash the British 11th Armored Division seized Antwerp on 4 September, at least theoretically pocketing the Fifteenth Army.[10]

Even in the catastrophe engulfing Army Group Center, Model had been able to exert more influence on the course of the battle than he did during his first week in command in France. Partly the difference came from the fact that in Belorussia the field marshal had at least had access to a handful of full-strength panzer divisions that could be used in short, sharp tactical jabs to keep the Soviets off balance. The relative mobility of the German and Red armies had also been much more equal than that of Model's forces when compared to Patton's. Finally, although the Russians had gained air superiority around Minsk, Vitebsk, and Bobriusk, nothing had prepared Model for the unrelenting air attacks of the western Allies. "Unlimited air dominance, similar to ours of 1940," he wrote on 29 August, allowed his opponent "to push through wherever it wants."[11]

On 28 August, at Fifth Panzer Army headquarters, in a meeting with Dietrich and the chiefs of staff of all three armies, the issue finally came to a head. Model was bending over the situation maps laying out an intermediate defensive line between the Seine and his "final position" along the Somme-Marne line and still speaking of phased withdrawals. Sepp Dietrich had been stomping around the room throughout the meeting, muttering to himself (not entirely an unusual occurrence), when he suddenly stopped and addressed the field marshal directly, "Do stop this, this is of no use at all." He then erupted into a prolonged diatribe against Hitler and OKW. Just as he had never corrected Speidel the many times he undoubtedly overheard his chief of staff characterizing Hitler as "that asshole in the Burgdorff," Model on this occasion made no reply.[12]

Instead, between 28 August and 4 September Model came to grips for the first time in his career with a disaster that he could not immediately ameliorate. In an order of the day to the troops scampering back toward the Reich's borders, the field marshal admitted publicly, "We have lost a battle, but I assure you of this:

We will win this war! I cannot tell you more at present, although I know that questions are burning on your lips. Whatever has happened, never lose your faith in the future of Germany." These words rang hollow when accompanied by the following bleak assessment:

> With the enemy's advance and the withdrawal of our front several hundred thousand soldiers are falling back. . . . In this stream are remnants of broken units. . . . Whenever orderly columns turn off the road to reorganize, streams of disorganized elements push on. With their wagons move whispers, rumors, haste, endless disorder and vicious self-interest. This atmosphere is being brought back to the rear areas, infecting units still intact.

Complaining of "stupid gossip, rumors and irresponsible reports," Model lectured his troops that the enemy could not be "everywhere at once," and that "if all the tanks reported by rumormongers were counted, there would be a hundred thousand of them." The mission had now become one of "gaining time, which the Führer needs to put new weapons and new troops into operation." "I appeal to your honor as soldiers," Model concluded.[13]

The desperate ring of this and other public orders represents only part of the evidence that the "lion of the defense" had at least momentarily lost some of his legendary aplomb. He also began besieging Hitler and OKW with increasingly strident demands for reinforcements that he must have known were absolutely unavailable. On 4 September, for example, he asked for twenty-five fresh infantry and six new panzer divisions. This was not Model manipulating Hitler for advantage; this was a man close to the edge of despair. A final example cements the case: By the time British tanks neared Antwerp, Model was preparing to sacrifice the entire Fifteenth Army. Seeing no other way to slow or halt the Allied armored strike into Belgium (and ultimately to the Rhine itself), he ordered von Zangen to launch his infantry divisions in a suicidal attack against the flanks of the British XXX Corps. Had these orders been carried out, at least an additional 65,000 to 85,000 troops would probably have ended up in Allied POW cages in short order.[14]

The attack never occurred. Model simply could not manage both the coordinating responsibilities of OB West and the operational requirements of Army Group B simultaneously, in part owing to circumstances but in equal measure because of temperament. By late August the two headquarters—colocated during the Normandy fighting—were sixty miles apart with complete parallel staffs. Given Allied air superiority, regular commuting was out of the question, and even the most organized officer could not have accomplished both. For Model this constituted an impossible challenge, given his habit of roaming the front lines for hours without communications and passing out orders directly to subordinate units about which he often forgot to inform his chief of staff or operations officer. Even men who had worked under Field Marshal Erwin Rommel's freewheeling leadership style found it difficult to keep Model's affairs untangled. Speidel and Siegfried Westphal (chief of staff at OB West) even coined a term for this behavior. "To Model"—as in "to muddle" or "to meddle"—was what they came to expect when the field marshal left headquarters; "to de-Model" was what had to be done in his wake.[15]

The staff eventually appealed in late August through the OKW operations chief, Colonel General Alfred Jodl, for the return of Field Marshal Karl Gerd von Rundstedt to exercise the senior command. Hitler had relieved the elderly (and alcoholic) but still capable von Rundstedt in favor of von Kluge on 5 July, citing his age and potential defeatism. With Rommel wounded (and suspected of complicity in the assassination plot), however, von Rundstedt was the most popular officer with the average German soldier left in Hitler's shrinking *Führerreserv*. The *Landser* credited him with the early victories in Poland, France, and southern Russia, whereas to most men in the western armies Model was an abstract name in

Wehrmacht communiqués that retained very little credibility any-way. Model learned of this proposal in late August—after it had al-ready been presented to Hitler—and astounded both Speidel and Westphal by commenting, "That is a good idea."[16]

Reappointed as OB West on 5 September, von Rundstedt made his first act in his new post the countermanding of Model's attack orders to the Fifteenth Army. Instead, he mandated that von Zan-gen evacuate as many men and weapons as possible across the Scheldt River estuary west of Antwerp before British infantry had a chance to catch up to their tanks and seal off the trap. This op-eration saved nearly 80,000 troops to fight again in the battles for Holland, Belgium, and the Rhine and gave Model the breathing space he needed to recover his equilibrium. (It also, however, set up a dynamic that would reemerge later: Having learned that his new commander was hardly infallible, von Zangen in months to come would be repeatedly ready to challenge or even ignore Model's directives.)[17]

This exchange of responsibilities also coincided with Model los-ing Speidel as his chief of staff. Already implicated in the 20 July plot by several forced confessions, OKW had attempted to pry Speidel loose from Model's headquarters in mid-August. Charac-terizing these charges as "rubbish," Model bluntly refused to send the "indispensable" Speidel to Berlin. Model knew exactly what Speidel thought, if not exactly his role in the conspiracy. The two men, Speidel wrote later, "had found ample opportunity to discuss the general situation," and the chief of staff had not been shy about advocating "the political and military measures which in his opinion ought to be taken." But like von Rundstedt and von Kluge before him, even though "Model saw clearly the hopelessness of the total situation," he "declined to speak to Hitler about these matters, which he called 'none of my business.'" Nor would Model approve "independent strategic decisions in the west, al-though the army leaders and field commanders repeatedly urged such a decision."[18]

All Model would do (again, as his predecessors had done before him) was shield Speidel personally for as long as possible and turn a deaf ear to such treasonous conversations as he might accidentally overhear. On 5 September, however, OKW peremptorily ordered Speidel to Berlin, where *Reichsführer* Heinrich Himmler had him arrested two days later. As a replacement, OKW again paired Model with the smooth-talking, intellectually shallow Hans Krebs, who arrived sometime around 9 September. To offset any political capital his earlier resistance might have cost him with Hitler, on Speidel's departure Model filed a formal request that Army Group B be sent a "National Socialist Leadership Officer," the quasi-commissar position created by Hitler the previous year for the Russian front. This move naturally did nothing to endear him to the circle of anti-Hitler officers with whom he now worked, though Model hardly cared.

Meanwhile, at least from a morale point of view, the picture began to grow more favorable. The troops corralled at collection points turned out to be more confused than defeated. After marching several hundred miles from Falaise to the borders of Belgium and Germany, those who intended to surrender had already done so. Most of the remainder, perhaps recalling the vitriol heaped on the German army in 1918 after giving up the fight before the Fatherland had even been invaded, wanted weapons and orders that would enable them to fight again. Wilhelm Prüller of the 9th Panzer Division, who had written on 12 August, "In the nights I often wonder how it is that I'm still here and not under a simple wooden cross," was one of those who avoided Allied captivity in the harrowing trek back toward the German border. He arrived footsore, but with his morale amazingly unimpaired, as can be gleaned from his letter home on 10 September:

You know my ever-present optimism; it's there now as it always was. I am sure everything will take a turn for the better. It can't be that a people to whom the world obviously owes everything could disintegrate. There's no nation more faithful, more courageous, more efficient. Our accursed enemies will not conquer us, even if now the bitter struggle for our beloved fatherland seems quite hopeless. . . . It is quite unthinkable that everything should have been for nothing.[19]

Additional good news reached headquarters in early September as Colonel General Kurt Student's newly raised First Parachute Army was thrown into the gap between the Fifteenth and Seventh Armies. Hastily organized around several parachute training regiments, and initially deploying only about twenty thousand men with few heavy weapons and limited infantry experience, the First Parachute nonetheless represented an invaluable nucleus around which stragglers like Prüller could coalesce. Moreover, as events would quickly prove, Student—as an expert in air assaults—would be exactly the right man to have in Holland that fall.

On 11 September a much more relaxed Model moved his headquarters to Oosterbeek, just outside the Dutch city of Arnhem on the banks of the lower Rhine. This location was convenient to the headquarters at Doetinchem of II SS Panzer Corps, whose two divisions were just beginning the process of being reorganized and refitted as Army Group B's new operational reserve. Oosterbeek, noted Lieutenant Gustav Sedelhauser of the headquarters staff, "had everything we wanted: a fine road net and excellent accommodations," especially the Hartenstein Hotel, which historian Cornelius Ryan describes as including a "broad expanse of crescent-shaped lawn, stretching back into park-like surroundings where deer roamed undisturbed, and the smaller two-story, tree shaded Tafelberg with its glassed-in veranda and paneled rooms." Like the rest of the staff (including Model), Sedelhauser "was looking forward to some peace and a chance to get my laundry done."[20]

Model and his staff were sitting there on the verandah of the Tafelberg in the early afternoon of 15 September. "Whenever he was at the headquarters, the Field Marshal was punctual to a fault," recalled Sedelhauser. "We always sat down to luncheon at precisely 1300 hours." A sudden series of explosive blasts wracked the building, knocking a glass of chilled Moselle wine from Model's hand. As the field marshal and his party dove beneath the heavy oak tables for cover from shrapnel, the army group operations officer, Colonel Hans von Templehoff, burst into the room, shouting, "What an absolute swine! There are one to two parachute divisions right on top of us!" "Right!" responded Model. "Everyone out!"

The sky outside was full of planes and parachutes as the British 1st Airborne Division began leaping into Arnhem, initiating "Operation Market-Garden," Field Marshal Bernard Law Montgomery's ambitious bid to breach the Rhine barrier with a carpet of three airborne divisions. Momentarily Model entertained the idea that what he saw was a raid designed to capture him and his headquarters staff, but the enormity of the Allied air armada quickly dispelled this conceit. Not even stopping for "his cap, pistol, and belt," or when his briefcase dropped and spewed out his underwear and toiletries across the sidewalk, Model leapt into a staff car and raced toward Doetinchem.[21]

This flurry of activity represented excitement rather than panic, as some of Model's detractors would later argue. He was back in his element, confronted by a dire tactical threat on a limited front, and the prospect energized him. The scope if not the intent of the Allied attack was clearly evident, but as he motored toward II SS Panzer Corps headquarters, Model realized that whoever had planned the 1st British Airborne Division's drop on Arnhem had committed a serious error. Instead of accepting the risks inherent in landing directly in an urban area to have the best possible chance of capturing both ends of the Arnhem bridge intact, the British paras opted to land in clear terrain on the outskirts of the city and then rush for their objective. This meant that there would an interval of as much as two hours before the enemy could materialize in downtown Arnhem, a delay Model intended to use.

Obergruppenführer Willi Bittrich, who had served intermittently under Model's command since January 1942, had already begun to react. Although his divisions were seriously understrength (the 9th SS *Hohenstaufen* had about 3,000 men and 30 armored cars but no panzers or heavy weapons; the 10th SS *Frundsberg* disposed 4,000 troops, a battalion of Pzkw Mk IVs, and 12 antitank guns), they were composed of veterans. More to the point, both divisions were now composed of seasoned veterans and by chance their location so near the British drop zone had gone unremarked upon by Allied intelligence. Bittrich had already ordered a local SS replacement battalion to block the paratroopers' line of march into Arnhem, based on the theory, as its commander, Sepp Krafft, later explained, that "it is not possible to destroy overwhelming airborne forces with slight forces" like his makeshift battalion, "but one can pin him down to secure time to prepare counter-measures."[22]

Bittrich and Model learned that the Allied airborne carpet extended from Arnhem south through Nijmegen (U.S. 82nd Airborne Division) and Eindoven (U.S. 101st Airborne Division) to the Maas-Escaut Canal, over which the heavily armored British XXX Corps was to advance across captured bridges all the way to the Rhine in seventy-two hours or less. Model believed that Arnhem might not be the ultimate Allied objective and that more airborne drops might be expected farther east in support of a British right turn toward the Ruhr, but this did not affect his early tactical decisions. The two men quickly decided that the 9th SS *Hohenstaufen* would oppose the British 1st Airborne Division at Arnhem, while the 10th SS *Frundsberg* moved south to reinforce the fragments of the garrison units dealing with the American landings at Nijmegen under control of the ad hoc *Korps* Feldt. Student's First Parachute Army would operate against the Americans at Eindoven and directly oppose the XXX Corps thrust.[23]

It was evident from these orders that Model intended to do far more than defend river crossings. Aided by a captured copy of the

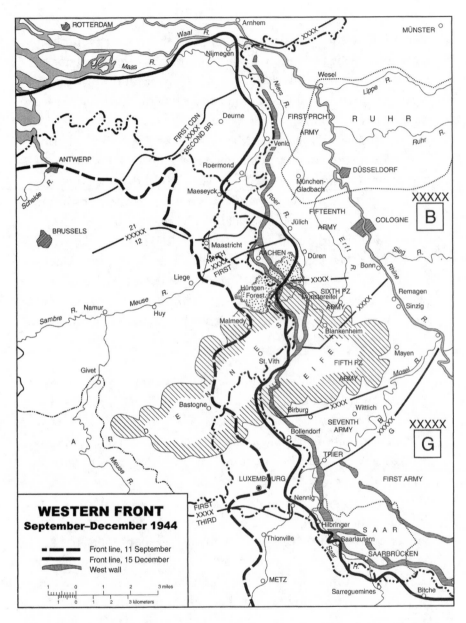

Although Allied histories emphasize the logistical difficulties of maintaining their advance into Germany after the breakout from the Normandy beachhead, Model's twin defensive victories at Arnhem and Hürtgen Forest stabilized the Western Front for the last time in the war.

entire British operational plan, the field marshal intended to inflict a stinging defeat on his opponents, possibly even clear southern Holland of Allied forces. To achieve this objective he could not afford to stymie the British advance by destroying all the bridges between the Maas-Escaut Canal and the Rhine, because he needed them to maneuver his own forces offensively.

This decision represented Model's most serious tactical error during the battle, and Bittrich argued the point with him from the beginning: "I suggested to Field Marshal Model that the Nijmegen bridge, which had already had a demolition charge in position, should be blown up. Field Marshal Model rejected this suggestion . . . arguing that the bridgehead might be the point of departure for future attacks towards the south." The argument surfaced again and again over the next few days, with Bittrich and Heinz Harmel (commanding the 10th SS *Frundsberg*) arguing passionately that the bridge over the Waal River had to be destroyed. After the war Harmel reflected:

> Model said don't blow the bridge because I need it for a counterstroke. By that he meant a counter-attack at the higher operational level. Bittrich and I believed it should be blown straight away. We realized we would never mobilize sufficient forces for an offensive on that scale. It was a case of cutting one's coat according to one's cloth. Model's shirt was always too short, it never reached!

Eventually, with British tanks approaching the bridge on 20 September, Harmel gave the order, "on my own responsibility, to blow the road bridge," but either through mischance or sabotage by the Dutch underground, the charges failed to detonate. "I was waiting to see the bridge collapse and the tanks plunge into the river," Harmel said. "Instead, they moved forward relentlessly, getting bigger and bigger, closer and closer."[24]

Aside from this error, which allowed XXX Corps ultimately to advance far enough to watch impotently from across the river as the Germans liquidated the 1st Airborne Division, and his inexplicably stubborn refusal to call off a senseless attack by the First Parachute Army against superior enemy forces on 28 September, Model fought an outstanding battle and handed the Allies a sharp defeat. Not only did the Rhine barrier hold, but the 1st Airborne lost 7,578 men out of the 10,005 who jumped into Arnhem (the division was never reconstituted). Total British casualties in the nine-day battle exceeded 17,000 (at least 13,226 British and 3,974 American). Model's methods were not pretty: The Germans probably lost between 9,800 and 13,300 troops in repelling the attack.[25]

Throughout the battle Model had commanded from the front lines, as he always did in the glory days at the Ninth Army. As one battalion commander recalled, "He was always feared, because he constantly demanded precise reports over the situation, available manpower, wounded, units involved and so on." This wandering field marshal syndrome discomfited Hans Krebs far less than it had Speidel because he had long been accustomed to dealing with it. On 23 September, for example, a question arose regarding whether a changed tactical situation on the front of the 59th Infantry Division meant that an attack mandated by Model on one of his jaunts should be canceled. The division commander brought the question to LXXXVIII Corps headquarters, which bucked it up to the Fifteenth Army, where the army chief of staff telephoned Krebs for clarification. The answer was succinct: "If the Field Marshal has ordered the attack then it should still happen." Lost in the moment perhaps was that critical "if" in Krebs's reply, which implied that he was enforcing compliance with an order about which he had never been informed.[26]

The German success at Arnhem cannot, however, be attributed solely to Walther Model. The Allied strategy suffered from serious flaws and might well have collapsed under their weight even without Model's presence. Model also benefited from the intelligence fiasco that caused the II SS Panzer Corps to be overlooked or at least discounted by enemy planners. Nor should the quality of

Model's subordinates be discounted. As at the Ninth Army, he was at his best with a strong supporting team; at Arnhem he had an airborne expert (Student) commanding an army, a gifted panzer leader (Bittrich) at the head of a corps, and seasoned veterans like Heinz Harmel, Gerhard Graf von Schwerin, and Kurt Chill leading divisions. Finally, the Arnhem battle was so obviously a tactical affair and so thoroughly under Model's control even at the height of the fighting that Hitler did not badger him excessively with unwanted orders, while von Rundstedt oversaw the arrival of limited but sufficient reinforcements to win the day.

Arnhem restored much of the self-confidence Model had lost during his first two weeks in the West. Gone were the moments of personal weakness when he publicly admitted in his orders that Germany faced defeat. Instead of appealing to the honor of his soldiers, he reverted to the stern language of the Eastern Front. One colonel, defending his sector in Aachen against an overwhelming American attack, received the following curt communiqué from Model's headquarters in mid-October: "Fight to the last man. If necessary, have yourself buried under the ruins!"[27] By November his rhetoric had become even more strident, to the point that it is difficult to believe that the same man who approved the September "We have lost a battle" announcement signed the order of the day delivered to German soldiers in the Hürtgen forest:

> The long-awaited enemy offensive has begun. . . . Disappointed peoples stand behind the mercenaries of America and England. Peoples who had been promised Germany's collapse this year. Behind them stand the greedy Jew, lusting after gain, and the murderous, bloodthirsty Bolshevist. Capture of the Ruhr, the collapse of the Reich, the *enslavement* of all Germans are but stages of their will to destroy. We must shock these hypocritical benefactors of mankind out of their expectations of a cheap victory. With terror they shall realize that here German soldiers battle stubbornly and

tenaciously for German home soil. Our women and children look on us. With blasting hatred and unceasing courage we will fight for the honor and security of the German fatherland. Every combat squad must be a repository of fanatic battle spirit in our holy struggle for life. Then the bitter strife of the Third Reich at Aachen will end with our success. Faith in the Führer will guarantee our victory.[28]

As the days grew shorter and colder with the approach of autumn, logistical difficulties inevitably slowed the Allied advance, while a final resurgence of the German war industry and Himmler's draconian mobilization of the Reich's final manpower reserve sent a steady trickle of reinforcements and new equipment to the front. These conditions, along with the obsolete but still formidable "West Wall" fortifications, allowed Model in large measure to stabilize the front. He could not prevent the Allies from advancing, but he could slow their progress, inflict casualties, and—above all—reestablish an essentially continuous line of defense.

His efforts to blunt the U.S. First Army's thrust through the West Wall in the Aachen–Hürtgen forest–Roer River dam area during October and November exemplified this pattern. Although Aachen itself fell after heavy street fighting on 21 October, Model managed to tie down the U.S. First (and subsequently the Ninth) Army in bloody protracted struggles that gutted successive American divisions without ever producing a decisive breakthrough. In the battle for Aachen proper, the U.S. 1st and 30th Infantry Divisions suffered between them nearly 5,000 casualties in less than three weeks; U.S. XIX Corps commander Major General Charles Corlett was relieved for his conduct of the battle. During the so-called first battle in the Hürtgen forest (6 October to 13 November) the U.S. 9th Infantry Division lost 4,500 men in ten days while gaining only two miles; the 28th Infantry Division suffered 6,184 casualties. Apparently undaunted, the U.S. First Army attacked into the woods again from 16 to 28 November, costing the 4th

Infantry Division alone 4,053 battle and 2,000 nonbattle casualties, while the 8th Infantry Division, Combat Command R of the 5th Armored Division, and the 2nd Ranger Battalion added another 4,000 combat losses and 1,200 nonbattle casualties to the toll. The Ninth Army's grinding approach to the Roer River from 16 November to 9 December fared no better, absorbing 10,000 battle casualties to push forward at most twelve miles without breaching the river barrier or even preventing the Germans from opening the dams to create an impenetrable flooded area that would secure the position for many weeks.[29]

Historian Charles Whiting comments bitterly that

> Naturally, the official history of the campaign in Europe glosses over what was a defeat of the first magnitude. . . . The fact that the Hurtgen [*sic*] had beaten them was conveniently swept beneath the carpet. That bold dash to the Rhine, which the Top Brass had been so confidently predicting ever since September 1944, had never come about. Field Marshal Model, defending the Forest, had stopped them dead.[30]

Again Model had profited from a series of what might be seen as lucky breaks. On the Allied side there was complacency; the inexperience of American soldiers at the type of confused fighting necessary to prevail in thick woods and city streets; supply constraints that limited the number of artillery shells that could be fired; and the dreary, cloud-filled skies, which often neutralized—at least temporarily—the dreaded fighter-bombers. As at Arnhem, the field marshal was also fortunate to have excellent subordinates conducting his battle (Erich Brandenberger at the Seventh Army and Gerhard Engel, Siegfried von Waldenburg, and Gerhard Wilck at various divisions) and to have a handful of excellent if weary divisions available (the 12th and 47th Volksgrenadier, the 3rd Panzergrenadier, the 9th and 116th Panzer). (In the Hürtgen forest the 47th Volksgrenadier Division also served notice that not all of Germany's "instant divisions," thrown together in a few weeks' time, were pushovers. Soldiers in the U.S. 1st Infantry Davison would later accord the 47th honors as "the most suicidal stubborn unit this Division has encountered.")[31]

The field marshal enjoyed other kinds of luck as well. How else to explain what happened on 3 November, as the U.S. 28th Infantry Division attacked toward the village of Schmidt? Model, Brandenberger, and LXXIV Corps commander Erich Staube had convened the previous day in Cologne to conduct a war game based on a renewed American division-level attack in the Hürtgen forest. During the morning of 3 November, as the staff officers were still laying out the flags on the situation maps, a telephone call from the front announced the 28th Infantry's advance and requested reinforcements. According to historian Charles McDonald, "Model promptly directed Erich Staube . . . to get back to his headquarters. Then he went on with the game, this time using actual reports from the front for the play," which allowed him to make a much earlier decision to commit the 116th Panzer Division than might otherwise have been the case. Certainly Napoleon Bonaparte would have conceded a role here for *La Fortune*.[32]

Yet for all these advantages, it was still Model's victory. If he interfered far less in the day-to-day tactical decisions than he had at Arnhem, he kept careful tabs on the ebb and flow of battle, making judicious decisions about reinforcements and tactical retreats. He visited the front every two or three days, as the occasion permitted, and personally assessed the combat-readiness of the divisions about to be fed into the fight. As McDonald concludes (not in the official history that Whiting derided but in the shorter account he published two years later):

A cagy, imperturbable army commander, Erich Brandenberger, guided by the master of improvisation of Army Group B, Field Marshal Walter Model, had hoarded his meager resources and fed them to the points of real crisis with an almost uncanny sense of timing.

So successful were Model and Brandenberger in using the forest to
advantage for the delaying action they required, despite limitations
in manpower, airpower, equipment, and supply, that little criticism
can be directed at the broad German conduct of the battle.[33]

Hitler of course could still criticize Model's performance, and
after the loss of Aachen, when the Führer summoned von Rundstedt and Model to East Prussia on 23 October for an immediate
conference, that was exactly what both men expected. Hours later,
however, a telephone call from OKW informed them that their
presence would not be required after all and that instead Siegfried
Westphal and Hans Krebs would make the trip as their delegates.

What the two chiefs of staff reported upon their return changed
everything, both for the course of the war and the ultimate fate of
Walther Model.

14

THE 10 PERCENT SOLUTION

Army Group B:
November 1944 to January 1945

HANS KREBS AND SIEGFRIED WESTPHAL RETURNED TO THEIR respective headquarters on 23 October shaken by the announcement Hitler had made to them. The Führer had decided that Germany's last, carefully hoarded reserves of men, tanks, aircraft, and fuel would be assembled for a grand offensive in the West. Recapturing the glories of his victory over France in 1940, Hitler intended to amass over two thousand panzers and two thousand planes for a surprise thrust through the lightly defended the Ardennes forest, followed by a lightning strike for the Meuse River. Crossing the Meuse south of the city of Liege, his panzers would then lunge forward to recapture Antwerp, surrounding the entire British 21st Army Group (as well as all of the U.S. Ninth and part of the U.S. First Armies) in a gigantic pocket. Even if the British managed a new Dunkirk evacuation of the continent, Hitler confidently expected to shatter the Anglo-American alliance and to buy

328

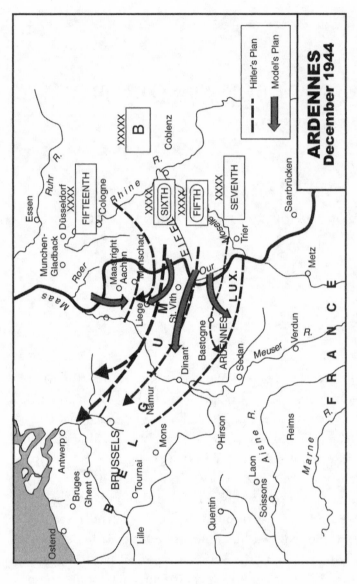

The disagreement during the planning over the strategic objectives to be pursued in the Ardennes offensive marked the beginning of the deterioration of the relationship of Model's influence with Adolf Hitler. While Hitler clung to the unrealistic possibility of driving all the way to Antwerp, Model argued unsuccessfully for the "small solution" that would cut off fifteen Allied divisions in the Aachen bulge.

himself precious time to stem the Soviet offensive in East Prussia and Poland.[1]

Army Group B, with the Fifth and Sixth Panzer Armies, and supported by the Eighth Army, was to carry out this attack no later than 25 November. Upon hearing this, Model remarked to Krebs, "This plan hasn't got a damned leg to stand on," then immediately picked up the telephone, called OKW, and demanded that General Jodl be placed on the line. In his usual brusque manner, and apparently without preamble, he barked, "You can tell *your* Führer from me, that Model won't have any part of it!"[2]

He would not of course have any choice.

The reaction from von Rundstedt was more temperate, but essentially the same. He later admitted, "When I received this plan early in November I was staggered. Hitler had not troubled to consult me about its possibilities. It was obvious to me that the available forces were far too small for such an extremely ambitious plan. Model took the same view of it as I did."[3]

Model and von Rundstedt, who had to this point had very little in common, abruptly found a cause to draw them together. Neither man believed Hitler's choice of Antwerp as a final strategic objective to be anything other than fantastic. On the other hand, both men agreed with the dictator that pursuing a purely defensive course (as Model continued to do from necessity in the Aachen–Hürtgen forest–Roer River sector) could do nothing other than delay Germany's ultimate defeat. They agreed that a strategic blow might provide the best chance of negotiated peace (at least with the Western Allies). "The only hope," von Rundstedt told Model, was "to wean Hitler from this fantastic aim by putting forward an alternative proposal that might appeal to him, and would be more practicable." So they determined to offer Hitler a more reasonable alternative, which came to be known as the "small solution."[4]

Model favored concentrating forces in the Ardennes but not driving all the way to the Meuse. Instead, after breaking American lines, he expected to wheel the panzer divisions north to cut off the two dozen Allied divisions in the immediate vicinity of Aachen. If such a *Kessel* (pocket) could be created, it would remove for months, if not a full year, any chance that the Allies might force the Rhine. Agreeing that the Aachen area represented Germany's best opportunity to deliver a strategic setback to the Allies, von Rundstedt disagreed only with the singularity of Model's approach; the elder field marshal suggested that augmented forces also be found for von Zangen's Fifteenth Army to make a subsidiary attack south toward Aachen.

Realizing that they could not afford to speak with anything but a united voice, von Rundstedt ordered Model to reconcile their plans, which the younger marshal did by adopting a scaled-down version of the Fifteenth Army attack. So prepared, von Rundstedt and Model met on 27 October with the three army commanders designated to lead the offensive: *Oberstgruppenführer* Sepp Dietrich (Sixth Panzer Army), General of Panzer Troops Hasso von Manteuffel (Fifth Panzer Army), and General of Panzer Troops Erich Brandenberger (Seventh Army). The meeting occurred at Model's headquarters. "When I saw Hitler's orders for the offensive I was astonished to find that these even laid down the method and timing of the attack," von Manteuffel later recalled.[5] Sepp Dietrich was less diplomatic, grousing to his Canadian interrogator following the war:

> I grew so big with these plans. . . . I had merely to cross a river, capture Brussels and then go on and take the port of Antwerp. And all this in the worst months of the year, December, January, February, through the countryside where snow was waist deep and there wasn't room to deploy four tanks abreast, let alone six armored divisions; when it didn't get light until eight in the morning and was dark again at four in the afternoon; with divisions that had just been reformed and contained chiefly raw, untried recruits, and at Christmas time.[6]

After several hours the two field marshals had guided their subordinates to the same conclusion: Although the drive on Antwerp was patently unrealistic, the "small solution" appeared possible. Thus fortified by the agreement of Dietrich, von Manteuffel, and Brandenberger, the field marshals took the unprecedented step of inviting Jodl to visit Model's headquarters to discuss the offensive. On 3 November von Rundstedt, Model, and von Manteuffel examined both plans in detail. Jodl listened—even appeared to agree with certain key points—but in the end he lacked the authority to change Hitler's plan even if he had wanted to do so. The best that the OKW operations officer could offer was the postponement of the attack from 25 November to 10 December.

Model had no intention of accepting this as a final answer. He had browbeaten or manipulated Adolph Hitler enough times in the past that he surely went into the mid-November briefings of his corps commanders and their chiefs of staff believing that in the end he would be able to evolve the plan into something more to his liking. Summoned on 23 November along with von Rundstedt, Westphal, Krebs, von Manteuffel, and Dietrich to a planning conference with Hitler in Berlin, Model raised his objections and his alternatives directly with the Führer. He emphasized that supplies to sustain the attack were more critical to success than achieving tactical surprise and that, given the sorry state of German logistics, a less ambitious counterattack near Aachen would be more realistic. The Americans, Model stressed, were exhausted after their "unsuccessful breakthrough battle in the larger area of Aachen," and he might have the chance to bag ten or twelve divisions. Then (the sop to Hitler) Model suggested that a drive toward the Meuse would become possible; it was, he suggested, a matter of capturing the "fat sparrow" first before attempting the "pigeon."[7]

The response shook him. At Moscow in 1941 Model had cowed the dictator into changing his attack orders. Eighteen months later, as the German army geared up for Operation Citadel, he had been able to secure a postponement of the attack over von Manstein's objections. Outside Leningrad and in Galicia, Model's *Schild und Schwert* rhetoric had convinced the Führer to allow him to make tactical withdrawals that had been denied other officers. Finally, in the debacle in Belorussia that consumed both the Fourth and Ninth Armies, Model had received unparalleled latitude to conduct operations as he saw fit. This day, however, Hitler remained unmoved, even mildly ridiculing Model's "small solution" as a "half solution." This marked a critical turning point in Model's life and career: For the first time Hitler had heard him out without giving an inch.[8]

Frustration sometimes nourishes strange alliances. Between Model and Hasso von Manteuffel few warm feelings existed. Some authors have suggested that the younger von Manteuffel, with his ancestors grounded firmly in the Prussian *Junker* elite, looked down on the son of a music teacher sporting a monocle and a field marshal's baton. Others have opined that von Manteuffel's abrupt rise to prominence in 1944 (through Hitler's patronage, he skipped directly from division to army command) might have made him appear too much the rival for Model's taste. Nor can it be dismissed that von Manteuffel's brother Günther had often been on the receiving end of Model's foul temper when the two served together in the 3rd Panzer Division in 1941. Whatever the reason, even von Manteuffel's most charitable postwar assessment of Model is tinged with distaste:

> Model was a very good tactician, and better in defense than in attack. He had a knack of gauging what troops could do, and what they could not do. His manner was rough, and his methods were not always acceptable in the higher quarters of the German Army, but they were both to Hitler's liking. Model stood up to Hitler in a way that hardly anyone else dared, and even refused to carry out orders with which he did not agree.[9]

Nonetheless, both men recognized that the Ardennes offensive, if carried out to Hitler's exact specifications, had no chance whatsoever. When von Manteuffel challenged Model directly regarding some of the more restrictive tactical requirements laid down in the Führer's planning documents, the field marshal responded sarcastically, "You'd better argue it out with the Führer." Undaunted, von Manteuffel replied, "All right, I'll do that if you'll come with me."[10]

In fact, Model, von Manteuffel, Dietrich, and Westphal all visited Hitler again in Berlin on 2 December. (Von Rundstedt—perhaps more fatalistic by this point—declined to accompany them and spent the day observing a map exercise at Dietrich's headquarters.) Model took the lead, presenting a command appreciation that recalled his lectures on Napoleonic strategy in the early 1930s. Even von Manteuffel found himself reluctantly impressed:

> Model was, as always, well prepared and had been well provided with the necessary factual bases for his arguments by his most competent first operations officer. He had a great day. Everyone in the large conference halls had to acknowledge his ability as he delivered his masterly summary. Even Hitler failed to interrupt him, and was visibly impressed. Model expressed his point of view with complete frankness and great force.[11]

Among the most important issues Model raised at this meeting was the rate of advance necessary to achieve Hitler's goal. Given that the U.S. First Army held the Ardennes front very weakly, Model believed that the Germans could concentrate sufficient infantry to break the American lines at multiple points in a single day. He then allowed a second day to traverse the worst of the tangled terrain of the Ardennes forest and two more days to reach the Meuse. Only by thrusting ahead that rapidly (to keep to the timetable the panzer spearheads would have to push ahead twenty-five miles per day), Model believed, could the Meuse be forced before the Allies reacted to defend it. Such an advance was comparable to the German penetration of the Ardennes in 1940, but in that campaign the Wehrmacht had enjoyed air superiority, good weather, and sufficient fuel to sustain prolonged operations. By contrast, Model explained, the same ninety-six-hour period could see the Germans shatter the American lines, throw out a strong defensive screen toward (but not over) the Meuse, and then pivot north to execute the Aachen operation. Nonetheless, Hitler remained unmoved, and although von Manteuffel received some tactical concessions, Antwerp remained the operational objective.[12]

To all outward appearances, following this rebuff Model threw himself into the final preparations for the offensive with his usual enthusiasm. He wandered the division and corps concentration areas fraternizing with the troops and haranguing their officers. When the chief of staff of the LVII Panzer Corps stopped him to complain of the disparity between the supplies that had been promised and those actually delivered, Model exploded, "If you need anything, take it from the Americans!" Likewise, in response to Major General Ludwig Heilmann, who observed that his 5th Parachute Division (spearhead of the Seventh Army's attack) lacked the training, heavy weapons, and vehicles necessary to achieve its mission, Model brushed him off, saying, "The parachute troops will find their way forward. I am confident of their courage!"[13]

On 4 December, with barely two weeks left to go, Model introduced his own bizarre wrinkle to the plan, suggesting that "a local Luftwaffe land operation"—which meant a parachute drop—might "hold open one or two important roads" in the sector designated for the 12th SS *Hitlerjugend* Panzer Division. This off-the-cuff suggestion then spiraled into the rapid creation of a poorly trained, ad hoc parachute regiment assigned to Colonel Augustus von der Heydte. A veteran of the Battle of Crete (the Luftwaffe's last large-scale airborne operation), the luckless von der Heydte struggled gamely to organize the unit, but by 14 December he had been brought to his wit's end. He appeared at Army Group

Even as preparation for the Ardennes offensive proceeded in the rear areas, Model roamed the front lines. Here he is seen speaking with two young officers responsible for the defenses in the Aachen sector on December 6, 1944.

B headquarters in the middle of the night on 14 December, less than forty-eight hours before his men were to board their planes. Model had already retired for the evening, and Krebs obviously intended merely to listen to the Luftwaffe officer complain for a few minutes before sending him on his way. As von der Heydte itemized problem after problem, however, the chief of staff soon realized that he would have to wake the field marshal.

Bleary-eyed and stone-faced, Model sat through von der Heydte's presentation. When the parachute commander finished, Model asked only one question: "Do you give the parachute operation a 10 percent chance of success?"

"Yes," answered von der Heydte.

"Well, then it is necessary to make the attempt, since the entire offensive has no more than a 10 percent chance of success," Model said, and then went back to bed.[14]

Perhaps part of this response had been conditioned three days earlier at a series of briefings Hitler held for commanders down to division level at his "Eagle's Nest" in Bavaria. The Führer gave the main address himself, standing rigidly behind a podium, his unmoving arms at his side. He invoked a variety of examples from history to prove his point that the Anglo-American alliance with the Soviet Union was both unnatural and seriously strained. One good blow could change the balance of power in Europe, but the alternative was a Germany destroyed by its enemies. Model's SS adjutant took down the dictator's closing sentences verbatim:

Gentlemen, if your breakthrough via Liege to Antwerp is not successful, we will be approaching an end to the war which will be extremely bloody. Time is not working for us, but against us. This is really the last opportunity to turn the fate of this war in our favor.

Much later, as Allied officers interviewed them in the POW cages, many German officers would claim that Hitler's rhetoric on this occasion had little effect on them. They realized the extent to which his promises were empty and his assumptions bankrupt, but could do nothing in the context of the People's Court except comply. Historian Wilhelm Tieke, however, reaches a different conclusion in his history of the II SS Panzer Corps. After carefully examining the extant records, Tieke notes that "the effect of this great, passionate speech was not lost," because "Hitler understood, as always, how masterfully to reawaken hope" in even his senior officers, and he succeeded in "convincing many that this offensive would have to be won, that it was a matter of the existence or extinction of the flayed Fatherland." Despite the presence of von Rundstedt, Model, and von Manteuffel, "no one contradicted, or even pointed out that anyone thought in terms of large and small solutions." Major General Siegfried von Waldenberg, newly appointed commander of the 116th Panzer Division, agreed with Tieke's assessment, as his operations officer, Heinz Günther Guderian, recalled: "The speech did not fail to impress the audience, in spite of many absurdities that are recognizable today."[15]

Neither Model nor Sepp Dietrich, however, had stopped thinking about the "small solution." As the Sixth Panzer Army began entering its assembly area on 8 December, Dietrich and his chief of staff had started drawing up an internal army plan that contradicted Hitler's orders. Instead of projecting his lead panzer divisions to pass south of Liege and then over the Meuse, Dietrich's work envisioned occupying both sides of the city in order to retain the logistical and tactical flexibility to turn north toward Aachen. Model certainly knew about this plan and by his silence gave Dietrich tacit permission to continue the work.

This noncompliance with Hitler's intention apparently did not pass unnoticed. During the night of 15 December, as the assault troops began moving into their final assembly positions, the Führer telephoned Model directly to insist for a final time that "there will be no deviation by the panzer units east of the Meuse toward the north. The Sixth Panzer Army must keep clear of the covering front to be built [by the Fifth Panzer Army] between

Monschau and Liege. Do not let Dietrich become involved in the fighting along his northern flank." He finished with a directive the like of which Model had never heard before: the field marshal and his army commanders were commanded to obey "all orders from the supreme command unconditionally, and to see that they are followed down to the lowest unit." Shaken, Model called Dietrich and told him that the game was up, then reconnected with Hitler to say, "All the efforts of Army Group B will be directed toward the thrust to Antwerp."[16]

Yet Model might as well have added to the end of that sentence, ". . . for as long as possible." His nightly supply report indicated that the Sixth Panzer Army's four SS panzer divisions were rolling into position with only 20 percent of the fuel that Army Group B had been promised back in November. The SS divisions had at least been rested out of the line for a few weeks and their ranks had refilled (if only with involuntary transferees from the navy and Luftwaffe), but Army panzer formations that had to be reha-bilitated "in the line," like the 2nd, 9th, and 116th Panzer Divi-sions, entered the battle with hundreds of new soldiers lacking even the most rudimentary training. Worse, the two panzer armies deployed between them only about 980 tanks, instead of the 2,000 Hitler had originally envisioned. Most of the army group's heavy artillery lacked prime movers and could not be moved forward to support subsequent attacks (not that the grandiosely titled *Volksartillerie Korps* possessed sufficient am-munition to conduct multiple bombardments). Brandenberger's Seventh Army—in reality a reinforced corps with the 5th Para-chute Division spearheading four untried volksgrenadier divi-sions—entered the battle in even worse condition. The field marshal's grim estimate to Colonel von der Heydte of a 10 percent chance of success began to look prescient.

Nonetheless, as the attack opened in the cloud-covered predawn hours of 16 December, Model optimistically wired Berlin at 6:00 A.M., "Up to now everything is on schedule and the beginning is going according to plan everywhere." A few hours later he authorized Krebs to inform OKW that "tactical and operational surprise is apparently successful. Till now very little enemy counterattack and decidedly little radio activity. Especially noticeable in all three attack armies is the very slight artillery fire. Due to weather conditions, air force action on both sides is not possible at this time." More realistically, von Rundstedt's headquarters reports as the day unfolded spoke of "stubborn resistance in major enemy strongpoints three to five kilometers behind the front lines" and grudgingly allowed that "the anticipated rapid advance of the panzer formations [has] not yet taken place."[17]

Obscured by careful phraseology (and often ignored even by Allied historians) was the fact that on 16 December, despite having achieved tactical surprise and a concentration of forces that in some sectors of the front exceeded ten-to-one, the German timetable had already been thrown off. Partly because of the operational decision not to commit Dietrich's panzers in the first wave of the assault, and partly because the disjointed but spirited defense of the eighteen-year-old draftees of the U.S. 106th Infantry Division far exceeded the Wehrmacht's expectations, the Americans had managed to cling to the critical road junction at St. Vith. Historian Danny Parker bluntly assesses Model's opening assault as "a failure. On the evening of the 16th only one clear breakthrough had been attained—in the Losheim Gap. Another appeared to be developing in the thin sector held by the 28th Division. But more than this was required." Model plainly understood that he had not achieved results that would carry his offensive to the Meuse in four days, but experience led him to couch his evening report to Hitler very carefully: "Quick exploitation of the successes of the first day of the attack will be decisive. The first objective is to achieve liberty of movement for the mobile units."[18]

When St. Vith still had not fallen by the next evening, Model informed von Manteuffel that he was releasing the *Führer Begleit* (Escort) Brigade—an oversized elite unit commanded by Colonel

Otto Remer—to assist with reducing the town on 18 December. Having wanted to retain Remer's brigade for the exploitation phase, von Manteuffel balked, but the field marshal overruled his objections. This disagreement became moot the next day, however, as the brigade required nearly seventy hours to filter forward over the infantry- and wagon-clogged roads immediately behind the front. The Fifth Panzer Army achieved a breakthrough farther south, but the St. Vith defenders still stubbornly held the ground.[19]

Meanwhile, it became evident to everyone except Hitler and Jodl that the Allied command had reacted more swiftly to the German counteroffensive than anyone had believed possible. Within the first twenty-four hours reinforcements had been routed toward the expanding German salient in the Ardennes. Most critically, the U.S. 101st Airborne Division would win the race with von Manteuffel's panzers to occupy Bastogne. Within a few more days the U.S. Third Army would receive orders to attack north into Brandenberger's flank of what was already becoming known as "the Bulge," while the British XXX Corps received orders to close on the Meuse and defend the crossings.

The enemy represented only half of Model's problem. On the morning of 18 December he informed OKW that to keep the offensive moving he would require at least six fuel trains per day sent forward from the Rhine. The Quartermaster Department responded that "in the best case situation we can only deliver up to four trains daily." Meanwhile, St. Vith still held, and the unit commanders of the I SS Panzer Corps, impatient to enter the battle, began on 19 December to edge south from their deployment areas into the roads needed by General Walther Lucht's LXVI Corps. When artillery ammunition for the bombardment of the 106th Infantry Division did not arrive (but reports of haughty SS officers throwing Wehrmacht supply trains off the road did), Lucht set up his own armed roadblocks to resist the SS incursion into his supply line.

"Kick them off so they stay off," von Manteuffel told Lucht. "Without artillery you'll never take St. Vith."

"I'll see to it," announced Model, walking up unannounced. Waving his baton, the field marshal leapt out of his vehicle and stalked into the nearest intersection, personally replacing the field police who were supposed to be directing traffic. As darkness fell, however, SS and army columns remained entangled, Remer's brigade had not made it forward to reinforce the attack, and the nearly encircled defenders of St. Vith held out for another critical day. That evening Sixth Panzer Army headquarters again proposed that the Fifteenth Army be reinforced for an attack around Aachen and that the thrust of the main offensive be turned north in accordance with the "small solution."[20]

Model instinctively realized that the time had not yet come to pass such ideas along to Hitler. Instead, on 20 December his reports to OKW played down the difficult situation at St. Vith and concentrated instead on the gains von Manteuffel had achieved in the south. "The third day of the attack is marked by the successful breakthrough on the broad front between Stavelot and Bastogne," he assured the Führer, adding that the U.S. First Army's front was decisively breached. He then suggested that the feasibility of "striking a shattering blow before the establishment of a new defensive line east of the Meuse is very great." That the field marshal recognized the disingenuous nature of this assessment was suggested by another radio message he sent the same day. In that communication Model asked the Luftwaffe to send out aerial reconnaissance assets to locate *Kampfgruppe* Peiper, the lead element of the 1st SS Panzer Division, which had broken through the American lines only to lose radio contact with the Sixth Panzer Army. It would be very difficult to strike that "shattering blow" until Army Group B located its designated spearhead unit.[21]

Colonel Remer's brigade finally managed to reach the battle for St. Vith on 21 December, but even the commitment of the *Führer Begleit* Brigade did not immediately result in the clearing of the critical road junction. Meanwhile, on the morning of 22 December Model received advance weather reports from East Prussia that identified a new high-pressure system moving west. Within three to four days that high would drive many if not all of the clouds from the Belgian sky, opening the door for the return of the dreaded U.S. Air Force. Given the prolonged failure to clear up the situation at St. Vith, the American paratroopers in Bastogne, and a rapidly deteriorating supply situation, both von Rundstedt and Model apparently concluded that evening that crossing the Meuse was beyond their capability. In the minds of both field marshals the "small solution" now represented the only alternative to disaster. Sepp Dietrich obviously sensed this sea change when he told visiting SS officer Leon Degrelle that day, "Aachen! Aachen! In the month of January I will be in Aachen."[22]

Hitler of course flatly refused to consider this option when the two field marshals presented it on Christmas Eve. Predictably, he reiterated his inflexible orders that von Manteuffel's spearhead units continue west and force a crossing of the Meuse. What Model thought of this decision can best be illustrated by the orders sent on 25 December to the fuel-starved 2nd Panzer Division, which had ground to a halt three miles short of the river at Foy-Notre Dame. Since Army Group B could not get fuel to the division, Model instead radioed orders to continue the advance on foot. It was an order that he knew neither could nor would be obeyed.[23]

The next day, with the U.S. Third Army tearing into Brandenberger's flank to relieve Bastogne, Model forwarded a detailed appreciation of what would be required to force the Meuse and drive on to Antwerp. He told OKW bluntly that

Army Group B not only assumes that all of the reserves, including OKW reserves, in his area will be available for deployment to achieve these objectives, but also expects the addition of three to four Panzer divisions from other theaters of war, for the formation of an operational reserve. As further prerequisites for the success of this operation, not only will sufficient supply, especially fuel, and sufficient manpower replacements be required, but also a weather situation that excludes unhindered actions of the enemy air forces.[24]

This memorandum was obviously calculated to highlight the impossibility of carrying out the original design, as Model knew quite well that Germany lacked the additional forces and fuel for which he asked. Moreover, the weather had already turned against him: Clear skies had allowed Allied air forces to fly 3,500 sorties over the battlefield in just over forty-eight hours, forcing Model to prohibit daylight movement of vehicles.

Model's message reached OKW the same day that Heinz Guderian also asked to have the Ardennes offensive suspended because otherwise he would be unable to build up a reserve to resist the inevitable Soviet offensive in Poland and East Prussia. Unmoved, Hitler responded: "We have had unexpected setbacks—because my plan was not followed to the letter. But all is not yet lost. Model can still cross the Meuse, *if* Brandenberger's Seventh Army regains its equilibrium in the south; *if* Bastogne is taken; *if* Manteuffel and Dietrich wipe out the great Allied force we have caught in the bend of the Meuse."[25]

Two days later the Führer announced to his astonished commanders that he not only expected them to continue the fight with their current resources but also intended a second strategic offensive by Army Group G in the Alsace Lorraine. "We will strike in a few days with 'Nordwind,'" Hitler proclaimed.

> Its certain success will automatically bring about the collapse of the threat to the left of the main offensive in the Ardennes, which will then be resumed with a fresh prospect of success. In the meantime, Model will consolidate his holdings and reorganize for a new attempt on the Meuse. And he will also make a final powerful assault on Bastogne. Above all, we must have Bastogne.[26]

Ironically, in the short term Hitler's dissipation of effort in Nordwind fit into Model's undiminished intent to evolve the offensive toward the "small solution." He still believed that if Bastogne fell he might successfully attack north toward Aachen while holding Patton at bay. At any rate, a concentration of force against Bastogne would finally provide a *schwerpunkt* (point of main effort) for the offensive, a place to "clench into a fist the hand which has till now been spread open." The decision to focus everything on Bastogne also allowed Model the excuse to issue orders to Dietrich and von Manteuffel that "the final target of Antwerp must be abandoned for the time being. The task which now presents itself is to strike at the enemy with annihilating force to the east of the Meuse and in the Aachen area." Only "after the successful conclusion of this partial attack" would it "be possible to develop the operation toward Antwerp."[27]

Model's penchant for conducting battles personally now reasserted itself, as if he intended to show Hitler and Jodl exactly how an attack should be planned. On 29 December, having been refused the use of the 11th Panzer and the 10th SS Panzer Divisions from the OKW reserve, Model stripped virtually all of the panzer assets from Dietrich, transferring both the I and II SS Panzer Corps to the Fifth Panzer Army. This did not mean that he planned to turn control of the attack over to von Manteuffel. Without notifying the army commander, Model then began ruthlessly interfering in the Fifth Panzer Army's organizational structure, subordinating XXXIX Panzer Corps to XLVII Panzer Corps.

Having concluded that Patton's relief corridor into Bastogne from the south could not be cut, Model clung to the possibility of breaking directly into the town in a frontal attack. When the U.S. 6th Armored Division launched furious (albeit tactically insignificant) attacks on both 31 December and 1 January, both Model and von Manteuffel realized that the tide of battle had now completely turned against them. The Fifth Panzer Army commander concluded that the time had come to give up the game and go over to the defensive; Model thought otherwise. On 2 January he demanded that I SS Panzer Corps, with the 9th SS Panzer, part of the

12th SS Panzer, and the bulk of the 340th Volksgrenadier Division, conduct a major daylight counterattack by the next morning. Corps commander Hermann Preiss pressed von Manteuffel for a day's delay or the conversion of the operation to a night attack; von Manteuffel told him simply that Model would never allow it. Nonetheless, the wiry young Prussian made the attempt, trying gamely to convince Model that Bastogne simply could not be taken.[28]

Even though he had already written in an appreciation to OKW that the tactically and strategically correct course for Army Group B was a "transition to the defensive on the whole Ardennes front," Model could not admit that to von Manteuffel. Refusing to cancel the order, on 3 January he engaged in a vicious shouting match with *Gruppenführer* Sylvester Stadler, the veteran commander of the 9th SS Panzer Division, who adamantly refused to make a daylight attack in the face of American air superiority. To the amazement of the staff officers witnessing this explosion, Model did not relieve Stadler on the spot (as had been his habit on more than one occasion) but uncharacteristically backed down. Stadler received ill-tempered assent to a night assault, which, predictably, achieved little.[29]

Although several thousand more German soldiers would fall in bitter defensive fighting from 4 to 16 January, the Ardennes offensive—even in the most limited sense—ended with Stadler's attack. Slowly but inevitably surrendering to American artillery and air power, the German salient shrank steadily over the next two weeks, and even Hitler was finally convinced that the attack had failed. On 16 January the U.S. First and Third Armies retook Houffalize in a combined attack; the same day OKW ordered the four badly battered SS panzer divisions of the Sixth Panzer Army out of the line for transfer to Hungary.

One of the casualties of the Ardennes was Walther Model's prestige with Adolph Hitler. In the past Model's many tactical successes had provided the foundation for his blunt, confrontational style with the Führer, and Hitler had always arguably seen the monocle-sporting Prussian as one of the few officers who always agreed with him regarding ends if not means. In the Ardennes, however, Model had banked heavily first on talking Hitler out of the drive on Antwerp before the attack opened, and then on his ability to present the dictator with a fait accompli while the battle raged. Neither stratagem worked, and both cost him credibility with an increasingly paranoid, inflexible Hitler. By mid-January 1945 one of the key elements of Walther Model's personal success had disappeared along with Germany's last panzer reserve: He had become just another willful field marshal who thought he knew better than his Führer.

15

THE LESSONS
OF ANTIQUITY

Army Group B:
January to April 1945

As some of the heaviest fighting in the campaign raged around Bastogne, Model took time on 31 December to wish Siegfried von Waldenburg a happy forty-sixth birthday and to write him the following greeting: "For our Fatherland, as well as for me, probably the most difficult year imaginable came to an end. . . . The last attack gave all of us a lift. Even if the major objectives have not been reached, we keep on hoping. We have to persevere or we will be ruined! . . . God be with us in the New Year, and may it finally bring us the long desired peace after victory!"[1]

Ruin, however, approached rapidly. The Battle of the Bulge had consumed Germany's last operational reserves of men, weapons, and fuel without achieving more than a momentary shift in the tactical initiative on the Western front. The constant disagreements with the generals involved—von Rundstedt, Model, von Manteuffel, and Dietrich—had finally convinced Hitler that none of his commanders could be trusted to execute his orders. "After the Ardennes failure, Hitler started a 'corporal's war,'" Hasso von Manteuffel reflected ruefully a few years later. "There were no big plans—only a multitude of piecemeal fights."[2] As the remnants of Army Group B dug in to defend the Rhineland, OKW promulgated a new Führer Directive on 21 January 1945:

The following order by the Führer is issued in its original text:

1. The Commanders of armies, corps and divisions will be personally responsible for all the following types of decisions or intentions reaching me early enough to enable me to exercise my influence on such decisions and for a counter-order to reach the front-line troops in time:
    (i) any decision involving an operational movement,
    (ii) any projected attack of divisional size or larger which is not covered by general orders issued by Supreme Headquarters,
    (iii) any offensive action on an inactive front exceeding normal patrol activity apt to draw the enemy's attention to that sector,
    (iv) any projected movement of withdrawal or retreat,
    (v) any contemplated abandonment of a position, a fortified town or fortress.

2. The Commanders of armies, corps and divisions, the Chiefs-of-Staff and every single General Staff Officer or staff officers will be personally responsible to me to see to it that any report addressed to me directly or through channels will contain nothing but the blunt truth. In future I will punish drastically any attempt at veiling facts, whether done on purpose or through negligence.[3]

For the first time in his career Model now discovered that these strictures applied to him as well. Against the advice of virtually every senior commander in the West, Hitler refused to countenance a fighting withdrawal to the Rhine and instead staked Army Group B's fate on an inch-by-inch struggle in front of the river. The latitude vouchsafed him at Arnhem and in Hürtgen now gone, Model found himself serving as merely the tactical executive of the Führer's orders. It was a functional demotion that led, predictably, to more drinking and more lashing out at the officers around him.

On 24 January, however, Model's staff surprised him by maneuvering the Reich's dying military bureaucracy to transport the field marshal's eighteen-year-old son Hansgeorg (an officer candidate in the *Grossdeutschland* organization) from Prussia to his father's headquarters for a birthday celebration. Hansgeorg spent several days accompanying the field marshal to the front, sat through several protracted drinking bouts, and even participated in a snowball fight conducted almost exclusively by General Staff officers. Eventually—inevitably—the visit came to an end, and as he drove off from the castle that headquartered Army Group B, Hansgeorg found himself looking back at the figure of his father, "very serious, almost lonely, as he stared after our departing car. Suddenly the realization seized me—I would never see my father again."[4]

That reunion with his son began a round of what in retrospect appeared to be Walther Model's good-byes to his family. In late February he visited his wife in Dresden a few days after Allied bombers had destroyed their home, along with most of the old city. Three weeks later, even as enemy armies encircled his command, Model paid a visit to Hella, his eldest daughter, who found him "as active as ever" and "even displaying a certain degree of optimism." The field marshal's final letters to his wife, however, suggest that his bright outlook had more and more become a facade. "All fear comes from the Devil," Walther told Herta on 24 March, but "we receive courage and joy from the Lord." He concluded ominously that "we must all die at some time or other."[5]

This is the look that Model's son might have seen as he waved a final good-bye to the Field Marshal in January 1945. Model's confidence is still visible, but there is an added element of resignation beneath it.

That letter was posted several weeks after the U.S. First Army seized the Ludendorff bridge at Remagen on 7 March, fatally breaching the Rhine barrier. While Model and von Zangen quarreled over the appropriate tactical response, Hitler sacked von Rundstedt (again!), replacing him with Field Marshal Albert Kesselring, famous for his tenacious defense of the Italian peninsula for the past two years. Preceding Kesselring's arrival, the Führer bombarded Model with a series of precise instructions about the counterattack necessary to throw the Americans back across the river. Germany's industrial czar, Albert Speer, found Model at his headquarters as those orders arrived. The field marshal, Speer recalled, was "in a state of fury." Model raged "that commands had just come in from Hitler to attack the enemy on flank at Remagen, using certain specified divisions" that, he said, "have lost their weapons and have no fighting strength at all. They would be less effective than a company! It's the same thing all over again: at headquarters they have no idea what is going on. . . . Of course, I'll be blamed for the failure."[6]

What Model did not tell Speer was that he had no intention of following Hitler's orders. After an initial probe resulted in heavy casualties, on his own authority the field marshal countermanded the directive for an immediate counterattack, telling his division commanders to take the time necessary to organize their forces. Two days later Kesselring arrived and with bland optimism reiterated Hitler's orders to "throw the Americans back across the Rhine," to which an insulted Model replied, "I'll try, but I don't think my forces are sufficient." Again this represented dissembling: Model not only had given up trying to eliminate the American bridgehead at Remagen but had covertly begun ordering large elements of Army Group B to evacuate the Rhineland and cross the river. On 25 March (the day after that final letter to his wife) Model unilaterally ordered the 12th Volksgrenadier and 176th Infantry Divisions across the Rhine without authorization and without even informing OKW. The next day he pulled back the entire Fifth Panzer Army (now commanded by his old subordinate Josef Harpe), again without Hitler's permission.[7]

The Führer responded to these maneuvers on 29 March with a proclamation just short of ordering Model's relief. Not only did he refuse to allow Army Group B to withdraw any further forces to or from the Rhine, but Hitler also specified that "each withdrawal, each surrender of a village is forbidden under pain of death. In every large populated area a responsible commander is to be assigned who will be responsible for carrying out this order." As the now-encircled Army Group B in the Ruhr was designated a fortress in the same communication, Model by default became that "responsible commander." It was the same formula that had condemned general officers from Kovel to Vitebsk to Aachen, and it now condemned Model as well.[8]

Incompatible mandates began to pile up on the field marshal. Hitler had insisted on the demolition of bridges, electric plants, and other elements of critical infrastructure as Germany's armies retreated, a policy intended to leave the Allies with only a devastated wasteland. Albert Speer, now thinking about a future beyond the Third Reich, had begun touring the front trying to convince senior officers to ignore these directives. He found Model maddeningly inconsistent: One day the field marshal would nod as if he understood and promise to attempt to keep the fighting away from such installations, but in a subsequent interview Model would then reject this course. Speer, like Speidel before him, marked Walther Model as possessing insufficient "moral courage" to do the right thing, completely missing the inner turmoil roiling behind the field marshal's monocle.[9]

When Model tried to follow OKW orders to mobilize the Hitler Youth and the *Volkssturm*, he met resistance everywhere. Even an old-line Nazi supporter like General Joachim von Kortfleisch told him that "supplying them with weapons is an indirect delivery of weapons to the U.S.A." General Vollrath Luebbe (whose 2nd Panzer Division Model had once blamed for failing to break through Russian defenses at Kursk) flatly refused to issue mobilization orders in his area. Model, who could never tolerate resistance from his subordinates, flew into one of his patented rages and threatened Luebbe's chief of staff with summary court-martial and execution if the orders were not issued by the next morning.

The unrepentant staffer shot back that none of them had that long to live anyway. Muttering threats, Model stalked off, and—to everyone's surprise—never returned.[10]

By 30 March Model had decided that his position was completely hopeless; he protested to Kesselring that having his troops pinned in the Ruhr pocket was insane: "To continue the defense in this position is absurd, as such defense cannot even pin down enemy forces." Communications had disintegrated to the point that Model could no longer even keep track of the battle. One officer described Army Group B headquarters as "a madhouse. Reports came flooding in all the time, the one contradicting the other. It was just the same with the orders and counter-orders being issued from the HQ." Kesselring understood Model's logic but had no authority to order either surrender or a breakout attack, so Model took matters into his own hands. He appointed Harpe as commander of the western half of the pocket and put von Zangen in charge of the eastern half, but he also directly ordered Fritz Bayerlein, commanding LIII Corps, to break out: "I order you to attack with available forces out of the Schmallenberg area to the east, south of the Edertal block, and make contact with a battle group committed from the northeast and together burst the ring of encirclement."[11]

Historian Leo Kessler believes that "Model thought a successful breakthrough to the east would allow him to withdraw his troops to fight another day in Central Germany," but contemporary evidence suggests otherwise. On 13 April, for example, Hitler plucked Colonel Günther Reichhelm, Model's operations officer, to become chief of staff to Walther Wenck's chimerical Twelfth Army, supposedly assembling west of Berlin to "drive a wedge between the English and American troops and reach Army Group B." "They must go all the way to the Rhine!" the Führer announced. In a fit of spontaneous anger, Model accused Reichhelm of deserting the army group at a critical moment and trying to save himself at everyone else's expense. After curtly dismissing Reichhelm, Model

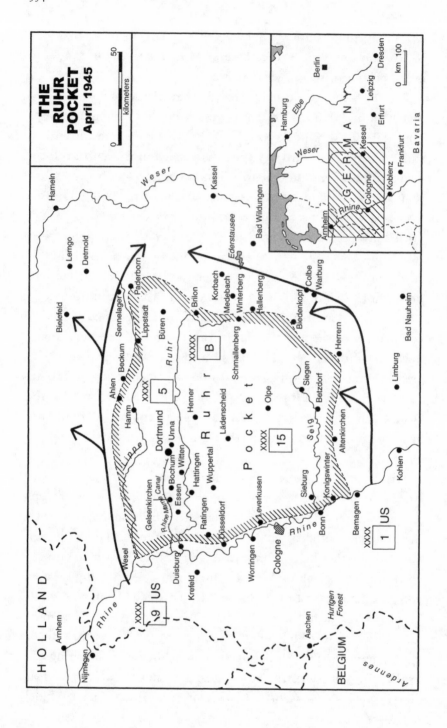

THE
RUHR
POCKET
April 1945

50
0 kilometers

0 km 100

HOLLAND

Arnhem
Nijmegen

Rhine

XXXX
9 US

Wesel

Rhine Maas Canal

Lippe

Duisburg
Krefeld

Worringen

Cologne

Bonn
Bad Godesberg

Remagen

XXXX
1 US

BELGIUM

Aachen

Hurtgen
Forest

Ardennes

Hameln

Lemgo
Detmold

Bielefeld

Paderborn

Sennelager
Lippstadt
Büren

Ahlen
Beckum
Hamm

Dortmund
Unna

Gelsenkirchen
Bochum
Essen
Ratingen
Düsseldorf

Witten
Hattingen
Wuppertal
Leverkusen

Hemer
Lüdenscheid

XXXX
5

R u h r

Ruhr

P o c k e t

Olpe

Sieg

Siegburg
Königswinter

XXXX
15

Weser

Kassel

Bad Wildungen

Ederstausee

Brilon
Korbach
Medebach
Winterberg
Hallenberg
Schmallenberg

Colbe
Warburg

Biedenkopf

Herrem

Siegen
Betzdorf

Altenkirchen

Kohlen

Limburg

Bad Nauheim

XXXX
B

Hamburg

Berlin
Leipzig
Dresden
Erfurt

Elbe

Weser

G E R M A N Y

Kessel

Frankfurt
Koblenz
Cologne

Rhine

Arnhem

B a v a r i a

crumpled Hitler's optimistic orders and consigned them to the trash.[12]

About the same time his chief of staff, Major General Karl Wagener, directly approached the field marshal about asking for Hitler's permission to surrender. Model rejected the idea out of hand: "I could hardly make such a proposal." Yet a few hours later, when Major General Gerhard Engel reported in for a similar transfer, Model's reaction was quite different, possibly because Engel, as Hitler's former adjutant, could provide him an indirect channel to the Führer. A "very earnest" Model asked Engel to convey the hopelessness of Army Group B's tactical situation to Hitler, emphasizing that in the last few days before the Americans reduced the Ruhr pocket Hitler might have his final chance to make peace. Engel recalled this moment years later:

> I think, despite everything, Model still felt there was a chance. Of course, most of us were blinded by Goebbels's propaganda at the time, believing that the Western Allies and Russia would go for each other in the end and that Germany might find a place fighting against the Russians in the Allied camp. But Model didn't cling to that kind of vain hope, I feel. Somehow I think on that Saturday he believed we could just stop the war, in the west at least, and walk away from it—to let somebody else pick up the pieces. You know, like those gallant officers in those romantic nineteenth-century paintings of the battlefields. All heroics and bleeding hearts. In essence, he was just sticking his head in the sand.[13]

By 15 April even sticking his head in the sand had ceased to be an option: The Americans had split the army group in half, and in reaction Hitler ordered an immediate, full-scale counterattack. Model again discarded the order; when he visited Harpe's headquarters later that afternoon, the new Fifth Panzer Army chief of staff, Friedrich-Wilhelm von Mellenthin (no Model fan since their paths had crossed in Galicia) saw something in the field marshal he had never observed before: indecision. "I had the feeling that he was wrestling with himself to find a solution to some inner conflict," von Mellenthin wrote. The two men "discussed the question of capitulation . . . but we both rejected any such idea." Neither man knew (or, if he knew, von Mellenthin did not tell Model) that Harpe had already made an independent decision to surrender the Fifth Panzer Army.[14]

Later that day Model received a letter from Major General Matthew Ridgway of the U.S. XVIII Airborne Corps, carried by an American captain brought blindfolded to his headquarters. It was not a typical surrender demand:

> Neither history nor the military profession records any nobler character, any more brilliant master of warfare, any more dutiful subordinate of the state, than the American general, Robert E. Lee. Eighty years ago this month, his loyal command reduced in members, stripped of its means of effective fighting and completely surrounded by overwhelming forces, he chose an honorable capitulation.
>
> The same choice is now yours. In the light of a soldier's honor, for the reputation of the German Officer Corps, for the sake of your nation's future, lay down your arms at once. The German lives you save are sorely needed to restore your people in their proper place in society. The German cities you will preserve are irreplaceable necessities for your people's welfare.

Holding the letter, Model asked Wagener before sending his response: "Has everything been done to justify our actions in the light of history? What can there be left for a commander in defeat? In antiquity, they took poison." In the end Model sent a verbal reply to Ridgway that he could not surrender given that he was still bound by his sworn oath to Hitler. "It would do violence to his sense of honor even to *consider* my message," Ridgway learned from Wagener, who had volunteered to carry back Model's answer (and then chose to stay as an American prisoner).[15]

Even before he knew that Wagener had surrendered himself, Model directed that all boys under eighteen years of age and the older *Volkssturm* members be discharged and sent home. On 17 April he ordered the army group's small remaining stocks of ammunition and supplies distributed to individual units, ceding authority to unit commanders to determine for themselves if they should surrender or fight on. At this point Model was adapting to events rather than influencing them: His soldiers had already begun throwing down their arms en masse—the battle of the Ruhr pocket was over. On 20 April Josef Goebbels's Propaganda Ministry formally condemned the "treacherous army of the Ruhr" as the cause of Germany's final defeat.[16]

What remained to be determined was only the fate of Walther Model himself. Accompanied by three staff officers and a handful of orderlies, the field marshal began his final odyssey, darting from village to village, seeking some crack in the American lines through which he might slip. At some point—probably on 20 April—Model encountered Sergeant Walther Maxeiner, an old campaigner from Russia, who was himself leading a small group of young soldiers. "We went up asking what we should do," Maxeiner wrote later. "With great astonishment our young soldiers looked at the officers with the stripes on their pants and their medals. Never before had they been so close to the big brass." Model always had time for the individual *Landser* when he toured the battlefield; for just a moment his depression broke, and he was back in his element. He asked each man's name, where he lived, and how long he had been a soldier. Maxeiner recalled that "for some time he discussed my tour of duty on the eastern front with me. It turned out I had been in a unit under his command at the time." What should they do now? That was the question on everyone's lips. "Go home, boys. The war is over for us," Model told them, shaking each man's hand. "Good luck on the trip home and tell your men not to lose courage and to continue to remain decent boys."[17]

His staff realized that Model had no intention of being captured, primarily because of his reaction when an intelligence officer mentioned the possibility that upon capture "the Western Powers would hand him over to the Russians." Suicide represented the only obvious alternative to captivity, but when they attempted to talk him out of it, the field marshal replied, "I simply cannot do it. The Russians have branded me a war criminal and the Americans would be sure to turn me over to them—for hanging. My hour has come." On 21 April 1945, near the village of Wedau, Walther Model told his officers again that "anything's better than falling into Russian hands." He then drew his service pistol from its holster, said, "You can bury me here," and walked into the woods.[18]

The single shot came only a few moments later.

Led by former members of the field marshal's staff, Hansgeorg Model came to Wedau in the spring of 1955 to recover his father's body. Like another field marshal's son—Manfred Rommel—Hansgeorg found the rest of his life somewhat overshadowed by his famous father. Manfred eventually rose to become lord mayor of Stuttgart in the Federal Republic of Germany, but his own accomplishments never quite rescued him from the image of "the Desert Fox." When I met him briefly in 1982 (along with two dozen other American servicemen participating in a "Meet the Mayor" event), someone inevitably asked him about his father. His answer was both polished and gracious, but I thought his smile a bit . . . weary. How many times must he have heard this question? But then how many fathers had been played by James Mason in a major international motion picture?

Hansgeorg Model finished the war fighting with *Grossdeutschland* units in northern Germany, where he had the good fortune to be captured by the British rather than the Soviets. Along with millions of other Germans, he and his family survived the hard winters that followed. Entering the reborn German army (*Die Bundeswehr*) in the 1950s, the younger Model advanced to become a brigadier general and an expert on training whose writing is still foundational to U.S. air force training doctrine today. Yet following retirement from active service, Hansgeorg found himself drawn back to his father's career; he would spend more than a decade collecting documents for some future biographer, because five decades after his suicide Walther Model not only languished in relative obscurity but was seen by many who knew his name as historian John Toland presented him: "a zealous disciple of Hitler, resolved to carry out his order to hold every foot of ground until the last moment."[19]

Part of the problem of course was that Walther Model spent much of his career in Russia, one of the "soldiers in the shadow," in B. H. Liddell Hart's parlance, while Rommel's North Africa campaign made him the "soldier in the sun." Ultimately, however, many German commanders emerged from those shadows—Heinz Guderian, Erich von Manstein, and Gerd von Rundstedt, to name only three. The crux of the matter lay beyond the view of Model as a "zealous disciple of Hitler": While Erwin Rommel had the good fortune to be presented to history by awed opponents and former German officers who worshiped the ground upon which he walked (at least posthumously), the men who introduced Walther Model to posterity loathed him.

And in many cases they were the same individuals.

The number of German General Staff officers who felt themselves to have been abused by Walther Model reads like a who's who of the men who made postwar careers out of providing what might well be considered a "politically correct" history of the Wehrmacht's conduct of World War II for their American captors. The list includes Fritz Bayerlein, Günther Blumentritt, Friedrich-Wilhelm von Mellenthin, Hans Speidel, Karl Wagener, Siegfried Westphal, August Winter, Otto Wohler, and Bodo Zimmermann. Throughout their writings run consistent themes that have influenced the historiography of the German army for decades: Hitler's responsibility for virtually every military blunder during the war, the ignorance of senior officers regarding the Holocaust, and the tragic nobility of those like Rommel who had finally joined the conspiracy to overthrow the Führer. On all three counts Model came out badly: He was a Hitler sycophant, a commander whose brutality toward the Russian population led the Soviets to declare him a war criminal, and—in the end—a man who understood that the war was lost but lacked the moral courage to act. Thus, the essentials of the mythical Walther Model came into existence.

What of the reality?

The first point that his postwar detractors sought to ignore was that Model's early career followed—almost to the letter—the preferred progression laid out for General Staff officers. When Hans von Seeckt selected Model for inclusion in the Reichswehr, he arguably did so primarily on the basis of the young officer's staff service with the Army High Command, the Guard Ersatz Division, and the 36th Reserve Division rather than his brief stint as a battalion commander in the trenches. During the early 1930s Model joined the small clique of officers interested in army motorization that formed beneath Walther von Brauchitsch, Heinz Guderian, Oswald Lutz, and Walther von Reichenau, an association that led him into relationships with Franz Halder, Friedrich Paulus, and even Hermann Göring. Model had been noted as a potential army chief of staff as early as 1938, when such preferment still remained solidly in the hands of the old-line army bureaucracy. His promotions to army chief of staff, panzer division commander, and panzer corps commander all resulted from the traditional mix of aptitude, seniority, and patronage (in Model's case from von Brauchitsch, then commander-in-chief of the German army). There exists not a shred of evidence either that Hitler even noticed him prior to late 1941 or that his supposed pro-Nazi views assisted his career advancement, as was true for men like Ernst Busch, Hermann Hoth, and Adolph Strauss. (The fact that Model was passed over in the round of promotions and awards after the French campaign strongly supports this observation.)

Model's appointment to command the Ninth Army, as examined in chapter 6, did not result from his relationship with Hitler but rather initiated that relationship. Moreover, in the early stages of that relationship it often appeared that Model, far from being the fawning disciple, was the dominant personality. Gerd von Rundstedt once dismissed him as having the makings of a "good regimental sergeant major" rather than a German field marshal, yet it was precisely that rough manner that apparently connected with the former corporal at the head of the Third Reich. Model's bluntness (perhaps even his coarseness) intimidated the Führer, and his hardness exceeded even what the dictator demanded from his generals.

Thus, Model acquired a great deal more latitude and freedom of action than many other generals. This psychological element was buttressed by the fact that Model rarely if ever called for relinquishing territory in order to conduct an "elastic defense," a mantra Hitler began to hear too often after 1942 from officers like Hermann Hoth, Ewald von Kleist, and Erich von Manstein. This did not, however, represent on Model's part some blind allegiance to Hitler's dogma of "not a step back"; instead, his reluctance to cede territory stemmed from his tactical situations and his understanding of defensive warfare. The Ninth Army held a static front for over a year with divisions that had been repeatedly stripped of armor, artillery, and transportation assets to feed equipment into the mobile battles farther south. Usually no more than two panzer divisions (often only one) constituted the army reserve, and those divisions rarely deployed more than a single tank battalion. Model and his officers developed a defensive doctrine of standing fast and fighting in depth because they literally had no alternative: If the Red Army ever succeeded in breaking the front open (as June to July 1944 would prove), the Ninth Army would have shattered.

Necessity, however, was only one of the parents of what might be called Model's defensive doctrine. As noted in chapter 7, there is considerable circumstantial evidence that Model and his subordinates carefully thought through the details of stopping the Soviets dead in their tracks. What Model developed was an unlovely, often quite bloody doctrine of attrition that made his enemies pay for every single inch of ground. He would demonstrate his mastery of the technique to the Russians especially at Rzhev and in the Orel salient, but he would also belie the critics who said he did not understand the special challenges of the Western front by ensnaring the Americans for months in the tangled vastness of the Hürtgen forest. These successes make Model a strong candidate for the title of the best purely defensive tactician in the German army during World War II.

On the other hand, Model enjoyed far less luck when he attacked. Although he could counterpunch quite effectively in the context of his defensive doctrine, the field marshal lacked the touch for offensive operations. The two set-piece offensives with which Model would be associated—Operation Citadel and the Ardennes—both turned into abysmal failures, and Model legitimately deserves criticism for mistakes in each. At Kursk he miscalculated the relative rates of Russian and German buildups around the salient, and his counsel convinced Hitler to delay the offensive. When the battle kicked off, Model's tactics were at best orthodox; more realistically speaking, they were flawed. His "rolling battle of attrition" against Soviet defenses at Ponyriy resembled the agonizing meat-grinder at Verdun twenty years earlier, with about the same results. In the Ardennes Model hindered himself horribly by promising Hitler that he truly had his sights set on Antwerp, while simultaneously scheming to manipulate the Führer into accepting the "small solution" as a fait accompli.

Nor was Model by any measure a strategist. Twice—once in each theater—he held commands that included control of multiple army groups. Twice, it must also be admitted, Model failed to pursue any coherent strategy. When he simultaneously commanded Army Groups Center and North Ukraine during the summer of 1944, Model attempted to stabilize the Belorussian front by pulling away the reserves from his Galician lines, a maneuver that eventually ended up with two army groups torn to shreds. Likewise, during Model's brief stint as OB West, he proved unable (primarily by temperament) to coordinate rather than leap into a command vehicle and head for the front. As a result, Model's own staff successfully petitioned OKW to have his job responsibilities downgraded again to army group commander. Little or nothing suggests that Walther Model ever broadened his horizons to look at what was happening along stretches of front he did not happen to command.

The Ardennes offensive also represented the beginning of Model's decline as Hitler's favorite field marshal. By then accustomed to seeing evidence of defeatism in every single communication from his generals, the Führer had ample reason to suspect Model of the same. After all, Model had vigorously protested the entire plan on multiple occasions, and it would have taken an idiot not to realize that during the battle he kept manipulating to have his preferred strategy replace Hitler's. Thus, by January 1945 Walther Model had become just another army group commander to the Führer, and not even a candidate to replace von Rundstedt when the elder field marshal was again retired. By late April the Third Reich's propaganda machine (about the only organism still functioning) had officially denounced both Army Group B and Model as traitorous.

Was Walther Model a Nazi? A staunch conservative, Model saw himself firmly in the tradition of the Prussian apolitical soldier (*nur-soldat*) and had arguably been overly impressed by the example of Erich Ludendorff during the Great War. He believed in order and an authoritarian government, and he possessed a strong sense of German nationalism. Underpinning those beliefs were many of the same racial and religious prejudices (against Slavs and

Jews) common to many Germans of his generation. Moreover, in the field at moments of crisis, more than one witness has recorded images of Walther Model not only cursing but also haranguing his soldiers to have faith in their Führer. There is also his acceptance of an SS aide and his repeated request to have National Socialist leadership officers attached to his commands during the last year of the war.

Yet it was also possible for a German officer to see Hitler (at least in the early years) as that necessary strong leader without buying the entire Nazi philosophy, as the example of Walther von Reichenau suggests. Likewise, it is critical not to forget the consistent cynicism that Model displayed in his dealings with Hitler. Rather than represent his acceptance of Nazi philosophy, both the SS aide and the Nazi officers assigned to him provided Model with cover to do as he pleased. The best (and, simultaneously, the worst) that can be said about Walther Model in this regard is that he had no more compunctions about using Hitler and the Nazis in achieving his own goals than they had about using him for the same purpose.

What then was Model's purpose in life? Having suggested that there are many parallels between Model and Rommel, here it becomes more useful to posit a similarity with certain aspects of George Patton. Both Model and Patton would have ascribed patriotism as their underlying motivation, but when their careers are examined in the aggregate, each of these commanders seems to have internalized almost an eighteenth-century model of the professional soldier, one who is detached from politics and serves primarily for the glory of the fight and the chance to rise to the top of his country's armed forces. There was in both the German and the American an essentially primal, single-minded focus on his own military success, almost to the exclusion of all other considerations. What was good for the Ninth Army (or the Third Army) was by definition good for the cause. Thus we have Patton maneuvering to acquire the supplies of neighboring forces in order to keep unsanctioned offensives rolling, and Model ruthlessly bleeding Army Group Center and OKH reserve units in the fight for Rzhev to spare his own troops.

The angst Model suffered during the last few weeks of the war, as all of his conceptions about Germany, honor, and Adolph Hitler came crashing down at once, would be more compelling if Model himself had manifested some saving grace, some final nobility of character. But it simply was not there. Model spent his last days nominally in command of a doomed army group, yet having been rendered functionally impotent to affect the military situation. The host of contradictory glimpses we receive from that period suggests mercurial changes of temperament, from apparently courting suicide at the front to arguing with Albert Speer over the destruction of German infrastructure or threatening Vollrath Luebbe with summary execution for failing to mobilize the *Volkssturm*. Once the soldier had been defeated, it seemed, there remained only a supremely tired man who could not come to terms with the loss of the only world he had ever known. There might be a place in the next Germany for Hasso von Manteuffel, but not for Walther Model. His suicide had less to do with the honor of Prussian field marshals or the fear of Soviet war-crimes tribunals than with the inability of the man who had held Rzhev against all odds to face his own future.

NOTES

Chapter 1: An Uncomfortable Subordinate

1. Theodor Wolff, *The Eve of 1914* (New York: Alfred A. Knopf, 1936), pp. 509, 517–518.

2. Walter Bloem, *The Advance from Mons 1914* (1930; reprint, New York: Tandem, 1967), pp. 23, 25.

3. Walter Görlitz, *History of the German General Staff, 1657–1945* (New York: Praeger, 1953), p. 157; Fritz Klein, ed., *Deutschland im esrten Weltkrieg*, 3 vols. (Berlin: Akademie-Verlag, 1971), vol. 1, pp. 306, 313.

4. Hermann von Kuhl and Friedrich von Bergmann, *Movements and Supply of the German First Army During August and September 1914* (Fort Leavenworth, KS: Command and General Staff School Press, 1929), p. 59; see also Alexander von Kluck, *The March on Paris and the Battle of the Marne 1914* (London: Edward Arnold, 1923), pp. 6–18.

5. Erich Ludendorff, *Ludendorff's Own Story*, 2 vols. (New York: Harper and Brothers, 1920), vol. 1, p. 18; Alistair Horne, *The Price of Glory, Verdun 1916* (New York: St. Martin's Press, 1962), p. 59; Robert B. Asprey, *The German High Command at War: Hindenburg and Ludendorff Conduct World War I* (New York: William Morrow, 1991), p. 166; *Histories of 251 Divisions of the German Army Which Participated in the War (1914–1918)* (Washington, DC: U.S. Government Printing Office, 1920), p. 109; Walter Görlitz, *Model: Strategie der Defensive* (Wiesbaden: Limes Verlag, 1975), p. 19; Kluck, *March on Paris*, p. 131.

6. Görlitz, *Model*, pp. 10–14; Carlo D'Este, "Model," in Correlli Barnett, ed., *Hitler's Generals* (New York: Grove Weidenfeld, 1989), pp. 319–320; Samuel W. Mitcham Jr., *Hitler's Field Marshals and Their Battles* (Chelsea, MI: Scarborough House, 1990), p. 313.

7. Görlitz, *Model*, p. 14; D'Este, "Model," p. 320; Klaus Theweleit, *Male Fantasies*, vol. 2, *Male Bodies: Psychoanalyzing the White Terror* (Minneapolis: University of Minnesota Press, 1989), pp. 143–145.

8. Theweleit, *Male Fantasies*, pp. 143–145.

9. *The German Army from Within, by a British Officer Who Has Served in It* (New York: George H. Doran, 1914), pp. 28–29.

10. Kenneth Macksey, *Guderian: Creator of the Blitzkrieg* (New York: Stein & Day, 1975), p. 25.

11. Wolf Keilig, *Das Deutsche Heer, 1939–1945*, 3 vols. (Friedburg: Podzun Verlag, 1956), III/211: pp. 145, 222; Görlitz, *Model*, pp. 14, 16.

12. Gustav A. Sigel, *Germany's Army and Navy of the Nineteenth Century* (1900; reprint, London: Bracken, 1989), p. 28; Dennis Showalter, *Tannenberg: Clash of Empires* (Hamden, CT: Archon, 1991), pp. 110–111; Keilig, *Das Deutsche Heer*, III/211: p. 145; Michael Howard, *The Franco-Prussian War* (New York: Collier, 1961), pp. 95–98, 147–154.

13. Görlitz, *Model*, p. 17.

14. Bloem, *Advance from Mons*, p. 31.

15. Howard, *Franco-Prussian War*, pp. 378–379.

16. Barbara Tuchman, *The Guns of August* (New York: Dell, 1962), pp. 255–257.

17. Tuchman, *Guns of August*, pp. 356–357; Joe H. Kirchberger, *The First World War: An Eyewitness History* (New York: Facts on File, 1992), p. 65; Bloem, *Advance from Mons*, p. 52; Werner Mader, ed., *Hitler's Letters and Notes* (New York: Harper & Row, 1974), p. 50.

18. Kirchberger, *Eyewitness History*, p. 65; Bloem, *Advance from Mons*, pp. 30–31; Hermann Balck, *Ordnung im Chaos: Erinnerungen 1893–1948* (Osnabrück: Biblio Verlag, 1981), pp. 16–18; Lyn McDonald, *1914–1918: Voices and Images of the Great War* (London: Michael Joseph, 1988), p. 38; Tuchman, *Guns of August*, pp. 199, 255–256.

19. Ludendorff, *Ludendorff's Own Story*, vol. 1, pp. 35–36; Kluck, *March on Paris*, pp. 25–26; Tuchman, *Guns of August*, p. 255.

20. Kluck, *March on Paris*, pp. 12–15; Kuhl and Bergmann, *First Army*, p. 19.

21. Tuchman, *Guns of August*, pp. 197, 403–404.

22. Bloem, *Advance from Mons*, p. 43; Balck, *Ordnung im Chaos*, p. 23.

23. Correlli Barnett, *The Swordbearers: Supreme Command in the First World War* (Bloomington: Indiana University Press, 1963), pp. 39–41.

24. Tuchman, *Guns of August*, p. 254; Kluck, *March on Paris*, p. 45.

25. C. S. Forester, *The General* (1947; reprint, Baltimore: Nautical and Aviation Publishing, 1987), p. 33; Tuchman, *Guns of August*, pp. 286–287.

26. Kluck, *March on Paris*, p. 88; Barnett, *Swordbearers*, p. 55.

27. James E. Edmonds, ed., *History of the Great War, Based on Official Documents: Military Operations, France and Belgium, 1914* (London: Macmillan and Co., 1937), p. 94n.

28. Ibid., pp. 80–81; John Terraine, *Mons: The Retreat to Victory* (London: B. T. Batsford, 1960), p. 94.

29. A. F. Wedd, ed., *German Students' War Letters* (New York: E. P. Dutton, 1929), p. 13.

30. Adolph Hitler, *Mein Kampf* (1927; reprint, Boston: Houghton Mifflin, 1971), p. 164.

31. Bloem, *Advance from Mons*, p. 108.

32. Ibid., p. 92.

33. Edmonds, *History*, p. 197n; Kluck, *March on Paris*, pp. 56, 69.

34. Kluck, *March on Paris*, p. 85; Tuchman, *Guns of August*, pp. 403–404, 445–446; Bloem, *Advance from Mons*, pp. 106–108.

35. Asprey, *German High Command*, pp. 99–103; Görlitz, *General Staff*, pp. 159–160.

36. Asprey, *German High Command*, pp. 99–103; Görlitz, *General Staff*, pp. 159–160.

37. Görlitz, *General Staff*, p. 162.

38. Bloem, *Advance from Mons*, p. 156.

39. Balck, *Ordnung im Chaos*, pp. 28–29.

40. Paul Fussell, *The Great War and Modern Memory* (New York: Oxford University Press, 1975), pp. 36–37; Werner Maser, ed., *Hitler's Letters and Notes* (New York: Harper & Row, 1973), pp. 61–63.

41. *Divisions of the German Army*, p. 109; Görlitz, *Model*, pp. 19–20.

42. German Werth, *Verdun* (Bergisch Gladbach: Gustav Lübber Verlag, 1979), pp. 66–67.

43. *Divisions of the German Army*, p. 109.

44. Charles Messenger, *The Last Prussian: A Biography of Field Marshal Gerd von Rundstedt, 1875–1953* (London: Brassey's, 1991), pp. 12–13; Sigel, *Germany's Army and Navy*, p. 78; Görlitz, *Model*, p. 20.

45. Asprey, *German High Command*, p. 266; Görlitz, *General Staff*, pp. 182, 192; Görlitz, *Model*, p. 20.

46. Ludendorff, *Ludendorff's Own Story*, vol. 2, pp. 4, 6.

47. Asprey, *German High Command*, pp. 304–305.

48. Erich Ludendorff, *The General Staff and Its Problems*, 2 vols. (New York: E. P. Dutton, n.d.), vol. 2, pp. 385, 387–388.

49. Görlitz, *Model*, pp. 20–21; Görlitz, *General Staff*, pp. 192, 231.

50. *Divisions of the German Army*, p. 28.

51. Ibid.; Dick Rustin, "The Kaiser's Battle: The German Offensive, March 1918," *Strategy and Tactics* 83 (November–December 1980): pp. 8, 12.

52. Conrad H. Lanza, ed., *The German Offensive of July 15, 1918, Marne Source Book* (Fort Leavenworth, KS: General Service Schools Press, 1923), p. 4.

53. *Divisions of the German Army*, p. 28; Rustin, "Kaiser's Battle," p. 8.

54. Rustin, "Kaiser's Battle," p. 8.

55. Rudolf Binding, *A Fatalist at War* (Boston: Houghton Mifflin, 1929), pp. 204, 206.

56. Ibid., pp. 206, 214.

57. Asprey, *German High Command*, pp. 422–425.

58. Binding, *Fatalist*, pp. 225–226.

59. Ibid.; Lanza, *German Offensive*, p. 176.

60. Lanza, *German Offensive*, p. 288.

61. Binding, *Fatalist*, p. 226; Herbert Sulzbach, *With the German Guns: Four Years on the Western Front, 1914–1918* (London: Leo Cooper, 1973), p. 202; Kurt

Hesse, "The Marne-Drama of July 15, 1918, Seen from the Angle of the Fighting Grenadier Regiment No. 5, 36th Infantry Division," in Charles F. Horne and Walter F. Austin, eds., *The Great Events of the Great War*, 7 vols. (New York: National Alumni Press, 1920;), vol. 6, p. 250.

62. Lanza, *German Offensive*, pp. 176, 253–254, 288.

63. Hesse, "Marne-Drama," p. 254; Sulzbach, *German Guns*, p. 201.

64. Binding, *Fatalist*, pp. 234–235; Lanza, *German Offensive*, pp. 539–541.

65. The narrative of events is provided in Binding, *Fatalist*, pp. 234–235. While he does not identify the division, a careful cross-checking of locations and reports (see Lanza, *German Offensive*, pp. 427, 517) makes it abundantly clear that he was describing the scene at the Guard Ersatz Division.

66. Lanza, *German Offensive*, pp. 564, 572, 576, 588, 617, 650.

67. Ibid., pp. 617–630.

68. Ibid., pp. 645–646; Sulzbach, *German Guns*, pp. 203, 208.

69. Mitcham, *Field Marshals*, pp. 21, 76, 146, 242, 284, 332; Barnett, *Generals*, pp. 40, 70, 336; Samuel W. Mitcham Jr. and Gene Mueller, *Hitler's Commanders* (Lanham, MD: Scarborough House, 1992), pp. 81, 125, 138–139; Robert J. O'Neill, *The German Army and the Nazi Party, 1933–1939* (New York: James H. Heinemann, 1966), pp. 190, 191.

70. *Divisions of the German Army*, pp. 423–424.

71. Ibid.; Günter Wegmann, ed., *Formationgeschichter und Stellenbesetzung der Deutschen Streitkräfte, 1815–1990*, 2 vols. [to date] (Osnabrück: Biblio Verlag, 1990–1992), vol. 1, p. 177; Görlitz, *Model*, p. 23.

Chapter 2: Suited for Higher Command

1. Raymond J. Sontag, *A Broken World, 1919–1939* (New York: Harper & Row, 1971), pp. 45–46; Robert G. L. Waite, *Vanguard of Nazism: The Free Corps Movement in Postwar Germany, 1918–1923* (New York: W. W. Norton, 1952), pp. 2–3.

2. Hitler, *Mein Kampf*, p. 201; Macksey, *Guderian*, p. 43; F. L. Carsten, *The Reichswehr and Politics, 1918 to 1933* (Oxford: Clarendon Press, 1966), p. 9; Waite, *Vanguard*, p. 7.

3. Görlitz, *Model*, p. 23.

4. Harold J. Gordon, *The Reichswehr and the German Republic, 1919–1926* (Princeton, NJ: Princeton University Press, 1957), pp. 15–16, 50.

5. Waite, *Vanguard*, pp. 5, 9.

6. John W. Wheeler-Bennett, *The Nemesis of Power: The German Army in Politics, 1918–1945* (New York: Viking, 1967), pp. 22, 28.

7. Waite, *Vanguard*, pp. 10–15.

8. Waite, *Vanguard*, is the best general introduction to the *Freikorps*; Gordon, *Reichswehr and the German Republic*, is also an excellent source for examining their relationship with the army.

9. B. H. Liddell Hart, *The German Generals Talk* (1948; reprint, New York: Quill, 1979), pp. 11–12; Albert Seaton, *The German Army* (New York: St. Martin's

Press, 1979), pp. 4–5; Charles L. Mee Jr., *The End of Order: Versailles 1919* (New York: E. P. Dutton, 1980), pp. 220–221.

10. Carsten, *Reichswehr and Politics*, pp. 29, 30, 40, 79, 104, 149, 154, 158, 172, 175–177n, 212, 248, 299, 300, 342–343, 389.

11. Gordon, *Reichswehr and the German Republic*, pp. 64–65, 437–438; Görlitz, *Model*, pp. 24–25; Waite, *Vanguard*, pp. 137–139.

12. Waite, *Vanguard*, pp. 45, 183–191; Carsten, *Reichswehr and Politics*, pp. 40, 79; Görlitz, *General Staff*, pp. 219–220.

13. Barnett, *Hitler's Generals*, p. 436; Mitcham, *Hitler's Field Marshals*, p. 340; Günther Fraschka, *Knights of the Reich* (Atglen, PA: Schiffer, 1994), p. 237; Friedrich-Wilhelm von Mellenthin, *German Generals of World War II as I Saw Them* (Norman: University of Oklahoma Press, 1977), pp. 175, 193, 240; Mitcham and Mueller, *Hitler's Commanders*, pp. 68–72.

14. Görlitz, *Model*, pp. 23, 32.

15. Ibid., pp. 18, 23; Gordon, *Reichswehr and Politics*, pp. 437–438; Waite, *Vanguard*, pp. 180–182; Nigel H. Jones, *Hitler's Heralds: The Story of the Freikorps, 1918–1923* (New York: Dorset, 1987), pp. 181–185.

16. Ibid., pp. 27, 32.

17. Robert M. Citino, *The Evolution of Blitzkrieg Tactics: Germany Defends Itself Against Poland, 1918–1933* (New York: Greenwood, 1987), pp. xii, 47–48, 185; Görlitz, *Model*, pp. 36–37; Adolf Reinicke, *Das Reichsheer, 1921–1934, Ziele, Methoden der Ausbildung und Erziehung owie der Diesntgestaltung* (Osnabrück: Biblio Verlag, 1986), p. 452.

18. Görlitz, *Model*, p. 37; Reinicke, *Reichsheer*, p. 158; Walther K. Nehring, *Die Geschichte der deutschen Panzerwaffe, 1916 bis 1945* (Berlin: Propyläen, 1969), pp. 53–57; Wolfgang Paul, *Das Potsdamer Infanterie—Regiment 9, 1918–1945, Preussiche Tradition in Krieg und Frieden* (Osnabrück: Biblio Verlag, 1985), pp. 59, 60, 81; Dermot Bradly, *Walter Wenck: General der Panzertruppe* (Osnabrück: Biblio Verlag, 1981), pp. 80–81.

19. Wilhelm Ritter von Leeb, "Von Leeb's Defense," in *Roots of Strategy*, book 3 (Harrisburg, PA: Stackpole, 1991), p. 13.

20. James Corum, *The Roots of Blitzkrieg: Hans von Seeckt and German Military Reform* (Lawrence: University Press of Kansas, 1992), p. 183; S. J. Lewis, *Forgotten Legions: German Army Infantry Policy, 1918–1941* (New York: Praeger, 1985), p. 48; Reinicke, *Reichsheer*, p. 92.

21. Görlitz, *Model*, p. 37; Reinicke, *Reichsheer*, p. 102; Reiner Wohlfeil, *Reichswehr und Republik (1918–1933)* (Frankfurt: Heer und Republik, n.d.), p. 320.

22. Görlitz, *Model*, pp. 41–43; Nehring, *Panzerwaffe*, pp. 41, 74; Reinicke, *Reichsheer*, p. 447; Telford Taylor, *Sword and Swastika: Generals and Nazis in the Third Reich* (New York: Simon & Schuster, 1952), p. 405; Yuri Dyakov and Tatyana Bushuyeva, *The Red Army and the Wehrmacht: How the Soviets Militarized Germany, 1922–1933, and Paved the Way for Fascism* (Amherst, NY: Prometheus, 1995), pp. 268–269.

23. Corum, *Roots of Blitzkrieg*, pp. 196–197; Citino, *Evolution of Blitzkrieg Tactics*, pp. 186–191; Nehring, *Panzerwaffe*, pp. 67–71.

24. Görlitz, *Model*, pp. 45–48; Seaton, *German Army*, pp. 55–58.

25. Johannes Steinhoff, Peter Pechel, and Dennis Showalter, eds., *Voices from the Third Reich: An Oral History* (Washington, DC: Regnery Gateway, 1989), p. 16; Carsten, *Reichswehr and Politics*, p. 311; Eberhard Zeller, *The Flame of Freedom: The German Struggle Against Hitler* (1967; reprint, Boulder, CO: Westview Press, 1994), p. 5; Ian Kershaw, *The "Hitler Myth": Image and Reality in the Third Reich* (New York: Oxford University Press, 1987), pp. 13–50.

26. Messenger, *Last Prussian*, p. 61; Albert Kesselring, *The Memoirs of Field-Marshal Kesselring* (1953; reprint, Novato, CA: Presidio, 1989), p. 27; O'Neill, *German Army and Nazi Party*, pp. 18–19; Macksey, *Guderian*, pp. 77–80; Görlitz, *General Staff*, pp. 274–275.

27. It is difficult to determine with any precision exactly when Model made the acquaintance of Goebbels and Goering. Neither the extensive biographies of each man nor Goebbels's diaries make any specific reference to Model until well after the beginning of the war. Yet it is clear from a remark in Halder's diary on 19 October 1939 that Model's friendship with Goering was already warm and well known throughout the army. It probably began during Model's assignment to *Abteilung 8*, when he served as an army liaison to Luftwaffe rearmament. The relationship with Goebbels is more problematic, but again, circumstantial evidence strongly suggests it predated the war. Görlitz, *Model*, p. 18; Arnold Lissance, ed., *The Halder Diaries: The Private War Diaries of Colonel General Franz Halder*, 2 vols. (Boulder, CO: Westview Press, 1976), vol. 1, pp. 107, 143.

28. Heinz Guderian, *Panzer Leader* (London: Michael Joseph, 1952), pp. 32–33; Matthew Cooper, *The German Army, 1933–1945: Its Political and Military Failure* (New York: Stein and Day, 1978), pp. 137–138; Nehring, *Panzerwaffe*, p. 74.

29. Görlitz, *Model*, pp. 52–53.

30. Ibid., pp. 54–58; Nehring, *Panzerwaffe*, p. 76; Walter J. Spielberger, *Sturmgeschütz and Its Variants* (Atglen, PA: Schiffer, 1993), p. 12.

31. Görlitz, *Model*, pp. 58–64; O'Neill, *German Army and Nazi Party*, p. 148; Seaton, *German Army*, p. 83; Cooper, *German Army*, pp. 77–78.

Chapter 3: As Fussy as a Field Marshal

1. Cooper, *German Army*, pp. 77–78; Keilig, *Das Deutsche Heer*, vol. 3, pp. 211/313; Taylor, *Sword and Swastika*, p. 400; Görlitz, *General Staff*, pp. 50–68.

2. Nehring, *Panzerwaffe*, p. 100.

3. Keilig, *Das Deutsche Heer*, vol. 3, pp. 211/27, 83, 119, 241, 363–364.

4. Görlitz, *Model*, pp. 64–67, 197; Siegfried Knappe and Ted Brusaw, *Soldat: Reflections of a German Soldier, 1936–1949* (New York: Orion, 1992), p. 122.

5. Seaton, *German Army*, pp. 56–57; Samuel W. Mitcham Jr., *Hitler's Legions: The German Army Order of Battle, World War II* (New York: Stein and Day, 1985), pp. 27–28; Victor Madej, ed., *German Army Order of Battle: The Replacement Army, 1939–1945* (Allentown, PA: Valor, 1984), p. 34.

6. Görlitz, *Model*, pp. 66–67; Williamson Murray, *The Change in the European Balance of Power, 1938–1939: The Path to Ruin* (Princeton, NJ: Princeton University Press, 1984), pp. 264–283.

7. Knappe and Brusaw, *Soldat*, p. 114; Keilig, *Das deutsche Heer*, vol. 1, pp. 10/2; vol. 2, 101/I/1, 11–14; Victor Madej, ed., *German Army Order of Battle: Field Army and Officer Corps, 1939–1945* (Allentown, PA: Valor, 1984), pp. 49, 56–57.

8. Alan Bullock, *Hitler and Stalin: Parallel Lives* (New York: Alfred A. Knopf, 1992), pp. 606–609; Anthony Read and David Fisher, *The Deadly Embrace: Hitler, Stalin, and the Nazi-Soviet Pact, 1939–1941* (New York: W. W. Norton, 1988), pp. 173–174; Hanson Baldwin, *Battles Lost and Won: Great Campaigns of World War II* (New York: Harper & Row, 1966), p. 3.

9. Read and Fisher, *Deadly Embrace*, pp. 227–228; Albert Speer, *Inside the Third Reich* (New York: Macmillan, 1970), p. 223.

10. Messenger, *Last Prussian*, pp. 81–86; Erich von Manstein, *Lost Victories* (Novato, CA: Presidio, 1982), pp. 22–24; Günther Blumentritt, *Von Rundstedt: The Soldier and the Man* (London: Oldham's, 1952), pp. 46–48.

11. Ibid.; J. E. Kaufmann and H. W. Kaufmann, *Hitler's Blitzkrieg Campaigns: The Invasion and Defense of Western Europe, 1939–1940* (Conshohocken, NJ: Combined Books, 1993), pp. 84–85, 343.

12. Kaufmann and Kaufmann, *Blitzkrieg Campaigns*, p. 68; Robert M. Kennedy, *The German Campaign in Poland (1939)* (Washington, DC: U.S. Department of the Army, 1956), p. 58; Burkhart Mueller-Hillebrand, *Das Heer 1933–1945*, 3 vols. (Darmstadt: E. S. Mittler & Sohn, 1954), vol. 1, p. 72.

13. Von Manstein, *Lost Victories*, pp. 49, 55; *Heeresgruppe Sud; Anlage zum Kriegtagebuch (Ia): Karten*, 31 August 1939, reel 240, T–311, U.S. National Archives, Washington, DC (hereafter cited as NA).

14. Von Manstein, *Lost Victories*, pp. 49, 55–56.

15. Knappe and Brusaw, *Soldat*, pp. 132–135; *Kriegtagebuch (Ia) IV Korps*, 28–31 August 1939, reel 215, T–314, NA.

16. *Kriegtagebuch (Ia) IV Korps*, 28–31 August 1939, reel 215, T–314, NA

17. Ibid.

18. Guderian, *Panzer Leader*, pp. 66, 73–74; Manstein, *Lost Victories*, pp. 24, 29; Kesselring, *Memoirs*, pp. 44–45; Friedrich-Wilhelm von Mellenthin, *Panzer Battles: A Study of the Employment of Armor in the Second World War* (New York: Ballantine, 1971), pp. xviii–xix.

19. Wilhelm Prüller, *Diary of a German Soldier* (London: Faber and Faber, 1963), p. 11; see also Omer Bartov, "Operation Barbarossa and the Origins of the Final Solution," in David Cesarani, ed., *The Final Solution: Origins and Implementation* (London: Routledge, 1994), pp. 126–131.

20. *Kriegtagebuch (Ia) IV Korps*, 1–5 September 1939, reel 215, T–314, NA; M. Norwid Neugebauer, *The Defence of Poland (September 1939)* (London: M. I. Koln, 1942), pp. 98–99.

21. *Heeresgruppe Sud; Anlage zum Kriegtagebuch (Ia): Karten*, 9 September 1939, reel 240, T–311, NA; Kaufmann and Kaufmann, *Blitzkrieg Campaigns*, p. 344.

22. *Kriegtagebuch (Ia) IV Korps*, 10 September 1939; *Anlage* 4, report of captured material at Radom, reel 215, T–314, NA; Janusz Piekalkiewicz, *Polenfeldzug: Hitler und Stalin zerschlagen die Polnische Republik* (Bergisch Gladbach: Gustav Lübbe Verlag, 1982), pp. 134–135; Neugebauer, *Defence of Poland*, p. 155; Kennedy, *Poland*, p. 103.

23. *Kriegtagebuch (Ia) IV Korps*, 12 September 1939, reel 215, T–314, NA; Piekalkiewicz, *Polenfeldzug*, p. 150; Kennedy, *Poland*, p. 104.

24. Heinz Hohne, *The Order of the Death's Head: The Story of Hitler's SS* (New York: Ballantine, 1971), p. 339; Messenger, *Last Prussian*, p. 90; Lissance, *Halder Diary*, vol. 1, pp. 22, 82–85, 89, 96; Ministry of Foreign Affairs, Republic of Poland, *German Occupation of Poland: Extract of Note Address to the Allied and Neutral Powers* (New York: Greystone, 1941), pp. 62–64, 225.

25. Prüller, *Diary*, pp. 15, 25; Messenger, *Last Prussian*, p. 91; James Lucas, *Battle Group! German Kampfgruppen Action of World War Two* (London: Arms and Armour, 1993), p. 13.

26. *Kriegtagebuch (Ia) IV Korps*, 16 September 1939, reel 215, T–314, NA; Lissance, *Halder Diary*, vol. 1, pp. 39, 54, 59, 81, 85, 87, 96, 98, 106–107; Richard C. Lukas, *Forgotten Holocaust: The Poles Under German Occupation, 1939–1944* (New York: Hippocrene, 1986), p. 3; Raul Hilberg, *The Destruction of the European Jews*, 3 vols. (New York: Holmes & Meier, 1985), vol. 1, 194, 199, 249.

27. *Kriegtagebuch (Ia) IV Korps*, 11 September–10 October 1939, reel 215, T–314, NA; Fritz Freiherr von Siegler, *Die höheren Dienstellen der deutschen Wehrmacht, 1933–1945* (Frankfurt: Instituts für Zeitgeschichte, 1956), p. 46.

28. *Kriegtagebuch (Ia) IV Korps*, 3–5 October 1939, reel 215; *OQu* 1, Fr/73, 19 October 1939, reel 218, T–314, NA; Hohne, *Order of the Death's Head*, pp. 339–344; Richard Breitman, *The Architect of Genocide: Heinrich Himmler and the Final Solution* (New York: Alfred A. Knopf, 1991), pp. 76–81; Lissance, *Halder Diary*, vol. 1, pp. 61, 85, 87, 94.

29. Lissance, *Halder Diary*, vol. 1, p. 107; Seaton, *German Army*, p. 119.

30. *(IIa) Grenzabschnitte Mitte, Sprach 4696/Fr 80*, 20 October 1939, reel 218, T–314, NA.

31. Lissance, *Halder Diary*, pp. 104, 107; Keilig, *Das deutsche Heer*, vol. 3, pp. 211/324.

32. Mitcham, *Hitler's Field Marshals*, pp. 270–273; Richard Brett-Smith, *Hitler's Generals* (San Rafael, CA: Presidio, 1977), pp. 196–197; Taylor, *Sword and Swastika*, p. 400.

33. Ibid.

34. Ernst Busch, "Has the Decisive Battle Role of the Infantry Ended?" in Ladislas Farago, ed., *The Axis Grand Strategy: Blueprints for the Total War* (New York: Farrar and Rinehart, 1942), pp. 189–190.

35. Görlitz, *Model*, p. 72. Note the lack of participation, or even mention, of either Busch or Model in the abortive 1940 coup attempt in Harold C. Deutsch, *The Conspiracy Against Hitler in the Twilight War* (Minneapolis: University of Minnesota Press, 1968), or in Zeller, *Flame of Freedom*, pp. 39–42.

36. Telford Taylor, *The March of Conquest: The German Victories in Western Europe, 1940* (New York: Simon & Schuster, 1958), pp. 156–162; Kaufmann and Kaufmann, *Blitzkrieg Campaigns*, pp. 133–138.

37. Lissance, *Halder Diary*, pp. 131, 153, 171.

38. Taylor, *March of Conquest*, p. 170; Kaufmann and Kaufmann, *Blitzkrieg Campaigns*, pp. 137–139.

39. Görlitz, *Model*, p. 75; Lissance, *Halder Diary*, vol. 1, pp. 213–215, 226–227, 230, 237, 243, 247; Guderian, *Panzer Leader*, p. 90.

40. Lissance, *Halder Diary*, pp. 213–215, 239; Guderian, *Panzer Leader*, p. 92.

41. Lewis, *Forgotten Legions*, p. 105.

42. Ibid.; Florian K. Rothburst, *Guderian's XIXth Panzer Corps and the Battle of France: Breakthrough in the Ardennes, May 1940* (New York: Praeger, 1990), p. 27.

43. Lissance, *Halder Diary*, vol. 1, pp. 95, 234; Tom Schactman, *The Phony War, 1939–1940* (New York: Harper & Row, 1982), p. 98; Seaton, *German Army*, p. 120.

44. Görlitz, *Model*, p. 77; Lissance, *Halder Diary*, vol. 1, pp. 247, 280.

45. *(Ia) Kreigsgleiderungen, Armeeoberkommando 16*, 20 April 1940 and 5 May 1940, reel 525, T–312, NA; Taylor, *March of Conquest*, pp. 400–407; Görlitz, *Model*, p. 80.

46. Lissance, *Halder Diary*, vol. 1, pp. 104, 107, 349; Reinhard Gehlen, *The Service: The Memoirs of General Reinhard Gehlen* (New York: World, 1972), pp. 25, 380.

47. Hans-Adolf Jacobsen, ed., *Dokumente zum Westfeldzug 1940* (Göttingen: Musterschmidt-Verlag, 1960), pp. 8–9; Lissance, *Halder Diary*, vol. 1, pp. 390, 393.

48. Ibid., pp. 17, 23, 28, 37, 42, 48, 50, 67, 75.

49. Jacobsen, *Westfeldzug*, pp. 80, 93, 104–105; Lissance, *Halder Diary*, vol. 1, p. 415.

50. Taylor, *March of Conquest*, pp. 409, 411; Jacobsen, *Westfeldzug*, pp. 109, 155, 158; *(Ia) Kreigsgleiderungen, Armeeoberkommando 16*, 1 June 1940 and 4 June 1940; *Artilleriegleiderung, Armeeoberkommando 16*, 3 June 1940; *OQu/Qu 1, Stellenbesatzung*, 1 June 1940, reel 525, T–312, NA. See Newton, *German Battle Tactics*, pp. 262–263, for a detailed explanation of corps commands.

51. Kaufmann and Kaufmann, *Blitzkrieg Campaigns*, pp. 270, 275–276.

52. Lissance, *Halder Diary*, p. 439; Jacobsen, *Westfeldzug*, pp. 104–105, 170, 173–174, 183.

53. Kaufmann and Kaufmann, *Blitzkrieg Campaigns*, pp. 265–266, 270; von Mellenthin, *Panzer Battles*, p. 27.

54. Kaufmann and Kaufmann, *Blitzkrieg Campaigns*, p. 274; Jacobsen, *Westfeldzug*, pp. 183, 188, 203.

55. Jacobsen, *Westfeldzug*, pp. 189, 191; *OQu/Qu 1, Stellenbesatzung*, 1 June 1940, reel 525, T–312, NA.

56. Jacobsen, *Westfeldzug*, pp. 195–196; Lissance, *Halder Diary*, vol. 1, p. 454.

57. Jacobsen, *Westfeldzug*, pp. 208–209; Lissance, *Halder Diary*, vol. 1, p. 462.

58. Jacobsen, *Westfeldzug*, pp. 219, 220, 222, 226, 228, 231, 233, 238, 240.

59. Taylor, *March of Conquest*, pp. 344–351, 405–407.

60. Görlitz, *Model*, p. 80; Taylor, *March of Conquest*, pp. 405–407.

61. Telford Taylor, *The Breaking Wave: The Second World War in the Summer of 1940* (New York: Simon & Schuster, 1967), p. 199.

62. Walter Warlimont, *Inside Hitler's Headquarters, 1939–1945* (London: Weidenfeld and Nicolson, 1964), p. 108; Frank Davis, "SEELÖWE: The German Plan to Invade Britain, 1940," *Strategy and Tactics* 40 (September–October 1973): pp. 21–22.

63. Taylor, *Breaking Wave*, pp. 216–218; Davis, "SEELÖWE," pp. 26–28.

64. Davis, "SEELÖWE," pp. 30–31.

65. Taylor, *Breaking Wave*, p. 253; Davis, "SEELÖWE," p. 28; Messenger, *Last Prussian*, pp. 124–125.

66. Peter Schenck, *Invasion of England 1940: The Planning of Operation Sealion* (London: Conway Maritime Press, 1990), pp. 29, 87, 88, 186–187.

67. Ibid., p. 188.

68. Davis, "SEELÖWE," p. 33.

Chapter 4: Guderian's Spearhead

1. Cooper, *German Army*, pp. 259–260; Barry A. Leach, *German Strategy Against Russia, 1939–1941* (New York: Oxford University Press, 1973), p. 106; Bryan I. Fugate, *Operation Barbarossa: Strategy and Tactics on the Eastern Front, 1941* (Novato, CA: Presidio, 1984), pp. 61–63; Albert Seaton, *The Russo-German War, 1941–1945* (New York: Praeger, 1971), pp. 52–53.

2. Seaton, *German Army*, pp. 150–157.

3. Lissance, *Halder Diary*, vol. 1, pp. 551, 557, 560, 574, 587, 600, 619, 621, 631, 674, 676, 677, 681, 689, 739, 754, 773.

4. Ibid., vol. 1, pp. 683, 684.

5. Görlitz, *Model*, pp. 82–85.

6. Stumpff commanded the 20th Panzer Division for only about a year before being sidetracked into recruiting, administrative, and replacement positions for the remainder of the war. After losing his command to Model, he was apparently never considered for corps command. Ibid.; Keilig, *Deutsche Heer*, vol. 3, pp. 211/334.

7. Lissance, *Halder Diary*, vol. 1, p. 700; Görlitz, *Model*, pp. 83–84.

8. Görlitz, *Model*, pp. 85–86.

9. Ibid. For examples of actions in which German panzer units were employed along straight organizational lines (panzers and infantry operating in separate groups, for example) in Poland and France, see Liddel Hart, *German Generals Talk*, p. 93; Guderian, *Panzer Leader*, pp. 104–110; Mellenthin, *Panzer Battles*, p. 20.

10. Görlitz, *Model*, p. 86; Keilig, *Deutsche Heer*, vol. 3, pp. 211/45, 210.

11. An idea of Audörsch's limited ability as a field commander can be gleaned from the fact that he spent only six months in combat commanding his regiment before being shelved again at OKH. Thereafter it was only in August 1944, after the disaster in Belorussia, that he was whisked through the division commander's course and given a panzer division. Effective regimental commanders in panzer di-

visions universally moved up to division and corps command much more quickly. Keilig, *Deutsche Heer*, vol. 2, pp. 103/II/2; vol. 3, pp. 211/9, 165.

12. Görlitz, *Model*, p. 87.

13. Lissance, *Halder Diary*, vol. 1, p. 739; Russell H. S. Stolfi, *Hitler's Panzers East: World War II Reinterpreted* (Norman: University of Oklahoma Press, 1991), p. 137.

14. Manstein, *Lost Victories*, p. 21.

15. Keilig, *Deutsche Heer*, vol. 1, pp. 34/7–13; Mueller-Hillebrand, *Das Heer*, vol. 2, pp. 192–193; Görlitz, *Model*, p. 92.

16. Seaton, *Russo-German War*, p. 116; Guderian, *Panzer Leader*, pp. 145, 513; Paul Carell, *Hitler Moves East, 1941–1943* (New York: Ballantine, 1971), pp. 6, 10.

17. Guderian, *Panzer Leader*, pp. 145–150; Seaton, *Russo-German War*, pp. 50–64; Fugate, *Operation Barbarossa*, pp. 61–94; Alan Clark, *Barbarossa: The Russian-German Conflict, 1941–1945* (New York: William Morrow, 1965), pp. 70–72, 77–80; Stolfi, *Hitler's Panzers East*, pp. 21–25; 77–79; Victor Madej and Shelby Stanton, "The Smolensk Campaign, 11 July–5 August 1941," *Strategy and Tactics* 57 (July–August 1976): p. 5.

18. Ibid.; Manstein, *Lost Victories*, pp. 185–186; Leach, *German Strategy*, p. 171; Alfred W. Turney, *Disaster at Moscow: Von Bock's Campaigns, 1941–1942* (Albuquerque: University of New Mexico Press, 1970), pp. 31–32.

19. Stolfi, *Hitler's Panzers East*, p. 137; Clark, *Barbarossa*, p. 71; Guderian, *Panzer Leader*, pp. 77–81; Turney, *Disaster at Moscow*, p. 40.

20. Wilhelm Keitel, *The Memoirs of Field-Marshal Keitel* (New York: Stein and Day, 1966), pp. 135–136; Lissance, *Halder Diary*, vol. 1, pp. 846–847.

21. Hilberg, *Destruction of the European Jews*, vol. 1, pp. 280–281, 284, 286, 289–290.

22. Theo J. Schulte, *The German Army and Nazi Policies in Occupied Russia* (New York: Berg, 1989), pp. 317, 312–322; Jürgen Förster, "The Wehrmacht and the War of Extermination Against the Soviet Union," in Michael R. Marrus, ed., *The Nazi Holocaust: Historical Articles on the Destruction of European Jews*, 9 vols. (Westport, CT: Meckler 1989), vol. 3, pt. 2, p. 501.

23. Jürgen Förster, "The Relation Between Operation Barbarossa as an Ideological War of Extermination and the Final Solution," in David Cesarani, ed., *The Final Solution: Origins and Implementation* (London: Routledge, 1994) p. 85; Guderian, *Panzer Leader*, p. 152; Messenger, *Last Prussian*, p. 134; Steinhoff, Pechel, and Showalter, *Voices from the Third Reich*, p. 141; von Manstein, *Lost Victories*, pp. 179–180.

24. Förster, "Operation Barbarossa as an Ideological War," pp. 89–90, 97; Christian Streit, "Wehrmacht, Einsatzgruppen, Soviet POWs, and Anti-Bolshevism in the Emergence of the Final Solution," in Cesarani, *Final Solution*, p. 110; Horst Fuchs Richardson, ed., *SIEG HEIL! War Letters of Tank Gunner Karl Fuchs, 1937–1941* (Hamden, CT: Archon, 1987), p. 124; Förster, "War of Extermination," pp. 497, 500–501; V. N. Denisov and G. I. Changuli, eds., *Nazi Crimes in Ukraine 1941–1944: Documents and Materials* (Kiev: Nuakova Dumka, 1987), pp. 184–186; Matthew Cooper, *The Nazi War Against Soviet Partisans, 1941–1944* (New York:

Stein and Day, 1979), pp. 21, 51–52; Omer Bartov, *Hitler's Army: Soldiers, Nazis, and War in the Third Reich* (New York: Oxford University Press, 1991), pp. 84–85.

25. Görlitz, *Model*, pp. 90–91.

26. Ibid., p. 90; Guderian, *Panzer Leader*, p. 148; Carell, *Hitler Moves East*, p. 9.

27. Rudolf Steiger, *Armour Tactics in the Second World War: Panzer Army Campaigns of 1939–1941 in German War Diaries* (Oxford: Berg, 1991), p. 20.

28. Paul Carell, *Unternehmen Barbarossa im Bild: Der Russlandkrieg fotograiert von Soldaten* (Berlin: Verlag Ullstein, 1967), p. 33; Clark, *Barbarossa*, p. 48.

29. Fugate, *Operation Barbarossa*, pp. 48, 111, 319, 322; Clark, *Barbarossa*, p. 48; Carell, *Hitler Moves East*, p. 17.

30. Seaton, *Russo-German War*, p. 120; Fugate, *Operation Barbarossa*, p. 111; Clark, *Barbarossa*, p. 51.

31. Fugate, *Operation Barbarossa*, pp. 322, 328–330; Michael Parrish, "Formation and Leadership of the Soviet Mechanized Corps in 1941," *Military Affairs* (April 1983): pp. 64, 66; Richard M. Armstrong, *Red Army Tank Commanders: The Armored Guards* (Atglen, PA: Schiffer, 1994), pp. 104–105; David M. Glantz, *The Role of Intelligence in Soviet Military Strategy in World War II* (Novato, CA: Presidio, 1990), pp. 16–17.

32. Ibid.; Görlitz, *Model*, p. 92; Horst Zobel, "3rd Panzer Division Operations," in David M. Glantz, ed., *The Initial Period of War on the Eastern Front: 22 June–August 1941, Proceedings of the Fourth Art of War Symposium* (London: Frank Cass, 1993), p. 242.

33. Fugate, *Operation Barbarossa*, pp. 111–114; Carell, *Hitler Moves East*, pp. 70–71.

34. Clark, *Barbarossa*, p. 49; Fugate, *Operation Barbarossa*, pp. 112–113; Carell, *Hitler Moves East*, p. 67.

35. Guderian, *Panzer Leader*, pp. 158–161; Fugate, *Operation Barbarossa*, pp. 115–116; Zobel, "3rd Panzer Division Operations," p. 244.

36. Görlitz, *Model*, p. 93; Clark, *Barbarossa*, p. 73; Guderian, *Panzer Leader*, p. 164; Fugate, *Operation Barbarossa*, pp. 117, 119; Zobel, "3rd Panzer Division," p. 395.

37. Fugate, *Operation Barbarossa*, p. 117.

38. Ibid., pp. 57–59; Louis Rotundo, "The Creation of Soviet Reserves and the 1941 Campaign," *Military Affairs* (January 1985): p. 25.

39. Clark, *Barbarossa*, p. 73; Fugate, *Operation Barbarossa*, pp. 117, 119, 325.

40. Ibid.; Steiger, *Armour Tactics*, p. 79; Zobel, "3rd Panzer Division," p. 394.

41. Guderian, *Panzer Leader*, pp. 166–169.

42. Fugate, *Operation Barbarossa*, pp. 118–119; Guderian, *Panzer Leader*, p. 168.

43. Leo Freiherr Geyr von Schweppenburg, *The Critical Years* (London: Allan Wingate, 1952), p. 53; Fugate, *Operation Barbarossa*, p. 118.

44. Fugate, *Operation Barbarossa*, p. 119.

45. *(Ia) Kreigtagebuch, 3.Panzerdivision*, 6 July 1941, reel 116, T–315, NA.

46. Carell, *Hitler Moves East*, pp. 82–83; Fugate, *Operation Barbarossa*, pp. 124–127.

47. Fugate, *Operation Barbarossa*, p. 117; Clark, *Barbarossa*, p. 86; Guderian, *Panzer Leader*, p. 176.

48. Fugate, *Operation Barbarossa*, pp. 150–153.

49. *(Ia) Kreigtagebuch, 3.Panzerdivision*, 16–23 July 1941, reel 116, T–315, NA; Janusz Piekalkiewitz, *The Cavalry of World War II* (New York: Stein and Day, 1980), p. 44.

50. *(Ia) Kreigtagebuch, 3.Panzerdivision*, 23–28 July 1941, reel 116, T–315, NA.

51. *(Ia) Kreigtagebuch, 3.Panzerdivision*, 28 July 1941, reel 116, T–315, NA; Guderian, *Panzer Leader*, p. 182; Fraschka, *Knights of the Reich*, p. 208.

52. Guderian, *Panzer Leader*, pp. 184–189; Clark, *Barbarossa*, pp. 95–96; Fugate, *Operation Barbarossa*, p. 187.

53. Ibid.; *(Ia) Kreigtagebuch, 3.Panzerdivision*, 4–15 August 1941, reel 116, T–315, NA.

54. *(Ia) Kreigtagebuch, 3.Panzerdivision*, 19–20 August 1941, reel 116, T–315, NA; Fugate, *Operation Barbarossa*, p. 195.

55. *(Ia) Kreigtagebuch, 3.Panzerdivision*, 21–24 August 1941, reel 116, T–315, NA; Guderian, *Panzer Leader*, pp. 202–203; Görlitz, *Model*, p. 94.

56. Guderian, *Panzer Leader*, p. 203; Fugate, *Operation Barbarossa*, pp. 258, 349.

57. Carell, *Hitler Moves East*, p. 113.

58. Ibid., pp. 114–117.

59. Guderian, *Panzer Leader*, pp. 207–208; Fugate, *Operation Barbarossa*, pp. 253–256; Görlitz, *Model*, p. 94.

60. Guderian, *Panzer Leader*, pp. 210, 212; Carell, *Hitler Moves East*, pp. 122–123.

61. Carell, *Hitler Moves East*, p. 112; James Lucas, *War on the Eastern Front, 1941–195: The German Soldier in Russia* (New York: Stein and Day, 1980), p. 111; Prüller, *Diary*, pp. 85, 104, 108; Guderian, *Panzer Leader*, p. 210.

62. *(Ia) Kreigtagebuch, 3.Panzerdivision*, 8–10 September 1941, reel 116, T–315, NA; Alexander Werth, *Russia at War, 1941–1945* (New York: E. P. Dutton, 1964), p. 240; Guderian, *Panzer Leader*, pp. 213–214.

63. Carell, *Hitler Moves East*, pp. 124–127; Guderian, *Panzer Leader*, pp. 214–215.

64. *(Ia) Kreigtagebuch, 3.Panzerdivision*, 12–14 September 1941, reel 116, T–315, NA; Guderian, *Panzer Leader*, pp. 218–219.

65. *(Ia) Kreigtagebuch, 3.Panzerdivision*, 13–14 September 1941, reel 116, T–315, NA; Guderian, *Panzer Leader*, pp. 218–219; Carell, *Hitler Moves East*, pp. 126–128.

66. *(Ia) Kreigtagebuch, 3.Panzerdivision*, 20 September 1941, reel 116, T–315, NA; Guderian, *Panzer Leader*, pp. 220–222; Carell, *Hitler Moves East*, pp. 129–130.

67. *(Ia) Kreigtagebuch, 3.Panzerdivision*, 12–14 September 1941, reel 116, T–315, NA; Klaus Reinhardt, *Die Wende vor Moskau: Das Scheitern der Strategie*

Hitlers im Winter 1941–42 (Stuttgart: Deutsche Verlags-Anstalt, 1972), p. 317; Lucas, *Battle Group*, pp. 60–61.

68. Seaton, *Russo-German War*, pp. 177–180; Albert Seaton, *The Battle for Moscow* (New York: Jove, 1983), pp. 82–92.

69. Guderian, *Panzer Leader*, pp. 232–233; Lucas, *Battle Group*, pp. 62–63; Hans von Greiffenberg et al., *The Battle of Moscow, 1941–1942*, MS T–28 (Washington, DC: U.S. Army, Europe, Historical Division, n.d.), p. 15.

70. John Erickson, *The Road to Stalingrad* (New York: Harper & Row, 1975), p. 215; Armstrong, *Red Army Tank Commanders*, pp. 38–42, 250–255; Guderian, *Panzer Leader*, pp. 239–240; Reinhardt, *Die Wende vor Moskau*, pp. 65, 79.

71. Görlitz, *Model*, p. 96; Kelig, *Deutsche Heer*, vol. 3, pp. 221/45, 222.

Chapter 5: Advance and Retreat

1. Görlitz, *Model*, pp. 98–99; Newton, *German Battle Tactics*, pp. 14, 52n.

2. Görlitz, *Model*, p. 100; Keilig, *Deutsche Heer*, vol. 3, pp. 211/7, 163, 222, 286, 348.

3. Görlitz, *Model*, p. 99.

4. Rolf O. G. Stoves, *Die 1.Panzer Division 1935–1945* (Dorheim: Podzun Verlag, 1962), p. 114; Carl Röttiger, "XXXXI Panzer Corps During the Battle of Moscow in 1941 as a Component of Panzer Group 3," in Steven H. Newton, *German Battle Tactics on the Russian Front, 1941–1945* (Atglen, PA: Schiffer, 1994), pp. 24–30.

5. Röttiger, "XXXXI Panzer Corps," pp. 28–30.

6. Erickson, *Road to Stalingrad*, p. 219; Robert G. Poirer and Albert Z. Conner, *The Red Army Order of Battle in the Great Patriotic War* (Novato, CA: Presidio, 1985), pp. 45, 50–51.

7. Röttiger, "XXXXI Panzer Corps," pp. 31–33; Reinhardt, *Die Wende vor Moskau*, p. 317.

8. Görlitz, *Model*, p. 99; Stoves, *1.Panzer Division*, p. 114; Röttiger, "XXXXI Panzer Corps," pp. 31–33; Greiffenberg, *Battle of Moscow*, p. 103.

9. Görlitz, *Model*, pp. 99–100.

10. Röttiger, "XXXXI Panzer Corps," pp. 33–34.

11. Ibid., p. 34.

12. Steinhoff, Pechel, and Showalter, *Voices from the Third Reich*, p. 128; Hans von Luck, *Panzer Commander: The Memoirs of Hans von Luck* (New York: Dell, 1989), p. 78; Röttiger, "XXXXI Panzer Corps," pp. 34–36; Albert Seaton, *The Battle of Moscow* (New York: Stein and Day, 1971), pp. 155–156.

13. Görlitz, *Model*, pp. 102–103; Röttiger, "XXXXI Panzer Corps," p. 35; Reinhardt, *Die Wende vor Moskau*, p. 317.

14. Görlitz, *Model*, pp. 101–102; Karl Heinrich Sperker, *Generaloberst Erhard Raus: Ein Truppenführer im Ostfeldzug* (Osnabrück: Biblio Verlag, 1988), pp. 67–69.

15. Stoves, *1.Panzer Division*, p. 114; Erhard Raus, "Military Improvisations During the Russian Campaign," in Peter G. Tsouras, ed., *The Anvil of War: Ger-*

man Generalship in Defense on the Eastern Front (London: Greenhill, 1994), p. 50; Röttiger, "XXXXI Panzer Corps," p. 36.

16. Erhard Raus, *Effects of Climate on Combat in Russia* (Washington, DC: U.S. Department of the Army, 1952), p. 4; Steinhoff, Pechel, and Showalter, *Voices from the Third Reich*, p. 128; Röttiger, "XXXXI Panzer Corps," pp. 38–39; Earl F. Ziemke and Magna E. Bauer, *Moscow to Stalingrad: Decision in the East* (New York: Military Heritage Press, 1988), p. 65; Reinhardt, *Die Wende vor Moskau*, pp. 223–224.

17. Georgi K. Zhukov, *The Memoirs of Marshal Zhukov* (London: Jonathan Cape, 1971), p. 339.

18. Raus, *Effects of Climate*, p. 4; Zhukov, *Memoirs*, pp. 339–340, 348; Poirier and Conner, *Red Army Order of Battle*, pp. 13, 41, 50.

19. Armstrong, *Red Army Tank Commanders*, p. 263; Carell, *Hitler Moves East*, p. 335; Röttiger, "XXXXI Panzer Corps," p. 39.

20. Carell, *Hitler Moves East*, p. 336; Reinhardt, *Die Wende vor Moskau*, p. 317.

21. Luck, *Panzer Commander*, pp. 81–82.

22. Carell, *Hitler Moves East*, p. 339.

23. Görlitz, *Model*, pp. 104–105; Röttiger, "XXXXI Panzer Corps," p. 39.

24. Carell, *Hitler Moves East*, pp. 340–341; Röttiger, "XXXXI Panzer Corps," p. 39.

25. Stoves, *1.Panzer Division*, p. 114; Carell, *Unternehmen Barbarossa*, p. 122.

26. Görlitz, *Model*, p. 104.

27. Stoves, *1.Panzer Division*, pp. 114–115; Oldwig von Natzmer, "Operations of Encircled Forces: German Experience in Russia," in Peter G. Tsouras, ed., *The Anvil of War: German Generalship in Defense on the Eastern Front* (London: Greenhill, 1994), pp. 235–237; Werth, *Russia at War*, p. 258.

28. Stoves, *1.Panzer Division*, pp. 114–115.

29. Helmut Ritgen, *The 6th Panzer Division, 1937–1945* (London: Osprey, 1982), p. 21; Raus, "Military Improvisations," p. 51; Röttiger, "XXXXI Panzer Corps," p. 41.

30. Raus, *Effects of Climate*, p. 16; Röttiger, "XXXXI Panzer Corps," p. 40.

31. Raus, *Effects of Climate*, p. 5; Röttiger, "XXXXI Panzer Corps," p. 41.

32. Raus, *Effects of Climate*, p. 5; Ritgen, *6th Panzer Division*, p. 23; Raus, "Military Improvisations," p. 34; Sperker, *Raus*, p. 70.

33. Röttiger, "XXXXI Panzer Corps," pp. 40–43.

Chapter 6: Who Commands the Ninth Army?

1. Carell, *Hitler Moves East*, p. 392; Mitcham, *Hitler's Field Marshals*, p. 315; Seaton, *Battle for Moscow*, pp. 268–269.

2. The best brief discussion of these promotions is found in Earl F. Ziemke and Magna E. Bauer, *Moscow to Stalingrad: Decision in the East* (New York: Military Heritage Press, 1988), pp. 80–88.

3. *Kriegsgliederung Armeeoberkommando 9*, 19 January 1942, reel 294, T–312, NA.

4. *Kriegstagbuch (Ia)*, *Armeeoberkommando 9*, 18 January 1942, reel 294, T–312, NA.

5. Ibid.; *Kreigsgleiderung Armeeoberkommando 9*, 19 January 1942, reel 294, T–312, NA; Halder, *War Diary*, pp. 602–603.

6. Carell, *Hitler Moves East*, pp. 392–397.

7. Hitler made this comment in his evening conversation with his inner circle the same day that Model was dispatched to the front. See Hugh Trevor-Roper, ed., *Hitler's Secret Conversations, 1941–1944* (New York: Farrar, Strauss and Young, 1953), pp. 180–181; Görlitz, *Model*, p. 114.

8. *Kriegstagbuch (Ia)*, *Armeeoberkommando 9*, 19–25 January 1942, reel 294, T–312, NA.

9. The discussion in this and the subsequent two paragraphs is drawn from ibid. and from *Kreigsgleiderung Armeeoberkommando 9*, 19 January 1942, reel 294, T–312, NA.

10. See Ziemke and Bauer, *Moscow to Stalingrad*, pp. 139–142.

11. Görlitz, *Model*, pp. 116–117; Ziemke and Bauer, *Moscow to Stalingrad*, pp. 166–169.

12. Trevor-Roper, *Hitler's Secret Conversations*, p. 187.

13. Halder, *War Diary*, p. 609.

14. Though dated and decidedly partisan in outlook, the best English-language rendition of this attack remains Carell, *Hitler Moves East*, pp. 397–402.

15. James Lucas, *Das Reich: The Military Role of the 2nd SS Division* (London: Arms and Armour, 1991), pp. 78–79; Mark C. Yerger, *Waffen SS Commanders: The Army Corps and Divisional Leaders of a Legend*, 2 vols. (Atglen, PA: Schiffer, 1997): vol. 2, pp. 25–28.

16. *Kriegstagbuch (Ia)*, *Armeeoberkommando 9*, 22–25 January 1942, reel 294, T–312, NA; *Tagekarte, Armeeoberkommando 9*, 25 January 1942, reel 295, T–312, NA.

17. At least the Ninth Army war diary recorded no protests from von Vietinghoff; see *Kriegstagbuch (Ia)*, *Armeeoberkommando 9*, 23–26 January 1942, reel 294, T–312, NA.

18. Ziemke and Bauer, *Moscow to Stalingrad*, pp. 167–169; James Lucas, *Battle Group! German Kampfgruppen Action of World War Two* (London: Arms & Armour, 1993), pp. 90–95.

19. Görlitz, *Model*, pp. 117–119; *Kriegstagbuch (Ia)*, *Armeeoberkommando 9*, 8 February 1942, reel 294, T–312, NA.

20. Erhard Raus, *Panzer Operations: The Eastern Front Memoir of General Raus, 1941–1945*, edited and translated by Steven H. Newton (New York: Da Capo, 2004), pp. 101–104.

21. Ibid.

22. Among the more senior German officers, Krebs stands out as lacking any serious biographical treatment (even an extended article), despite having held senior staff positions at army and army group level throughout the war and ending up as the last chief of the Army General Staff. Alan Clark, *Barbarossa: The Russo-German Conflict, 1941–1945* (New York: William Morrow, 1965), p. 402.

23. *Kreigsgleiderung Armeeoberkommando 9*, 25 January 1942, reel 294, T–312, NA.

24. Ludwig Heidrich Dyck, "Loyal to Their Deaths," *World War II History* (September 2004): pp. 74–76.

25. Ibid., pp. 76–78.

26. Carell, *Hitler Moves East*, pp. 402–407.

27. *Kriegstagbuch (Ia), Armeeoberkommando 9*, 26 January–19 February 1942, reel 294, T–312, NA.

28. *Kriegstagbuch (Ia), Armeeoberkommando 9*, 6 and 11 February 1942, reel 294, T–312, NA.

Chapter 7: We Must Not Break

1. William B. Folkestad, *Panzerjäger: Tank Hunter* (Shippensburg, PA: Burd Street Press, 2000), pp. 38–39.

2. *Kriegsgleiderung Armeeoberkommando 9*, 10 May 1942, reel 297, T–312, NA; Ziemke and Bauer, *Moscow to Stalingrad*, pp. 283–296; Glantz and House, *When Titans Clashed*, pp. 103–105.

3. Helmut Hörner, *A German Odyssey: The Journal of a German Prisoner of War*, edited by Alan Kent Powell (Golden, CO: Fulcrum, 1991), pp. 11–12; Alex Buchner, *The German Infantry Handbook, 1939–1945* (Atglen, PA: Schiffer, 1991), pp. 126–128.

4. *Kriegsgleiderung Armeeoberkommando 9*, 10 May 1942, reel 297, T–312, NA.

5. Ibid.

6. Buntrock later (in December 1944) acquired responsibility for all *Abwehr* (German military intelligence) units operating at the front. For a general treatment of German frontline intelligence assessment, see David Kahn, *Hitler's Spies: German Military Intelligence in World War II* (New York: Da Capo, 1978), pp. 101–113. For a specific appreciation of Buntrock's activities at the Ninth Army, see David M. Glantz, *Zhukov's Greatest Defeat: The Red Army's Epic Disaster in Operation Mars, 1942* (Lawrence: University Press of Kansas, 1999), pp. 31–35. See also Newton, *German Battle Tactics*, pp. 137–142; Folkestad, *Panzerjäger*, p. 22.

7. Newton, *German Battle Tactics*, p. 72.

8. Ibid., p. 40.

9. Görlitz, *Model*, p. 125.

10. Helmuth Später, *The History of the Panzerkorps Grossdeutschland*, 3 vols. (Winnipeg, Man.: J. J. Fedorowicz, 1992), vol. 1, p. 391; Ziemke and Bauer, *Moscow to Stalingrad*, pp. 398–406.

11. Später, *Grossdeutschland*, vol. 1, pp. 420–429.

12. Später's history even omits the worst indignity suffered by his division during the period, the week during which Model subordinated *Grossdeutschland* to headquarters, 72nd Infantry Division, because he reportedly did not trust Hörnlein and his staff. Ziemke and Bauer, *Moscow to Stalingrad*, p. 404; Später, *Grossdeutschland*, vol. 1, pp. 434–437.

13. *Kriegsgleiderung Armeeoberkommando 9*, 10 May 1942, reel 297, T–312, NA; *Kriegsgleiderung Armeeoberkommando 9 und Panzerarmeeoberkommando 2*, 22 July 1943, reel 322, T–312, NA.

14. *(Ia) Kriegtagbuch, Armeeoberkommando 9*, 26–28 February 1943; *(Ia), Armeeoberkommando 9*, 727/43, 2 February 1943, and 800/43, 4 February 1943; all reel 308, T–312, NA; Franz X. Gabl, *Franzl II: From Four Years on the Russian Front, 1941–1945, to Standing on the Olympic Podium in 1948* (Missoula, MT: Pictorial Histories, 2000), p. 130.

15. Görlitz, *Model*, pp. 124–127; Ziemke and Bauer, *Moscow to Stalingrad*, pp. 398–404.

16. Ziemke and Bauer, *Moscow to Stalingrad*, pp. 398–404.

17. Görlitz, *Model*, p. 140.

18. The definitive account of this battle, from which this summary has been taken, is of course Glantz, *Zhukov's Greatest Defeat*; unfortunately, no comparable work has yet been written regarding the earlier summer battle.

19. Earl F. Ziemke, *Stalingrad to Berlin: The German Defeat in the East* (Washington, DC: Office of the Chief of Military History, 1968), pp. 115–117; Paul Carell, *Scorched Earth: The Russian-German War 1943–1944* (Boston: Little, Brown, 1970), pp. 304–307.

20. *1.(Zentr.)Abt., Heerespersonalamt* 440/44, 28 June 1944, reel 39, T–78, NA.

Chapter 8:
Criminal Buffaloes and Imaginary Panthers

1. Peter Hoffmann, *The History of the German Resistance, 1933–1945* (Cambridge, MA: MIT Press, 1977), pp. 283–289.

2. *Ia/9AOK to OKH/OrgAbt(1)*, 12 February 1943, reel 308, T–312, NA.

3. *Ia/9AOK, (Ia)* 800/43, 4 February 1943, reel 308, T–312, NA.

4. *Ia/9AOK, (Ia)* 960/43, 11 February 1943, reel 308, T–312, NA; Ben Shepherd, *War in the Wild East: The German Army and Soviet Partisans* (Cambridge, MA: Harvard University Press, 2004), p. 189.

5. *Ia/9AOK, (Ia)* 960/43, 11 February 1943, reel 308, T–312, NA.

6. *Ia/9AOK to HGr Mitte*, 26, 27, and 28 February 1943; *Ia/9AOK (Ia)* 727/43, 2 February 1943, reel 308, T–312, NA.

7. Cited in David M. Glantz and Jonathan M. House, *The Battle of Kursk* (Lawrence: University Press of Kansas, 1999), p. 356.

8. Steven H. Newton, *Kursk: The German View* (New York: Da Capo, 2002), pp. 371–380.

9. Ziemke, *Stalingrad to Berlin*, pp. 129–130.

10. Newton, *Kursk*, pp. 371–380; Niklas Zetterling and Anders Frankson, *Kursk 1943: A Statistical Analysis* (London: Frank Cass, 2000), pp. 11, 20–21.

11. Newton, *Kursk*, pp. 102–105.

12. Ibid.; Wilhelm Hertlein, *Chronik der 7.Infanterie-Division* (Munich: Bruckmann, 1984), pp. 168–169.

13. Werner Haupt, *Army Group Center: The Wehrmacht in Russia, 1941–1945* (Atglen, PA: Schiffer, 1999), pp. 148–152; *Armeeoberkommando 9 Kriegsgleiderung*, 30 June 1943, reel 322, T–312, NA.

14. Newton, *Kursk*, pp. 120–127.

15. Nehring, *Panzerwaffe*, pp. 296–297.

16. Zetterling and Frankson, *Kursk 1943*, pp. 181–182.

17. The bland details of this issue are recorded in Thomas L. Jentz, *Germany's Tiger Tanks: Tiger I and II: Combat Tactics* (Atglen, PA: Schiffer, 1997), p. 85; for the repercussions within the Ninth Army itself, see *Ia/9AOK* to *XXXXVII PzK*, 4 July 1943, reel 322, T–312, NA.

Chapter 9: Conflagration at Kursk and Orel

1. This and subsequent excerpts from the KTB (Kriegtagesbuch, or war diary) of the 292nd Infantry Division are quoted in Nehring, *Panzerwaffe*, p. 36.

2. David M. Glantz and Harold S. Orenstein, eds., *The Battle for Kursk 1943: The Soviet General Staff Study* (London: Frank Cass, 1999), p. 107.

3. To give but two examples, Glantz and House devote only twenty-two pages (including the subsequent battle for the Orel salient) to the northern front, while covering Army Group South's offensive with well over one hundred pages; my own *Kursk: The German View* is, if not equally skewed, at least demonstrative of this bias: Only four of fifteen articles deal specifically with the northern front.

4. *Notz fur Kriegtagesbuch* (hereafter cited as NFKTB), reel 322, T–312, NA.

5. NFKTB; Franz Kurowski, *Operation "Zitadelle": The Decisive Battle of World War II* (Winnipeg, Man.: J. J. Fedorowicz, 2003), pp. 50–54.

6. Kurowski, *Zitadelle*, pp. 52–54; Glantz and House, *Kursk*, pp. 87–89.

7. NFKTB.

8. Ibid.

9. Ibid.; Kurowski, *Zitadelle*, pp. 53–55.

10. NFKTB; Glantz and House, *Kursk*, pp. 87–89.

11. NFKTB.

12. Ibid.; Kurwoski, *Zitadelle*, pp. 53–54.

13. NFKTB.

14. Both quoted in Kurwoski, *Zitadelle*, p. 50.

15. Zetterling and Frankson, *Kursk 1943*, pp. 43–44, 58–67.

16. Jentz, *Panzer Truppen*, vol. 2, p. 85.

17. Kurowski, *Zitadelle*, p. 53; Nerhing, *Panzerwaffe*, p. 36.

18. Glantz and House, *Kursk*, pp. 88–92; Kurowski, *Zitadelle*, pp. 53–56.

19. NFKTB.

20. Ibid.; *Fernschrieben 9AOK*, 1 and 6 July 1943, reel 322, T–312, NA.

21. NFKTB.

22. Ibid.; Guderian, *Panzer Leader*, pp. 227, 228, 233, 237, 250; Louis B. Lochner, ed., *The Goebbels Diaries* (New York: Award, 1971), p. 414.

23. NFKTB.

24. Ibid.; Kurowski, *Zitadelle*, p. 55; *Fernschrieben 9AOK*, 6 July 1943, reel 322, T–312, NA.

25. NFKTB.

26. Kurowski, *Zitadelle*, pp. 55–56.

27. NFKTB.

28. Ibid.

29. Zetterling and Frankson, *Kursk 1943*, pp. 113–115.

30. Jentz, *Panzer Truppen*, vol. 2, pp. 87–88; Zetterling and Frankson, *Kursk 1943*, pp. 125–127.

31. Newton, *Kursk*, pp. 408–411.

32. NFKTB.

33. Ibid.

34. Ibid.

35. Ibid.

36. Ibid.; *Fernscrieben 9AOK*, 6 and 7 July 1943, reel 322, T–312, NA.

37. Zetterling and Frankson, *Kursk 1943*, pp. 113–119.

38. *Armeeoberkommando 9 (Ia)*, 324/43, 8 July 1943, reel 322, T–312, NA.

39. Glantz and Orenstein, *Battle for Kursk*, pp. 107–118.

40. Kurowski, *Zitadelle*, p. 56.

41. Robert Michulec, *4.Panzer-Division on the Eastern Front(1) 1941–1943* (Hong Kong: Concord, 1999), pp. 5–6; Andrei Kinski, Tomasz Nowakowski, Mriusz Skotnicki, and Robert Sawicki, *4.Dywizja Pancerna Kursk 1943* (Warsaw: Wudawnictwo Militaria, 1999), pp. 19–20.

42. Kurowski, *Zitadelle*, pp. 55–58.

43. Ibid.

44. Michulec, *4.Panzer-Division*, p. 6; Kurowski, *Zitadelle*, pp. 57–58.

45. *Armeeoberkommando 9 (Ia)*, 331/43, 9 July 1943, reel 322, T–312, NA.

46. Kurowski, *Zitadelle*, pp. 332–333.

47. *Armeeoberkommando 9 (Ia)*, 348/43, 13 July 1943, reel 322, T–312, NA; Kurowski, *Zitadelle*, pp. 332–333.

48. *Armeeoberkommando 9 (Ia)*, 340/43, 12 July 1943, reel 322, T–312, NA.

49. Zetterling and Frankson, *Kursk 1943*, pp. 77, 113.

50. Newton, *Kursk*, p. 25.

51. Kurowski, *Zitadelle*, pp. 335–337.

52. Glantz and House, *Kursk*, pp. 290–306.

53. Newton, *Kursk*, pp. 104–105, 120–133, 139.

54. Ibid., pp. 135–136.

55. Ibid., pp. 108–114; Später, *Grossdeutschland*, vol. 2, pp. 134–145.

56. Newton, *Kursk*, pp. 217–226.

57. Ibid.; Kurowski, *Zitadelle*, pp. 340–347.

58. Kurowski, *Zitadelle*, pp. 340–381.

59. Newton, *Kursk*, p. 190.

60. Ibid., p. 169.

61. Zetterling and Frankson, *Kursk 1943*, pp. 77, 113.

Chapter 10: *The Swine of the Baltic*

1. Görlitz, *Model*, p. 158.

2. Ibid., p. 159.

3. David M. Glantz, *The Battle for Leningrad, 1941–1944* (Lawrence: University Press of Kansas, 2002), p. 368.

4. Ziemke, *Stalingrad to Berlin*, pp. 257–258.

5. Görlitz, *Model*, pp. 161–163.

6. Glantz, *Leningrad*, p. 370.

7. Görlitz, *Model*, p. 163.

8. Ibid., p. 164.

9. *(Ia), Armeeoberkommando 18* 732/44, 5 February 1944, (reporting strength 30 January 1944); *(Ia), Heeresgruppe Nord* 1a/1d 554/44, 4 February 1944; both reel 70, T–311, NA.

10. Steven H. Newton, *Retreat from Leningrad, 1944–1945* (Atglen, PA: Schiffer, 1995), pp. 42–48.

11. Glantz, *Leningrad*, p. 329.

12. *(Ia), Heeresgruppe Nord* 1a 238/44, 2 February 1944, reel 70, T–311, NA.

13. Wilhelm Tieke, *Tragedy of the Faithful: A History of the III. (germanische) SS-Panzer-Korps* (Winnipeg, Man.: J. J. Fedorowicz, 2001), p. 55.

14. Görlitz, *Model*, pp. 165–168.

15. Ziemke, *Stalingrad to Berlin*, pp. 258–260.

16. See correspondence in Army Group North engineering files, reel 70, T–311, NA.

17. *(Ia), Heeresgruppe Nord* 1a/1d 784/44, 28 February 1944; reel 70, T–311, NA.

18. Glantz, *Leningrad*, pp. 398–401.

19. Ziemke, *Stalingrad to Berlin*, pp. 265–266.

20. Görlitz, *Model*, p. 170.

Chapter 11: *Interlude in the Carpathians*

1. Manstein, *Lost Victories*, pp. 544–547.

2. *Unterlagen für gross Kraftegegenenübstellung*, reel 463, T–78, NA; W. Victor Madej, ed., *Russo-German War: Summer 1944* (Allentown, PA: Valor, 1987), pp. 62–63.

3. Samuel W. Mitcham Jr., *Crumbling Empire: The German Defeat in the East, 1944* (Westport, CT: Praeger, 2001), pp. 14–16.

4. Manstein, *Lost Victories*, p. 522; Raus, *Panzer Operations*, pp. 279–283.

5. Mellenthin, *Panzer Battles*, pp. 324–325.

6. Raus, *Panzer Operations*, pp. 174–282.

7. Von Mellenthin, although he disagreed with Raus's tactical approach, apparently respected the Austrian, for in his memoir he voiced his criticisms so abstractly (and without the use of proper names) that it is often difficult to make out exactly to which officer he is referring. Comparing the context of his comments

with command assignments, however, makes this quite clear. Note also that both von Mellenthin and Balck took pains to associate the zone defense strategy with Model rather than Raus. See Mellenthin, *Panzer Battles*, pp. 335–337; Balck, *Ordnung im Chaos*, pp. 514–516.

8. Balck, *Ordnung im Chaos*, pp. 514–516.

9. Alex Buchner, *Ostfront: The German Defensive Battles on the Russian Front, 1944* (Atglen, PA: Schiffer, 1991), pp. 73–97; Raus, *Panzer Operations*, pp. 269–273.

10. Buchner, *Ostfront*, pp. 73–97.

11. Wilhelm Tieke, *In the Firestorm of the Last Years of the War: II. SS-Panzer-Korps with the 9. and 10. SS-Divisions "Hohenstaufen" and "Frundsberg"* (Winnipeg, Man.: J. J. Fedorowicz, 1999), pp. 44–60; Michael Reynolds, *Sons of the Reich: The History of II SS Panzer Corps in Normandy, Arnhem, the Ardennes, and on the Eastern Front* (Havertown, PA: Casemate, 2002), pp. 4–12.

Chapter 12: More Hole Than Front

1. Gerd Niepold, *Battle for White Russia: The Destruction of Army Group Centre June 1944* (London: Brassey's, 1988), pp. 139–140; Peter von der Groeben, *Collapse of Army Group Center and Its Combat Activity Until Stabilization of the Front (22 June to 1 September 1944)* (MS T–31) (Neustadt, FRG: U.S. Army, 1947), pp. 19–20.

2. Niepold, *Battle for White Russia*, pp. 140–143.

3. Groeben, *Collapse of Army Group Center*, pp. 20–22; Niepold, *Battle for White Russia*, pp. 143–146.

4. Niepold, *Battle for White Russia*, p. 146.

5. Helmut Heiber and David M. Glantz, eds., *Hitler and His Generals: Military Conferences 1942–1945* (New York: Enigma, 2003), p. 466.

6. Buchner, *Ostfront*, p. 201; Carell, *Scorched Earth*, p. 591; Mitcham, *Crumbling Empire*, pp. 45–47.

7. Niepold, *Battle for White Russia*, pp. 146–150.

8. Buchner, *Ostfront*, pp. 190–202; Haupt, *Army Group Center*, pp. 199–201; Paul Adair, *Hitler's Greatest Defeat: The Collapse of Army Group Centre, June 1944* (London: Arms and Armour, 1994), pp. 114–118; Niepold, *Battle for White Russia*, pp. 159–161, 168–171.

9. Niepold, *Battle for White Russia*, pp. 161–162, 171–173, 181–182, 191–193; Groeben, *Collapse of Army Group Center*, pp. 20–22, 29.

10. Niepold, *Battle for White Russia*, pp. 161–162, 171–173, 181–182, 191–193.

11. Adair, *Hitler's Greatest Defeat*, pp. 119–133.

12. Niepold, *Battle for White Russia*, p. 180.

13. Ibid., p. 256.

14. Madej, *Russo-German War*, p. 44; Groeben, *Collapse of Army Group Center*, pp. 29–33.

15. Groeben, *Collapse of Army Group Center*, pp. 35–36; Glantz and House, *When Titans Clashed*, pp. 212–213.

16. Groeben, *Collapse of Army Group Center*, pp. 35–36; Madej, *Russo-German War*, pp. 44–51.

17. Guderian, *Panzer Leader*, pp. 334.

18. Even Guderian's praise of Model for his early actions at Army Group Center was personal rather than professional. He lauded Model as a "bold, inexhaustible soldier, who knew the front well and who won the confidence of his men by his habitual disregard for his personal safety. . . . He was the best possible man to perform the fantastically difficult task of reconstructing a line in the centre of the Eastern Front." But while Guderian mentioned that Model's deputy at Army Group North Ukraine, Josef Harpe, was "a former panzer officer," he pointedly omitted any reference to Model's history with mobile troops. See ibid., pp. 336–337.

19. Ibid., pp. 340–341, 356.

20. Mitcham, *Crumbling Empire*, pp. 96–99.

Chapter 13:
With Blasting Hatred and Unceasing Courage

1. Hans Speidel, *Invasion 1944* (London: Regnery, 1950), pp. 128–129; Bodo Zimmermann, "France 1944," in Seymour Freiden and William Richardson, eds., *The Fatal Decisions* (New York: William Sloane, 1956), pp. 216–217.

2. A. A. Jillani, "The Riddle of the Ruhr Pocket—1945: An Open Letter to Brigadier Hansgeorg Model of the Bundeswehr," *Defence Journal* (April 2002), available at: http://www.defencejournal.com/2002/march/riddle.htm.

3. Hoffmann, *History of the German Resistance*, pp. 470–478.

4. Paul Carell, *Invasion: They're Coming!* (New York: E. P. Dutton, 1963), pp. 290–292.

5. Ibid.; Kazimierz Moczarski, *Conversations with an Executioner*, edited by Marianna Fitzpatrick (Englewood Cliffs, NJ: Prentice-Hall, 1981), pp. 219–234.

6. Zimmermann, "France 1944," pp. 218–219; Speidel, *Invasion 1944*, pp. 130–131.

7. Heinz Günther Guderian, *From Normandy to the Ruhr with the 116th Panzer Division in World War II* (Bedford, PA: Aberjona Press, 2001), pp. 85–86, 92, 95; Speidel, *Invasion 1944*, pp. 131–133.

8. Russell F. Weigley, *Eisenhower's Lieutenants: The Campaign of France and Germany, 1944–1945* (Bloomington: Indiana University Press, 1981), pp. 192–219; Carell, *Invasion: They're Coming!* pp. 273, 311–313.

9. Speidel, *Invasion 1944*, pp. 134–135; Zimmermann, "France 1944," pp. 221–222.

10. Weigley, *Eisenhower's Lieutenants*, pp. 209–211, 238–253.

11. Guderian, *From Normandy to the Ruhr*, pp. 92, 94–95, 99.

12. Charles Messenger, *Sepp Dietrich: Hitler's Gladiator* (London: Brassey's, 1988), pp. 140–143; David Irving, *The Trail of the Fox* (New York: E. P. Dutton, 1978), pp. 405–407, 417–418, 435–437.

13. Cornelius Ryan, *A Bridge Too Far* (New York: Simon & Schuster, 1974), pp. 40–41.

14. Ryan, *A Bridge Too Far*, pp. 53–59.

15. Messenger, *The Last Prussian*, pp. 203–205, 209–210; Günther Blumentritt, *Von Rundstedt: The Soldier and the Man* (London: Odhams, 1952), pp. 240–243.

16. Blumentritt, *Von Rundstedt*, pp. 240–243.

17. Ryan, *A Bridge Too Far*, pp. 57–61; Messenger, *The Last Prussian*, pp. 205–207.

18. Speidel, *Invasion 1944*, pp. 137–138; Irving, *Trail of the Fox*, p. 513; Görlitz, *Model*, pp. 201–203, 270.

19. Wilhelm Prüller, *Diary of a German Soldier*, edited by H. C. Robbins Landon and Sebastian Leitner (London: Faber and Faber, 1953), p. 176.

20. Ryan, *A Bridge Too Far*, pp. 116–117.

21. Ibid., pp. 218–219; Robert J. Kershaw, *"It Never Snows in September": The German View of MARKET-GARDEN and the Battle of Arnhem, September 1944* (London: Ian Allen, 1990), pp. 68, 75.

22. Sawyer, *"It Never Snows in September,"* pp. 75–77, 312; Tieke, *In the Firestorm of the Last Years of the War*, pp. 228–233.

23. Sawyer, *"It Never Snows in September,"* pp. 75–77.

24. Ryan, *A Bridge Too Far*, pp. 253–256, 284, 379–453, 464, 472–473; Sawyer, *"It Never Snows in September,"* pp. 192–194; Reynolds, *Sons of the Reich*, pp. 151–152.

25. Sawyer, *"It Never Snows in September,"* p. 260.

26. Ibid., pp. 123, 260, 271–274, 311, 339–340.

27. Charles Whiting, *The Battle of Hürtgen Forest: The Untold Story of a Disastrous Campaign* (New York: Simon & Schuster, 1989), p. 37.

28. Robert Sterling Rush, *Hell in Hürtgen Forest: The Ordeal and Triumph of an American Infantry Regiment* (Lawrence: University Press of Kansas, 2001), p. 144.

29. Weigley, *Eisenhower's Lieutenants*, pp. 356, 370–372, 420–421, 430–431.

30. Whiting, *Hürtgen Forest*, pp. xi–xiv, 271–274.

31. Weigley, *Eisenhower's Lieutenants*, pp. 430–431.

32. Charles B. McDonald, *The Battle of the Hürtgen Forest* (Philadelphia: J. P. Lippincott, 1963), pp. 102–103.

33. Ibid., p. 197.

Chapter 14: The 10 Percent Solution

1. Charles B. McDonald, *A Time for Trumpets: The Untold Story of the Battle of the Bulge* (New York: William Morrow, 1985), pp. 11, 34–35.

2. McDonald, *Time for Trumpets*, p. 35; John Toland, *Battle: The Story of the Bulge* (New York: Random House, 1959), p. 26; Danny S. Parker, *Battle of the Bulge: Hitler's Ardennes Offensive, 1944–1945* (Philadelphia: Combined Books, 1991), pp. 17–23.

3. Liddell Hart, *German Generals Talk*, p. 275.

4. Ibid., pp. 275–277; Messenger, *The Last Prussian*, pp. 205–207; McDonald, *Time for Trumpets*, pp. 86–87.

5. Hasso von Manteuffel, "The Ardennes," in Freiden and Richardson, *The Fatal Decisions*, pp. 240–252.

6. Messenger, *Sepp Dietrich*, p. 149.

7. Guderian, *From Normandy to the Ruhr*, pp. 283–287.

8. Manteuffel, "The Ardennes," p. 247.

9. Liddell Hart, *German Generals Talk*, p. 70.

10. Manteuffel, "The Ardennes," pp. 242–247; Liddell Hart, *German Generals Talk*, pp. 279–281.

11. Messenger, *Sepp Dietrich*, pp. 148–150; Manteuffel, "The Ardennes," pp. 247–248.

12. Parker, *Battle of the Bulge*, pp. 51–52, 147–154.

13. Guderian, *From Normandy to the Ruhr*, pp. 281, 286–288; Mellenthin, *German Generals of World War II*, p. 154; Parker, *Battle of the Bulge*, pp. 81, 164.

14. Parker, *Battle of the Bulge*, pp. 116–118.

15. Guderian, *From Normandy to the Ruhr*, p. 287; Tieke, *In the Firestorm of the Last Years of the War*, pp. 308–309.

16. Messenger, *Sepp Dietrich*, p. 148; Michael Reynolds, *Men of Steel: I SS Panzer Corps, the Ardennes and Eastern Front, 1944–1945* (New York: Sarpedon, 1998), pp. 47–53.

17. Parker, *Battle of the Bulge*, pp. 83–85.

18. Ibid., p. 85.

19. McDonald, *Time for Trumpets*, pp. 326–327; Charles Whiting, *Decision at St. Vith* (New York: Ballantine, 1969), pp. 85–86.

20. Whiting, *Decision at St. Vith*, pp. 137–138.

21. Parker, *Battle of the Bulge*, pp. 113, 142–145.

22. Messenger, *Sepp Dietrich*, p. 159.

23. McDonald, *Time for Trumpets*, pp. 565–566, 569, 574, 576–577.

24. Ibid., pp. 587–588; Parker, *Battle of the Bulge*, pp. 197–202, 209–214.

25. Toland, *Battle*, p. 284.

26. Ibid.

27. Guderian, *From Normandy to the Ruhr*, pp. 330–337; McDonald, *Time for Trumpets*, pp. 587–588; Manteuffel, "The Ardennes," pp. 272–275.

28. Parker, *Battle of the Bulge*, pp. 229–234; Tieke, *In the Firestorm of the Last Years of the War*, pp. 328–333.

29. Ibid.

Chapter 15: The Lessons of Antiquity

1. Guderian, *From Normandy to the Ruhr*, p. 344.

2. Liddell Hart, *German Generals Talk*, p. 292.

3. Messenger, *The Last Prussian*, p. 224.

4. Görlitz, *Model*, pp. 232–233; Leo Kessler, *The Battle of the Ruhr Pocket* (Chelsea, MI: Scarborough House, 1989), p. 2.

5. Görlitz, *Model*, pp. 237–238.

6. Albert Speer, *Inside the Third Reich* (New York: Macmillan, 1970), pp. 560–564.

7. John Toland, *The Last 100 Days* (New York: Random House, 1966), p. 245; Franz Kurowski, *Hitler's Last Bastion: The Final Battles for the Reich, 1944–1945* (Atglen, PA: Schiffer, 1998), pp. 122–136.

8. Kurowski, *Hitler's Last Bastion*, pp. 135–138.

9. Speer, *Inside the Third Reich*, pp. 562, 564, 567, 580.

10. Toland, *Last 100 Days*, pp. 233–234.

11. Ibid., pp. 249, 353; Kurowski, *Hitler's Last Bastion*, pp. 126–136; Kessler, *Ruhr Pocket*, pp. 113–114.

12. Kessler, *Ruhr Pocket*, pp. 113–114; Toland, *Last 100 Days*, p. 425; Görlitz, *Model*, pp. 255–256.

13. Kessler, *Ruhr Pocket*, pp. 97–98; Görlitz, *Model*, pp. 255–256.

14. Mellenthin, *Panzer Battles*, pp. 420–421; Mellenthin, *German Generals of World War II*, pp. 155–156.

15. Toland, *Last 100 Days*, pp. 425–426; Görlitz, *Model*, pp. 263–265.

16. Charles B. McDonald, *The Last Offensive* (Washington, DC: Center for Military History, 1973), pp. 368–369.

17. Kessler, *Ruhr Pocket*, p. 206.

18. Ibid., pp. 206–207; Görlitz, *Model*, pp. 265–266; McDonald, *Last Offensive*, pp. 371–372.

19. Toland, *Last 100 Days*, p. 214.

BIBLIOGRAPHY

Adair, Paul. *Hitler's Greatest Defeat: The Collapse of Army Group Centre, June 1944*. London: Arms and Armour, 1994.

Armstrong, Richard M. *Red Army Tank Commanders: The Armored Guards*. Atglen, PA: Schiffer, 1994.

Asprey, Robert B. *The German High Command at War: Hindenburg and Ludendorff Conduct World War I*. New York: William Morrow, 1991.

Balck, Hermann. *Ordnung im Chaos: Erinnerungen 1893–1948*. Osnabrück: Biblio Verlag, 1981.

Baldwin, Hanson. *Battles Lost and Won: Great Campaigns of World War II*. New York: Harper & Row, 1966.

Barnett, Correlli. *The Swordbearers: Supreme Command in the First World War*. Bloomington: Indiana University Press, 1963.

Bartov, Omer. *Hitler's Army: Soldiers, Nazis, and War in the Third Reich*. New York: Oxford University Press, 1991.

———. "Operation Barbarossa and the Origins of the Final Solution." In *The Final Solution: Origins and Implementation*, edited by David Cesarani. London: Routledge, 1994.

Binding, Rudolf. *A Fatalist at War*. Boston: Houghton Mifflin, 1929.

Bloem, Walter. *The Advance from Mons 1914*. New York: Tandem, 1967, reprint of 1930 edition.

Blumentritt, Günther. *Von Rundstedt: The Soldier and the Man*. London: Oldham's, 1952.

Bradley, Dermot. *Walter Wenck: General der Panzertruppe*. Osnabrück: Biblio Verlag, 1981.

Breitman, Richard. *The Architect of Genocide: Heinrich Himmler and the Final Solution*. New York: Alfred A. Knopf, 1991.

Brett-Smith, Richard. *Hitler's Generals*. San Rafael, CA: Presidio, 1977.

Buchner, Alex. *The German Infantry Handbook, 1939–1945*. Atglen, PA: Schiffer, 1991.

———. *Ostfront: The German Defensive Battles on the Russian Front, 1944*. Atglen, PA: Schiffer, 1991.

Bullock, Alan. *Hitler and Stalin: Parallel Lives*. New York: Alfred A. Knopf, 1992.

Busch, Ernst. "Has the Decisive Battle Role of the Infantry Ended?" Reprinted in *The Axis Grand Strategy: Blueprints for the Total War*, edited by Ladislas Farago. New York: Farrar and Rinehart, 1942.

Captured German records. Washington, DC: U.S. National Archives.

Poland (1939)

> *Heeresgruppe Sud*, T-311
> *IV Armeekorps*, T-314
> *Grenzabschnitte Mitte*, T-314

France (1940)
> *Armeeoberkommando 16*, T-312

Russia (1941–1944)
> *3.Panzerdivision*, 1941, reel 116, T-315
> *XXXXI Armeekorps (mot.)*, T-314
> *Armeeoberkommando 9*, T-312
> *Heeresgruppe Nord*, T-312
> *Heeresgruppe Nordukraine*, T-311
> *1.(Zentr.)Abt., Heerespersonalamt*, T-78

Carell, Paul. *Scorched Earth: The Russian-German War 1943–1944*. New York: Ballantine, 1966.

———. *Unternehmen Barbarossa im Bild: Der Russlandkrieg fotograiert von Soldaten*. Berlin: Verlag Ullstein GmbH, 1967.

———. *Hitler Moves East, 1941–1943*. New York: Ballantine, 1971.

———. *Invasion! They're Coming*. New York: Ballantine, 1972.

Citino, Robert M. *The Evolution of Blitzkrieg Tactics: Germany Defends Itself Against Poland, 1918–1933*. New York: Greenwood, 1987.

Clark, Alan. *Barbarossa: The Russian-German Conflict, 1941–1945*. New York: William Morrow, 1965.

Collins, Larry, and Dominique LaPierre. *Is Paris Burning?* New York: Simon & Schuster, 1965.

Cooper, Matthew. *The German Army, 1933–1945: Its Political and Military Failure*. New York: Stein and Day, 1978.

———. *The Nazi War Against Soviet Partisans, 1941–1944*. New York: Stein and Day, 1979.

Corum, James. *The Roots of Blitzkrieg: Hans von Seeckt and German Military Reform*. Lawrence: University Press of Kansas, 1992.

Davis, Frank. "*SEELÖWE*: The German Plan to Invade Britain, 1940." *Strategy and Tactics* 40 (September–October 1973).

Denisov, V. N., and G. I. Changuli, eds. *Nazi Crimes in Ukraine 1941–1944: Documents and Materials*. Kiev: Nuakova Dumka, 1987.

D'Este, Carlo. "Model." In *Hitler's Generals*, edited by Correlli Barnett. New York: Grove Weidenfeld, 1989.

Deutsch, Harold C. *The Conspiracy Against Hitler in the Twilight War*. Minneapolis: University of Minnesota Press, 1968.

Dyakov, Yuri, and Tatyana Bushuyeva. *The Red Army and the Wehrmacht: How the Soviets Militarized Germany, 1922–1933, and Paved the Way for Fascism.* Amherst, NY: Prometheus, 1995.

Dyck, Ludwig Heidrich. "Loyal to Their Deaths." *World War II History* (September 2004).

Edmonds, James E., ed. *History of the Great War, Based on Official Documents: Military Operations, France and Belgium, 1914.* London: Macmillan and Co., 1937.

Erickson, John. *The Road to Stalingrad.* New York: Harper & Row, 1975.

Folkestad, William B. *Panzerjäger: Tank Hunter.* Shippensburg, PA: Burd Street Press, 2000.

Forester, C. S. *The General.* Baltimore: Nautical and Aviation Publishing, 1987, reprint of 1947 edition.

Förster, Jürgen. "The Wehrmacht and the War of Extermination Against the Soviet Union." In *The Nazi Holocaust: Historical Articles on the Destruction of European Jews,* edited by Michael R. Marrus, 9 vols. Westport, CT: Meckler 1989.

———. "The Relation Between Operation Barbarossa as an Ideological War of Extermination and the Final Solution." In *The Final Solution: Origins and Implementation,* edited by David Cesarani. London: Routledge, 1994.

Fraschka, Günther. *Knights of the Reich.* Atglen, PA: Schiffer, 1994.

Fugate, Bryan I. *Operation Barbarossa: Strategy and Tactics on the Eastern Front, 1941.* Novato, CA: Presidio, 1984.

Fussell, Paul. *The Great War and Modern Memory.* New York: Oxford University Press, 1975.

Gabl, Franz X. *Franzl II: From Four Years on the Russian Front, 1941–1945, to Standing on the Olympic Podium in 1948.* Missoula, MT: Pictorial Histories, 2000.

Gehlen, Reinhard. *The Service: The Memoirs of General Reinhard Gehlen.* New York: World, 1972.

The German Army from Within, by a British Officer Who Has Served in It. New York: George H. Doran, 1914.

Glantz, David M. *The Role of Intelligence in Soviet Military Strategy in World War II.* Novato, CA: Presidio, 1990.

———. *Zhukov's Greatest Defeat: The Red Army's Epic Disaster in Operation Mars, 1942.* Lawrence: University Press of Kansas, 1999.

———. *The Battle for Leningrad, 1941–1944.* Lawrence: University Press of Kansas, 2002.

Glantz, David M., and Jonathan M. House. *The Battle of Kursk.* Lawrence: University Press of Kansas, 1999.

Glantz, David M., and Harold S. Orenstein, eds. *The Battle for Kursk 1943: The Soviet General Staff Study.* London: Frank Cass, 1999.

Gordon, Harold J. *The Reichswehr and the German Republic, 1919–1926.* Princeton, NJ: Princeton University Press, 1957.

Görlitz, Walter. *History of the German General Staff, 1657–1945.* New York: Praeger, 1953.

———. *Model: Strategie der Defensive*. Wiesbaden: Limes Verlag, 1975.

Greiffenberg, Hans von, et al. *The Battle of Moscow, 1941–1942*. MS T-28. Washington, DC: U.S. Army, Europe, Historical Division, Europe, n.d.

Groeben, Peter von der. *Collapse of Army Group Center and Its Combat Activity Until Stabilization of the Front (22 June to 1 September 1944)*. MS T-31. Neustadt, FRG: U.S. Army, 1947.

Guderian, Heinz. *Panzer Leader*. London: Michael Joseph, 1952.

———. *From Normandy to the Ruhr: With the 116th Panzer Division in World War II*. Bedford, PA: Aberjona, 2001.

Haupt, Werner. *Army Group Center: The Wehrmacht in Russia, 1941–1945*. Atglen, PA: Schiffer, 1999.

Heiber, Helmut, and David M. Glantz, eds. *Hitler and His Generals: Military Conferences 1942–1945*. New York: Enigma, 2003.

Hertlein, Wilhelm. *Chronik der 7.Infanterie-Division*. Munich: Bruckmann, 1984.

Hesse, Kurt. "The Marne-Drama of July 15, 1918, Seen from the Angle of the Fighting Grenadier Regiment No. 5, 36th Infantry Division." In *The Great Events of the Great War*, edited by Charles F. Horne and Walter F. Austin, 7 vols. New York: National Alumni Press, 1920.

Hilberg, Raul. *The Destruction of the European Jews*. 3 vols. New York: Holmes & Meier, 1985.

Histories of 251 Divisions of the German Army Which Participated in the War (1914–1918). Washington, DC: U.S. Government Printing Office, 1920.

Hitler, Adolph. *Mein Kampf*. Boston: Houghton Mifflin, 1971, reprint of 1927 edition.

Hoffmann, Peter. *The History of the German Resistance, 1933–1945*. Cambridge, MA: MIT Press, 1977.

Hohne, Heinz. *The Order of the Death's Head: The Story of Hitler's SS*. New York: Ballantine, 1971.

Horne, Alistair. *The Price of Glory: Verdun 1916*. New York: St. Martin's Press, 1962.

Hörner, Helmut. *A German Odyssey: The Journal of a German Prisoner of War*, edited by Alan Kent Powell. Golden, CO: Fulcrum, 1991.

Howard, Michael. *The Franco-Prussian War*. New York: Collier, 1961.

Irving, David. *The Trail of the Fox*. New York: E. P. Dutton, 1977.

Jacobsen, Hans-Adolf, ed. *Dokumente zum Westfeldzug 1940*. Göttingen: Musterschmidt-Verlag, 1960.

Jentz, Thomas L. *Panzer Truppen: The Complete Guide to the Creation and Combat Employment of Germany's Tank Force*. 2 vols. Atglen, PA: Schiffer, 1996.

———. *Germany's Tiger Tanks: Tiger I and II: Combat Tactics*. Atglen, PA: Schiffer, 1997.

Jones, Nigel H. *Hitler's Heralds: The Story of the Freikorps, 1918–1923*. New York: Dorset, 1987.

Kahn, David. *Hitler's Spies: German Military Intelligence in World War II*. New York: Da Capo, 1978.

Kaufmann, J. E., and H. W. Kaufmann. *Hitler's Blitzkrieg Campaigns: The Invasion and Defense of Western Europe, 1939–1940.* Conshohocken, NJ: Combined Books, 1993.

Keilig, Wolf. *Das Deutsche Heer, 1939–1945.* 3 vols. Friedburg, FRG: Podzun Verlag, 1956.

Keitel, Wilhelm. *The Memoirs of Field-Marshal Keitel.* New York: Stein and Day, 1966.

Kennedy, Robert M. *The German Campaign in Poland (1939).* Washington, DC: U.S. Department of the Army, 1956.

Kershaw, Ian. *The "Hitler Myth": Image and Reality in the Third Reich.* New York: Oxford University Press, 1987.

Kershaw, Robert. *"It Never Snows in September": The German View of MARKET-GARDEN and the Battle of Arnhem, September 1944.* London: Ian Allen, 1990.

Kesselring, Albert. *The Memoirs of Field-Marshal Kesselring.* Novato, CA: Presidio, 1989, reprint of 1953 edition.

Kessler, Leo. *The Battle of the Ruhr Pocket.* Chelsea, MI: Scarborough House, 1989.

Kinski, Andrei, Tomasz Nowakowski, Mriusz Skotnicki, and Robert Sawicki. *4.Dywizja Pancerna Kursk 1943.* Warsaw: Wudawnictwo Militaria, 1999.

Kirchberger, Joe H. *The First World War: An Eyewitness History.* New York: Facts on File, 1992.

Klein, Fritz, ed. *Deutschland im ersten Weltkrieg.* 3 vols. Berlin: Akademie-Verlag, 1971.

Kluck, Alexander von. *The March on Paris and the Battle of the Marne 1914.* London: Edward Arnold, 1923.

Knappe, Siegfried, and Ted Brusaw. *Soldat: Reflections of a German Soldier, 1936–1949.* New York: Orion, 1992.

Kuhl, Hermann von, and Friedrich von Bergmann. *Movements and Supply of the German First Army During August and September 1914.* Fort Leavenworth, KS: Command and General Staff School Press.

Kurowski, Franz. *Hitler's Last Bastion: The Final Battles for the Reich, 1944–1945.* Atglen, PA: Schiffer, 1998.

———. *Operation "Zitadelle": The Decisive Battle of World War II.* Winnipeg, Man.: J. J. Fedorowicz, 2003.

Lanza, Conrad H., ed. *The German Offensive of July 15, 1918: Marne Source Book.* Fort Leavenworth, KS: General Service Schools Press, 1923.

Leach, Barry A. *German Strategy Against Russia, 1939–1941.* New York: Oxford University Press, 1973.

Leeb, Wilhelm Ritter von. "Von Leeb's Defense." In *Roots of Strategy,* book 3. Harrisburg, PA: Stackpole, 1991.

Lewis, S. J. *Forgotten Legions: German Army Infantry Policy, 1918–1941.* New York: Praeger, 1985.

Liddell Hart, B. H. *The German Generals Talk.* New York: Quill, 1979, reprint of 1948 edition.

Lissance, Arnold, ed. *The Halder Diaries: The Private War Diaries of Colonel General Franz Halder*. 2 vols. Boulder, CO: Westview Press, 1976.

Lochner, Louis B., ed. *The Goebbels Diaries*. New York: Award, 1971.

Lucas, James Sidney. *War on the Eastern Front, 1941–1945: The German Soldier in Russia*. New York: Stein and Day, 1980.

———. *Das Reich: The Military Role of the 2nd SS Division*. London: Arms and Armour, 1991.

———. *Battle Group! German Kampfgruppen Action of World War Two*. London: Arms and Armour, 1993.

Luck, Hans von. *Panzer Commander: The Memoirs of Hans von Luck*. New York: Dell, 1989.

Ludendorff, Erich. *The General Staff and Its Problems*. 2 vols. New York: E. P. Dutton, n.d.

———. *Ludendorff's Own Story*. 2 vols. New York: Harper and Brothers, 1920.

Lukas, Richard C. *Forgotten Holocaust: The Poles Under German Occupation, 1939–1944*. New York: Hippocrene, 1986.

MacDonald, Charles B. *The Battle of the Hürtgen Forest*. Philadelphia: J. P. Lippincott, 1963.

———. *The Siegfried Line Campaign*. Washington, DC: U.S. Department of the Army, 1963.

———. *The Last Offensive*. Washington, DC: Center for Military History, 1973.

———. *A Time for Trumpets: The Untold Story of the Battle of the Bulge*. New York: William Morrow, 1985.

Macksey, Kenneth. *Guderian: Creator of the Blitzkrieg*. New York: Stein and Day, 1975.

Madej, Victor, ed. *German Army Order of Battle: Field Army and Officer Corps, 1939–1945*. Allentown, PA: Valor, 1984.

———, ed. *German Army Order of Battle: The Replacement Army, 1939–1945*. Allentown, PA: Valor, 1984.

———, ed. *Russo-German War, Summer 1944*. Allentown, PA: Valor, 1987.

Madej, Victor, and Shelby Stanton. "The Smolensk Campaign, 11 July to 5 August 1941." *Strategy and Tactics* 57 (July–August 1976).

Mader, Werner, ed. *Hitler's Letters and Notes*. New York: Harper & Row, 1974.

Manstein, Erich von. *Lost Victories*. Novato, CA: Presidio, 1982.

Manteuffel, Hasso von. "The Ardennes." In *The Fatal Decisions*, edited by Seymour Freiden and William Richardson. New York: Berkeley, 1958.

McDonald, Lyn. *1914–1918: Voices and Images of the Great War*. London: Michael Joseph, 1988.

McKee, Alexander. *The Race for the Rhine*. New York: Zebra, 1971.

Mee, Charles L., Jr. *The End of Order: Versailles 1919*. New York: E. P. Dutton, 1980.

Mellenthin, Friedrich-Wilhelm von. *German Generals of World War II as I Saw Them*. Norman: University of Oklahoma Press, 1977.

———. *Panzer Battles: A Study of the Employment of Armor in the Second World War*. New York: Ballantine, 1971.

Messenger, Charles. *Sepp Dietrich: Hitler's Gladiator*. London: Brassey's, 1988.

———. *The Last Prussian: A Biography of Field Marshal Gerd von Rundstedt, 1875–1953*. London: Brassey's, 1991.

Michulec, Robert. *4.Panzer-Division on the Eastern Front(1) 1941–1943*. Hong Kong: Concord, 1999.

Ministry of Foreign Affairs, Republic of Poland. *German Occupation of Poland: Extract of Note Addressed to the Allied and Neutral Powers*. New York: Greystone, 1941.

Mitcham, Samuel W., Jr. *Hitler's Legions: The German Army Order of Battle, World War II*. New York: Stein and Day, 1985.

———. *Hitler's Field Marshals and Their Battles*. Chelsea, MI: Scarborough House, 1990.

———. *Crumbling Empire: The German Defeat in the East, 1944*. Westport, CT: Praeger, 2001.

Mitcham, Samuel W., Jr., and Gene Mueller. *Hitler's Commanders*. Lanham, MD: Scarborough House, 1992.

Moczarski, Kazimierz. *Conversations with an Executioner*. Englewood Cliffs, NJ: Random House, 1983.

Mueller-Hillebrand, Burkhart. *Das Heer 1933–1945*, 3 vols. Darmstadt, FRG: E. S. Mittler & Sohn, 1954.

Murray, Williamson. *The Change in the European Balance of Power, 1938–1939: The Path to Ruin*. Princeton, NJ: Princeton University Press, 1984.

Natzmer, Oldwig von. "Operations of Encircled Forces: German Experience in Russia." In *The Anvil of War: German Generalship in Defense on the Eastern Front*, edited by Peter G. Tsouras. London: Greenhill, 1994.

Nehring, Walther K. *Die Geschichte der deutschen Panzerwaffe, 1916 bis 1945*. Berlin: Propyläen, 1969.

Neugebauer, Norwid. *The Defence of Poland (September 1939)*. London: M. I. Koln, 1942.

Newton, Steven H. *German Battle Tactics on the Russian Front, 1941–1945*. Atglen, PA: Schiffer, 1994.

———. *Retreat from Leningrad, 1944–1945*. Atglen, PA: Schiffer, 1995.

———. *Kursk: The German View*. New York: Da Capo, 2002.

Niepold, Gerd. *Battle for White Russia: The Destruction of Army Group Centre June 1944*. London: Brassey's, 1988.

O'Neill, Robert J. *The German Army and the Nazi Party, 1933–1939*. New York: James H. Heineman, 1966.

Parker, Danny S. *Battle of the Bulge: Hitler's Ardennes Offensive, 1944–1945*. Philadelphia: Combined Books, 1993.

Parrish, Michael. "Formation and Leadership of the Soviet Mechanized Corps in 1941." *Military Affairs* (April 1983).

Paul, Wolfgang. *Das Potsdamer Infanterie-Regiment 9, 1918–1945: Preussiche Tradition in Krieg und Frieden*. Osnabrück: Biblio Verlag, 1985.

Piekalkiewicz, Janusz. *The Cavalry of World War II*. New York: Stein and Day, 1980.

————. *Polenfeldzug: Hitler und Stalin zerschlagen die Polnische Republik.* Berg-isch Gladbach, FRG: Gustav Lübbe Verlag, 1982.

Poirer, Robert G., and Albert Z. Conner. *The Red Army Order of Battle in the Great Patriotic War.* Novato, CA: Presidio, 1985.

Prüller, Wilhelm. *Diary of a German Soldier.* London: Faber and Faber, 1963.

Raus, Erhard. *Effects of Climate on Combat in Russia.* Washington, DC: U.S. De-partment of the Army, 1952.

————. "Military Improvisations During the Russian Campaign." In *The Anvil of War: German Generalship in Defense on the Eastern Front,* edited by Peter G. Tsouras. London: Greenhill, 1994.

————. *Panzer Operations: The Eastern Front Memoir of General Raus, 1941–1945,* edited and translated by Steven H. Newton. New York: Da Capo, 2004.

Read, Anthony, and David Fisher. *The Deadly Embrace: Hitler, Stalin, and the Nazi-Soviet Pact, 1939–1941.* New York: W. W. Norton, 1988.

Reinhardt, Klaus. *Die Wende vor Moskau: Das Scheitern der Strategie Hitlers im Winter 1941–1942.* Stuttgart: Deutsche Verlags-Anstalt, 1972.

Reinicke, Adolf. *Das Reichsheer, 1921–1934: Ziele, Methoden der Ausbildung und Erziehung owie der Diesntgestaltung.* Osnabrück: Biblio Verlag, 1986.

Reynolds, Michael. *Men of Steel: 1st SS Panzer Corps, the Ardennes, and Eastern Front, 1944–1945.* New York: Sarpedon, 1999.

————. *Sons of the Reich: The History of II SS Panzer Corps in Normandy, Arn-hem, the Ardennes, and on the Eastern Front.* Havertown, PA: Casemate, 2002.

Richardson, Horst Fuchs, ed. *"Sieg Heil!": War Letters of Tank Gunner Karl Fuchs 1937–1941.* Hamden, CT: Archon, 1987.

Ritgen, Helmut. *The 6th Panzer Division, 1937–1945.* London: Osprey, 1982.

Rothburst, Florian K. *Guderian's XIXth Panzer Corps and the Battle of France: Breakthrough in the Ardennes, May 1940.* New York: Praeger, 1990.

Röttiger, Carl. "XXXXI Panzer Corps During the Battle of Moscow in 1941 as a Component of Panzer Group 3." In *German Battle Tactics on the Russian Front, 1941–1945,* edited by Steven H. Newton. Atglen, PA: Schiffer, 1994.

Rotundo, Louis. "The Creation of Soviet Reserves and the 1941 Campaign." *Mili-tary Affairs* (January 1985).

Rustin, Dick. "The Kaiser's Battle: The German Offensive, March 1918." *Strategy and Tactics* 83 (November–December 1980).

Ryan, Cornelius. *A Bridge Too Far.* New York: Simon & Schuster, 1974.

Schactman, Tom. *The Phony War, 1939–1940.* New York: Harper & Row, 1982.

Schenck, Peter. *Invasion of England 1940: The Planning of Operation Sealion.* Lon-don: Conway Maritime Press, 1990.

Schulte, Theo J. *The German Army and Nazi Policies in Occupied Russia.* New York: Berg, 1989.

Schweppenburg, Leo Freiherr Geyr von. *The Critical Years.* London: Allan Wingate, 1952.

Seaton, Albert. *The Battle of Moscow.* New York: Stein and Day, 1971.

————. *The Russo-German War, 1941–1945*. New York: Praeger, 1971.

————. *The German Army, 1933–1945*. New York: St. Martin's Press, 1979.

Shepherd, Ben. *War in the Wild East: The German Army and Soviet Partisans*. Cambridge, MA: Harvard University Press, 2004.

Showalter, Dennis. *Tannenberg: Clash of Empires*. Hamden, CT: Archon, 1991.

Siegler, Fritz Freiherr von. *Die höheren Dienstellen der deutschen Wehrmacht, 1933–1945*. Frankfurt: Instituts für Zeitgeschichte, 1956.

Sigel, Gustav A. *Germany's Army and Navy of the Nineteenth Century*. London: Bracken, 1989, reprint of 1900 edition.

Sontag, Raymond J. *A Broken World, 1919–1939*. New York: Harper & Row, 1971.

Später, Helmuth. *The History of the Panzerkorps Grossdeutschland*. 3 vols. Winnipeg, Man.: J. J. Fedorowicz, 1992.

Speer, Albert. *Inside the Third Reich*. New York: Macmillan, 1970.

Speidel, Hans. *Invasion 1944*. New York: Pocket Books, 1953.

Sperker, Karl Heinrich. *Generaloberst Erhard Raus: Ein Truppenführer im Ostfeldzug*. Osnabrück: Biblio Verlag, 1988.

Spielberger, Walter J. *Sturmgeschütz and Its Variants*. Atglen, PA: Schiffer, 1993.

Steiger, Rudolf. *Armour Tactics in the Second World War: Panzer Army Campaigns of 1939–1941 in German War Diaries*. Oxford: Berg, 1991.

Steinhoff, Johannes, Peter Pechel, and Dennis Showalter, eds. *Voices from the Third Reich: An Oral History*. Washington, DC: Regnery Gateway, 1989.

Stolfi, Russell H. S. *Hitler's Panzers East: World War II Reinterpreted*. Norman: University of Oklahoma Press, 1991.

Stoves, Rolf O. G. *Die 1.Panzer Division 1935–1945*. Dorheim, FRG: Podzun Verlag, 1962.

Streit, Christian. "Wehrmacht, Einsatzgruppen, Soviet POWs and Anti-Bolshevism in the Emergence of the Final Solution." In *The Final Solution: Origins and Implementation*, edited by David Cesarani. London: Routledge, 1994.

Sulzbach, Herbert. *With the German Guns: Four Years on the Western Front, 1914–1918*. London: Leo Cooper, 1973.

Taylor, Telford. *Sword and Swastika: Generals and Nazis in the Third Reich*. New York: Simon & Schuster, 1952.

————. *The March of Conquest: The German Victories in Western Europe, 1940*. New York: Simon & Schuster, 1958.

————. *The Breaking Wave: The Second World War in the Summer of 1940*. New York: Simon & Schuster, 1967.

Terraine, John. *Mons: The Retreat to Victory*. London: B. T. Batsford, 1960.

Theweleit, Klaus. *Male Fantasies*, vol. 2, *Male Bodies: Psychoanalyzing the White Terror*. Minneapolis: University of Minnesota Press, 1989.

Tieke, Wilhelm. *In the Firestorm of the Last Years of the War: II. SS-PanzerKorps with the 9. and 10. SS-Divisions "Hohenstaufen" and "Frundsberg."* Winnipeg, Man.: J. J. Fedorowicz, 1999.

————. *Tragedy of the Faithful: A History of the III. (germanische) SS-Panzer-Korps*. Winnipeg Man.: J. J. Fedorowicz, 2001.

Toland, John. *Battle: The Story of the Bulge*. New York: Random House, 1959.

————. *The Last 100 Days*. New York: Random House, 1966.

Trevor-Roper, Hugh, ed. *Hitler's Secret Conversations, 1941–1944*. New York: Farrar, Strauss and Young, 1953.

Tuchman, Barbara. *The Guns of August*. New York: Dell, 1962.

Turney, Alfred W. *Disaster at Moscow: Von Bock's Campaigns, 1941–1942*. Albuquerque: University of New Mexico Press, 1970.

Waite, Robert G. L. *Vanguard of Nazism: The Free Corps Movement in Postwar Germany, 1918–1923*. New York: W. W. Norton, 1952.

Warlimont, Walther. *Inside Hitler's Headquarters, 1939–1945*. London: Weidenfeld and Nicolson, 1964.

Wedd, A. F., ed. *German Students' War Letters*. New York: E. P. Dutton, 1929.

Wegmann, Günter, ed. *Formationgeschichter und Stellenbesetzung der Deutschen Streitkräfte, 1815–1990*. 2 vols. (to date). Osnabrück: Biblio Verlag, 1990–1992.

Weigley, Russell F. *Eisenhower's Lieutenants: The Campaign for France and Germany, 1944–1945*. Bloomington: Indiana University Press, 1981.

Werth, Alexander. *Russia at War, 1941–1945*. New York: E. P. Dutton, 1964.

Werth, German. *Verdun*. Bergisch Gladbach: Gustav Lübber Verlag, 1979.

Wheeler-Bennett, John W. *The Nemesis of Power: The German Army in Politics, 1918–1945*. New York: Viking, 1967.

Whiting, Charles. *Bloody Aachen*. New York: Stein and Day, 1976.

————. *The Battle of Hürtgen Forest*. New York: Crown, 1989.

Wohlfeil, Reiner. *Reichswehr und Republik (1918–1933)*. Frankfurt: Heer und Republik, n.d.

Wolff, Theodor. *The Eve of 1914*. New York: Alfred A. Knopf, 1936.

Yerger, Mark C. *Waffen SS Commanders: The Army Corps and Divisional Leaders of a Legend*. 2 vols. Atglen, PA: Schiffer, 1997.

Zeller, Eberhard. *The Flame of Freedom: The German Struggle Against Hitler*. Boulder, CO: Westview Press, 1994, reprint of 1967 edition.

Zetterling, Niklas, and Anders Frankson. *Kursk 1943: A Statistical Analysis*. London: Frank Cass, 2000.

Zhukov, Georgi K. *The Memoirs of Marshal Zhukov*. London: Jonathan Cape, 1971.

Ziemke, Earl F. *Stalingrad to Berlin: The German Defeat in the East*. Washington, DC: Office of the Chief of Military History, 1968.

Ziemke, Earl F., and Magna E. Bauer. *Moscow to Stalingrad: Decision in the East*. New York: Military Heritage Press, 1988.

Zobel, Horst. "3rd Panzer Division Operations." In *The Initial Period of War on the Eastern Front, 22 June–August 1941: Proceedings of the Fourth Art of War Symposium*, edited by David M. Glantz. London: Frank Cass, 1991.

INDEX